主编 陈枫

一生必用的应用文写作案例大全

英汉双语版

中国水利水电出版社
www.waterpub.com.cn

内容提要

英语应用文最佳范文大集合，Wherever/Whenever 方法与案例完美结合！私人和公务场合均适用，中英双语全都能参考，妙笔生花你也能！

本书精选七类你一生必用的应用文，让你快速检索即学即用："社交公关"、"商务往来"、"跨洋求学"、"人力资源管理文书"、"行政文书"、"日常事务"及"电邮与短信"。书中体例清晰，内容全面，"应用文体介绍"、"书写注意事项"、"写作'三步走'"、"常用句型"和"各类范文"等栏目融为一体，便于读者活学活用，举一反三。各类英语文书的写作万能模板，拥有它，你就能写出"简洁有力"且"表达正确"的美丽文书和得体信函。

图书在版编目（CIP）数据

一生必用的应用文写作案例大全：英汉双语版 / 陈枫主编. — 北京：中国水利水电出版社，2012.9
ISBN 978-7-5170-0091-4

Ⅰ. ①一… Ⅱ. ①陈… Ⅲ. ①英语-应用文-写作 Ⅳ. ①H315

中国版本图书馆CIP数据核字(2012)第195307号

策划编辑：陈 蕾　责任编辑：陈艳蕊　加工编辑：于丽娜　曹亚芳

书　　名	一生必用的应用文写作案例大全（英汉双语版）
作　　者	主编 陈枫
出版发行	中国水利水电出版社 （北京市海淀区玉渊潭南路1号D座　100038） 网　址：www.waterpub.com.cn E-mail：mchannel@263.net（万水） 　　　　sales@waterpub.com.cn 电　话：（010）68367658（发行部）、82562819（万水）
经　　售	北京科水图书销售中心（零售） 电　话：（010）88383994、63202643、68545874 全国各地新华书店和相关出版物销售网点
排　　版	北京万水电子信息有限公司
印　　刷	北京市蓝空印刷厂
规　　格	148mm×210mm　32开本　16.5印张　644千字
版　　次	2012年9月第1版　2012年9月第1次印刷
印　　数	0001—6000册
定　　价	39.80元（赠1CD）

凡购买我社图书，如有缺页、倒页、脱页的，本社发行部负责调换

版权所有·侵权必究

特色速递

Practical English Writing for Everyday Use

英语应用文最佳范文大集合，
Wherever/Whenever 方法与案例完美结合！

私人和公务场合均适用，中英双语全都能参考，妙笔生花你也能！

精选七类你一生必用的应用文，超快速检索使用

1. "社交公关"囊括了邀请信、祝贺信、感谢信、告别信、慰问信等 98 篇模板
2. "商务往来"包括业务咨询与往来、信用证、投诉、理赔等 76 篇模板
3. "出国留学"罗列有求学简历、个人陈述、推荐信等 45 篇模板
4. "人力资源管理文书"精选招聘广告、求职简历、推荐信等 62 篇模板
5. "行政文书"包含证明、奖状、通知、备忘录、新闻稿、致辞等 46 篇
6. "日常事务"涵盖便条、启事、海报、字据、账单、授权书、约会等 60 篇模板
7. "电邮与短信" 搜集最新网络文体：电子邮件、短消息等 18 篇模板

序

零压力、超轻松万用信函模板，你值得拥有！

当岁月的年轮悄然拂过21世纪的门槛，关山万里仅需鼠标轻点就宛如眼前，全球化已成为现代世界中最重要的主题，用英语流畅自如地进行交流和信函写作是职场精英必备的技能。但是，随着生活节奏的加快，人们用于阅读的时间越来越少。因此，选择正确的阅读材料对忙碌的各种人群来说尤为重要。如果你打算在最短的时间内领略最实用、最规范、最得体、最优雅的各类英文信函，这本书将是你最具慧眼的选择。书中提供的各类英文信函范文是最佳的万能写作模板，拥有本书，你就能"写得出、写得好、写得快"。

本书收集了各类最新、最全的英语信函，包罗万象，满足各种不同场合的需求。本书分为七大部分，即"社交公关"、"商务往来"、"跨洋求学"、"人力资源管理文书"、"行政文书"、"日常事务"及"电邮与短信"。其中"社交公关"囊括了工作中各种公关活动以及生活中婚丧嫁娶各礼仪所需信函文本，如"邀请信"、"祝贺信"、"感谢信"、"告别信"、"慰问信"等；"商务往来"包括日常商业活动的各种具体细节，如"业务咨询与往来"、"信用证"、"资信调查"、"货运与保险"、"投诉、索赔、理赔"等；"跨洋求学"罗列海外求学需要的各种手续和信函，如"求学简历"、"申请出国个人陈述"、"推荐信"等；"电邮与短信"则搜集最新的网络文体，包括"电子邮件"和"短消息"等。

本书秉持"内容至上、读者第一"的创作理念，查阅了大量资料，力求所选范文案例都新颖独特、实用规范。拥有本书，日常生活、商务工作英文信函写作再也不用愁！

特色速览：

1. **实战性强** 各类信函范文和常用信函句型，地道的原汁原味英文模板，随时套用、立刻上手！
2. **母语助读** 每个模板都有顺畅、精炼的译文，让你对英文信函内容理解顺畅。
3. **写作点拨** 应用文体介绍和书写注意事项，精炼、准确，让你一目了然。
4. **提升思维** 写作"三步走"，简明扼要，分条阐述，让你的写作有章可循。
5. **省时省力** 疑难词句加适当的脚注，省去你查单词的时间。
6. **方便查找** 体例清晰，编排有序，查找容易，使用方便。

本书集实用信函写作与原汁原味的英文于一体，再加上丰富全面的范文案例、清晰流畅的栏目设置、简约的版式设计，倾力打造全国第一本"零压力、超轻松"上班族、SOHO族等一生必备的英语信函读本。让你在愉悦的氛围中写出"简洁有力"且"表达正确"的美丽文书和得体信函！

本书专为广大上班族、白领人士和海外出差、留学人士打造，同时也适合各高校大学生、具有初中级英语水平且希望提高应用文写作水平的各界人士以及和老外互动的网友阅读。

编者
2012年初秋于北京

参 编

杨金鑫　刘　晓　刘　欢　陈俐娜　马　梦　林　静　石家宜　葛　俊　白　烨
孙　帅　高爱琴　刘　纯　郭美兰　王　霞　张艳萍　吴淑严　武少辉　成　琳
王　琴　曾丽文　祝万伟　何长领　梁俊茂　韩红梅　薛　博　王建军

目 录

Chapter 01

社交公关
Social Letters

Unit 1
邀请信
Letters of Invitation

常用句型 –2
1. 邀请朋友吃饭 –3
2. 接受朋友邀请 –3
3. 谢绝朋友邀请 –3
4. 邀请朋友参加生日聚会 –4
5. 接受朋友邀请 –5
6. 谢绝朋友邀请 –5
7. 宴会或晚会邀请函 –6
8. 接受宴会或晚会邀请 –6
9. 谢绝宴会或晚会邀请 –7
10. 招待会邀请函 –7
11. 接受招待会邀请 –8
12. 谢绝招待会邀请 –8
13. 展览会邀请函 –9
14. 接受展览会邀请 –9
15. 谢绝展览会邀请 –10
16. 开业邀请函 –11
17. 接受开业邀请 –12
18. 谢绝开业邀请 –12
19. 写给亲属的订婚通知 –13
20. 婚礼邀请信 –14

Unit 2
祝贺信
Congratulations Letters

常用句型 –15
21. 祝贺生日 –16
22. 祝贺订婚 –16
23. 祝贺结婚 –17
24. 祝贺生子 –18
25. 祝贺毕业 –19
26. 祝贺获得奖学金 –20
27. 祝贺找到工作 –21
28. 祝贺晋升 –21
29. 祝贺退休 –22
30. 祝贺获奖 –23
31. 祝贺开业 –24

Unit 3
感谢信
Thank-you Letters

Unit 4
告别信
Farewell Letters

Unit 5
慰问信
Letters of Sympathy

常用句型 –25
32. 感谢老师 –26
33. 感谢亲人 –26
34. 感谢领导 –27
35. 感谢同事 –27
36. 感谢其他单位 –28
37. 感谢志愿者 –29
38. 感谢款待 –30
39. 感谢帮助 –30
40. 感谢祝贺 –31
41. 感谢奖励 –31
42. 感谢捐赠 –32
43. 感谢赠送生日礼物 –33
44. 感谢赠送结婚礼物 –34
45. 感谢慰问 –34
46. 感谢吊唁 –35

常用句型 –37
47. 给朋友的告别信 –38
48. 给父母的告别信 –38
49. 给妻子的告别信 –39
50. 给员工的告别信 –40
51. 给老板的告别信 –41

常用句型 –42
52. 慰问病人 –43
53. 慰问伤员 –44
54. 慰问同事 –44
55. 上级对下级的慰问 –45
56. 对其他单位人员的慰问 –46
57. 对受灾单位的慰问 –46

Unit 6 吊唁信 Letters of Condolence

常用句型 –48
58. 吊唁好友丧母 –49
59. 吊唁好友丧偶 –49
60. 吊唁好友丧子 –50
61. 吊唁好友 –51
62. 吊唁领导 –51
63. 吊唁同事 –52
64. 吊唁德高望重的师长 –53
65. 吊唁商业伙伴 –53
66. 吊唁国家领导人逝世 –54

Unit 7 道歉信 Letters of Apology

常用句型 –58
67. 为不当言行道歉 –59
68. 为约定期限内未完成某事道歉 –60
69. 医疗道歉信 –61
70. 为客户投诉道歉 –61
71. 给女友道歉 –62
72. 给好友道歉 –63

Unit 8 正式致词 Speeches

常用句型 –65
73. 欢迎词 –66
74. 答谢词 –67
75. 开幕词 –68
76. 闭幕词 –70
77. 颁奖词 –71
78. 领奖词 –73

Chapter 02 商务往来 Business Letters

Unit 1 业务咨询与往来 Business Consultation and Communication

常用句型 –97
1. 索要商品目录 –98
2. 回复对商品目录的索要 –98
3. 索要产品信息 –99
4. 回复对产品信息的索要 –99
5. 要求寄送样本 –101
6. 推销商品 –101
7. 跟进函 –102
8. 要求澄清具体条款 –103
9. 澄清具体条款 –104

Unit 2 询价报价、发盘还盘 Inquiry & Quotation, Offer & Counter-offer

常用句型 –107
10. 询价 –107
11. 报价 –108
12. 主动报价 –109
13. 还盘 –109
14. 反还盘 –110

Unit 9
祝词
Speeches

常用句型 –75
79. 祝酒词 –76
80. 婚礼祝词 –77
81. 生日祝词 –79
82. 市区政府领导人祝词 –81
83. 国家领导人祝词 –82

Unit 10
请柬、名片、贺卡
Invitation Cards, (Business) Cards, Greeting Cards

84. 宴会请柬 –86
85. 舞会请柬 –86
86. 招待会请柬 –87
87. 展览会请柬 –87
88. 婚礼请柬 –88
89. 私人名片 –89
90. 商务名片 –89
91. 新年贺卡 –90
92. 圣诞贺卡 –90
93. 教师节贺卡 –91
94. 结婚贺卡 –91
95. 生日贺卡 –91
96. 晋升贺卡 –92
97. 成就贺卡 –92
98. 升学贺卡 –92

特别奉献

一 表示心情的词汇中英对照 –94
二 常见食物名称中英对照（一）–95

Unit 3
订单
Order

常用句型 –112
15. 下订单 –113
16. 确认订单 –114
17. 拒绝订单 –115
18. 取消订单 –115
19. 对方确认取消订单 –116

Unit 4
付款
Payment

常用句型 –118
20. 付款信（现金电汇 T/T）/ 119
21. 付款信（付款交单 D/P）/ 120
22. 付款信（L/C）/ 121
23. 请求延期付款 –121
24. 同意延期付款 –122
25. 拒绝延期付款 –123
26. 第一次催款 –124
27. 第二次催款 –125
28. 第二次以后的催款 –126
29. 最后一次催款 –128
30. 收款代理机构的催款信 –129

Unit 5
信用证
Letters of Credit (L/C)

常用句型 –130
31. 申请商务信用证 –131
32. 申请具体信用额度 –132
33. 接受商务信用证的申请 –132
34. 拒绝商务信用证的申请 –133
35. 要求对方开证 –134
36. 通知已开证 –135
37. 要求改证和展证 –136
38. 终止赊账权利 –136

Unit 6 资信调查
Credit Inquiries

常用句型 –138
39. 通过银行进行资信调查 –139
40. 通过相关公司企业进行资信调查 –140
41. 通过专业信用机构进行资信调查 –141
42. 积极的回复 –141
43. 消极的回复 –142

Unit 7 货运与保险
Shipment & Insurance

常用句型 –144
44. 通知发货情况 –144
45. 货运通知 –145
46. 通知运输推迟 –146
47. 通知运货出错 –147
48. 回复运输推迟通知 –148
49. 给保险公司的信（询问保险率）–148
50. 买方请求卖方代为投保 –149
51. 给保险公司的信（投保）–150

Unit 10 合同协议
Contracts & Agreements

66. 买卖合同 –166
67. 经销协议 –175
68. 销售代理协议 –185

Unit 11 感谢函及其他
Letters of Thanks & Others

常用句型　191
69. 感谢给予合作机会 –191
70. 感谢购买产品 –192
71. 感谢安排见面 –193
72. 告知对方其提议已得到通过 –194
73. 邀请捐款 –195
74. 捐款函 –195
75. 回复捐款函 –196
76. 表示终止业务往来 –197

Unit 8 投诉、索赔、理赔
Complaints & Claims & Settlements

常用句型 –152
52. 投诉送货延迟 –152
53. 投诉送错货物 –153
54. 投诉货物不达标 –154
55. 投诉货物损坏 –155
56. 回复对送货延误的投诉 –156
57. 回复对送错货物的投诉 –157
58. 回复对货物质量的投诉 –157
59. 回复对货物损坏的投诉 –158
60. 索赔 –159
61. 回复索赔 –160

Unit 9 代理与合作
Agency & Cooperation

常用句型 –161
62. 请求代理 –162
63. 要求独家代理 –163
64. 不知对方是否已有代理，请求代理 –164
65. 批发商托销 –165

特别奉献

一　外贸术语中英对照 –199
二　金融术语中英对照 –201
三　中国主要银行名称中英对照 –205

Chapter 03

跨洋求学

Unit 1
求学简历
CVs

1. 本科生简历 —208
2. 硕士简历 —212
3. 博士简历 —216

Unit 2
申请出国个人陈述
Personal Statements

4. 文科生 —222
5. 理工科生 —226

Unit 5
申请奖学金
Scholarship

27. 提出奖学金申请 —251
28. 索取奖学金申请表 —252
29. 寄回填好的奖学金申请表 —253
30. 感谢给予奖学金 —253

Unit 6
经济资助（助学金）及资助证明
Financial Aid & Certificates

31. 递交申请材料 —255
32. 询问申请进展 —256
33. 学校通知获得经济资助 —256
34. 感谢提供经济资助 —257
35. 国家留学基金管理委员会出具的公派资助证明 —258
36. 单位出具的公派资助证明 —259
37. 家长资助证明 —260
38. 家长担保函 —260
39. 资助人的单位收入证明 —261

Unit 3 推荐信
Letters of Recommendation

6. 老师为学生写的推荐信（理工类）–231
7. 老师为学生写的推荐信（文科类）–232
8. 管理人员为员工深造写的推荐信 –233
9. 邀请推荐人写推荐信 –235
10. 感谢老师写的推荐信 –237

Unit 4 申请过程中与大学的各种联络信件
Application Correspondences

11. 索取入学申请表 –238
12. 校方对索取信息的回复 –239
13. 告知校方已填好入学申请表 –239
14. 告知校方各项材料正分别寄出 –240
15. 询问申请材料是否收到 –241
16. 告知校方 TOEFL 和 GRE 成绩已寄出 –241
17. 告知已按要求补寄经济资助证明和成绩单等 –242
18. 询问申请进展情况 –243
19. 录取通知书 –243
20. 拒绝通知书 –245
21. 申请者表示同意入学 –246
22. 申请者谢绝入学 –247
23. 询问住宿问题 –247
24. 申请住校 –248
25. 申请延期入学 –248
26. 通知校方已获得护照和签证 –249

Unit 7 学历、学位、奖励、工作经历证明
Relevant Certificates

40. 本科学历证明 –263
41. 硕士学历证明 –264
42. 本科学位证明 –264
43. 硕士学位证明 –265
44. 奖励证明 –266
45. 工作经历证明 –266

❋ 特别奉献

一 世界著名高校名称中英对照 –268
二 世界名校校训中英文对照 –269
三 美国各州州名中英对照 –270

Chapter 04

人力资源管理文书

Unit 1 招聘广告 Recruitment Advertising

1. 生产部门 —274
2. 行政部门 —274
3. 销售部门 —276
4. 实习生招聘 —277

Unit 2 求职简历 Resumes

5. 会计求职简历 —280
6. 金融分析师求职简历 —282
7. 计算机行业求职简历 —285
8. 市场营销求职简历 —288
9. 人力资源职位求职简历 —290
10. 行政助理求职简历 —292

Unit 5 工作岗位的申请和回复 Employment Correspondences

26. 用人单位收到简历后的初步回复 —313
27. 用人单位审阅求职信后的面试邀请 —314
28. 用人单位审阅求职信后的回绝 —314
29. 求职者对面试邀请的拒绝 —315
30. 用人单位面试后的回绝 —316
31. 求职者面试后的感谢信（争取工作机会）—316
32. 录用通知（正式职位）—317
33. 申请人接受工作岗位 —318
34. 申请人拒绝工作岗位 —319

Unit 6 申请和批复 Applications & Replies

35. 病假申请 —320
36. 产假申请 —321
37. 事假申请 —322
38. 休假申请 —323
39. 加薪申请 —324
40. 晋升申请 —325
41. 调动工作申请 —326
42. 事假批复 —327
43. 休假批复 —328
44. 加薪批复 —329
45. 晋升批复 —330

Unit 3 求职信 Cover Letters

11. 应届毕业生的求职信 –296
12. 略有经历的求职者的求职信 –297
13. 职场老手求职信 –298
14. 在校生实习求职信 –299

Unit 4 推荐信和工作证明 Recommendations & References

15. 求职者要求提供推荐 –301
16. 原工作单位领导推荐 –302
17. 原雇主推荐 –303
18. 同事推荐 –304
19. 朋友推荐 –305
20. 老师推荐 –306
21. 求职者要求提供工作证明 –307
22. 用人单位要求提供工作证明 –308
23. 工作证明（好评）–309
24. 工作证明（中评）–310
25. 工作证明（差评）–311

Unit 7 企业各类人事通知 Notices & Announcements

46. 晋升通知 –331
47. 年终奖通知 –332
48. 警告通知 –333
49. 辞退通知 –334
50. 裁员通知 –335
51. 职务空缺通知 –336
52. 介绍新员工 –336
53. 员工辞职通知 –337
54. 员工退休通知 –337
55. 员工死亡通知 –338
56. 假期安排通知 –339
57. 开会通知 –339

Unit 8 辞职信 Letters of Resignation

58. 由于找到其他工作而辞职 –342
59. 由于身体原因而辞职 –342
60. 由于搬家而辞职 –343
61. 由于与公司人员意见不合而辞职 –344
62. 接受辞职 –345

❈ 特别奉献

一　世界著名企业名称中英对照 –346
二　企业部门及职位中英对照 –348
三　形容个人品质的词汇中英对照 –352

Chapter 05

行政文书

Unit 1
证明
Certificates

1. 身份证明 –355
2. 简历证明 –356
3. 在读证明 –357
4. 工作证明 –357
5. 离职证明 –358
6. 收入证明 –359
7. 夫妻关系证明 –359

Unit 2
奖状
Certificates of Merit

8. 优秀学生奖状 –360
9. 学科竞赛奖状 –361
10. 杰出市民奖状 –361
11. 模范领导组织奖 –362
12. 杰出教练奖状 –362
13. 季度优秀员工奖 –363

Unit 5
备忘录
Memorandum (Memo)

26. 交代员工做事的备忘录 –383
27. 要求提供进度报告的备忘录 –384
28. 公司规定变更备忘录 –384
29. 公司更名备忘录 –385
30. 会议通知备忘录 –386

Unit 6
会议议程和会议纪要
Meeting Agendas & Minutes

31. 会议议程（简约版）–390
32. 董事会会议纪要 –392
33. 公司全体年会会议纪要 –394
34. 部门会议纪要 –396

Unit 3 通知 Notices & Announcements

14. 搬迁通知 —364
15. 设立分支办公地点通知 —365
16. 拓展业务通知 —366
17. 收购通知 —367
18. 公司周年庆祝通知 —367
19. 公司更名通知 —368
20. 开会通知 —369

Unit 4 报告 Reports

21. 市场调查报告 —371
22. 可行性报告 —374
23. 进度报告 —376
24. 年度报告 —378
25. 故障调查报告 —381

Unit 7 新闻稿 Press Releases

35. 新品发布 —401
36. 人事任命 —403
37. 宣布新规定 —405

Unit 8 致词 Speeches

38. 表示欢迎 —407
39. 表示欢送 —408
40. 表示告别 —409
41. 表示勉励 —409
42. 表示感谢 —410
43. 表示祝贺 —411

Unit 9 其他行政文书 Other Official Writings

44. 规定 —414
45. 预算 —416
46. 营销计划 —419

❀ 特别奉献

一 重要政府部门中英对照 —422
二 世界主要国家和地区名称中英对照 —423

Chapter 06

日常事务

Unit 1 便条和通知 Notes & Notices

1. 便条（日常交流）—429
2. 便条（意见）—429
3. 便条（建议）—430
4. 便条（托事）—430
5. 学习通知—430
6. 讲座通知—431
7. 参观通知—431
8. 喜报—432
9. 放假通知—433
10. 停水通知—434

Unit 2 启事 Notices

11. 寻人启事—435
12. 寻物启事—436
13. 招领启事—436
14. 征婚启事—437
15. 开业启事—437
16. 停业启事—438
17. 更名启事—438
18. 出租启事—438
19. 求租启示—439
20. 搬迁启事—440
21. 鸣谢启事—440
22. 更正启事—441

Unit 5 字据、账单与租赁 I.O.U., Receipt & Bill & Renting Issues

32. 借据—452
33. 收据—453
34. 账单—453
35. 房主告知房客租约即将到期—453
36. 房客要求续约—454

Unit 6 约会 Appointments

37. 朋友约会—456
38. 恋人约会—457
39. 闺蜜约会—457
40. 和长辈约会—457
41. 和晚辈约会—458
42. 商务约会—458

❋ 特别奉献

一 常见食物名称中英对照（二）—482
二 重要标识英文表述法—483

Unit 3 海报 Posters

23. 学术报告类海报 –442
24. 文艺晚会海报 –443
25. 体育比赛海报 –443
26. 电影海报 –444
27. 社团开会海报 –444

Unit 4 广告 Advertisements

28. 店铺广告 –446
29. 促销广告 –448
30. 服务广告 –449
31. 出租广告 –450

Unit 7 授权书 Authorization Letters

43. 授权他人领取物品 –460
44. 授权代领薪水 –461
45. 授权某人进入自己家 –462
46. 医疗授权书 –462
47. 法律授权书 –465

Unit 8 其他 Other Writings

48. 建议书（给个人）–467
49. 建议书（给单位）–468
50. 抱怨信（质量低劣）–469
51. 抱怨信（多收运费）–470
52. 索赔信（人寿保险）–471
53. 索赔信（车险）–471
54. 索赔信（意外险）–472
55. 售后服务承诺书 –473
56. 免责声明 –474
57. 道歉声明 –474
58. 求助信 –478
59. 举报信 –479
60. 倡议书 –480

Chapter 07

电邮与短信
E-mails & Messages

Unit 1 电子邮件 E-mails

1. 公司对客户 —489
2. 公司对公司 —489
3. 客户对公司 —490
4. 发给关系较好的业务伙伴 —492
5. 发给下属 —493
6. 发给同事 —494
7. 发给亲人 —494
8. 发给心仪恋人 —496
9. 发给朋友 —497

Unit 2 短消息 Short Messages

10. 发给亲人 —500
11. 发给爱人 —500
12. 发给朋友 —500
13. 发给同学 —500
14. 发给老师 —500
15. 发给同事 —501
16. 发给上级 —501
17. 发给下级 —501
18. 短信祝语 —501

❀ 特别奉献

一 网络常用符号及其释义 —504
二 最新汉语潮词英译 —507

Chapter 01

社交公关 Social Letters

　　社交信函是人们日常生活、工作中不可缺少的交流思想的工具和载体。随着社会的进一步发展、融合，国内外人际交往频繁，文秘工作者在日常工作中处理礼节性往来信件也日益增多。社交类信函一般包括：邀请信、祝贺信、感谢信、告别信、慰问信、吊唁信、道歉信等等。由于这类书信使用频繁、是连接人际的纽带，因此写好这类信件就显得尤为重要。

　　社交类信函的写作，主要有以下几点要求：
1. 准确（Accuracy）：选择的文体要准确，表达的意思要准确，所说的内容要准确。
2. 简洁（Brevity）：要说明写信的理由、支持理由的事实以及对收信人的要求。句句切中主题，切勿繁琐冗长。
3. 清晰（Clarity）：尽量使用短的段落、句子和简单的词汇。因为社交信件不是炫耀文学功底的地方，一切以达到目的为准，以免让人反感。

　　公关礼仪类的应用文主要是用来调整人与人之间关系的。"人在江湖漂"，难免会遇到各种各样的公共场合，有的还需要你出来说上几句，发表点看法或者明确一下态度。所以写好公关礼仪类的应用文是非常重要的。恰当的措辞、华美的言语，不是对世俗的溜须拍马和逢场做戏，而是对对方的一种尊重，是写作者或发言者个人素质的集中体现。这类应用文一般包括：祝词、演讲、请柬、贺卡、题词、讣告、悼词、对联等等。虽然文体不一，难以做出总体性概括，但写作时都需要注意：选材恰当、长度恰当、用词恰当、言辞诚恳。

Unit 1　邀请信　　　　　　　　　　　Letters of Invitation

邀请信（Letters of Invitation）包括宴会、舞会、晚餐、聚会、婚礼等各种主题，形式上大体分为两种：一种为正式格式（formal correspondence），亦称请柬；一种是非正式格式（informal correspondence），即一般的邀请信。它在形式上不如请柬那样正规，但也是很讲究的。

书写时应注意：邀请信一定要将邀请的时间（年、月、日、钟点）、地点、场合写清楚，不能使接信人存在任何疑虑。例如："I'd like you and Bob to come to Luncheon next Friday."这句话中所指的是哪个星期五并不明确，所以应加上具体日期"I'd like you and Bob to come to luncheon next Friday, May the fifth."。

写作"三步走"：说明邀请目的——说明活动安排——期待尽早回复。

提示：信中要说明关于活动的详细信息，包括活动时间、地点、内容，有时还需要说明参加活动的人员。语气要热情真挚，但不要强人所难。

✻ 常用句型

1. I am writing to invite you to…
   我写信是想邀请您……

2. The reception will be held in …, on …
   招待会定于……在……举行。

3. We sincerely hope you can come.
   我们期待您的光临。

4. We have decided to have a party in honor of the occasion.
   为此我们决定举办一次晚会。

5. Please confirm your participation at your earliest convenience.
   是否参加，请早日告之。

1. 邀请朋友吃饭

Dear Mr. Lee,

  Can you and Mrs. Lee join a few other friends and us on Thursday evening, June the seventh, for dinner? Later we plan to go to the piano concert in downtown. Dinner will be at five thirty so as to allow plenty of time for driving there. We do hope you can come.

Yours sincerely,
Jack Joyce

亲爱的李先生：

  您和李太太能于6月7日（周四）晚上与我们及几位朋友共进晚餐吗？晚餐后我们计划去市中心听一场钢琴音乐会。为了有足够的时间驾车前往会场，晚餐将会在五点半开始。我们殷切希望你们能来。

诚挚的 杰克·乔伊斯

2. 接受朋友邀请

Dear Mr. Joyce,

  We shall be delighted to come to the dinner on Thursday evening, June the seventh. I appreciate your idea about the concert, and we are looking forward to meeting you.

Sincerely yours,
Tom Lee

亲爱的乔伊斯先生：

  我们很高兴能参加6月7日（周四）的晚餐。我很赞赏您观看钢琴音乐会的提议。我们期待与您相见。

诚挚的 汤姆·李

3. 谢绝朋友邀请

Dear Mr. Joyce,

  I'm certainly sorry that we may not be able to dinner on Thursday evening, June the seventh. You may not know, my wife has been not feeling good these days and her doctor asks her to have a good rest at home for at least two weeks. Both my wife and me highly appreciate your kind invitation to the dinner and the concert. We hope next time we can invite you to my place.

Sincerely yours,
Tom Lee

亲爱的乔伊斯先生：

　　实在抱歉我们可能无法参加6月7日（周四）的晚餐了。也许您不知道，我的夫人近些日子身体不甚舒服，医生建议她至少在家休息两周。我们都非常感谢您盛情邀请我们参加晚餐和音乐会。希望下次请您到我们这儿来坐坐。

诚挚的 汤姆·李

4. 邀请朋友参加生日聚会

Dear Mikha,

With great honor, we would like to request for your presence on this coming Sunday, 15th January at 3:00p.m. for the 14th birthday of Jessica.

The venue for the said event will be at the Victoria's garden restaurant and dress code will be casual attire.

We wish that you will find time to be present on the party. Please let us know whether you can or cannot join us for whatever reason. Contact me as soon as possible.

Hoping to meet you in the venue.

Best regards,
J. D. Jefferson

亲爱的米卡：

　　我们很荣幸邀请您于1月15日（本周日）下午3点前来参加杰西卡的14岁生日聚会。

　　聚会地点定于维克多利亚花园餐厅，着便装即可。

　　我们希望您能抽空出席聚会。无论出于何种原因，请务必告知我们您是否可以出席。请尽快与我联系。

期待在餐厅与您相见。

美好的问候
J. D. 杰弗森

5. 接受朋友邀请 ✉

Dear Isabel,

  I am delighted to accept your invitation to come to your home for your birthday party next Tuesday afternoon, June the eighth.

  It's very nice of you to invite me to the party and I'm looking forward to seeing you and wishing you happy birthday.

Cordially yours,
Janet

亲爱的伊莎贝尔：

  我很高兴接受你的邀请，在下周二，即6月8日下午到你家参加生日聚会。我要感谢你的邀请，也期待着与你见面并祝你生日快乐。

杰尼特 谨上

6. 谢绝朋友邀请 ✉

Dear Isabel,

  I am so sorry that I cannot come to your home for your birthday party next Tuesday afternoon, June the eighth. I'm leaving for Paris tomorrow and will not come back until November.

  Thank you so much for asking me! I hope we will get together some other time.

Cordially yours,
Janet

亲爱的伊莎贝尔，

  非常抱歉我无法于下周二，即6月8日下午到你家参加你的生日聚会了。

我明天就要前往巴黎,直到 11 月才会回来。

非常感谢你对我的邀请!希望我们日后能够相聚。

诚挚的 杰尼特

7. 宴会或晚会邀请函

Mr. & Mrs. Robinson,

We greatly appreciate your cooperation and help. We are cordially inviting you to an evening party on Sunday, July 8, in the Recreation Center of the company.

Looking forward to the pleasure of seeing you.

Yours faithfully
Jack Hanson

罗宾森夫妇:

我们非常感谢你们的合作和帮助。在此诚挚地邀请你们参加 7 月 8 日(周日)的晚宴,地点位于公司的文娱中心。

期待与你们相见。

杰克·汉森 敬上

8. 接受宴会或晚会邀请

Dear Mr. Hanson,

Mr. & Mrs. Robinson thank you for your kind invitation to the evening party on Sunday, July 8, and have much pleasure in accepting.

Yours truly,
Mr. and Mrs. Robinson

亲爱的汉森先生,

罗宾森夫妇感谢您邀请参加于 7 月 8 日(周日)举办的晚宴。我们非常高兴接受您的邀请。

罗宾森夫妇 敬上

9. 谢绝宴会或晚会邀请

Dear Sir,

    I do appreciate your kind invitation, but I am sorry that I cannot dine with you at Holiday Inn on Saturday, December the fifteenth, at seven o'clock p.m. Unfortunately, I have already made and engagement for that evening.

    I hope we shall have the opportunity to say YES at some future time.

Very sincerely yours,
Mike Lock

亲爱的先生：

    非常感谢您善意的邀请，但是非常抱歉，我无法于12月15日（周六）晚7点与您在假日酒店共进晚餐。非常不凑巧，我那晚已有安排。

    希望我们下次能有机会共进晚餐。

麦克·洛克 谨上

10. 招待会邀请函

Dear Professor Chapman,

    To celebrate the sixtieth anniversary of the founding of the People's Republic of China, we request the honor of your presence at a reception which is to be held in Bell Tower Hotel, on Sunday, (the 29th Sept. , 2009) from 7 p.m. to 9 p.m. .

    We would be glad if you could come.

Sincerely yours,
Secretariat

亲爱的查普曼教授：

    为庆祝中华人民共和国成立60周年，兹定于2009年9月29日（周日）晚7时至9时在钟楼饭店举行招待会。

    敬请光临。

秘书处 谨上

11. 接受招待会邀请

Dear Sir,

Thank you very much for your invitation to join the sixtieth anniversary of the founding of the People's Republic of China at Bell Tower Hotel on the 29th Sept.

I will be happy to be there at 7:00 p.m. to take part in the reception, and look forward to it with pleasure.

Sincerely yours,
Chapman

敬启者：

非常感谢您邀请本人参加为庆祝中华人民共和国成立 60 周年，于 9 月 29 日在钟楼饭店举行的活动。

我很高兴于晚 7 时参加招待会，并欣然期待它的举行。

诚挚的 查普曼

12. 谢绝招待会邀请

Dear Sir,

Thank you for your invitation to attend the reception for the 60th anniversary of the founding of the People's Republic of China to be held at Bell Tower Hotel on the 29th, Sept. I had hoped that it would be possible for me to be there, but I now find the rush of work makes it impractical.

Please accept my regrets, and I'll try to make it next year.

Cordially yours,
Chapman

敬启者：

感谢邀请本人参加为庆祝中华人民共和国成立 60 周年，于 9 月 29 日在钟楼饭店举办的招待会活动。本人原定参加活动，但今由于事务繁多，无法赴会。请接受本人的歉意，来年将会尽可能参加。

诚挚的 查普曼

13. 展览会邀请函

Dear Mr. Homann,

  It is an honor to be given the privilege to invite you to the Home Decor Exhibit. This event will be held at the Expo House on October 2 to 5, 2009. Exhibit will start at 8:00 in the morning until 7:00 in the evening.

  This upcoming event is organized for the benefit of individuals of families who wish to find a new home decor and gives a chance for everyone to meet each other.

  Hoping for your presence in the said event.

Cordially Yours

Donald Swan

亲爱的霍曼先生：

  很荣幸能够邀请您参加家庭装潢展览会。本次展览会将于 2009 年 10 月 2 日至 5 日在博览园举办。展览时间为上午 8 时至晚 7 时。

  本次即将召开的展会旨在服务期待改变家居装潢的个人和家庭，并为大家提供一个相互认识的契机。

  敬请光临。

诚挚的 多纳德·斯万

14. 接受展览会邀请

Dear Sirs,

  We have received your letter of invitation dated August 1st with thanks. Your exhibition is of great interest to us. We think it will benefit both of us a great deal, so we have decided to visit your exhibition held on Sept. 10th, 11th, and 12th. Since the exhibition is about a month ahead, we cannot decide specifically when we will arrive at Xi'an. However, once we make a specific decision, we will notify you by fax.

  For your information, there is a heavy demand for printers in the market here. We hope we can place large orders during this visit.

Faithfully yours,

Jack Carter

敬启者：

　　我们很荣幸收到您 8 月 1 日发来的邀请函。我们对本次展览有着浓厚的兴趣。由于本次展览能使双方互利互惠，因此我们决定参加此次定于 9 月 10 日至 12 日举办的展览。但由于距离展览还有将近一个月的时间，所以我们无法确定何时将抵达西安。如果做出具体的决定，我们将通过传真告知您。

　　根据您的信息，目前市场上需要大量的打印机。我们希望此次行程中我们能签下大订单。

诚挚的 杰克·卡特

15. 谢绝展览会邀请

Dear Sirs,

Thank you for your kind invitation. However, we cannot accept it since we are no longer dealing in light products. Last May we shifted to handling the import and export of native products.

We think you may be pleased to invite the largest dealer of printers in this area and their address is as follows:

Messers, Parson & Co.

37 Sunshine Ave.

Los Angeles, CA 90300

Faithfully yours,
Jack Carter

敬启者：

　　感谢您的善意邀请，但由于我们不再处理轻便产品，所以很遗憾，我们不能接受此次邀请。我们已经在去年五月份将工作转移到处理本地产品的进出口上。

　　我想你们会乐意邀请本地区最大的打印机交易商，他们的地址如下：
加利福尼亚州 洛杉矶 阳光大道 37 号梅瑟斯·帕森公司，邮编：90300

诚挚的 杰克·卡特

16. 开业邀请函

Dear Mr. Folder,

  We would like to invite you to attend the inauguration of our business located at Lispher Bldg. on September 12, 2009, at 8:00 a.m. . It is our honor to have you as our loyal customer in our other businesses. We are hoping that we will get the same support from you. We have been in this business for quite some time now yet we have always managed to stay on top of our competitors. This is not possible if not with your support to our business. We have prepared something for you as our patrons as a way of saying thank you. Please come early so that we can find a comfortable seat for you and so that you will be there as we acknowledge our loyal customers and you are definitely in the list.

  Please let us know if you are attending the said event or not by September 2, 2009.

  We hope for your presence on that day. And we are looking forward to more fruitful business deals with you.

Sincerely Yours,
Aaron Green

亲爱的福尔德先生：

  我们诚邀您参加我公司的开业典礼，典礼将于2009年9月12日早8点在利斯弗大楼举行。我们很荣幸在其他业务上有您这位忠实的顾客。我们期望在新的业务上能获得您同样的支持。目前我们已在这一业务涉猎多时，我们一直努力使自己保持在竞争对手之上。没有您对我们业务的支持，就没有我们的今天。为表谢意，我们为您这位老顾客精心准备了礼物。请您早些来到现场，这样我们可以给您安排个好位置，这是我们为忠实顾客准备的，而您自然是他们中的一员。

  请您在2009年9月2日前告知我们是否有空参加此次活动。

  我们期望您能出席当日的典礼。希望日后与您在生意上的合作硕果累累。

阿伦·格林 谨上

17. 接受开业邀请

Dear Mr. Brown,

I am writing this letter to express our honor in announcing that we are accepting your proposal for a venture dated June 12, 2009.

With optimism, we are expecting a fruitful relationship with you in the days to come as we go to business together.

Thank you and more power.

Respectfully Yours,
Wilma Joseph

尊敬的布朗先生：

　　我们很荣幸地通知您，我们接受您提出的于 2009 年 6 月 12 日举办开业典礼的邀请。

　　我们以乐观的态度，期盼日后与您的合作能取得丰硕的成果。

　　谢谢您并祝您成功！

威尔玛·约瑟夫 敬上

18. 谢绝开业邀请

Dear Mr. Brown,

Thank you so much for inviting me to your inauguration of your business. I'm really flattered by the great honor you give me and I'm more than willing to come.

However, I have planned to go to France during that time, so I am afraid that maybe I cannot make it there this time.

I really feel sorry about that because you are my good friend. Please accept my regret. And good luck to your new endeavor.

Faithfully yours,
Wilma Joseph

亲爱的布朗先生：

　　感谢您邀请本人参加贵公司的开业典礼。我很荣幸您能给我如此高的礼遇，并且十分愿意出席。

但是我已计划在那段时间前往法国，因此恐怕我无法参加您的典礼。

拒绝您这样的好友，我深表歉意。请接受我的歉意，愿您的新事业一帆风顺！

威尔玛·约瑟夫 敬上

19. 写给亲属的订婚通知

Dear Aunt Mary and Uncle Jack,

Good news! You've been asking how long I was intending to keep up my bachelor existence. The answer is, not long.

I've just got engaged to a girl I met eight months ago at a company party. Her name is Eleanor and she works as a designer at our head office. Her family live near Enfield but come originally from Trinidad.

Needless to say, I think she is wonderful. Mum and Dad seem quite taken by her too. I hope you get the chance to make up your own minds soon.

No date fixed as yet for the wedding, but we are both keen to have it fairly soon. September perhaps.

I trust all the family are keeping well. We both look forward to seeing you in the near future.

Best wishes to you and cousins Kate and Michael.

Yours sincerely,
Roger

亲爱的杰克叔叔、玛丽阿姨：

我要告诉你们一个好消息！你们曾经问过我打算光棍多久，我的答案是，我马上就要"脱光"了。

我刚刚和一个女孩订了婚，她是我八个月前在一个公司的派对上认识的。她名叫埃莉诺，在我们的总公司担任设计师。她家在埃菲尔德附近，但她的老家是特立尼达。

毋庸置疑，我认为她很棒。我的父母似乎也被她打动了。我希望你们趁这个机会，也快点儿对她有个印象。

我们还没确定婚礼日期，但我们都希望能尽快完婚。婚礼也许会在九月举办吧。

我相信所有的亲戚一切都好，我们期盼着不久后能够见到你们。

祝你们、凯特表妹和迈克尔表弟万事顺意！

罗格 谨上

20. 婚礼邀请信

Dear Mr. and Mrs. Johnson,

As the parents of the bride, I would like to take this opportunity to invite you to the wedding of our daughter, Sandra Green to her fiancé, Adam Locke. On this joyous occasion, we wish to share the day with our closest friends and family members.

Children grow faster than any of us can imagine, the time is upon us to watch our child grow and flourish into a new stage of their life. He proposed while the two of them were on vacation, she happily accepted and now they are to be married.

The formal event will be located at the Fire Lake Golf and Country Club on the fifteenth of August at three o'clock, two thousand and nine.

Please RSVP by the fifteenth of June to ensure attendance.

We hope to see you there to enjoy this special day with friends and family.

Sincerely Yours,
Jim & Lucy

亲爱的约翰逊先生和夫人：

作为新娘的父母，我们愿借此机会邀请你们参加小女桑德拉·格林的婚礼，新郎是亚当·洛克。我们希望能和我们的亲朋好友一同分享这个美妙的时刻。

孩子们成长的速度超乎我们的想象，这一刻我们将见证自己的孩子走向成熟，踏上人生中一个新的阶段。新郎在度假时向她求婚，她愉悦地接受了，如今他们即将走进婚姻的殿堂。

正式婚礼将于8月15日下午三时在火湖高尔夫和乡村酒吧举行。

为确定参加人数，请于6月15日前回复。

我们期待在婚礼上与你们相见，与亲朋好友共度这美好的时刻。

吉姆和露西 敬启

Unit 2　祝贺信

Congratulations Letters

祝贺信 (Congratulations Letters) 是社交中的一种礼仪性信函。通常包括以下几个方面的内容：说明祝贺事由，表达热烈、诚挚的祝贺；围绕祝贺事件表述贺喜内容；表达美好祝福。

写作"三步走"：说明事由并表达自己衷心的祝贺——展开评论事件、赞扬收信人——再次表达良好祝愿

提示：在写作主要内容的时候，可以重点赞扬一下当事人的优秀能力和取得成就的原因、并展望他将来的美好发展前景等。

✻ 常用句型

1. Heartfelt congratulations on…

   真心祝贺……

2. Congratulations, all of us feel proud of your remarkable achievements!

   祝贺你，我们都为你所取得的巨大成就感到骄傲。

3. I wish you further success!

   预祝你取得更大的成功！

4. Please accept our sincerest congratulations and very best wishes for all the good future.

   谨向你表示由衷的祝贺和美好的祝福。

5. I take pride in your achievements and would like to avail myself of this opportunity to extend my best wishes for your success.

   对你取得的成就我深感自豪，我愿借此机会对你的成功表示由衷的祝贺。

21. 祝贺生日

Dear Anne,

A little bird told me that you have a big birthday coming up, so I want to send you huge congratulations! The little bird also told me that you will be over the hill as you turn 40, but I just want to say "hogwash" to that! You will always be young in my heart, and you've always looked younger than you are anyway.

I would love to get together so we can celebrate your birthday in person, so please give me a call sometime soon and we can make plans. It will be so much fun to give you a big birthday hug and enjoy some birthday cake together. Best wishes for much more happy and healthy decades, and again, congratulations on celebrating this exciting milestone!

Sincerely yours,
Lucy

亲爱的安妮：

　　一只小鸟告诉我你的生日即将到来，所以我想把最好的祝福送给你。这只小鸟还告诉我你过了40岁就要走下坡路了，但我只想对它说声"去你的"！在我心中，你将青春永驻，而且你总是显得很年轻。

　　我真想和你相聚，这样我们就可以亲自为你庆祝生日，所以请尽快给我来电，这样我们就可以好好计划一番。如果能给你一个生日拥抱，一起分享生日蛋糕，那应该会很开心吧。祝愿你日后拥有更多的开心和健康，再次祝贺你迎来这个闪亮的里程碑。

露西 敬启

22. 祝贺订婚

Dear Jenny,

My mom just told me the most exciting news that I have heard all year–you're engaged! Congratulations! I am so happy for you and Mark that I can hardly contain myself. I have always been so inspired and encouraged by your strong relationship and know your marriage will be happy and fulfilling.

I hear there will be an engagement party coming up sometime this month, so I look forward to hearing all the details about that. I for sure plan to be there to help you celebrate. If you have a moment, feel free to call me so I can congratulate you over the phone. Like I said, huge congratulations are coming your way from me. Looking forward to hearing more!

Sincerely yours,
Emmy

亲爱的珍妮：

我妈妈刚才告诉我你订婚了，这是我今年听到的最爆炸性的新闻！祝贺你！我难以抑制自己的喜悦之情，我为你和马克感到高兴。我总是被你们强大的爱情所鼓舞，相信你们的婚姻将会是快乐而美满的。

我听说这个月的某一天将有场订婚典礼，我希望能了解典礼的细节。我十分乐意出席庆典，并帮你们一起庆祝。如果你有时间就打我电话吧，这样我就可以在电话里给你道喜了。就像我说的那样，我会再次隆重地祝贺你。期待能听到更多的好消息！

诚挚的 艾米

23. 祝贺结婚

Dear Sophie and Luke,

Hearty congratulations on your recent marriage, I am writing to send you my very best wishes for your married life and bright your future together. I know that you two were made for each other, and now you have tied the bond of love and can look forward to a lifetime of happiness together.

Charles Dickens wrote "Have a heart that never hardens, and a temper that never tires, and a touch that never hurts". My sincere wish is that your married life together will have this principle all through, and that your love for each other grows each passing day.

Thank you for inviting Peter and myself to your wedding. It was such a wonderful occasion to be at. We were both so pleased being there to be able to share your very special day and to celebrate your marriage.

Sending you our heartfelt best wishes for your future together.

Congrats again!

Your friend always,
Love,
Elizabeth

亲爱的苏菲和卢克：

你们最近步入了婚姻的殿堂，我对此表示衷心的祝贺。祝愿你们的婚后生活一帆风顺，两人白头偕老。我知道你们是天生的一对，现在你们为爱而结合，并将携手走向终生的幸福。

查尔斯·狄更斯曾说："拥有一颗心，永远柔软；一种脾性，永不疲倦；一种触摸，永无伤害。"我衷心希望这句话贯穿于你们的婚姻生活，也希望你们对彼此的爱与日俱增。

谢谢你们邀请我和皮特参加婚礼，婚礼举办得太好了。能和你们分享这个特殊的日子并庆祝你们的结合，我们都感到万分欣喜。

为你们的明天献上我们最诚挚的祝福。

再次祝贺你们！

你们永远的朋友
挚爱的 伊丽莎白

24. 祝贺生子

Dear friend Ronald,

I heard the good news and I am very happy for you that you have become a father. I want to convey my hearty congratulations to you regarding your new baby. It is really a good thing that a baby boy has taken birth in your house. I know your joy will have no bonds.

But as a good friend, I would also like to remind you that you have many challenges to face for the upbringing of the child. It is really good to know that your wife and your son is not having any complication regarding their health. You two now need to take care of their health for a couple of months. Give proper medicines and vaccinations to your child as the new borns are at a threat of being getting many diseases. I pray to God that he blesses your child and gives him a good and bright future.

>Yours affectionately,
>Tom Riddle

亲爱的罗纳德：

　　欣闻你做了父亲，我甚是高兴。我对你家中添丁表示衷心的祝贺。在家里产下一名男婴真是件好事，你一定沉浸在无边无际的幸福中吧。

　　但作为好友我也要提醒你，要把孩子带大，你还得吃些苦头。现在你的妻儿没有出现任何问题，这真是太好了。在接下来的几个月里，你也要承担起照顾妻儿健康的重任。由于新生儿容易染上许多疾病，你要给他适当用药，加强免疫。我祈祷上苍，愿他保佑你的孩子，并给予他美好的未来。

>汤姆·里德尔 谨上

25. 祝贺毕业

Dear Jim,

　　Huge congratulations to you on the significant milestone of your college graduation! I know how hard you have worked to get to this point in your academic career, and I am extremely proud of you for this achievement. We look forward to seeing you at your graduation this weekend and to celebrating with you at the party that your parents are holding afterwards.

　　I know great things are ahead of you in life-in your career, in your personal life, everything. You have so much potential, and I look forward to seeing what opportunities present themselves to you. Remember, keep reaching for your goals and dreams. Never forget your ability to achieve them. Congratulations, and may you always be abundantly blessed.

>Sincerely,
>Emmy

亲爱的吉姆：

　　恭喜你迎来了人生中一个重要的里程碑——完成大学学业！我知道，为了这一天，你在象牙塔中加倍努力学习，最终取得成就，因此我为你感到骄傲。我们期待能在周末的毕业典礼上与你重逢，然后在你父母举办的派对上好好庆祝一番。

　　我相信无论在你的事业还是个人生活中，你必将前途似锦。你是个潜力无穷的孩子，我期待看到成功的机遇一个个地来到你的面前。记住，在实现目标和梦想的道路上要马不停蹄，同时也不要忘记自己有达成目标的实力。恭喜你，愿你永远受到幸运之神的眷顾。

艾米 敬启

26. 祝贺获得奖学金

Dear Ms. Jennifer

We are honored and pleased to inform you that you have cleared the scholarship exam which was held in your St. Martins College of Arts and Commerce on 1st September, 2010. Knowing you can give the entrance exam for MBA and after you clear the entrance exam your scholarship fees will get stated from the same month of your course. This entire fees for MBA including your college as well as tuition fees everything will come under this scholarship. Apart from these two fees all your books and related material will also be come under this fee. Your college and tuition fees amount will directly to be given to their respective source and a monthly stipend of rupees five thousand will be given to you every month. We require all your related certificates and documents for submission purpose so contact us as soon as possible.

Yours Sincerely,
Mr. Harlan S. Diaz

亲爱的詹尼佛小姐：

我们很荣幸地通知你，在2010年9月1日圣马丁大学艺术与商业学院的奖学金考试中，你脱颖而出，获得奖学金。你可以参加工商管理硕士入学考试，在此之后你的奖学金将于课程开始的当月生效。工商管理硕士的全部学费，包括你的择校费和学费，所有的开支将包含在此奖学金之下。此外，所有的课本及相关资料花费也将包含其中。你的学杂费数额将直接由相应的渠道支付，此外你每月将收到一笔五千卢布的生活津贴。为了提交申请，我们需要你提供相应资料和文件，请你尽快联系我们。

哈伦·S·迪亚兹 敬启

27. 祝贺找到工作

My dear Michael,

  I am very happy to hear that you have secured a job in the Microsoft as a software engineer. Congratulations my dear friend and keep it up. It's a great achievement to get a job in such an huge multinational software company. You will feel the presence of very intelligent and professional personals in the office.

  Now you must work hard to stay among them and learn more and more things from them. You are very hardworking and I know your colleagues will enjoy working with you. During the weekends if possible come and meet your old pals as we all want to see the genius. Well jokes apart and all the best for your new job. May God bless you.

Yours Sincerely
Alex

亲爱的迈克尔：

  听说你成功应聘为微软的软件工程师，我感到十分高兴。恭喜你，我的好朋友，希望你能坚持不懈。能成功应聘这样一家大型跨国软件公司，真是不小的胜利。你将开始和办公室里聪明而专业的同事们打交道。

  现在你必须努力工作，才能保证不被淘汰，并不断从你的同事那儿学到东西。你吃苦耐劳，我相信你的同事会乐于和你合作。如果可以，周末出来见见你的老朋友吧，他们都想和你这个天才见个面。抛开玩笑，祝你工作顺意。愿上帝保佑你！

艾利克斯 敬启

28. 祝贺晋升

Dear Mr. Michael

  We are pleased and honored to inform you that you have been promoted from Junior Accounts Officer to Senior Accounts Officer in the organization. I congratulate to you on behalf of the company for this achievement of yours. As your post grows in the company your responsibility towards your work will also increase. You have achieved this promotion within a span of one year with all your hard work and dedication towards your work. We expect the same behavior from you in future even though you got a promotion. Your new salary structure and details about compensation everything will be mentioned in the official promotional letter which will be given to you very soon. If you find any queries or difficulties related to this matter you can contact the Human Resource Department on the intranet of the companies' website. Once again many congratulations to you and all the best for future growth.

Yours Sincerely,
Ms. Lynn F. Hoskins

亲爱的迈克尔先生：

  我们很高兴也很荣幸地通知你，你已经从初级会计师被提拔到我们集团的高级会计师。我谨代表公司，祝贺你所取得的成就。随着职位的提升，你的工作责任也将相应增加。你在过去的一年中，献身工作，兢兢业业，因此获得了提升的机会。尽管你得到了提拔，我们仍希望你日后继续保持优良作风。你的新工资结构以及薪水的细节将在官方升职信中提及，不久你将收到。如果你对此还有疑问，你可以通过公司内网联系人力资源部。最后，再次恭喜你获得升迁，祝你未来的事业蒸蒸日上。

林恩·F·霍斯金斯小姐
敬上

29. 祝贺退休

Dear friend Robbin,

  I am writing this letter to congratulate on your retirement. I got this news yesterday. I am very happy that you will enjoy leisure. You had a very good work experience. Your work used to be appreciated every year in the office. Many times you got the award for best employee in your office. You sincerely carried out the post of senior sales manager in your company and served your company for 50 years. The company will always remember your service and contribution towards your job.

  I still remember when we were in college and used to discuss about our career. But you made it towards your dream job. I also remember the day when you were appointed in your company. Anyway this is your leisure time.

You should now utilize your time for relaxing purpose. You should enjoy all the activities that you missed out when you were supposed to do. I know you must have planned to spend most of your time on your farmhouse.

May God give you happiness.

Your affectionately,
Tom Hogg

亲爱的罗宾：

　　我写这封信，特来对你的退休表示祝贺。我昨天得知了这个消息，一想到你将颐养天年，我就十分开心。你有着很好的工作经验，你的工作每年都得到办公室同仁的认可，在你的办公室里你甚至拿了很多次最佳员工奖。在公司里，你很好地诠释了高级销售经理这一职位，五十年如一日地把精力奉献给公司。公司将永远记住你的付出和贡献。

　　我依然记得，我们在大学深造时曾经探讨过我们的事业，只有你在自己梦想的工作上获得了成功。我依然记得你被公司任命的那天。无论如何，你现在迎来了闲暇时光。你要用你的时间好好放松一下。你应该好好享受那些曾经应该做却没有做的事。我知道，你应该已经做好了计划，打算把大部分的时间花在你的农场里。

　　愿上帝赐予你快乐。

你最亲爱的
汤姆·霍格

30. 祝贺获奖

Dear Tom,

　　I have read with great delight your name published in today's morning newspaper. You have won the George Washington Award for 2011, one of the most coveted prizes for men of literature in our country. Your untiring industry, dedicated perseverance, and devotion and immense service to English literature have won you this honor.

　　My sincerest wishes are with you. I join with your friends and admirers in offering you my heartiest congratulations. May your unremitting endeavor in the service of English Literature go on with undiminished vigor!

Yours sincerely,
Elizabeth

亲爱的汤姆:

  当我在今天的早报上看到你的名字时,我心中充满了愉悦之情。你赢得了2011年度的乔治·华盛顿奖,这是我国文学界最令人垂涎的奖项之一。你不知倦怠的工作、忘我的坚持以及对英语文学的投入和倾心服务为你赢得了这项荣誉。

  我把最衷心的祝福献给你。我和你的朋友以及仰慕者一同向你表示最诚挚的祝贺。愿永不熄灭的活力伴随着你,以不懈的努力继续为英语文学增光添彩!

伊丽莎白 谨致

31. 祝贺开业

Dear John,

  Congratulations on your new venture. I'm sure that the Irvington Company will be a great success. You are very savvy to have started early on in businesses of this kind.

  I would think we'll see many more cropping up in the next few years, and you will have the advantage of experience and an established client base.

  I'm looking forward to doing business with you.

Regards,
Olivier

亲爱的约翰:

  祝贺你的公司开业!我相信欧文顿公司将大获成功。像你这样富有见识的人,才会及早进军这片商业领域。

  也许在接下来的几年里,我们将见证越来越多的类似企业诞生,但你将拥有经验上的优势和牢固的客户基础。

  我期盼着能和你合作。

谨致问候
奥利维亚

Unit 3　感谢信

Thank-you Letters

感谢信（Thank-you Letters）通常带有浓厚的感情色彩，具有比较浓的人情味。感谢信通常分为正式感谢信和非正式感谢信，前者行文得体、语气礼貌谦恭、用词正式正规；后者语气则更加亲切热情。

写作"三步走"：表达感谢之情并说明原因——提及自己曾受到对方的帮助——再次感谢并表达回报愿望

提示：表达的感激之情要恰到好处，不要过于夸张；建议在结尾尽量表达希望回报对方的愿望，显得更加真诚。

✽ 常用句型

1. Thank you very much for …

   十分感谢……

2. I am truly grateful to you for …

   为了……，我真心感激您

3. It was good (thoughtful) of you …

   承蒙好意（关心）……

4. You were so kind to send …

   承蒙好意送来……

5. Thank you again for your wonderful hospitality and I am looking forward to seeing you soon.

   再次感谢您的盛情款待，并期待不久见到您。

6. I find an ordinary "thank-you" entirely inadequate to tell you how much…

   我觉得一般的感谢的字眼完全不足以表达我对您多么……

32. 感谢老师

Dear Miss Lai,

  I hope you know how much I've been missing you for all these years! I really love your class and I know I learned a ton. You have a way of making dry subjects really interesting. I only wish all the best for you and your family, especially your lovely son.

  Thank you!

Sincerely yours,
Martin

亲爱的赖老师：

  我希望您知道这些年我有多么想念您！我非常喜欢您讲的课，也从中获益匪浅。您能让枯燥的知识变得有趣。我只愿您和您的家人吉祥如意，尤其是您那可爱的儿子。

  谢谢您！

马丁 谨致

33. 感谢亲人

Dear Mom,

  Best wishes to you on Mother's Day, when I get to officially declare you the Best Mom Ever. Though I may not always say it (or show it), you mean the world to me. Thank you for being there. I don't know what I'd do without you. I love you!

Your son,
Jack

亲爱的妈妈：

  母亲节快乐！我在此正式宣布您获得史上最佳妈妈奖。尽管我不会经常说这句话或这样表达，但是您对我来说就是全世界。谢谢您对我的关怀。我不知道，如果没有您我将会变成什么样。我爱您！

您的儿子
杰克

34. 感谢领导

Dear Mr Rogerson

 I would like to thank you for taking your valuable time out from your busy schedule to discuss the insurance matters of the company with me. I was not able to handle the important investment deals as well as economic issues of the company due to lack of knowledge. Now, I am fully satisfied with the discussion which has helped me gain knowledge and experience that are agreeing with the needs of our company.

 I am thankful to you for organizing an hour long conference to explain internal financial ventures of the company with me. I truly appreciate your dedication towards work and various working techniques that you use in this organization. I will certainly try my best to bring out the best of work with excellent results.

 Thank you once again for your kind support.

Yours Sincerely,
Erin Rose

亲爱的罗格森先生:

 您在百忙之中抽出宝贵的时间,和我探讨公司的保险业务,为此我深表感谢。因为业务不熟,我难以应付公司的重要投资交易以及经济问题。我对我们的讨论十分满意,它让我获得了与公司需要相符的知识和经验。

 感谢您抽出了一小时的时间,给我解释了公司内部的财务项目。我很欣赏您在集团中献身工作的精神,以及使用的各种工作技巧。我将尽我最大的努力,以最好的状态给工作带来累累硕果。

 再次感谢您的鼎力支持!

艾琳·罗斯 敬上

35. 感谢同事

Dear friends,

 Good day to all. After the serious and deep thoughts, I have come to a decision to put an end to my job in this company. The company gave me many benefits and the greatest thing that I experience here is to have you as my colleagues. I would like to extend my sincerest thanks to all of you people by writing this letter. You are so amazing.

　　This might be a surprise to you, however I decided to work in the ABC Videocon Electronics, my job commencing will be this coming August 21. You know that it is my dream to work in multi-national company and now that the opportunity has come, I will not let this pass, and I am pleasured to work there. Nevertheless, prior to my resignation, I would like to handover the responsibilities.

　　I wish you great success in future! From my deepest, thank you.

Sincerely,
Gopi Kiran.

亲爱的朋友们：

　　大家好。经过深思熟虑之后，我终于决定从公司辞职。公司曾给予我许多好处，但最美好的莫过于和各位同事相处的经历。通过这封信，我想对你们所有人表达我最诚挚的谢意。你们都棒极了。

　　然而，我决定加盟 ABC 视频录像电子公司，并于 8 月 21 日开始上班，这对你们来说可能太突然了。你们知道，在跨国企业工作一直是我的梦想，现在机遇降临在我的身上，我不能失之交臂，我喜欢在那儿工作。尽管如此，在辞职之前，我会将我的工作职责移交。

　　祝愿你们在未来都能大有作为！我从内心深处向你们致以谢意。

戈皮·齐兰 敬上

36. 感谢其他单位

Dear Company X,

We are thrilled to hear you've decided to work with us. We know you'll be happy with our products and I personally will make sure you've got all the assistance you need going forward.

Our company prides itself on customer service, as does yours, and I look forward to being in touch to answer any questions or just see that all is going smoothly. Thank you for your business.

Sincerely,
Tom Jackson

亲爱的 X 公司：

  听说贵公司已决定与我们合作，我们都为之振奋不已。我们相信，贵公司将对我们的产品十分满意，而且我个人保证在前进的道路上，我将给予你们必要的帮助。

  客户服务是我们公司的骄傲，也是你们的骄傲。我期待着我们能保持联系，以便我能回答任何问题，或是仅看看是否一切进展顺利。非常感谢您的合作。

汤姆·杰克森 谨致

37. 感谢志愿者

Dear Mr. Chen,

  I would like to thank you from the bottom of my heart on behalf of our department for sparing your precious time and serving us in the celebration of the 60th anniversary of the founding of the People's Republic of China.

  It was possible only with the assistance of volunteers like you that we have been capable to take up such fantastic services in the event.

  We genuinely thank you once more and expect that you would carry on widening your precious support in our upcoming events also.

  Thanking You!

Sincerely,
Li Ming

亲爱的陈先生：

  在中华人民共和国 60 周年华诞庆祝活动圆满成功之际，我谨代表本部门，向百忙中抽空帮助服务的您致以最诚挚的谢意！

  只有在以您为代表的志愿者的帮助下，我们才能在庆祝活动中献上如此完美的服务。

  为此，我们再次感谢您的支持，希望您在我们接下来的活动中再接再厉，继续发扬宝贵的奉献精神。

  此致
敬礼！

李明 敬上

38. 感谢款待

Dear Nina and Dean,

Thank you so much for the wonderful visit at your house. We always have a great time whenever we're with you. We just wish we saw you more often.

Thank you so much for the lovely meals you made for us. David loved the Chicken Paprikash and of course I'm always a fan of the zucchini quiche. I'm always inspired whenever I'm with you because you have the amazing ability to create such lovely meals with ease.

But even if we're eating Jimboy's Tacos, we love sharing meals with you. We hope to see you more often in the new year.

Warm Regards,
Green

亲爱的妮娜和迪安：

非常感谢你们对我的盛情款待。无论我们何时在一起，总能享受一段美好的时光。我们只希望以后能多多聚会。

非常感谢你们为我们烹制的美味佳肴。大卫很喜欢红椒鸡肉，而我自然是南瓜酥壳饼的忠实粉丝。无论我们何时在一起，我总能受你启发，因为你在烹饪方面真是天赋异禀。

但就算我们去吃吉姆男孩的炸玉米饼，我们也乐于和你们分享美食。我们期盼在新年里与你们多见面。

诚挚的 格林

39. 感谢帮助

Dear Miss Liu,

Thank you so much for providing my son with tutoring assistance related to his French studies. Because of your help, he is earning better grades and enjoying French classes so much more. It is so encouraging to see this progress.

We will be in touch soon to schedule more tutoring sessions. Thanks again for all of your help.

> Sincerely,
> Mrs. Cooper

亲爱的刘小姐：

  非常感谢您给我儿子补习法语课。在您的关怀下，他取得了更好的成绩，比以前更喜欢上法语课。看到这样的进展，我感到非常受鼓舞。

  我们很快会与您联系，以安排更多的私人辅导环节。再次感谢您的帮助！

> 库珀太太 敬上

40. 感谢祝贺

Dear Mr. James Pound,

  Thank you very much for your note of congratulation on my graduating from college.

  It was good of you to take the time and trouble to write, and I sincerely appreciate your kindness.

> Cordially yours,
> Li Ming

亲爱的詹姆斯·庞德先生：

  非常感谢您为我大学毕业写来祝贺信。

  您在百忙中抽出时间给我写信，对此我由衷感激。

> 你诚挚的 李明

41. 感谢奖励

Dear Boss,

  I was so thrilled and surprised to receive the company's Employee of the Year award this week. What a honor-thank you. It is so gratifying to know that my hard work and efforts have been noticed and appreciated.

  Thank you again for such an important recognition.

> Sincerely,
> Michael Lee

亲爱的老板：

  本周我收到了公司的年度最佳员工奖，为此我感到十分惊喜和意外。谢谢您给了我这一殊荣。自己的辛勤工作和努力得到了大家的注意和认可，这令我十分欣慰。

  再次感谢您对我的认可。

迈克尔·李 敬上

42. 感谢捐赠

Dear Ms. Hamilton,

  Thank you for your generous gift of $ 5000 to Edukids, California. Thanks to your contribution and commitment to the cause of education in third world countries, we are able to increase awareness and raise funds for kids from countries who are unable to provide even basic education to children, due to various factors. We appreciate your effort and all that you have done to ensure that more kids get educated and therefore, have a brighter future.

  Our mission as an organization is to educate those kids who have never even stepped into the hallways of a school, lacking not just the money to go to an educational institute but also lacking the infrastructure for a school. With the help of donations that we receive from patrons such as yourself, and other events that we organize like fetes, book collections drives, etc. We raise money and collect books to donate to the cause. The money is used to build schools and buy books, primarily in areas in Nepal and Bangladesh. The money that you have donated is being used primarily to build a school in the Kathmandu district of Nepal.

  As we successfully fulfill our mission of educating more children in lesser developed countries, we also aim at educating their parents to enable them to help their kids cope with their studies. It is only due to the patronage of people like you that we have managed to work towards achieving our mission.

  Thank you again for all your contributions to our cause.

Yours sincerely,
Carla Dorian

亲爱的汉密尔顿女士：

非常感谢您为加利福尼亚儿童教育基金会捐赠的 5,000 美元。谢谢您为第三世界国家的教育事业做出的贡献。为此我们得以提高知名度；为那些因故不能为儿童提供基础教育的国家的儿童募集资金。我们很欣赏您为了更多的孩子能上学并拥有一个美好的明天而作出的努力。

作为一个组织，我们的使命是教育那些没能走进学堂上课的孩子，但我们不仅缺乏发展为国际组织的资金，还缺少学校的基础设施。只有通过像您这样的人士的捐助，以及为我们组织的募捐游乐会、书籍捐赠等活动，我们才能收集资金和书籍以完成我们的使命。这些资金将主要花费在尼泊尔和孟加拉国等地，帮助学校建立校舍、购买图书。您所捐赠的钱款将主要用于建设尼泊尔加德满都地区的一所学校。

当我们成功实现我们的使命，使更多欠发达国家的孩子走进学堂时，我们也致力于教育他们的父母，使他们能帮助自己的孩子完成学业。多亏了像您这样的企业总裁的援助，我们才能朝着我们的目的坚持着走下去。

再次感谢您为我们的事业做出的贡献！

卡拉·多瑞安 敬上

43. 感谢赠送生日礼物

Dear Toby,

If you had asked me what I wanted for my birthday, I would have said, "A unique necktie" You just couldn't have selected anything I would like more! The color and the material are both magnificent!

Thank you, Toby. You have a marvelous genius for selecting the right gift!

With much love,
Edward

亲爱的托比：

如果你问我最想要什么生日礼物，我会说："我要一条独特的领带！"没有什么能比你给我的礼物更讨我欢心了，它的颜色和面料都棒极了。

谢谢你，托比。你真是个选礼物的天才！

艾德伍德 致以最诚挚的爱

44. 感谢赠送结婚礼物

Dear Ms.Wilma

  I am happy that you could make it to my wedding anniversary. James's and yours presence made a lot of difference to our special day. Thanks for making the day all the more memorable and cherish able with your company. You are very near to our heart and your presence means a lot to us.

  In addition, thank you for the beautiful antique wall painting gifted by both of you on our anniversary. The painting is a masterpiece and the beautiful and intricate work on the frame is a matter to marvel. I am waiting to flaunt it on our bedroom wall of our new home.

  Please accept appreciation from both of us.

  Thank you once more for making us feel so unique and making us so important.

  Hoping to meet you soon.

Mr & Mrs Conklin

亲爱的威尔玛小姐：

  我很高兴你能抽空参加我的结婚典礼。你和詹姆斯的出席为我们这个特殊的日子增添了不少喜气。谢谢您的陪伴，让我们的这一天变得更有纪念意义，更值得珍惜。你离我们的心很近，你的出席对我们来说有很多的意义。

  另外，谢谢你们为我们的婚礼准备的精美古典墙画。这幅画作巧夺天工，复杂精美的画框做工真是令人叹为观止。我正等着把它摆在新家的卧室墙上，好好地炫耀一番。

  请接受我们诚挚的谢意。

  你让我们感到自己如此独特、如此重要，对此我们再次表示感谢。

  期待着再次与你相见。

康克林夫妇 敬上

45. 感谢慰问

Dear Mrs. Cai,

  I am writing to express my most heartfelt thanks to you for being such a compassionate and competent caregiver for my mother during the time that she has been recovering from surgery and other illnesses. It is so difficult to see her going through these health challenges but such a reassurance to know that someone like you is looking after her needs so closely.

As always, please let me know whenever you have questions or need to provide me with medical updates about my mother. I will also be sure to keep you informed on anything that you need to know. I truly value our communication and our ability to work together as a team on my mother's behalf. Thank you again so very much for everything you do.

Sincerely,
T. J. London

尊敬的蔡女士：

您是一位称职并富有同情心的保姆，使我的母亲从手术和其他疾病中迅速康复，为此我写这封信以表达我最诚挚的谢意。我不忍心看她老人家与疾病抗争，但知道有像您这样的人贴身照顾她的起居后，我就打消了所有的担忧。

和往常一样，如果您有疑问，或者要向我提供我母亲最新的医疗状况，请及时告知我。如果我有什么需要让您知道的，我也会告诉您。为了我的母亲，我们应该及时沟通并团结合作。再次感谢您为我母亲所做的一切。

T J. 兰登 敬上

46. 感谢吊唁

Dear Mrs. Thompson,

I shall always remember with gratitude the letter you wrote me when you learned of Joan's death. No one but you, who knew my wife and loved her as her own family did, could have written that letter. It brought me comfort, Mrs. Thompson, at a time when I needed it badly.

Thank you from the bottom of my heart, for your letter and for your many kindness to Joan during her long illness.

Sincerely,
Jude Steven

亲爱的汤普森夫人:

  当您知晓琼的死讯时,您特意写了封信给我,为此我将永远铭记于心。没有人能像您这样了解我的妻子,像亲人一样关心她,并写出那样的一封信。正是在我需要安慰之时,您的信安慰了我受伤的心。

  我从心底感激您的来信,以及您在琼生病期间对她的照顾。

祖德·斯蒂芬 谨致

Unit 4　告别信

Farewell Letters

"天下没有不散的宴席",很多时候,我们在离开某地或某人前需要预先告知对方,这时就需要写一封告别信(Farewell Letters)。告别信可以是写给亲朋好友也可以是写给企业单位等。告别信一定要说明告别的原因,表示自己对这次告别的态度,同时对收信人要表示安慰、祝福、勉励等情感,这样的一封告别信才是真诚的、饱满的。

写作"三步走":开门见山说明离开原因——展开原因——必要时应表达感谢和祝福

提示:措辞要委婉、恳切,力求以情动人。

❋ 常用句型

1. Time is flying away, and years are passing by. Farewell, my friend! Take care, my friend!

   时光飞逝,岁月匆匆。朋友,再见!朋友,珍重!

2. Don't be disappointed on the journey of life. There are friends in the world. Seize your chance and value your opportunities. May our friendship be everlasting.

   人生路上何须惆怅,天涯海角总有知音。把握机会珍惜缘分,祝愿我们友谊长存。

3. I am writing this letter to you so that you have something that you can keep to remind you of our friendship, to bid you a proper farewell, so you will never forget our friendship and the times of joy as well as sadness, we have spent together.

   我给你写这封信,是以让你记住我们的友谊,同时也是向你告别,切莫忘记我们的友谊,以及那些我们一起经历的悲喜。

4. On my retirement, I hold every confidence in you as my team to carry on in my footsteps, and I wish you all, and the company all the best for your future endeavors!

   在退休之际,我坚信团队中的你们一定会继续我的步伐,我也祝你们以及整个公司在未来的旅途上一路顺风!

47. 给朋友的告别信

Dear Ella,

The past three years with you have been fantastic, but the best of friends must apart.

Imagine if Mrs. Thin had not made us sit next to each other, then we would never have become such firm friend that we are today.

My cell phone number and e-mail are the same as always. Please stay in touch, you are a life-long friend to me, and I wish you all the best for whatever your ventures are for the future.

Yours Truly
Janice Perkins

亲爱的艾拉:

与你共度的三年是美妙的,但天下没有不散的宴席。

如果辛夫人没有把我们安排为同桌,我们也不可能成为如此要好的朋友。

我的电话号码和邮箱地址都没有变。一定要保持联系。你是我一生的朋友,祝愿你未来一帆风顺,万事如意。

贾尼斯·帕金斯 敬启

48. 给父母的告别信

Dear Mum and Dad,

I am writing this letter to you both, to bid you a fondest of farewells as I fly the nest to start my college studies. I know we have already said our goodbyes, but I want to write this letter to you, for you to keep.

Thank you so much for doing such a good job in preparing me for the future, in nurturing me, and shaping me for the outside world. Your guidance has been more important than you realize.

I am so happy that you support my decision to pursue my education by going on to do further education at college. This is all a little scary for me, but I will always have with me all that you have taught me to give me a helping hand wherever I may go.

              Your loving daughter
              Jan

亲爱的爸妈：

  我写这封信，是想在远去求学之际向你们道声再见。虽已道过别，但我仍想留书一封，愿你们以此为念想。

  感谢你们为我的未来所做的准备，感谢你们的养育之恩，也感谢你们教会我如何面对外面的世界。你们的教导比你们想的要重要得多。

  当我决定进入大学继续学习时，你们的支持令我甚是欣喜。尽管有一丝怯意，但我会谨记你们的教诲，相信不管身处何方，它都能助我一臂之力。

              爱你们的女儿
              简

49. 给妻子的告别信

Dear Lillian,

  It has been twenty years since we took our wedding vows, and promised to cherish each other for life, and since that very day, not a day has gone by when you have not been by my side.

  Times are hard now and I have been forced to accept the job in New Delhi, forcing us to spend weeks, if not months apart. And I'm writing you this letter to bid you a goodbye.

  You have stood by me through the good and the bad for the past twenty years, especially when times got tough, always been there for me. I sincerely hope that you will continue your support to me even though we have been forced to live apart. I will send you my new contact details just as soon as I have them–my new address and cell phone number.

              Your loving husband
              Ali Hafed

亲爱的莉莲：

  自我们彼此在婚礼上结下誓言、承诺今生互相珍惜以来已有二十年。这么些年你一直都陪伴在我身边。

但时事无情,我迫不得已接受新德里的工作,为此我们要分别数周甚至数月。故写此信与你告别。

过去二十年,你随我同甘共苦;纵是时得艰难,你亦不离不弃。即将分开的这段日子,我真心希望你能继续做我的后盾。我会尽快告诉你我新的地址和电话号码。

爱你的丈夫
阿里·哈菲德

50. 给员工的告别信

Dear Team,

I am writing you this letter as, after ten years with the company, it has now come around for it to be my time to take my retirement. Throughout these ten years, I have received nothing less than support, cooperation, hard work and diligence from you. The great success of the company is a direct result of such dedication.

On my retirement, I hold every confidence in you as my team to carry on in my footsteps, and I wish you and the company all the best for your future endeavors. I will leave my cell phone and e-mail with the receptionist, you are all welcome to keep in touch, and please do not hesitate to contact me if need be on any company problem with which I may be of assistance.

Best regards
Philip McMahon

亲爱的伙伴们:

我在公司工作已有十年,如今也到了退休的时候,因此给你们写了这封告别信。在这十年中,你们给予我的全是支持、合作与兢兢业业。是你们的奉献造就了公司的巨大成功。

虽然我即将退休,但我坚信作为队友的你们能随我的步伐继续前进。祝愿你们和公司日后的事业一切顺利。我会将电话和邮箱留给接待员,望保持联系,若公司事务上有需要的地方,请随时告诉我。

致敬
菲利普·麦克马洪

51. 给老板的告别信

Dear Mr. Perrin,

As I am sure you are aware, today is my last day working for UBA group, but I find it appropriate to write you this letter in order to take a moment to thank you for all your support that you have given me during my time with the company, I have learned a great deal from you.

I will take with me my experiences and all that I have learned, your leadership in this company being second to none, always keeping everyone together as a team.

I wish to thank you again for giving me the confidence you have given, for giving me the ability to stand up against any challenge, and for truly allowing me to flourish and prosper both personally and professionally.

Please keep in touch.

My sincerest regards
J smith

尊敬的佩林先生：

相信您已知道，今天是我为 UBA 集团效力的最后一天，故致信给您，借此机会感谢您在我工作期间对我的支持。从您那儿，我学到了很多。

您在我们公司的领导能力首屈一指，总能把众人凝聚为一个团队，我会铭记在公司的工作经历，谨记所学到的一切。

再次感谢您帮助我树立信心，使我不畏艰难，在个人和职业中绽放自我。

请保持联系。

最真挚的问候
J. 史密斯

Unit 5　慰问信　　　　　　　　　　Letters of Sympathy

　　慰问信（Letters of Sympathy）是表示向对方（一般是同级、或上级对下级单位、个人）关怀、慰问的信函。它是有关机关或者个人，以组织或个人的名义在他人处于特殊的情况下（如战争、自然灾害、事故），或在节假日，向对方表示问候、关心的应用文。慰问信包括两种：一种是表示同情安慰；另一种是在节日表示问候。信应写得态度诚恳、真切。

　　写作"三步走"：说明写慰问信的原因，或是对受害者深表同情——叙述对方的模范事迹或遇到的困难时表现出来的高尚品质，并向对方表示慰问——写一些鼓励和祝愿的话

　　提示：
- 要根据所慰问的不同对象，确定信的内容。
- 慰问信的抒情性较强，语言亲切、生动，使受慰问者在精神上得到安慰和鼓励，增强克服困难的勇气和继续前进的信心。

✽ 常用句型

1. We are very sorry to learn of…

   我们非常遗憾地获悉……

2. I felt very sorry indeed when I heard of your illness.

   得知你生病的消息我非常难过。

3. In the next few days I think you should have a good rest and take the doctor's advice.

   在接下来的几天内，你要好好休息，谨记医嘱。

4. With the best wishes for your quick and complete recovery.

   希望你早日康复。

5. If there is anything I can do, give me a call.

   如果有我能帮忙的，请打电话通知我。

52. 慰问病人

Dear Nickolai,

I am deeply saddened to hear that you are not in good health at this time. When I saw you last month during the Ski Trip at Big Bear, you appeared to be well. This news most definitely comes as a shock to the rest of our church choir group and myself.

Words cannot express how glad I am that you were able to get yourself checked by the doctor sooner than later, so that there is still time to get back up from this illness.

I understand that with your job as an editor for the Cochran newspaper, you are mostly sitting throughout the day. Despite this, I suggest you take the time to exercise regularly and eat well. These are crucial in assuring that you fight this illness. Do not forget to drink plenty of water. Also, doing some daily breathing exercises, slowly inhaling and exhaling, will help reduce any additional stress you may have. This will put you on the road to good health.

I hope you do all you can do for yourself to get better when you are by yourself. Keep in mind that your family and friends are here for you to provide you with anything that you need. You will be in our thoughts and prayers. Please call me to let me know how you are doing when you are ready to talk.

Love,
Thalia

亲爱的尼可莱:

得闻你此刻抱恙,深感痛心。上月在大熊山滑雪时,你身体看上去还不错,此时却得了病,我们教堂歌唱队的成员们都甚是惊讶。

听闻你尽早去看了医生,定能及早痊愈,我感到无比欣慰。

我知道,作为一名科克伦报纸编辑的你,每天的大部分时间都要在办公椅上度过。但是,我建议你能抽出时间定期锻炼,并保持健康饮食,这对抵抗疾病是非常重要的。要记得多喝水,同时每天做呼吸运动(缓慢地吸气呼气)会有降压的效果。这些都会助你恢复健康。

一个人生活的时候，希望你能好好照顾自己。记住，如果有任何需要，家人和朋友们随时都可以帮助你。我们会想念你，为你祈祷。有空时给我打电话，让我了解你的近况。

爱你的 塔利亚

53. 慰问伤员

Dear Helen,

I could not believe that you broke a hone in skiing. Be patient. Take good care of it and recover soon. Do not worry about your lessons! Fred, Isabelle, Sophie, Jimmy and others all promise to help you make up. We are sending you a PSP. I hope you like it, and that it will help to pass the time pleasantly.

With every good wish for your swift recovery!

Sincerely yours,
Grace

亲爱的海伦：

惊悉你在滑雪时不幸骨折，令人难以置信。这段时间你要保持耐心，注意伤处，尽快康复。不要担心课程，弗雷德、伊莎贝拉、索菲、吉米，还有其他人都说会帮你补课。希望你喜欢我们给你送去的 PSP，让它帮你轻松地打发掉时间。

衷心祝愿你迅速康复。

格雷斯 谨上

54. 慰问同事

Dear Mike,

It was sad to listen about your severe illness and absence from work. The whole staff members are missing you so much. I am writing this letter with a hope that this will cheer you up and make you feel better.

The whole team is terribly missing you because they said there is no fun or liveliness in anything without you. The disease is not fun, but please be relieved that the doctors have ruled out treatment even for a severe illness.

I suppose you will have to give up hot peppers and chili and I know that it is not easy for you but this is better for your health and stay you out of the doctor's office.

I'm glad that you are home from the hospital and doing better.

Get well soon, so you can come and see us again.

With Love,
John

亲爱的迈克:

获悉你得了重病,无法工作,我很难过。全体员工都很想念你,我写这封信是希望你振作起来,身体早日康复。

整个团队对你甚是思念,没有你在一切都了无生趣。生病不是好玩的事,但即使是重病,医生也有办法治疗,你尽可宽心。

我建议你别吃辣椒,我知道这对你来说并非易事,但这样有益于你的身体健康,可以让你少生病。

很高兴你已经出院回家,并且逐渐康复。

希望你早日痊愈,这样就可以再见到我们了。

约翰 谨上

55. 上级对下级的慰问

Dear Frank,

I was sorry to learn of your illness.

Everybody in the company misses you, and we hope you will be all right soon. While you are away from the office, Nathan will do your share of the job, so you don't need to worry.

If there's anything else I could do for you, do not hesitate to let me know.

With my sincere wishes for your speedy recovery.

Yours sincerely,
Martin

亲爱的弗兰克：

得知你生病，我很难过。

同事们都很想念你，希望你尽快康复。你无法上班的这段时间，南森会完成你的工作，所以不要担心。

有什么需要的地方，请及时告诉我。

衷心祝愿你尽早康复。

马丁 谨上

56. 对其他单位人员的慰问

Dear Mr. Lin,

I was so sorry to hear that you had been injured in a traffic accident and am anxious to know how you are getting on now.

Through talking with your colleague, I know that your company's business is going well and has received many orders for your improved productivity. I believe everything will go well.

I'm hoping for your quick and complete recovery.

Yours faithfully,
Mark

尊敬的林先生：

听闻你因车祸受伤，我深感难过，不知现况如何。

在与你的同事交谈时得知，你公司的业务进展顺利，生产率的提高给你们带来了很多订单。我相信一切都会顺利。

祝愿你早日痊愈。

马克 敬上

57. 对受灾单位的慰问

Red Cross Society of Shanxi

Dear Sirs,

We were shocked to learn that the strong earthquake around the area in eastern Shanxi unfortunately caused heavy casualties and material losses to the inhabitants. Shaanxi people express deep sympathy and solicitude for the afflicted people and donate the sum of RMB one and a half million yuan as an expression of our concern for them. Your Society is requested to transmit this sum to the people in the affected areas and convey the profound solicitude of the Red Cross Society of Shaanxi and Shaanxi people to them.

The Red Cross Society of Shaanxi

山西红十字会的诸位工作人员：

惊悉山西东部地区发生强烈地震，给当地人民造成了巨大的人员伤亡和物质损失。陕西人民对受灾人民表示深切地同情和慰问，并捐款一百五十万人民币，以示关切。请贵会将此款转交给受灾地区的人民，并传达陕西红十字会和陕西人民对灾区人民的亲切关怀。

陕西红十字会

Unit 6　吊唁信

Letters of Condolence

吊唁信（letters of condolence）是社交活动中最难写的信。这类信主要是表达对死者的哀悼和怀念，并给其家属、亲人以真挚的安慰和问候。

写作"三步走"：对死者深表同情和怀念——给其亲人慰问——送出自己的祝福

提示：写吊唁信时要注意以下几点：

- 语言精炼概括，文字简短为宜。
- 内容充实，情感真挚。一般来说，包括这些内容：
  1) 听到噩耗后的惊讶和悲痛心情；
  2) 失去死者是难以弥补的缺憾；
  3) 简述死者生前的品德和功绩；
  4) 表示继承死者遗愿；
  5) 对死者亲属表示慰问以及传达有关方面的慰问。
- 语言要深沉、淳朴、自然、催人泪下，全文渗透悲痛和悼念的情调，切忌滥用修饰语或是夸大其词，给人油腔滑调之感。

✸ 常用句型

1. I was terribly sorry to hear of the death of Prof. Smith.

   听到史密斯教授去世的消息，我万分难过。

2. We have just learned with deep sorrow the sad news.

   得知这一悲伤的消息，我们极其悲痛。

3. I can't tell you how deeply we feel for you in your sorrow.

   我无法描述由于你的悲伤，我们是多么沉痛。

4. I wish there were some way in which we could lighten your burden of sorrow.

   希望有什么方法能减轻你的痛苦。

5. I hasten to offer you my most profound sympathy for the great grief that has fallen upon you and your household.

   我谨向你和你全家表示深切的慰问，万望节哀。

58. 吊唁好友丧母

Dear Walter,

I got to know about the death of your mother. I would like to express my sorrow about this unfortunate happening. I know that mother have special importance in everyone's life and it is very depressing to loss her. But everyone has to go one day and we have to accept this truth. May you all well.

Feel free to tell me if there is anything that I can do for you. My warmest love and wishes are with you and may God bless you.

Sincerely yours,
Todd M. Lowery

亲爱的沃尔特：

  惊悉你母亲去世，对此不幸，我很难过。母亲对于每个人来说都特别重要，她的逝世是令人悲痛的，但人固有一死，我们要接受现实。希望你一切安好。

  若有需要帮忙的地方，请随时联系我。谨致以最温暖的爱和祝愿，愿上帝保佑你。

托德·M·洛厄里 谨上

59. 吊唁好友丧偶

Dear Ray,

It may be not the right time for you to read the letter but I wish to express my deep condolences on the untimely death of your wife due to serious accident. I know that this is a very difficult situation for you but you have to keep patience and strength to bear this loss.

I wanted to go there and meet you but at this time it is not possible for me as I am out of station for some official meeting. I will definitely come at your place after coming back. Please tell me if you need any help.

Sincerely,
John

亲爱的雷：

　　尽管现在可能不是一个恰当的时间让你读这封信，但我仍想对你妻子在重大事故中的不幸早逝表示深切哀悼。我很了解，此时此刻对于你来说十分艰难，但请你一定要保持冷静，坚强地面对这次伤痛。

　　我想要去看望你，但我正出差赶赴会议，估计是不可能了。回去后我定会去拜访。需要什么帮助就请告诉我。

诚挚的　约翰

60. 吊唁好友丧子

Dear Mr. David

　　With very heavy heart I want to give you the sad news of death of your son. He has lost his life while fighting against the terrorists. He was a brave soldier and has great sentiments for the country. He have fought against terrorists so many times and saved the nation from them. We can never forget his contribution in saving the country.

　　Please accept my deep condolences on the behalf of President on his unfortunate death. For his bravery, we wish to give him a medal that will be given by President himself. Please come on January 26th to accept the medal. I will discuss more about it later.

Yours faithfully,
Jeffrey

尊敬的大卫先生：

　　我怀着沉痛的心情来告知您儿子的死讯。他在与恐怖分子作斗争时牺牲了。作为一名勇敢的战士，他对祖国有着深厚的感情，曾多次对抗恐怖分子，拯救国家。我们将永远铭记他的贡献。

　　我谨代表总统对您儿子的不幸逝去表示深切哀悼。我们希望授予他由总统亲自颁发的勋章以纪念他的英勇。请于2月26日来受领。不久我会与您讨论具体事宜。

杰弗里　敬上

61. 吊唁好友

Dear John & Family,

Thank you for passing along the sad news of Mark's death. He was a friend that I cherished and someone that touched many people's hearts. While I don't know your family very well, Mark shared things about you often. It was clear you meant so much to him. Please know that my thoughts and prayers are with you during this time.

Warmest Regards,

Bradley

亲爱的约翰一家：

感谢你们告知我马克不幸去世的消息。我非常珍惜马克这位朋友，他是个能触动他人内心的人。虽然我不怎么熟悉你们家族，但马克经常与我分享你们的事情，你们对他而言真的很重要。这段时间里，请记得我与你们同在，为你们祈祷。

最真挚的问候

布兰德利

62. 吊唁领导

Dearest Eric,

I am greatly saddened by the sudden death of Mr. David, your father. Your father and I were colleagues at work as I worked under his supervision. Working with him was one of my greatest wish in my career. Your father was very good in business and he has a good personality as well.

I do sympathize with how you are feeling and I know that it is far beyond any consolation as of the moment. Now, you will be facing another challenge in managing the company without the guidance of your father. Don't worry, be strong and do not stop believing in yourself and in our God as he will be with you to protect you. Please count on me if ever you need some help. I am always here if you need my service. Again, my condolences to you and to the rest of your family.

Praying for the repose of your father's soul.

With love and prayers,
Ervin Flores.

最亲爱的艾里克：

　　惊闻你父亲大卫先生突然离世，我深感悲痛。他曾是我的同事，我的领导。与他共事是我职业生涯中的最大心愿。你的父亲不仅业务能力强，个性也很好。

　　我理解你现在的感受，也知道此刻任何的安慰都是苍白的。现在的你要面对另外一个挑战：离开父亲的指导独自管理公司。别担心，坚强起来，切莫失去自信，相信上帝会与你同在、保佑你的。若有难处请告诉我，我随时都会帮助你。再次向你和你的家人表示哀悼。

　　愿你父亲的灵魂得到安息。

　　　　　　　　　　　　　　　　　　　　　　　　致以爱和祈祷
　　　　　　　　　　　　　　　　　　　　　　　　欧文·弗洛勒斯

63. 吊唁同事

Dear Madam,

Please accept my deep condolences on the death of your husband Mr. West. We were working on the same project and he was very hard-working and enthusiastic member of our team. It is really very tough for me to believe that now he is not with us.

But as we know that it is the circle of life and we have to accept hard realities of death. I know that you and your children have hard time ahead so my all best wishes are with you. May God help you and give you strength to overcome from this tough time. You are free to ask for any help from me.

　　　　　　　　　　　　　　　　　　　　　　　　Thanks
　　　　　　　　　　　　　　　　　　　　　　　　John

尊敬的夫人：

　　惊悉维斯先生离世，深表悲痛。我与他曾在一项工程中共事，在我们队伍中他工作努力、充满热情。很难相信他已离开了我们。

　　但这是生命循环使然，我们要接受这残酷的事实。想来您和您的孩子将来要度过艰难的时日，所以我要把最好的祝福送给您，愿上帝能帮助您，赐予您克服困难的力量。我会随时给您帮助的。

请节哀
约翰

64. 吊唁德高望重的师长

Dear Walter,

  I got to know about the death of your mother, Mrs. Carter. I would like to express my sorrow about this unfortunate happening. I know that your mother, Professor Carter, have special importance in everyone's life. She was my best teacher in the university and was loved by all her students. We feel greatly sad about the loss of the honored professor and academic authority. But everyone has to go one day and we have to accept this truth.

  Feel free to tell me if there is anything that I can do for you. My warmest love and wishes are with you and may God bless you.

Thanks
Todd M. Lowery

亲爱的沃尔特：

  痛悉你母亲卡特夫人逝去，对此不幸，我深表悲伤。你的母亲卡特教授对很多人来说都具有特殊的意义。她是我最喜欢的大学老师，全体学生也都很爱戴她。失去她这位受人尊敬的教授和学术权威，我们都极度悲痛。但是人都有老去的一天，我们要接受事实。

  若有任何需要，请告诉我。向你致以最真挚的爱和祝福，愿上帝保佑你。

节哀顺变
托德·M·洛厄里

65. 吊唁商业伙伴

Dear Manager Veronica,

  We were sorry to know that your chairman, Mr. Harrison had passed away and I am writing on behalf of my colleagues to express our deep sympathy.

I had the privilege of knowing Mr. Harrison for many years and always regarded him as a friend. By his untimely passing our industry has lost one of the ablest leaders. We at the representative office in Shanghai recall his many kindnesses and the pleasure of doing business together with him. Mr. Harrison will be greatly missed by all of us who have known him and worked with him in building a better relationship between our two businesses.

Please accept our deepest sympathy and convey our best wishes to Lady Harrison and her family.

With sincere sympathy,
Adam Keats

尊敬的维罗妮卡经理:

痛悉贵公司董事长哈里森先生去世的消息,我谨通过此函代表全体同事表达我们深切的关心和慰问。

我与哈里森先生相识多年,一直视其为好友。他的离去使我们这一行业失去了一名优秀的领军人物。我们上海办事处的同事们将铭记他的友善以及与他生意往来时的愉快经历。所有和哈里森先生相识或与之共创双方和谐关系的人们都会深深地怀念他。

谨致以最真挚的慰问,并请您向哈里森夫人及其家人传达我们最美好的祝愿。

致以最诚挚的问候
亚当·济慈

66. 吊唁国家领导人逝世

【模板】

Pyongyang

Central Committee of the Workers' Party of Korea

Central Military Commission of the Workers' Party of Korea

National Defense Commission of the Democratic People's Republic of Korea

Presidium of the Supreme People's Assembly of the Democratic People's Republic of Korea

Cabinet of the Democratic People's Republic of Korea:

We are shocked to learn that general secretary of the Workers' Party of Korea, chairman of the DPRK National Defense Commission and supreme commander of the Korean People's Army comrade Kim Jong Il passed away and we hereby express our deepest condolences and most sincere regards to the DPRK people.

Comrade Kim Jong Il is a great leader of the Worker's Party of Korea and the DPRK. He has dedicated the whole of his life and rendered immortal service to the great undertaking of socialist construction of the DPRK people.

Comrade Kim Jong Il is a close friend of the Chinese people. He has carried on and further developed the traditional friendship between China and DPRK which was built and cultivated by the older generation of revolutionaries of the two countries, established profound friendship with the Chinese leaders and pushed forward vigorously the good-neighborly friendship and cooperation between China and the DPRK. The CPC, the Chinese government and people are deeply saddened by the demise of comrade Kim Jong Il who will be remembered forever by the Chinese people.

Comrade Kim Jong Il has passed away, but he will always live in the heart of the DPRK people. We believe that the DPRK people will definitely carry on at the behest of comrade Kim Jong Il, closely unite around the Worker's Party of Korea, turn their grief into strength under the leadership of comrade Kim Jong Un and make unremitting efforts for the construction of a strong socialist country and the realization of sustainable peace and stability on the Korean Peninsula.

China and the DPRK are close neighbors and stand together in good or bad times. The CPC and the Chinese government have always adhered to the policy of continuously consolidating and developing traditional friendship with the DPRK. We firmly believe that the traditional party-to-party, state-to-state and people-to-people friendship between the two countries will be carried on and further developed with the joint efforts of both sides. The Chinese people will always stand side by side with the DPRK people!

Eternal glory to Comrade Kim Jong Il!

Central Committee of the Communist Party of China

Standing Committee of the National People's Congress of the People's Republic of China

State Council of the People's Republic of China

Central Military Commission of the People's Republic of China

December 19, 2011

Beijing

平壤
朝鲜劳动党中央委员会
朝鲜劳动党中央军事委员会
朝鲜民主主义人民共和国国防委员会
朝鲜民主主义人民共和国最高人民会议常任委员会
朝鲜民主主义人民共和国内阁：

惊悉朝鲜劳动党书记、国防委员会委员长、朝鲜人民军最高司令官金正日同志不幸与世长辞，我们谨以无比沉痛的心情向全体朝鲜人民致以最深切的哀悼和最诚挚的慰问。

金正日同志是朝鲜劳动党和朝鲜民主主义人民共和国的伟大领导者，他把毕生的精力献给了朝鲜人民，为建设朝鲜社会主义强盛国家的伟大事业建立了不朽的历史功勋。

金正日同志是中国人民的亲密朋友，他以极大的热情继承和发展了由两国老一辈革命家亲自缔造和培育的中朝传统友谊，同中国领导人结下了深厚友谊，有力地推动了中朝睦邻友好合作关系不断向前发展。中国共产党、政府和中国人民对金正日同志的逝世深感悲痛，中国人民将永远怀念他。

金正日同志虽已溘然长逝，但他将永远活在朝鲜人民心中，我们相信朝鲜人民必将继承金正日同志的遗志，紧密团结在朝鲜劳动党的周围，在金正恩同志的领导下化悲痛为力量,为建设社会主义强盛国家,实现朝鲜半岛的持久和平继续前进。

  中朝两国山水相连,休戚与共,不断巩固和发展中朝传统友好合作关系是中国共产党和政府的一贯方针,我们坚信在双方共同努力下,中朝两党两国和两国人民的友谊必将巩固和发展下去,中国人民将永远与朝鲜人民站在一起。金正日同志永垂不朽。

中国共产党中央委员会

中华人民共和国全国人民代表大会常务委员会

中华人民共和国国务院

中华人民共和国军事委员会

2011 年 12 月 19 日于北京

Unit 7　道歉信

Letters of Apology

　　我们在工作或生活中，有时难免会犯一些错误，写封道歉信就显得很有必要。道歉信（Letters of Apology）通常包括以下内容：1）表示歉意；2）道歉的原由；3）出现差错的原因；4）提出弥补措施；5）请求原谅。写道歉信的语言要诚挚，解释的理由要真实，不要显示出丝毫的虚情假意。好的道歉信不仅会取得对方的谅解，还会增进彼此的感情。

　　写作"三步走"：表示歉意——说明具体原因、提出补救办法——再次致歉、希望得到理解

　　提示：在写作过程中，尽可能提供比较合理的理由。如果违反生活常识将导致扣分；在解释完原因后，尽量提供一个合适的补救办法，使行文更加完满。

✽ 常用句型

1. I am writing to apologize for … /I am writing to say sorry for…
   我写这封信是因……向你致歉。
2. I am indeed very sorry for what I said/did, but believe I had no intention to…
   对于我说的话／做的事，我确实感到很抱歉。但请相信，我并非故意要……
3. Please forgive me for a stupid choice of words.
   请原谅我说话欠妥。
4. I feel awfully sorry about it and want you to know what happened.
   为此我感到非常内疚，所以想告诉你实情。
5. I sincerely hope you can understand my situation/think in my position and accept my apologies.
   我真心希望你能理解我的处境／设身处地地为我考虑，并接受我的道歉。
6. Once again, I'm sorry for any inconvenience caused/you have sustained.
   对于造成的不便，我再次表示歉意。

67. 为不当言行道歉

Dear Mr. Goldie,

    I am writing this letter to humbly express my deepest apology for my last week's misconduct at work. This incident was due to several factors and stress is one of the leading factors which I had experienced during recent project. My child is also hospitalized and in previous days his condition was too critical. I love my family too much and this situation deviate my attention toward several things. I am a professional person and value my work a lot. My whole performance record is excellent since I was employed in this company. It saddens me that I have caused a mar in my record.

    I personally talked to my direct superior to explain the matter but I know a formal apology letter to you for violating company rules is also necessary. I am aware of company rules, regulations and the work ethics that every employee need to follow. I am awaiting the penalty as a result of my actions and will willingly accept it.

    I will undergo the due process and face the consequences of my action as per company rules. Rest assured that the incident will not happen again and I will do everything again to gain your complete trust back in my capacity.

    Accept my sincere apologies again.

Sincerely,
Mr. Leola Meir

尊敬的戈尔戴先生：

    我写此信，谨对我上周工作中的不佳表现致以深深的歉意。造成这次事故的原因有数个，其中近期那个项目给我带来的的压力是最主要的原因。我的孩子也生病住院了，前些天他的病情甚是严重。我太爱我的家庭了，面对这样的情况，我的注意力就转移到别的事情上了。我很有事业心，对工作非常重视。自我进入公司以来，我的总体表现记录是良好的。此次在自己的职业记录上留下污点，我甚感痛心。

    我已当面向我的直接负责人解释了情况，但我认为有必要给您写一封正式的道歉信，表达我对违反公司规章制度一事的歉意。我深知公司有其规章制度，员工有其职业操守。对于因我的错误行为造成的恶果,请予以处罚,我没有怨言。

我会承受应有的处罚,直面这次违规造成的后果。我保证这样的事故不会再有第二次。我会尽我所能,重新赢得您对我工作能力的充分信任。

再一次诚挚地道歉。

里欧拉·梅尔 谨上

68. 为约定期限内未完成某事道歉

Dear Mr. Rockefellow,

We understand that Angel and John Associates are supposed to submit your income tax return and pay the taxes due thereon. We are very sorry that we missed yesterday's deadline for filing the income tax. We admit our negligence and hope to settle the problem amicably.

Angel and John Associates have come personally to Internal Revenue Office to ask for an extension of filing the return without increments. The good news is they allowed the filing until today. The team is now on its way to pay your taxes. We regret that this event occurred.

To ensure that this does not happen again, we have modified our standard operating procedures. We apologize for any inconvenience this delay has caused you.

Sincerely Yours,
Parker How

尊敬的洛克费罗先生:

我们知道安琪儿 & 约翰联合公司应当上交贵处的所得税收益并立即支付到期的税款。但我们未能在昨日的最后期限之前整理好所得税数据,对此我们深表歉意。我们承认工作中的疏忽大意,并希望此事能以友善的方式得以解决。

安吉尔 & 约翰联合公司已经亲自到国税办公室,申请在没有额外支出基础上的收益备案延期。让人高兴的是,他们同意将期限延长至今日。我处相关小组正在支付贵处的税收。对于此次延期,我们表示抱歉。

为确保此事不再发生,我们修改了标准操作程序。对于这次延期给贵处造成的不变,我们表示歉意。

帕克·郝 谨上

69. 医疗道歉信

Dear Mr. Philip

  I, Mr. Seth E. Bullock, Chief Executive Officer of Wockard Hospital, sincerely apologies to you on behalf of the entire medical team of the hospital. As your mother admitted in the hospital for 1 month because she had to undergo for a Brain Tumor operation and the operation won't be successful due to which she found dead. I take up a responsibility to explain you the whole scenario that your mother was at the last of tumor and her age was 75. At this stage of age there is less chances of living after the operation and it was clearly mentioned in our preoperative contract which is already signed by you. But still on your demand, our highly qualified doctors had took a chance and operated her. They had tried their best from their side but please consider it as God's wish. I truly respect your feelings for your mom and with the bottom of my heart I apologies to you and your family. I will pray to God that your mother's soul would leave in peace.

Mr. Seth E. Bullock

尊敬的飞利浦先生：

  本人是沃卡得医院的首席执行官瑟斯·E·布洛克。我谨代表我院医疗团队全体成员，向您表示诚挚的歉意。您的母亲由于需要进行脑肿瘤手术，接受了为期一个月的住院治疗。但她在住院期间辞世，因此手术没有成功。我负责向您解释整件事情。您母亲的肿瘤已经到了晚期，而且她已是75岁高龄。在生命的这一阶段，术后痊愈的机会相对较少；这点在我们的手术合同上也明确陈述，并且您也在上面签了字。但尽管如此，在您的要求下，我们的资深医生没有放弃机会，对她进行了手术。他们已经拼尽了全力，请您就把这看作是上帝的意愿吧。我真心地尊重您对母亲的感受，并从心底对您和您的家人表示歉意。我会向上帝祈祷，希望您母亲的灵魂平静地离开。

瑟斯·E·布洛克

70. 为客户投诉道歉

Dear Mr. Jackie,

  I, Mr. Derek E. Dalrymple, Customer Relation Manager on behalf of my company Hindustan Unilever Pvt. Ltd., sincerely apologies to you. As we receive a notice from your side that you had purchased an expired medicine of our company. We hereby inform you that this was unintentional and the packet of expired medicine was undoubtedly gone along with the unexpired packets. I know if you would have consumed the medicine, the result would be dangerous, therefore we always advice that please see the date of expiry before consuming any of the products. We are ready to pay to the fine amount mentioned by you in your notice. But we request you that please don't take the matter to the consumer court. I hope you will accept our apology and kindly act in favor of us. Hope to hear the needful from your side.

Faithfully yours,
Mr. Derek E. Dalrymple

尊敬的杰克先生：

　　本人是印度斯坦乌尼列夫公司的客户关系部经理德瑞克·E·达尔林颇。我谨代表公司，对您表示诚挚的歉意。我们收到了您的来信，信上说您购买了一份我公司的过期药品。在此我们向您澄清，此乃无心之失，过期药品的包装一定是混进了未过期药品的包装里。我们知道，如果您购买了这样的药品，后果可能会很危险，因此我们一直建议顾客，请在购买任何药品之前查看失效日期。我们愿意支付您信中提到的赔款。但请求您不要将此事诉诸消费者法庭。希望您接受我们的道歉，并能善意地为我公司着想。静候佳音。

德瑞克·E·达尔林颇 谨上

71. 给女友道歉

Dear Kate,

I know that we have been going through hard times lately, and so I decided to write this letter to show how much I care for and love you. I know you are upset with what happened, but I also want you to know how I feel. You are the whole world to me and I really get sad when you are hurt. I am sorry for the mistakes I have done, and I promise not to do them or any sort in our future.

I am trying to improve on what bad qualities and habits I have, which were a hurt to you. For the mistakes I have done, I am learning it the hard way. All of it taught me about my mistakes, and what it would take for me, to be the best man in your life.

You mean a lot to me, and I just cannot afford to lose you. You can talk to me whenever you think is the correct time, but until then, take care of yourself.

Loads of Love
Sam

亲爱的凯特：

我知道最近我们的感情出现了危机，因此我决定给你写这封信，让你知道我是多么地在乎你、爱你。我知道你对那件事很生气，但是我也要告诉你我的所想。对我来说，你就是整个世界。你受到了伤害，我真的很伤心。我对自己犯的错道歉，我保证今后再也不会做这样或者类似的事了。

我会试图改掉身上的不良品质和坏习惯，这些都让你受到了伤害。对于我犯下的错误，我正在努力地从中吸取教训。这件事给了我教训，它告诉我要怎样付出才能成为你生命中最合适的那个人。

你对我来说太重要了，我不能失去你。只要你认为时间适合，你随时可以找我聊聊。但在那之前，要好好照顾自己。

无尽的爱
山姆

72. 给好友道歉

Dear Margaret,

I am really sorry for the way I behaved with you at Jen's birthday party. I was in a really bad mood because of the project I am doing at college and also because of the argument I had with my brother, before coming to the party. However, this is no excuse for the things I said to you that day.

The reason I have decided to write this letter is that I understand that I was a total fool to shout at you. I want you to know that your friendship means a lot to me and I do not want to lose you because of my stupid behavior.

After whatever I said to you that day, I know, it will be difficult for you to forgive me. But, please give me another chance and I promise this will never happen again. You really mean a lot to me and I will hate to lose a friend like you. Waiting for your reply.

Love,
Samantha

亲爱的玛格丽特：

  在简的生日派对上我对你态度粗鲁，对此我深表歉意。我当时心情糟透了，参加派对前，我被学校里的一个项目缠身，哥哥也和我大吵一架。然而，这些无法为我那天对你的激烈言辞开脱。

  之所以要写这封信，是因为我知道自己对你那样大喊大叫实在是愚蠢透了。我希望你知道，你的友谊对我来说意义重大，我不想因为自己的愚蠢行为而失去你这个朋友。

  我知道，在我那天对你说的一通话之后，我是难以得到你的宽恕的。但请你再给我一次机会，我保证这样的事情绝不会发生第二次。你对我来说真的很重要，我不希望失去你这样的朋友。我期待着你的回复。

爱你的 沙满莎

Unit 8　正式致词

Speeches

正式致词（Speeches）一般指在举行会议或某种仪式时请具有一定身份的人讲话。一般包括：欢迎词、答谢词、开幕词、闭幕词、颁奖词、领奖词等。正式致词一般都有发言稿，也就是说，需要在发言前进行写作。稿子的质量对发言人临场的效果有着至关重要的作用，因而影响到了发言人的社交或公关效果。致词在后面的章节中还会有进一步介绍，本单元将提供欢迎词、答谢词、开幕词、闭幕词、颁奖词、领奖词等范文供各位读者朋友参考。

✱ 常用句型

1. I really appreciate your making time in your schedules to attend today.

   我非常感谢你们今天抽空来参加这个会议。

2. Thank you for giving me this opportunity to speak about myself in this special occasion.

   感谢您给我这个机会在这个特别的场合介绍我自己。

3. It is my honor to introduce the president of our company, Mr. Jones.

   我很荣幸介绍我们公司总裁琼斯先生。

4. On behalf of our entire company, I want to thank you for inviting us to such an enjoyable Christmas party.

   我代表全公司，我想感谢您邀请我们参加这样一个令人愉快的圣诞晚会。

5. Thank you from the bottom of my heart for giving me this chance to speak to you today.

   我从心底感谢你们今天给了我这个机会在你们前面讲话。

73. 欢迎词

Remarks by President Obama at Official Arrival Ceremony (Abstract)

Good morning, everyone. President Hu, members of the Chinese delegation, on behalf of Michelle and myself, welcome to the White House. And on behalf of the American people, welcome to the United States.

Three decades ago, on a January day like this, another American President stood here and welcomed another Chinese leader for the historic normalization of relations between the United States and the People's Republic of China. On that day, Deng Xiaoping spoke of the great possibilities of cooperation between our two nations.

……

Mr. President, we can learn from our people. Chinese and American students and educators, business people, tourists, researchers and scientists, including Chinese Americans who are here today – they work together and make progress together every single day. They know that even as our nations compete in some areas, we can cooperate in so many others, in a spirit of mutual respect, for our mutual benefit.

What Deng Xiaoping said long ago remains true today. There are still great possibilities for cooperation between our countries. President Hu, members of the Chinese delegation, let us seize these possibilities together. Welcome to the United States of America. Hwan-ying.

美国总统奥巴马在白宫欢迎胡锦涛主席的致词（有删节）

各位早上好。胡锦涛主席，中国代表团的诸位成员，我谨代表米歇尔和我本人，欢迎诸位莅临白宫。同时，我也代表美国人民，欢迎诸位来到美国。

三十年前，也是这样一个元月的日子，另一位美国总统站在此处，欢迎另一位中国国家领导人，从此开始了中美关系的正常化。那天，邓小平说，中美两国之间的合作潜力无限。

……

总统先生，我们可以向两国人民学习。在他们当中，有中美两国学生和教育从业者、商人、游客、研究人员、科学家，他们中还有许多今天到场的华裔美国人——每一天，他们都携手共事，共同进步。他们知道，尽管两国在一些领域存在竞争，但是我们依然可以本着相互尊重的精神，在许多其他领域为着共同的利益而展开合作。

邓小平先生多年前的讲话放在今日仍然没有过时。中美两国之间的合作依旧潜力无限。胡锦涛主席，中国代表团的诸位成员，让我们一起把握住这些潜力吧。欢迎莅临美利坚合众国。欢迎！

74. 答谢词

Ladies and Gentlemen,

I feel very pleased to attend your reception and have the opportunity to talk with all the Chinese friends here, and thank you for your nice welcome.

Following the continuous development of the friendly relations between our two countries, many government officers, scientists, artists and businessmen exchange their visits. I have been looking forward to this trip, and now I have been more than rewarded.

I feel very much honored to be given this opportunity to meet so many well-known personages like you. I am sure my stay here will be fruitful and enjoyable. I do hope to learn much from you while I am here.

Thank you!

女士们，先生们：

能够出席你们的招待会，有机会与在场的中国朋友交谈，我感到非常高兴。感谢你们的热情迎接。

随着两国友好关系的不断发展，许多政府官员、科学家、艺术家和商人互访。这次旅行，我盼望已久，而现在终于如愿以偿了。

特别使我感到荣幸的是，这次有机会见到你们多位知名人士。我坚信，这次在华的访问一定是卓有成效且令人愉快的。我非常希望访华期间多向诸位请教。

谢谢！

75. 开幕词

Opening Speech of 2008 Beijing Olympic Games by Jacques Rogge, President of IOC

Mr. President of the People's Republic of China,

Mr. LIU Qi,

Members of the Organising Committee,

Dear Chinese friends,

Dear athletes:

For a long time, China has dreamed of opening its doors and inviting the world's athletes to Beijing for the Olympic Games.

Tonight that dream comes true. Congratulations, Beijing.

You have chosen as the theme of these Games 'One World, One Dream'. That is what we are tonight.

As one world, we grieved with you over the tragic earthquake in Sichuan Province. We were moved by the great courage and solidarity of the Chinese people. As one dream, may these Olympic Games bring you joy, hope and pride.

Athletes, the Games were created for you by our founder, Pierre de Coubertin. These Games belong to you. Let them be the athletes' Games.

Remember that they are about much more than performance alone. They are about the peaceful gathering of 204 National Olympic Committees-regardless of ethnic origin, gender, religion or political system. Please compete in the spirit of the Olympic values: excellence, friendship and respect.

Dear athletes, remember that you are role models for the youth of the world. Reject doping and cheating. Make us proud of your achievements and your conduct.

As we bring the Olympic dream to life, our warm thanks go to the

Beijing Organising Committee for its tireless work. Our special thanks also go to the thousands of gracious volunteers, without whom none of this would be possible.

Beijing, you are a host to the present and a gateway to the future. Thank you.

I now have the honour of asking the President of the People's Republic of China to open the Games of the XXIX Olympiad of the modern era.

国际奥委会主席雅克·罗格在2008年北京奥运会开幕式上的演讲
尊敬的中华人民共和国主席,
尊敬的刘淇先生,
尊敬的组委会成员,
亲爱的中国朋友,
亲爱的运动员们：

在过去很长一段时间里,中国梦想着打开大门邀请来自世界各地的运动员们到北京参加奥运会。今晚,这个梦想实现了！祝贺你,北京！

你们选择的主题"同一个世界,同一个梦想"就是我们今晚的意义！

同一个世界,我们为四川大地震的悲剧感到痛心。我们为中国人民的坚强不屈和团结一致而感动。同一个梦想,愿奥运会能带给你们欢乐、希望和自豪。

运动员们,奥运会是我们的奠基人皮埃尔·德·顾拜旦为你们而创造的。这场比赛属于你们。让他成为运动员们的奥运会吧！

请大家牢记,奥运会不仅仅意味着比赛成绩,奥运会是和平的聚会。204个国家和地区相聚于此,跨越了民族、性别、宗教以及政治制度的界限,请大家本着奥林匹克的精神——卓越、友谊和尊重,投身于比赛。

亲爱的运动员们,请记住你们是世界年轻人的榜样。杜绝兴奋剂和舞弊。让我们为你们的成就和品格感到骄傲。

当我们将奥林匹克之梦注入生命,我们要对北京奥组委的不懈努力表示热诚的感谢。我们特别感谢千千万万亲切的志愿者们,没有他们就没有今天的一切。

北京,作为现今的东道主以及通往未来的大门,谢谢你！

现在,我很荣幸地邀请中华人民共和国主席为第29届北京奥林匹克运动会开幕。

76. 闭幕词

Closing Speech of 2008 Beijing Olympic Games by Jacques Rogge, President of IOC

Dear Chinese friends,

Tonight, we come to the end of 16 glorious days which we will cherish forever. Thank you to the people of China, to all the wonderful volunteers and to BOCOG!

Through these Games, the world learned more about China, and China learned more about the world. Athletes from 204 National Olympic Committees came to these dazzling venues and awed us with their talent.

New stars were born. Stars from past Games amazed us again. We shared their joys and their tears, and we marveled at their ability. We will long remember the achievements we witnessed here.

As we celebrate the success of these Games, let us altogether wish the best for the talented athletes who will soon participate in the Paralympic Games. They also inspire us.

To the athletes tonight: You were true role models. You have shown us the unifying power of sport. The Olympic spirit lives in the warm embrace of competitors from nations in conflict. Keep that spirit alive when you return home.

These were truly exceptional Games!

And now, in accordance with tradition, I declare the Games of the XXIX Olympiad closed, and I call upon the youth of the world to assemble four years from now in London to celebrate the Games of the XXX Olympiad.

Thank you!

国际奥委会主席雅克·罗格在 2008 年北京奥运会闭幕式上的演讲

亲爱的中国朋友们：

今晚，我们即将走到 16 天光辉历程的终点。这些日子，将在我们的心中永远珍藏，感谢中国人民，感谢所有出色的志愿者，感谢北京奥组委。

通过本届奥运会，世界更多地了解了中国，中国更多地了解了世界，来自204个国家和地区的运动健儿们在光彩夺目的场馆里同场竞技，用他们精湛的技能博得了我们的赞叹。

新的奥运明星诞生了，往日的奥运明星又一次带来惊喜，我们分享着他们的欢笑和泪水，我们钦佩他们的才能与风采，我们将长久铭记这次见证的辉煌成就。

在庆祝奥运会圆满成功之际，让我们一起祝福才华洋溢的残奥会运动健儿们，希望他们在即将到来的残奥会上取得优秀的成绩。他们同样令我们倍感鼓舞。

今晚在场的每位运动员们，你们是真正的楷模，你们充分展示了体育的凝聚力。来自冲突国家竞技对手的热情拥抱中闪耀着奥林匹克精神的光辉。希望你们回国后让这种精神生生不息，世代永存。

这是一届无与伦比的奥运会！

现在，遵照惯例，我宣布第29届奥林匹克运动会闭幕，并号召全世界青年四年后在伦敦举办的第30届奥林匹克运动会上再相聚。

谢谢大家！

77. 颁奖词

The Nobel Peace Prize for 2009

The Norwegian Nobel Committee Oslo,

October 9, 2009

The Norwegian Nobel Committee has decided that the Nobel Peace Prize for 2009 is to be awarded to President Barack Obama for his extraordinary efforts to strengthen international diplomacy and cooperation between peoples. The Committee has attached special importance to Obama's vision of and work for a world without nuclear weapons.

Obama has as President created a new international climate. Politic multilateral diplomacy has regained a central position, with emphasis on the role that the United Nations and other international institutions can play. Dialogue and negotiations are preferred as instruments for resolving even the most difficult (international) conflicts. The vision of a world free from nuclear arms has powerfully stimulated disarmament and arms control negotiations. Thanks to Obama's initiative, the United States is now playing a more constructive role in meeting the great climatic challenges the world is confronting. Democracy and human rights are to be strengthened.

Only very rarely has a person to the same extent as Obama captured the world's attention and given its people hope for a better future. His diplomacy is founded in the concept that those who are to lead the world must do so on the basis of values and attitudes that are shared by the majority of the world's population.

For 108 years, the Norwegian Nobel Committee has sought to stimulate precisely that international policy and those attitudes for which Obama is now the world's leading spokesman. The Committee endorses Obama's appeal that "Now is the time for all of us to take our share of responsibility for a global response to global challenges."

2009 年诺贝尔和平奖
挪威诺贝尔奖委员会，奥斯陆
2009 年 10 月 9 日

挪威诺贝尔委员会决定将 2009 年诺贝尔和平奖授予巴拉克·奥巴马总统，表彰他为加强国际外交和人民之间合作所作的杰出贡献。委员会尤其注重奥巴马提出的无核武器世界的愿景和他为之做出的努力。

作为总统，奥巴马创造了国际政治的新气象。多边外交重新占据中心位置，突出联合国和其他国际机构的作用。对话和协商被作为解决即使是最困难的国际冲突的首选手段。无核武器世界的愿景有力推动了裁军和军备控制谈判。由于奥巴马的主张，美国现在在应对世界面临的巨大气候挑战中发挥出了更富有建设性的作用。民主和人权将得到加强。

世界上鲜有人具有奥巴马这样的全球感召力并让自己的人民对更美好的未来充满希望。他的外交所基于的理念是，世界领袖必须按照世界大多数人所认同的价值和观念去行动。

108 年来，挪威诺贝尔委员会一直致力于促进的正是这种国际政策与姿态，而现在奥巴马是它在世界上的主要代表。委员会赞同奥巴马的呼吁："现在是我们大家承担自身责任，对全球性挑战作出全球性回应的时候了。"

78. 领奖词

Nobel Prize Acceptance Speech by Mr. Ernest Hemingway

Having no facility for speech-making and no command of oratory nor any domination of rhetoric, I wish to thank the administrators of the generosity of Alfred Nobel for this Prize.

No writer who knows the great writers who did not receive the Prize can accept it other than with humility. There is no need to list these writers. Everyone here may make his own list according to his knowledge and his conscience.

It would be impossible for me to ask the Ambassador of my country to read a speech in which a writer said all of the things which are in his heart. Things may not be immediately discernible in what a man writes, and in this sometimes he is fortunate; but eventually they are quite clear and by these and the degree of alchemy that he possesses he will endure or be forgotten.

Writing, at its best, is a lonely life. Organizations for writers palliate the writer's loneliness but I doubt if they improve his writing. He grows in public stature as he sheds his loneliness and often his work deteriorates. For he does his work alone and if he is a good enough writer he must face eternity, or the lack of it, each day.

For a true writer each book should be a new beginning where he tries again for something that is beyond attainment. He should always try for something that has never been done or that others have tried and failed. Then sometimes, with great luck, he will succeed.

How simple the writing of literature would be if it were only necessary to write in another way what has been well written. It is because we have had such great writers in the past that a writer is driven far out past where he can go, out to where no one can help him.

I have spoken too long for a writer. A writer should write what he has to say and not speak it. Again I thank you.

海明威接受诺贝尔文学奖的领奖词

我不善辞令,缺乏演说的才能,只想感谢阿尔雷德·诺贝尔评奖委员会的委员们慷慨地授予我这个奖项。

没有一个作家,当他知道在他之前不少伟大的作家并没有获得此项奖的时候,能够心安理得领奖而不感到受之有愧。这里无须一一列举这些作家的名字。在座的每个人都可以根据他们的学识和良心提出自己的名单来。

要求我国的大使在这儿宣读一篇演说,把一个作家心中所感受到的一切都说尽是不可能的。一个人作品中的一些东西可能不会马上被人理解,在这点上,他有时是幸运的;但是它们终究会十分清晰起来,根据它们以及作家所具有的点石成金本领的大小,他将青史留名或被人遗忘。

写作,在最成功的时候,是一种孤寂的生涯。作家的组织固然可以排遣他们的孤独,但是我怀疑它们未必能够促进作家的创作。一个在稠人广众之中成长起来的作家,自然可以免除孤苦寂寥之虑,但他的作品往往流于平庸。而一个在岑寂中独立工作的作家,假若他确实不同凡响,就必须天天面对永恒的东西,或者面对缺乏永恒的状况。

对于一个真正的作家来说,每一本书都应该成为他继续探索那些尚未到达的领域的一个新起点。他应该永远尝试去做那些从来没有人做过或者他人没有做成的事。这样他就有幸会获得成功。

如果已经写好的作品,仅仅换一种方法又可以重新写出来,那么文学创作就显得太轻而易举了。我们的前辈大师们留下的伟大业绩,正因为如此,一个普通作家常被他们逼人的光辉驱赶到远离他可能到达的地方,陷入孤立无助的境地。

作为一个作家,我讲得已经太多了。作家应当把自己要说的话写下来,而不是讲出来。再一次谢谢大家。

Unit 9　祝词

Speeches

　　祝词（Speeches）也称祝辞，是泛指对人、对事表示祝贺的言辞或文章。祝词多用在喜庆的仪式上，如各种工程开工庆典、寿辰和重要节日及其他社会活动，表示良好的愿望或庆祝。

　　祝词根据祝贺的内容不同可以划分为祝事业、祝酒、祝寿、祝婚、祝节日等类型；从表达形式上划分有韵文（诗、词）体和散文体两种类型。

　　祝酒：用于宴会、酒会上，传达祝酒者美好的愿望。

　　祝事业：多用于重大会议开幕、工厂开工、商店开业、展览剪彩以及其他纪念活动等，祝愿此事业顺利进行，早日成功。

　　祝寿：一般是对祝寿对象表示良好的愿望，希望他们健康长寿。

　　祝婚：一般是祝愿新婚夫妇幸福美满。

　　写作"三步走"：首先应向受祝贺的单位或人员表示祝贺、感谢或问候，或者说明写祝辞的理由或原因——其次常常对已做出的成就进行适当评价或指出其意义——再次写表示祝愿、希望、祝贺之语，也可以给被祝者以鼓励

　　祝词在大大小小的场合都用得上，小到一个生日聚会，大到国家领导人的宴请，因此写好祝词是很有用处的。本单元介绍了各种场合的几类祝词，供大家参考。

　　提示：祝词感情色彩强烈，针对性、场合性也很强。

✽ 常用句型

1. Warm greetings and best wishes for happiness and good luck in the coming year.

   衷心祝福来年快乐、幸运！

2. I wish you a gay and merry Christmas. All affection and best wishes to you and yours.

   以我所有的爱心与真心祝你及全家圣诞快乐。

3. May the beauty and joy of Christmas remain with you throughout the new year!

愿圣诞美景与欢乐常伴随你！

4. I on behalf of all my class to give you our best wishes from the bottom of our heart--Happy Teacher's Day to you! May smiles smile on your face everyday !

我代表全班同学由衷祝愿老师您：教师节快乐！愿您笑口常开！

5. I now propose a toast, to our common cause of world peace and development, to greater friendship and cooperation between China and other countries, and to the health and happiness of you all. Cheers!

现在，我提议：为促进世界和平发展的共同事业，为中国与各国友好合作不断加强，为各位来宾、朋友的健康幸福，干杯！

79. 祝酒词

Toast by Foreign Minister Yang Jiechi at the New Year Reception (Abstract)

Your Excellency State Councilor Dai Bingguo,

Your Excellencies Diplomatic Envoys,

Representatives of International Organizations and Your Spouses,

Dear Colleagues,

Ladies and Gentlemen,

Dear Friends:

　　We are once again gathered here on this joyful occasion to celebrate the New Year. And we are especially pleased to have with us today State Councilor Dai Bingguo and officials of relevant government agencies to renew friendship with Your Excellencies and other friends, old and new. Over the past year, Your Excellencies Ambassadors and your spouses and other diplomats have worked tirelessly to enhance our mutual understanding and promote friendship and cooperation and made invaluable contributions. On behalf of the Ministry of Foreign Affairs and in my own name, I wish to extend festive greetings to you and express heartfelt thanks to all the friends who have shown care and support for China's diplomacy.

　　……

With the beginning of the new year, everything takes on a new look. We look forward to continuing our good cooperation in the coming year for the sustained growth of our relations.

I now propose a toast,

to our common cause of world peace and development,

to greater friendship and cooperation between China and other countries, and

to the health and happiness of you all.

Cheers!

外交部长杨洁篪在 2011 年新年招待会上的祝酒辞（有删节）

尊敬的戴秉国国务委员，

尊敬的各位使节、代表和夫人，

各位同事，

女士们、先生们、朋友们：

今天，我们再次在这里欢聚一堂，共迎新年。令我们特别高兴的是，戴秉国国务委员和有关部门的负责人能够出席今天的晚会，与各位使节和新老朋友共叙友谊。一年来，各位驻华使节和夫人以及各位外交官们为增进相互了解、促进友好合作付出了辛勤的劳动，做出了宝贵贡献。我谨代表外交部并以我个人名义，向各位来宾致以最美好的节日祝福，向所有关心和支持中国外交的朋友们表示衷心的感谢！

……

一元复始，万象更新。在新的一年里，我们期待着继续与各位使节和朋友保持良好合作，共同为推动双边关系发展而不懈努力！

现在，我提议：

为促进世界和平发展的共同事业，

为中国与各国友好合作不断加强，

为各位来宾、朋友的健康幸福，

干杯！

80. 婚礼祝词

Friends, family and especially Mark and Judy, I first knew something was up when Mark skipped our annual Maine fishing trip to attend Judy's family reunion 2 years ago.

Of course, we razzed him quite a bit for that and we will never let him forget how he had his priorities mixed up, but when I see how happy he is today, how happy they are, I know that he probably made the right choice. Of course, I'll never admit that again and there better not be any excuses for next year's fishing trip!

Mark has been my best friend since 5th grade. We've been through a lot together, fun times and a few jams here and there. One thing I learned about Mark is that when he does something, he does it all the way. Once he commits himself to something he follows through and makes it the best it can possibly be.

I remember the year we agreed to paint my parent's lake house and the week we planned to do it, it rained every day. I was ready to throw in the towel. I mean, we had a good excuse! But Mark wouldn't agree to it. He insisted that we go up there for the next three weekends to get it done. I didn't appreciate it at the time but now I see that that kind of commitment is something to admire and emulate.

Judy, I'm sure you appreciate the value of it too. You have a great guy there and, from having gotten to know you over the past couple of years I know that, as usual, Mark has chosen well for himself.

I wish you both endless joy and love. A toast to Mark and Judy for a long and happy life together!

朋友们，家人们，尤其是马克和茱蒂：两年前，当马克在我们年度缅因州钓鱼之旅中放我们鸽子，到茱蒂家参加家庭聚会的时候，我就知道肯定里面"有鬼"。

当然，我们为那件事奚落了他一阵子，我们要让他永远记住他那是颠倒主次。但当我看到他今天有多么高兴，他们今天有多么高兴，我知道也许他那时的选择是对的。当然，我不会允许那样的放鸽子事件再次发生，明年的钓鱼之旅最好别再找什么借口！

从五年级开始，马克就一直是我最好的朋友。我们一起经历了很多事情，有喜有忧。我观察到马克的一个品质就是，一旦他着手做一件事情，他就会一直做下去。一旦他决心做一件事情，他就会持之以恒，力求完美。

我记得有一年，我们说好要给我爸妈湖边的房子刷漆，但我们打算动工的那周，雨下个不停。我都打算丢掉刷布了。我是说，我们其实有很好的理由！但是马克坚决不同意。他说我们在接下来的三个周末都去刷，直到刷完。当时我不太赞同他，但现在看来，那样的责任感是值得赞赏和学习的。

茱蒂，我相信你也会赞赏这种责任感。你找到了个好丈夫。而从我这些年对你的了解来看，马克也给他自己做了个正确的选择。

祝你们享受无尽的欢乐和爱。让我们为了马克和茱蒂的白头偕老干杯！

81. 生日祝词

Welcome friends, to Elizabeth's semi-centennial party! As you know, Elizabeth likes to celebrate everything so today we're just a little more dressed up than usual.

As you can see here, in 50 years Elizabeth has made a lot of friends. I suspect that like me, she befriended most of you by offering to help you in some way.

In my case, Elizabeth helped me tie my shoe on the first day of school back in kindergarten. I hadn't quite mastered that skill yet but Elizabeth was way ahead of me. I guess I've felt that way ever since then but not in a bad way, in an inspiring way.

I love that my dear friend always challenges me to move forward and achieve more and to always be true to myself.

I'd like to talk a little about Elizabeth's passion. I'm sure that all of you know of her involvement in the Leukemia/Lymphoma Society since the loss of her sister Ali to lymphoma 10 years ago.

Maybe that is not the most uplifting thing to mention at a 50th birthday party but it is an integral element of Elizabeth's life. I bring it up to remind us all to remember Ali today, and I am sure she is here in spirit, and also to remind all of you that in lieu of gifts, Elizabeth has asked us to contribute to the Leukemia/Lymphoma Society. Please contribute generously.

Elizabeth, 50 years is a good long time to live–I should know! And it is truly something to celebrate.

In the presence of your family here, your husband Rick, your daughters,

Alice and Susan and your parents, Joan and Bob I'd like to say that we here appreciate you and all you have done for so many of us. We celebrate the 50 years you have lived and we wish you many more.

I, for one, am looking forward to speaking again at your centennial party! To Elizabeth, congratulations and many more!

欢迎各位朋友参加伊丽莎白五十岁的生日派对！正如大家所知，伊丽莎白喜欢庆祝各种事情，所以今天我们就稍微庆祝了一下。

在五十年里，伊丽莎白结交了不少朋友，这个大家有目共睹。我想正如我一样，大家和伊丽莎白交上朋友是因为伊丽莎白在这个或那个方面对我们慷慨相助。

说说我的例子吧。在我上幼儿园的第一天，伊丽莎白就帮我系鞋带。当时我还不是很会系，但是伊丽莎白比我强多了。我从那时起就觉得她比我强，但这不让我嫉妒，而让我羡慕。

我这位亲爱的朋友一直鞭策我向前进，让我更有作为，也让我认清自己。

我想稍微谈谈伊丽莎白的热情。我想大家都知道，自从她的妹妹阿里十年前因为淋巴瘤而去世之后，伊丽莎白就将精力倾注到白血病/淋巴瘤协会里了。

也许把这放到一个五十岁生日聚会来说，并不是什么振奋人心的事情。但这件事却是伊丽莎白生命中不可或缺的一部分。今天我提起这件事，就是想让大家记住阿里，我相信她的精神与我们同在。我也想提醒大家，伊丽莎白说，我们可以不给什么生日礼物，但请给白血病/淋巴瘤协会一点儿捐助。请大家慷慨解囊。

伊丽莎白，五十年很长，能度过五十年很美好——这我也该知道！这个生日的确值得庆祝。

你的丈夫里克、你的女儿爱丽丝和苏珊、你的父母乔安和鲍勃今天都来了，当着你家人的面我想说，我们对你和你为大家所做的一切表示感谢。我们祝贺你度过了五十年的时光，也祝你长命百岁。

就我个人而言，我希望我能在你百岁寿辰上再度演讲！让我们为伊丽莎白干杯，祝福你，一切尽在不言中！

82. 市区政府领导人祝词

2010 New Year's Speech delivered by Zhou Ping, Governor of Zhabei District (Abstract)

On the occasion of the arrival of New Year, On behalf of the government of Zhabei District, I would like to extend my most sincere greetings and heartfelt thanks to people in this district and comrades and friends who care for and support the development of Zhabei

The year 2009, which is soon to be over, is the most difficult year for China's economic development since entering the new century. Faced with the impact of international financial crisis and severe and complicated economic situation, people throughout this district proceeded with confidence, took the bull by the horns and strove to turn challenges into opportunities. Hence, we effectively contained the trend of a marked decline in economic growth and kept stable and rapid social and economic development. In the Year 2009, we continuously improved the quality of our district's economic development and further accelerated structural adjustment; we made remarkable achievements in redevelopment of existing urban areas and completed the relocation of the North Plaza III; we achieved noticeable results in the work of greeting the World Exposition in 2010, enhanced the level of civilization and improved our district's environment; we devoted great efforts to improve the employment environment, relieved the poor in various ways, gave aid to the reconstruction work of Daguan Town in Dujiangyan and made new progress in the work of ensuring the people's livelihood and all other social undertakings.

……

The Year 2010 is of significance for Zhabei District to accelerate economic and social development. Let's dedicate ourselves heart and soul to the same cause, be indomitable, proceeded with confidence, accelerate development and strive to build a harmony new Zhabei under the leadership of the municipal Party committee and the municipal government.

Finally, I would like to extend my sincere wishes to you again. I wish you a happy New Year, a well-being life and good luck for everything.

上海市闸北区区长周平 2010 年新年致词（有删节）

值此新年到来之际，我谨代表闸北区人民政府，向全区人民以及区内外关心和支持闸北发展的同志们、朋友们，致以最诚挚的新年问候和衷心的感谢！

即将过去的 2009 年，是新世纪以来我国经济发展最为困难的一年。面对国际金融危机冲击和严峻复杂的经济形势，全区人民坚定信心、迎难而上，努力化挑战为机遇，有效遏制经济增长明显下滑的态势，保持了全区经济社会的平稳较快发展。一年来全区经济发展质量不断提高，产业结构调整步伐进一步加快；旧区改造取得显著成绩，北广场三期动迁全面完成；迎世博各项工作成效显现，城区文明程度和区域环境不断改善；大力做好就业工作，积极开展形式多样的帮困活动，切实推进对口支援都江堰大观镇灾后重建工作，民生保障和社会各项事业工作取得了新的进展。

……

2010 年是闸北加快推进经济社会发展的重要一年，让我们在市委、市政府的领导下，同心同德、顽强拼搏，坚定信心、加快发展，为建设和谐新闸北而努力奋斗！

最后，再次祝愿全区人民新年快乐、阖家幸福、万事如意！

83. 国家领导人祝词

Promoting the Wellbeing of the World's People Together (Abstract)

– 2011 New Year Speech delivered by Hu Jintao, President of the People's Republic of China

Ladies and gentlemen, comrades and friends,

The New Year's bell is about to ring, and 2011 will soon begin. At this beautiful moment of bidding farewell to the old and ushering in the new, via China Radio International, China National Radio and China Central Television, I am delighted to extend New Year greetings to Chinese of all ethnic groups, to compatriots in Hong Kong and Macao Special Administrative Regions and Taiwan, to overseas Chinese and to friends all over the world!

......

At present, the world is moving further towards multi-polarity and globalization while the innovation of science an technology is brewing new breakthroughs. But, at the same time, the recovery of world economy is still facing many hardships; global issues such as climate change, energy, resources, food and public sanitary security are prominent; and international and regional hot spots are popping up. World peace and development face grave challenges. To strengthen global cooperation and meet the challenges in a joint way is to the best interest of the people of all countries. I would like to take this opportunity to reaffirm that China will uphold the banner of peace, development and cooperation and adhere to an independent and peaceful foreign policy. We will unswervingly take the road of peaceful development and implement a strategy of opening up for mutual benefit and win-win situation, actively develop friendly cooperation with all countries on the basis of the Five Principles of Peaceful Coexistence, actively participate in efforts by the international community to deal with the global issues, and strive to build a harmonious world with lasting peace and common prosperity.

At this moment on this planet we inhabit, there are still people who are suffering the effects of war, poverty, sickness and natural disasters. The Chinese people have great sympathy for their pain, and are always willing to do all we can to help them overcome the difficulties. I believe, with sustained efforts of people of all countries, the world is sure to progress, and humanity's well-being is certain to improve.

Finally, from here in Beijing, I would like to wish you all happiness, peace and health in the New Year!

共同增进各国人民福祉（有删节）
——中国国家主席胡锦涛 2011 年新年贺词

女士们，先生们，同志们、朋友们，

新年钟声即将敲响，人类就要进入 2011 年。在这辞旧迎新的美好时刻，我很高兴通过中国国际广播电台、中央人民广播电台和中央电视台，向全国各族人民，向香港特别行政区同胞、澳门特别行政区同胞、台湾同胞和海外侨胞，向世界各国的朋友们，致以新年的祝福！

……

当前，世界多极化、经济全球化深入发展，科技创新孕育着新突破，但世界经济复苏进程仍将艰难曲折，气候变化、能源资源安全、粮食安全、公共卫生安全等全球性问题更加突出，国际和地区热点问题此起彼伏，世界和平与发展面临的机遇和挑战都前所未有。加强国际合作，携手应对人类共同面临的严峻挑战，符合各国人民共同利益。借此机会，我愿重申，中国将继续高举和平、发展、合作旗帜，坚持独立自主的和平外交政策，始终不渝走和平发展道路，始终不渝奉行互利共赢的开放战略，在和平共处五项原则的基础上积极发展同各国的友好交往和互利合作，积极参与应对全球性问题的国际合作，继续同各国人民一道推动建设持久和平、共同繁荣的和谐世界。

此时此刻，世界上还有不少民众经受着战火、贫困、疾病、自然灾害等带来的苦难。中国人民对他们的不幸遭遇表示深深的同情，衷心希望他们早日摆脱困境。中国人民将一如既往向他们提供力所能及的帮助。我相信，只要各国人民携手努力，世界发展前景一定会更加美好，各国人民福祉一定会不断增进。

最后，我在北京祝大家在新的一年里幸福安康！

Unit 10 请柬、名片、贺卡 Invitation Cards, (Business) Cards, Greeting Cards

请柬（Invitation Cards），又称请帖或简帖，是为了邀请客人参加某项活动而发的礼仪性书信。使用请柬，既可以表示对被邀请者的尊重，又可以表示邀请者对此事的郑重态度。凡召开各种会议，举行各种典礼、仪式和活动，均可以使用请柬。

请柬写作的注意事项：

1. 文字要美观，用词要谦恭，要充分表现出邀请者的热情与诚意。

2. 语言要精炼、准确，凡涉及到时间、地点、人名等一些关键性词语，一定要核准、查实。

3. 语言要得体、庄重。

请柬与邀请函区别：

请柬是为了邀请客人参加某项活动而发的礼仪性书信。它一般有两种样式：一种是单面的，直接由标题、称谓、正文、敬语、落款构成。一种是双面的，即折叠式；一为封面，写"请柬"二字，一为封里，写称谓、正文、敬语、落款等。而邀请信是邀请亲朋好友或知名人士、专家等参加某项活动时所发的请约性书信。在国际交往以及日常的各种社交活动中，这类书信使用广泛。

名片（Cards），是标示姓名及其所属组织、公司单位和联系方法的纸片。名片是新朋友互相认识、自我介绍的最快有效的方法。交换名片是商业交往的第一个标准官式动作。其文字信息应包含单位名称、名片持有人名称、头衔和联系方法。部分商业名片还有经营范围，多种文字选择，单位的座右铭或吉祥字句。

贺卡（Greeting Cards）是人们在遇到喜庆的日期或事件的时候互相表示问候的一种卡片。人们通常赠送贺卡的日子包括生日、圣诞、新年、母亲节、教师节、情人节等。贺卡上一般有一些祝福的话语。贺卡的产生源于人类社交的需要。由于贺卡是沟通人与人之间情感的交往，而此种交往又往往以短句表达，令人一看亦言简意赅，久而久之，贺卡祝福语就出现了程式化——讲究喜庆，互送吉语，传达人们对生活的期冀与憧憬。

84. 宴会请柬

INVITATION

Come and join us at a Dinner Party!
Given by Susan & John Swift
at
200, Main Street, Knightsbridge
on Sunday May 17
at 7.30 in the evening

Let's get together and
eat, drink and be merry!

R.S.V.P. Tel: Susan 223-768-2603
E-mail susan@swiftmail.com

请 柬

苏珊·斯威夫特和约翰·斯威夫特于 5 月 17 日（周日）晚 7 点 30 分在骑士桥大街 200 号举行宴会，欢迎光临！贤友毕至，觥筹交错，尽享欢愉！请回复。电话：苏珊 223.768.2603; E-mail: susan@swiftmail.com

85. 舞会请柬

INVITATION

Mr. and Mrs. Marlin Ryder
Miss Jane Ryder
at home
Saturday, May the Fourteenth
Dallas Country Club

Dancing   semi-formal
7:00 to 10:00 p.m.   No dates

请　柬

马林·莱德先生和夫人及女儿珍妮于 5 月 14 日周六下午 7 时至 10 时在达拉斯乡村俱乐部举行舞会。

敬请

光临

无需着晚礼服

不一定带舞伴

86. 招待会请柬

INVITATION

On the occasion of the forty-fifth
anniversary of the founding
of the Witburn & Company
the Board of Directors
requests the honor of
Mr. and Mrs. Herman Wilde's
presence at a reception
On Monday, the tenth of October
at eight o'clock p.m.
37 willow street
Reserve

请　柬

为庆祝威尔伯恩公司成立 45 周年，兹定于 10 月 10 日（周一）晚 8 时在里瑟夫市柳林街 37 号举行招待会。

敬请赫曼先生和夫人光临。

威尔伯恩公司董事会　谨订

87. 展览会请柬

INVITATION

The Organizing Committee of
The Beijing International Forum on Friendly

People-to-People Exchanges
requests the pleasure of
Mr. and Mrs. Prodi's
presence at the Opening Ceremony
on Tuesday, September the sixth
J. W. Warriott Hotel
at eight o'clock a.m.
R.S.V.P.

请　柬

北京国际民间友好论坛开幕式兹定于9月6日（周二）上午8时在J. W. 万豪酒店举行。敬请普罗迪先生和夫人光临。

请赐复

北京国际民间友好论坛组委会　谨订

88. 婚礼请柬

INVITATION

Mr. and Mrs. Smith
request the pleasure of your
company on the occasion of
the marriage of their daughter
Andrea Marie
With
Jeff Leyland,
at St Paul's, Knightsbridge
on Friday, 30th May 2009
at 2.30 o'clock
and afterwards at
The Mernmaid Hotel,
200, Main Street, Knightsbridge
R.S.V.P.

请　柬

　　史密斯夫妇之女安德拉·玛丽与杰夫·雷兰德的婚礼兹定于 2009 年 5 月 30 日下午 2 点 30 分在骑士桥的圣保罗教堂举行，随后将于骑士桥主街 200 号举行宴请。诚邀您的光临。

　　请赐复

89. 私人名片

Prof. Fan Aiguo

China Foreign Affairs University

24 Exhibition Rd., Xicheng District, Beijing 100037 PRC

Tel: 6800000　　　　　　Mobil:12345678901

E-mail: fansylovecfau@cfau.edu.com

外 交 学 院

范 爱 国　教授

地址：中国北京市西城区展览路 24 号

电话：6800000　　　　手机：12345678901

邮编：100037　　　　　E-mail: fansylovecfau@cfau.edu.com

90. 商务名片

Pharmacia

Wong Siu Lung, Alma
Assistant Sales Manager

Pharmacia (China) Ltd.	Beijing Rep. Office:
6F Regency Centre	Rm 1202/1204, Beijing Yanchen Hotel
39 Wong Chuk Hang Road	56 Haidian Road, Beijing
Hong Kong	Tel: 2563388
Tel: 58148421	Mobile: 12345678900
Mobile: 12345678901	Fax: 2565803
Fax: 58734550	E-mail: wsl@hotmail.com

Pharmaic 公司
黄少龙
助理营业经理

Pharmacia (China) Ltd.

北京代表处：北京市海淀路 56 号香港黄竹坑道 39 号伟晋中心 6 楼燕山大酒店 1202/1204 房间

电话：5148421	电话：2563388　手机：12345678900
手机：12345678901	传真：2565803
传真：58734550	电子邮箱：wsl@hotmail.com

91. 新年贺卡

Dear Judy,

　　The New Year's Day is drawing near. I wish you every success in the coming year and good health to your parents. Happy New Year!

Yours,
Sam

亲爱的茱蒂：

　　新年就要到了。祝你来年马到功成，愿你的父母身体健康。新年快乐！

山姆 谨上

92. 圣诞贺卡

To my best buddy,

How have you been? Hope things are all right with you.
Thinking of you and wishing you a beautiful Christmas season.

Yours,
Joe

给我最好的朋友：

　　近来安好？但愿万事顺意。
　　非常想你，祝你度过一个美妙的圣诞节。

你的 乔

93. 教师节贺卡

Dear Mr. Johnson,

You have been the mentor of life. Though I did not realize it earlier. Now it feels great to have someone who guided me to the right track in life. Happy Teacher's Day!

Your student,

Victor

亲爱的约翰森先生:

您是我的人生导师,虽然我早该认识到这一点。此刻,一想到有人将我引入了正确的人生道路,我就非常激动。祝您教师节快乐!

您的学生

维克多

94. 结婚贺卡

Dear Ethan & Holly,

Let the arguing begin.

Yours,

Tom

亲爱的伊森和红丽:

又有一对儿要开始过打口水战的日子了。

你们的

汤姆

95. 生日贺卡

My sweetheart,

Once upon a time, there lived a little girl. And tomorrow she will be 20 years old. Do you know who she is?

Your boyfriend

小甜心：

很久很久以前，曾经有个小姑娘。明天她就要20岁了。你知道她是谁吗？

你的男友

96. 晋升贺卡

Dear Carl,

My warmest congratulations to you on being promoted to department chairman. You have my best wishes for your continued success.

Jones

亲爱的卡尔：

热烈祝贺你荣升系主任。祝你日后事业一帆风顺。

琼斯

97. 成就贺卡

Dear Mart,

Let me congratulate you on your company's being ranked as the 50th strongest company in New Zealand. I wish you all the best and good luck with your future endeavors!

Yours

Jerry

亲爱的马特：

祝贺你的公司成为新西兰的第五十强。愿你一切安好，未来事业披荆斩棘！

你的 杰里

98. 升学贺卡

Dear nephew,

I'm more than delighted to learn about your success in getting admitted to China Foreign Affairs University. Your efforts in the past few years have finally been paid. It's an excellent university and you will definitely learn a lot there. Be a good diplomat. Don't let me down!

Your uncle

亲爱的外甥：

听说你被外交学院录取，我高兴极了。你这些年来算是没白努力。外交学院是个好大学，你一定可以学到很多东西。做个好外交官。别让我失望！

你的舅舅

特别奉献

一　表示心情的词汇中英对照

1. 悲伤、难过、后悔、失望
   depressed 焦虑的，挂念的
   rue 悲伤的，悔恨的
   sore 伤心的，悲痛的
   sorrowful 悲伤的，伤心的
   downcast 垂头丧气的，萎靡不振的
   forlorn 孤独的，凄凉的
   gloomy 阴郁的；忧郁的
   glum 闷闷不乐的；忧郁的
   grievous 令人悲痛的，极严重的
   miserable 凄惨的；
   melancholy 忧郁的，郁闷的

2. 快乐、兴奋
   happy 高兴的
   excited 兴奋的
   joyful 快乐的
   chirrupy 快活的
   delectable 令人愉快的，使人高兴的
   gladsome 高兴的/可喜的
   good-humored 心情愉快的，脾气好的
   hedonic 快乐的
   merry 愉快的，兴高采烈的

3. 生气、愤怒
   upset, mad 和 angry 的生气程度相当于"不爽"，"生气"，和"愤怒"
   irate 发怒的，生气的
   provoking 使人愤怒的，难熬的
   shirty 不高兴的，生气的
   vexed 焦急的，恼怒的

特别奉献

二 常见食物名称中英对照（一）

A. 肉品类

Fresh Grade Leg 大鸡腿
Fresh Grade Breast 鸡胸肉
Chicken Drumsticks 小鸡腿
Chicken Wings 鸡翅膀
Minced Steak 绞肉
Pigs Liver 猪肝
Pigs Feet 猪脚
Pigs Kidney 猪腰
Pigs Hearts 猪心
Smoked Bacon 醺肉
Lard 猪油
Hock 蹄膀
Stewing Beef 小块的瘦肉
Steak & Kidney 牛肉块加牛腰
Frying Steak 可煎食的大片牛排
Mimced Beef 牛绞肉
Rump Steak 大块牛排
Barnsley Chops 带骨的腿肉
Shoulder Chops 肩肉
Chuck Steak 头肩肉筋（油较多）
Pig Bag 猪肚

B. 海产类

Herring 鲱
Salmon 鲑
Cod 鳕
Tuna 鲔鱼
Plaice 比目鱼
Octopus 章鱼
Squid 乌贼
Carp 鲤鱼
Hake 鳕鱼类
Oyster 牡蛎
Crab 螃蟹
Prawn 虾
Crab Stick 蟹肉条
Peeled Prawns 虾仁
King Prawns 大虾
Winkles 田螺
Shrimps 小虾米
Cockles 小贝肉
Lobster 龙虾

Chapter 02

商务往来 Business Letters

商务信函写作关键之处在于，用简单朴实的语言，准确地表达自己的意思，让对方清楚地了解您想说什么，而非华丽的词句。下面总结了几方面的写作要点，希望对您写作商务信函起到抛砖引玉的作用。

◆语言真诚

不管是生活中的交往还是生意上的合作，真诚是最重要也是最基础的。不管说什么，都要带着您的诚意去说。

◆礼貌适度

我们这里所说的礼貌，并不是简单用一些礼貌用语，而是要体现一种为他人考虑、多体谅对方心情和处境的态度。但礼貌过了头，可能会变成阿谀奉承。所以，最关键的还是要把握好"度"，才能达到预期的效果。

◆数据精确

当涉及到数据或者具体的信息时，比如时间、地点、价格、货号等，尽可能做到精确。这样会使交流的内容更加清楚，更有助于加快事务的进程。

◆收件人明确

请在邮件中写上对方公司的名称，或者在信头直接称呼收件人的名字。这样会让对方知道这封邮件是专门给他的，从而表示对此的重视。

除了上面的写信技巧外，要是发出去的信没有回复，也可能有网络的原因。因为国外好多国家都对中国的 IP 地址发过去的邮件全都当垃圾邮件处理，对方可能根本没收到就被服务器删掉了，这就要查查你的网络服务商的邮箱系统是否是可靠了。

Unit 1　业务咨询与往来　Business Consultation and Communication

不管是一个刚刚建立的公司，还是一个老牌企业，都需要不断扩大自己的业务以寻求发展，因此要与潜在的客户沟通。沟通手段包括：函电、展销会、贸易团访问等，其中函电是最经常使用的手段。只有经过沟通，才能建立业务关系，继而实现交易。

建立业务关系的函电书写步骤及注意事项：

1. 向对方说明信息来源，即如何得知对方姓名、地址等信息。
2. 自我推介。说明自己现在的经营情况、条件和产品。
3. 表达己方意图，或出口或进口。欲进口则索取产品目录，价目表和样品，同时说明采购方案；欲出口则介绍拟出口的商品。
4. 若必要，须向对方提供己方的资信证人。
5. 一般来说，函电最后部分是重申想要建立贸易关系的意图，并表示希望早日收到回复。
6. 应尽早回复此类信函，不然轻则失礼，重则有损商誉。

✱ 常用句型

1. Having obtained/had your name and address from …
   从……得知贵公司的名称及地址。
2. We have learned from …
   从……得知。
3. We are one of the leading importers/exporters of …
   我们是……的主要进口商 / 出口商。
4. See if we can establish/enter into business relation with you.
   不知能否与贵方建立业务关系。
5. I'm interested in …
   我们对……感兴趣。
6. We are looking forward to your earlier reply/receiving your reply.
   我们期待你的早日回复。

1. 索要商品目录

Dear Mr. Johnson,

A business associate of ours, Scott Fox of the X company, mentioned your name and showed us your company's brochure. We own and operate 11 household appliances factories here in China and are looking for reliable components such as electric wires and buttons. Could you mail us your latest sales catalogue and price list? Thank you very much.

Sincerely,
Helen Reed

强生先生:

  X 公司的司各特·福克斯先生是我方的一位商业伙伴,他曾提及您的名字并向我们展示贵公司的小册子。而我方在中国经营着 11 家家用电器工厂,正欲购一批可靠的电器零部件,如电线、按钮等,不知贵方能否电邮一份最新的销售目录和价格表。非常感谢。

诚挚的 海伦·里德

2. 回复对商品目录的索要

Dear Mr. Chou,

  Thank you for your inquiry of 12 September asking for the latest edition of our catalogue.

  We are pleased to enclose our latest brochure. We would also like to inform you that it is possible to make purchases online at <http://jacksonbros.com>.

  We look forward to welcoming you as our customer.

Yours sincerely
Dennis Jackson

周先生:

  感谢您于 9 月 12 日发来的索要我方最新商品目录的询盘。

  我方乐于随函附上最新小册子,同时贵方也可进入 <http://jacksonbros.

com> 在线购买，望知晓。

热切期盼并欢迎贵方成为我们的客户。

丹尼斯·杰克森 谨上

3. 索要产品信息

模板

Dear Mr. Paul,

I am writing this letter to ask some details of your product. I am interested in purchasing your Model X21 in-home theatre system and writing this letter to request some additional information about this product. Particularly I need to know complete details about wiring or other system requirements needed for installation. I will also need handling details of Model X21 along with necessary precautions.

Please send this Model X21 information by May 30, 2013. I would like to make my decision for the purchase of this product by June 15. Your early reply will be highly appreciated.

Sincerely,
Karin Johns

保罗先生：

兹以此函索求贵公司产品的一些细节说明。我方对贵公司的 X21 型号家庭影院系统非常感兴趣，特索要该产品的相关信息。特别要指出的是，我方需要了解安装时有关接线的全部细节及其他系统要求。另外，希望能收到 X21 型号操作方法和必要防预措施。

请于 2013 年 5 月 30 日前寄送上述信息，我方将于 6 月 15 日前做出购买决定。企盼早日复函。

诚挚的 卡琳·约翰

4. 回复对产品信息的索要

模板

Dear Sir.

Re: Request for product information about ZoomPlusMax

I refer to your recent inquiries concerning our new Digital Video

Camera, the ZoomPlusMax.

We've put together an info package which should give you a good overview of this exciting new camera.

Enclosed please find:

- A DVD promotional and tutorial video.
- Product specifications for the new model ZoomPlusMax 2 due for release in store in July this year, as requested.

Additional materials:

Please check out the ZoomPlusMax Fans site, <http://www.zoomplusmaxfanzone.com>, which contains some spectacular examples of the fabulous suite of applications ZoomPlusMax has pioneered, including the famous animation software.

I hope this information gives you what you need. If you have any further queries, or need updates on the new camera, please feel free to contact us.

Yours sincerely
Adam Bull

敬启者：

回复：索要 ZoomPluxMax 产品信息要求。

此函回复贵方近期对我们的新型数码摄像机 ZoomPluxMax 的询盘。

我们整合了一个数据包，可帮助贵方对这款产品有个全面的初步了解。

随函附上：

• 一份 DVD 宣传和教学视频

• 遵照所嘱，附上一份将于今年七月在商店公布的最新 ZoomPluxMax2 产品规格。

额外材料：

请查阅 ZoomPluxMax 粉丝网站 <http://www.zoomplusmaxfanzone.com>，该网站提供一些经典范例，是 ZoomPluxMax 处于领先地位的极好的应用程序套件，其中包括有名的动画软件。

希望此信息能满足您的需求。若有其他问题或需要升级新款摄影机，请随时联系我们。

亚当·布尔 谨上

5. 要求寄送样本

Gentlemen,

Here at Wen Lin Press, we publish various textbooks and readers for Taiwan's high school and university students studying English, French and German. As such, we are always searching for new and interesting teaching materials.

In this connection, we would like to ask you to send us a sample copy of the following title by airmail for examination.

SLANGUAGE

If feasible, we would like to introduce the material for use in language education in Taiwan.

Please let us know the amount as soon as possible if payment is required in advance.

Yours sincerely,

Juliana Tseng

敬启者：

敝出版社（文林出版社）专为台湾的高中和大学出版学习英语、法语和德语所需的各种教科书及读本，故此我们不断探求新的、有趣的教材。

因此，烦请贵社以航空寄送下列书本一册，作为样本。

SLANGUAGE

若内容合适，我们想将其用于台湾的语言教学上。

若需预付书款，请尽早告知金额。

朱莉安娜·曾 谨上

6. 推销商品

Dear Ms Courtney,

I recently met Mr. Frank Dawson at a trade fair in Hanoi organized by the Australian Chamber of Commerce. He mentioned that Modern Elegance would shortly be reviewing their contracts with suppliers of finished clothing articles, and I am therefore writing to introduce my company.

Victor operates three production plants, and supplies high quality articles of dress clothing to a number of fashion houses in Europe and the USA. At present, we have no business arrangements in Australia, but we are keen to expand our market.

I will be pleased to provide some samples of our finished goods for your approval, together with any other information you may require about Victor. You might also wish to visit our website.

Please do not hesitate to contact me if I can be of further assistance. I look forward to hearing from you.

Yours sincerely
Albert Back

考特尼女士：

　　我近日于澳大利亚商会在河内组织的商展会上会见了弗兰克·达森先生，通过他得知，"现代优雅"近期将复审其与成衣供应商的合同。故以此函推介我方公司。

　　维克特公司经营着三家制衣厂，为欧美众多时装公司提供高质服装。目前，我方在澳大利亚尚无贸易，但我方渴望扩大市场。

　　我很乐意提供我公司的成品样品，希望能获得您的赞许。我方还可提供任何您想了解的有关维克特的信息。另外，您也可以访问我们的网页。

　　如有任何我方能帮上忙的，请随时联络。盼早日复函。

艾伯特·巴克 谨上

7. 跟进函

Dear Mr. Hand,

The catalogue and price list faxed to you last week provided descriptions of our professional video recorders. However, you may have some specific questions on these new models. For that reason, I would welcome the opportunity to answer your questions and, if possible, advise you on how these new models can best suit your company's requirements.

I would be happy to arrange a brief demonstration for you and key members of your staff at a mutually agreeable time. There is, of course, no cost or obligation. Please, contact me so that I can reserve a date for you.

Sincerely,
Vera Finger

汉德先生：

上周传真给贵方的目录和价目表里，提供了对我方的专业摄像机的描述。然而，贵方可能会对这些新的型号有一些具体的问题。因此，我方乐意回答贵方的问题，并且有可能的话，就它们的使用上提出一些建议，以满足贵公司要求。

若双方时间方便，我方乐意为贵方及贵方核心员工进行一次简短的演示。当然，这是免费的。请尽早联系我们，以方便为贵方留出时间。

诚挚的 薇拉·芬格

8. 要求澄清具体条款

Dear Miss Vanessa Brain,

Re: Quote for installation of air conditioning at 395 Kuanping Road, Changchun.

We acknowledge receipt of your quote dated 8 December 2011.

We would like to raise several points for clarification:

1. It's unclear if the installation is conditional on acceptance of the quote prior to 8 February 2012.

2. The quote includes two options, one of which (Option 1) is cheaper, but appears to have no provisions for servicing by your firm, unlike the other option.

3. The wattage for the two systems appears to be the same, but the quoted area of air conditioning is noticeably smaller in Option 2. Please clarify this apparent anomaly.

We are currently considering various suppliers for this contract. We would appreciate your response to these points prior to 8 January 2012. If no response is received it will be assumed you no longer wish to tender for this installation.

103

If you wish to discuss any of the matters raised, please contact me on the above phone number or e-mail.

Yours sincerely
Barry Cotton

瓦内萨·布雷恩女士：

回复：对长春市宽平大路 395 号空调安装的报价

兹确认，我方已收到你方于 2011 年 12 月 8 日发出的报价。

尚有几点待明确：
1. 安装是否以我方在 2012 年 2 月 8 日前接受报价为条件。
2. 贵方的报价包括两个选项，选项一价格低，但似乎无法享受贵公司的服务。另一选项则不然。
3. 两套系统的瓦数似乎是相同的，但选项二中空调的报价区明显更小。请对此异常给予陈清。

对该合同，我方目前正考虑是否选择其他供应商。请在 2012 年 1 月 8 日前复函解释上述几点，不胜感激。若我方未收到回复，则视为贵方无意愿提供安装。

若贵方有意就提出的事项进行讨论，请按以上电话或邮箱联系我们。

巴里·克顿 谨上

9. 澄清具体条款

Dear Sir,

Please forgive us for the inconvenience produced due to the confusion about prices.

The clarification is as the following:

(1) No.13 is $6 for each.

(2) No.32 is $22 for each.

Concerning the quantity prices you would like to know, our products are subject to 10% discount for orders exceeding (including) 10 thousand units.

Thank you.

Yours truly,
James Lee

敬启者：
　　对于价格上的疑惑造成贵方的不便，敬请谅解。
　　以下是澄清事项：
　　（1）13号单价为6美元。
　　（2）32号单价为22美元。
　　贵方可能想知道大宗交易价，我方对不少于一万件的订单提供9折优惠价。
　　谢谢。

詹姆斯·里 敬上

Unit 2　询价报价、发盘还盘　Inquiry & Quotation, Offer & Counter-offer

　　询价（inquiry）也叫询盘，是指交易的一方准备购买或出售某种商品，向对方询问买卖该商品的有关交易条件。询盘内容包括有：商品价格、规格、品质等，其中以询价为主。询价信函书写时应当清晰明确地表达出自己的意图。
　　询价函写作步骤：1. 首先介绍己方公司，告知信息来源；2. 询问商品信息；3. 向对方提供的帮助表示感谢。

　　卖方在收到询价函后，通过考虑自己产品的成本、利润、市场竞争力等因素，报出可行性价格，此为报价（Quotation）。即使未收到询价函，卖家也可主动向潜在客户报价。进行报价时，内容要准确无误，不能含糊其辞，语气要委婉。此外，要明确指出报价有效期限。报价函中若包括其他条款，此类信函就有点类似于发盘。
　　报价函写作步骤：1. 对询问进行答复；2. 报价；3. 结尾。

　　发盘（Offer）是一种意思表示行为，指的是交易中一方为了要购买或销售商品，向另一方提出交易条件，并表示愿意按这些条件达成交易。必须明确的是，发盘有实盘（Firm Offer）和虚盘（Non-firm Offer）之分。两者区别可总结为三点：
　　1. 虚盘意思表示一般很含糊，没有一个肯定的表示，如"中间价格"、"数量可能不会太多"等；
　　2. 虚盘的合同要件包括商品的品质、数量、交货期、价格条款及支付方式等一般不齐全；
　　3. 有些报盘虽然意思明确，要件齐全，但带有一定的保留条件，也属于虚盘，如"以我方最后确认为准"、"以我货未先售出为准"及"仅供参考"等。
　　由于实盘和虚盘的法律效力不同，在发盘函的写作中要特别注意实盘和虚盘的区别，以免为以后的争议埋下祸根。发盘时还需注意准确阐明各项主要交易条件并声明此发盘的有效期及其他约束条件。
　　发盘函写作步骤与报价几乎相同，只是在报价时还需列出一些细节，如折扣、交货期等。

　　还盘（Count-offer）是受盘人对发盘内容不完全同意而提出修改或变更的表示，对发盘条件进行添加，限制或其他更改的答复。在交易磋商中，由于双方需要磋商的交易条件很多，因此，在还盘时一般只对发盘中不同意的部分提出修改的表示，而对于表示同意的部分，则不必在还盘中提出。通俗来讲，还盘相当于还价，但不应局限于价格，要综合分析，灵活运用交易条件。可以降低无关紧要的条件，迫使对方减价；也可以在对方价格坚持不降的情况下，再提出其他增加对方义务的条件，达到讨价还价的目的。

还盘函写作步骤：1. 对发票函表示感谢；2. 提出修改或变更，说明原因；3. 提出期望的交易日期，并试图劝说对方接受；4. 希望尽快得到回复。

✽ 常用句型

1. Please quote us the lowest price...

   请报给我们……的最低价。

2. …have pleasure in sending you a copy of our latest catalogue and price-lists for…

   乐于寄上我们……的最新目录和报价单各一份。

3. We thank you for your letter of Aug. 27.

   感谢贵方 8 月 27 日来函。

4. We find your price too high and out of line with the prevailing market level.

   你方的价格过高，与现行市场行情有出入。

5. We hope you will consider our counter-offer and let us know your acceptance at your early convenience.

   希望贵方考虑我方还盘，并早日告知接受。

6. Let's meet each other half way.

   让我们各退一步。

10. 询价

Gentlemen,

　　We are interested in your Giant Brand bicycles for men, women and children.

　　Please quote us for the supply of the items listed on the estimate sheet enclosed, giving your lowest possible C.I.F. San Francisco prices. Will you please also state your earliest shipping time, terms of payment and discounts for regular purchases?

If the quality of your bicycles is satisfactory and the prices are attractive, we expect to place regular orders for fairly large numbers. We look forward to your early reply.

Faithfully yours,
Emily Hill

敬启者:

我方对你们的捷安特牌男式、女士和儿童自行车很感兴趣。

请按随函寄去的报价单上所列的目录以 CIF 旧金山价报出贵方最低价。还请告诉我方你们最早装船时间、支付方式和长期订货的折扣。

若贵方的自行车质量很好,价格又吸引人,那么我们会长期以较大的数量订货。盼早复函。

艾米丽·希尔 谨上

11. 报价

Dear Sirs,

We thank you for your letter of July 25th and have pleasure in sending you a copy of our latest catalogue and price-lists for all electronic products we hold in stock. Our prices are subject to a trade discount of 20% and an additional commission of 4%, if your annual purchases form us exceed US$120,000.

We are early awaiting your order.

Yours truly,
Kate Rice

尊敬的先生:

感谢你们 7 月 25 日的来信。兹寄上我们现有存货的所有电子产品的最新目录和报价单各一份,请收阅。如果每年的成交总额超过 12 万美元,我们可给予 20% 的批发折扣,另加 4% 的提成。

我们热切地期待着你们的订单。

凯特·赖斯 谨上

12. 主动报价

Dear Mr. Brown,

We have seen your name and advertisements in various US trade periodicals and note that you are a major importer of quality vacuum cleaner. Since 1998, our company has been the export agent for the well-known cleaner brands in China, and we are confident that we can offer your company a great variety of high-quality cleaners at very competitive prices.

We enclose a copy of our most recent sales catalog and price list and hope you will be encouraged to place a trial order with us.

Sincerely,

Chen Jianwei

尊敬的布朗先生：

我们在各种美国贸易期刊上看到贵公司的名字和广告，发现贵公司是高档真空吸尘器的主要进口商。自 1998 年以来，我公司就一直担任中国驰名吸尘器品牌的出口代理。我们相信，我们能够为贵公司提供一系列质量高、价格合理的吸尘器。

随函附上我们最新的商品目录及价目表，希望您能尝试从我们这里下订单。

诚挚的 陈建伟

13. 还盘

Dear Sirs,

<u>Apples</u>

We thank you for your letter of Aug. 27 offering us 200 tons of the subject goods at $125 per ton CIF Shanghai.

Although we are in urgent need of such product, we find your price too high and out of line with the prevailing market level. Your quoted price will deprive us of any profit. To tell you the truth, we have received quotations 11% lower than yours. Should you be prepared to reduce your price by, say 10%, we might come to terms.

Considering our long business relations, we make you such a counter-offer. As you know, this year's apple harvest was good and the market is declining, though there is a heavy demand for apples. We hope you will consider our counter-offer most favorably and let us know your acceptance at your early convenience.

Hope to hear from you soon.

Yours faithfully,
Jacob Brook

敬启者：

苹果

感谢贵方 8 月 27 日的来函，报盘 200 吨上述货物，价格为每吨 CIF 上海价 125 美元。

尽管我方急需此货，但是你方的价格过高，与现行市场行情有出入。贵方报价会使我方利益受损。实不相瞒，我们已收到了低于你们 11% 的报价。如果贵方愿意减价，譬如说减 10%，也许能达成交易。

鉴于我们双方长久的业务关系，我方才作出以上还盘。尽管苹果需求量大，但如贵方所知，今年苹果丰收，市价在下跌。希望贵方以理解的态度考虑我方还盘，并早日告知能否接受。

望早日收到复函。

乔库·布鲁克 谨上

14. 反还盘

【模板】

Dear Sirs,

<u>Apples</u>

Upon receipt of your counter-offer of Sept. 6, we have made a very careful study.

As our two companies have done business with each other for so many years, we should like to grant your request to lower the price by 10%. However, such practice will mean nil profit to us. Our apples are of higher quality and thus of higher cost than that of others. It is impossible for us to reduce the price by 10% without lowering the Grade of apples. Considering our long-standing mutual relationship, let's meet half way. We suggest a reduction of 5% on orders of 300 tons. Only on orders of this size can we manage to make the reduction without lowering the Grade of apples.

We hope our counter-suggestion will be acceptable to you and look forward to your orders, we remain.

Sincerely yours,
Zhang Qijun

敬启者：

苹果

方收到贵方 9 月 6 日的还盘，我方做了认真的研究。

我们两家公司业务往来多年，理应满足贵方降价 10% 的要求。然而，这将使我方利益受损。我们的苹果质量上乘，所以成本也会比别家的高。降价 10% 而又不影响苹果质量等级是不可能的。鉴于我们长期合作的关系，就各让一半吧。我们建议订货数量超过 300 吨，减价 5%。只有订货数量达 300 吨时，减价才不至于影响货物质量。

希望你们接受这一反还盘。我们依然等待贵方的订单。

张启俊 谨上

Unit 3 订单

Order

　　交易一方明确接受另一方的交易条件，交易即达成，然后签订具有合同性质的文件。如果买方发出订购函，寄出订单或者购货确认书，要求卖方按上面所列出的条件供货，就是对自己订货的确认。订单函通常需要明确以下条件：商品名称、质量要求和规格、订购数量、价格及价格条件、总额等。买方通常强调交货时间或者敦促对方尽快交货，根据需要还可能提出付款方式、供现货等其他条件。

　　买卖双方可以通过往来函电确认成交，也可以在往来函电达成交易的基础上，订制销售合同或者销售确认书、购货确认书，以确定双方之间的合同关系。

　　卖方收到订单函后，如果接受就应立即确认；如果因为无货可供，或者无法接受对方的交易条件，或者价格和规格发生变化等原因而不能接受订单时，应立即回复，回复函中通常需要解释拒绝订单的原因，也可推荐适合的替代品供对方参考。

买方下订单的步骤：
1. 表达对报价和样品或对上次订购的满意。
2. 订单内容。
3. 对包装、装运、付款方式等要求。
4. 希望尽早收到销售确认。

卖方回复订单步骤：
1. 对收到订单表示感谢。
2. 确认订单中交易条件。
3. 对所订购货物加以说明和讨论。
4. 拒绝订单理由。
5. 保证认真处理订单，希望收到更多订单。

✲ 常用句型

1. We are glad that, after long discussions, we have come to an agreement on this matter.
   我们很高兴经过长时间的讨论后，对此问题终于达成了协议。
2. Would you please take special care of the quality and the package of this order?

烦请贵方关照该订单的质量和包装。

3. We will order more if the first order with you proves to be satisfactory.

若首次订购满意，我方将继续下订单。

4. We hereby confirm receipt of your order for the following goods.

兹确认收到贵方订单，货品如下。

15. 下订单

Dear Sir,

After serious consideration, we have decided to place the order. Please dispatch to us 10,000 pairs of sheep leather gloves as per the terms stated in your offer of March 25.

Would you please take special care of the quality and the package of this order? The leather should be of the quality and the pair in an airtight polythene bag, a dozen pairs of gloves in a box and then 20 boxes to a strong seaworthy wooden case. We are enclosing our Purchase Confirmation No. 2006-398 in a duplicate for your signature. Please sign and return one copy for our file. Upon receipt of your confirmation, an L/C will be issued.

We will order more if the first order with you proves to be satisfactory. Please work on our order without delay and advise us a few days prior to its completion.

Yours truly,
Ethan William

敬启者：

经过认真考虑，我方决定从贵方下订单。请根据贵方 3 月 25 日的发盘条款内容发给我方 1 万双羊皮革手套。

烦请贵方关照该订单的质量和包装：皮革质量应当上乘，每副手套用塑料袋密封，每 12 副装一盒，每 20 盒装一坚固耐海运的木箱。随函附寄我方的购买确认书，编号为 No.2006-398，一式两份，请贵方签字后复函一份供我方存档。一收到贵方的确认，我方会立即开出信用证。

若首次订购满意，我方将订购更多。请即时处理我方订单并于完成前几日通知我方。

伊桑·威廉 敬上

16. 确认订单

Dear Sirs,

As requested, we hereby confirm receipt of your order for the following goods:

    20 Alpha 900 litre fridges

    10 Alpha 2000 litre freezers

    8 Alpha deep fryers Model AD23

    10 Beta washing machines Model BW333

    10 Beta dryers Model 334

    15 Gamma air conditioners Model GG5885

    20 Epsilon Barbecue Deluxe Models 6605

As requested, the purchase value of these goods is confirmed as $25,209.00, not including delivery or other costs.

Please contact me if you require any additional information regarding your request for confirmation of your purchase order.

Yours sincerely
Logan Miller

敬启者:
    遵照所嘱，兹确认收到贵方订单，货品如下：
    阿尔法 900 公升冰箱 20 台
    阿尔法 2000 公升冰箱 10 台
    阿尔法 AD23 油炸机 8 台
    贝塔 BW333 洗衣机 10 台
    贝塔 334 型号烘干机 10 台
    伽马 GG5885 空调 15 台
    艾司隆 6605 型号豪华烤肉架 20 台

按贵方要求，经确认这批货物总价为 25 209 美元整，不包括运费及其他费用。

若贵方还对订单确认事宜有其他要求，需要任何信息，请联系我方。

洛根·米勒 谨上

17. 拒绝订单

Dear Sir,

In our circular letter of May 21 (a copy of which is enclosed with this letter), we advised our customers of price increases in our entire camera line which would become effective on June 1. For that reason, we regret that we cannot accept your order No. BHJ-36 of June 15 which uses the expired price list.

Please advise us whether you want to confirm this order in accordance with our current price list.

We look forward to hearing from you soon.

Sincerely,

Noah Lee

尊敬的先生：

在 5 月 21 日的报单中（请看附件中的复印件），我们已经通知我们的客户，我们将全线上调我方照相机的价格，并于 6 月 1 日起生效。因此，很遗憾，我们不能接受贵方 6 月 15 日用过期价格发出的订单，订单编号为 No. BHJ-36。

如贵方有意按照当前价格确认此次订购，请通知我们。

希望尽快收到贵方的回复。

诚挚的 诺亚·李

18. 取消订单

Dear Sir,

We are sorry to inform you that we must cancel our order No. TPL-

1428 of November 3 due to the inexcusable delay in the shipment of the goods, which we still have not yet received.

Sincerely yours,
Ben Bush

敬启者：

　　我们很遗憾地通知您，由于贵方在装船方面造成拖延，致使我们至今仍未收到货物，这一错误不可原谅。因此我们必须取消11月3日的订单，订单编号为TPL-1428。

诚挚的 本·布什

19. 对方确认取消订单

Dear Sirs,

I refer to your letter of October 7 requesting cancellation of Order No. GLD-563.

Please be advised this order has now been cancelled:

♣ A refund of monies paid will be forwarded within 10 business days of the date of this letter by direct deposit, as requested.

♣ The materials delivered will be picked up by our couriers from your premises as soon as possible. Our staff will contact you directly to arrange suitable pickup times.

If you have any inquiries, please contact me on the above phone number or e-mail.

Yours sincerely
Zoe Henry

敬启者：

　　我方已查阅贵方10月7日要求取消订单的信件，订单号为GLD-563。
兹通知贵方，该订单已取消。

　•遵照所嘱，已付款将以直接存款的方式，在十个工作日内退还，时间以本函日期为始。

· 我方会尽快派遣快递员到贵方厂房直接收取已送达的原料。我方员工将直接联系贵方安排适当取回时间。

如有疑问，请按以上电话或邮箱联系我方。

佐伊·亨利 谨上

Unit 4　付款

Payment

外贸常用的付款方式有三种：

1. 信用证（Letter of Credit，简称 L/C），种类繁多；信用证实为不信任的产物，此种付款方式通过银行担保，在国际贸易中最常使用。信用证在 Unit 3 将有详细介绍，故在此不付赘言。

2. 汇付，主要包括电汇（Telegraphic Transfer，简称 T/T）、信汇（Mail Transfer，简称 M/T）和票汇（Demand Draft，简称 D/D）三种；

3. 托收（Collection），主要包括付款交单（Documents against Payment，简称 D/P）和承兑交单（Documents against Acceptance，简称 D/A）两种。

付款函的书写分三步：首先，买方下订单或卖方确认订单，紧接着提出付款方式；其次，解释原因并表示感谢；最后，希望对方采取行动、及时回复。

在国际贸易中经常会遇到买家不能按时付给卖家货款的情况。对于买家来说，无法按时付款很可能会降低公司的信用等级，严重的可能受到卖方的控告，因此就产生了买家向卖家申请延期付款的必要。请求延期付款的函电中，买方必须认真说明无法按时付款的原因，使得卖家因为考虑双方的合作关系，或者其他原因而不得不延长付款期限。

而对于卖家来说，不能按时收回货款会影响整个公司资金的运转，给公司带来经营上的困难，也因此出现卖方提醒或催促买方付款的函件。催款函的原则是既要达到索款目的，又要与客户保持友好关系。写此类信要求文字简练、表意明确。还需注意不能轻易怀疑对方故意拖欠不付，以免伤害对方感情，不利于达到索款的目的，更影响到以后的业务往来。对于某些屡催不付款或故意逃款的客户，则要语气强硬，措辞坚决，必要时让其了解拖欠的法律后果，"逼迫"对方付款。

✻ 常用句型

1. In terms of the payment, our usual practice is to accept orders against confirmed, irrevocable L/C at sight, valid for 3 weeks after shipment is made and allow transshipment and partial shipments.

   我方的惯例是：接受保兑的、不可撤销的、有效期为装船后三周的即期信用证，允许转船和分批装运。

2. I refer to your letter of 8 August explaining your need for an extension

of time for payment on your account with us due to changed business circumstances.

兹已查阅你方 8 月 8 日来函，解释由于经营状况的变化，你方需要延期付款。

3. I regret to inform you the proposed terms are not acceptable, due to…

   我方遗憾地通知贵方，贵方的提议未得到采纳，原因是……

4. If you have already paid this account, please disregard this notice.

   若贵方已付款，则忽略此通知。

5. Please note that our policy is to institute collection procedures upon failure to respond to two reminder notices.

   请注意，若两次催款通知无回复，我方将启动收款程序。

6. If you are having difficulty paying this account, it may be possible to…

   如果贵方支付有困难，可……

7. We are writing to request immediate payment on the amount…

   兹以此函要求贵方立即付清……

20. 付款信（现金电汇 T/T）

Dear Sir,

  It is a pleasure to receive your order of July 2 for cell phones. We hope that this is the first of many orders which you may place with us. Your letter does not mention your method of payment. You are no doubt aware of the custom of the wholesale trade that opening orders are payable in cash. If you wish us to send the cell phones immediately we shall be glad to do so on receipt of your remittance for $15,000. We are looking forward to your remittance.

Yours faithfully,
Lucas Lake

尊敬的先生：

  很高兴收到您 7 月 2 日的手机订单。我们希望今后会收到您更多的订单。

来信中没有提到付款方式。毫无疑问，您一定知道批发行业的惯例，即初次订货是以现金结账。如果您想要我们立即发运手机，等收到您 15 000 美元的货款后我们将立即发货。

期待着您的汇款。

卢卡斯·雷克 谨上

21. 付款信（付款交单 D/P）

Dear Sirs,

Subj.: Shoes

We are pleased to inform you that the subject goods under your order 1162A68 have been shipped to you today per S.S. "Elizabeth", due at Liverpool on Dec. 20. We hope you will be satisfied with our goods.

Our custom is to accept payment by L/C. but in order to facilitate your efforts in introducing our products to your market, we are now giving you a special accommodation by granting D/P. you are requested to honor our draft on presentation.

Thank you again for your order.

Truly yours,
James Smith

敬启者：

事由：鞋

很高兴通知贵方，贵方 1162A68 订单下的鞋今天已经装上"伊丽莎白号"轮，12 月 20 日抵达利物浦港。希望贵方能够对货物满意。

我们的惯例是以信用证方式付款。但为了协助贵方将我方产品引进贵方市场，我方给贵方特别优惠，同意贵方以付款交单方式支付。请见票即付。

再次感谢贵方的订货。

詹姆斯·史密斯 谨上

22. 付款信（L/C）

Dear Sirs,

We thank you for your order No. 1745 for 1 500 bicycles and appreciate your intension to push the sales of our products in your country. In terms of the payment, our usual practice is to accept orders against confirmed, irrevocable L/C at sight, valid for 3 weeks after shipment is made and allow transshipment and partial shipments.

As per the above terms we have done substantial business. We hope you will not hesitate to come to agreement with us on payment terms so as to get the first transaction concluded.

Your favorable reply will be highly appreciated.

Yours sincerely,

Jimmy Hunter

敬启者：

感谢贵方订购 1 500 辆自行车的 1745 号订单，以及贵方想在贵国推销我方产品的愿望。提及付款事宜，我方的惯例是：接受保兑的、不可撤销的、有效期为装船后三周的即期信用证，允许转船和分批装运。

根据以上条件，我方已经做成多笔交易。我们相信贵方也会毫不犹豫地接受我方的支付条件，达成第一笔交易。

恭候佳音。

吉米·亨特 谨上

23. 请求延期付款

Dear Sirs,

Your invoice No. 8719 for US$23,000 worth of goods supplied on June 12 is due for payment at the end of July.

These days our business capacity has become quite expanded and we have to take more time to check it and complete payment.

We shall appreciate it deeply if you can grant us this extension of payment time.

Faithfully yours,
Paul Reed

敬启者：

就6月12日提交的货物，贵方开具的23 000美元发票，我方本应于7月底付清。

然而，由于现今经营能力的较大提升，我方需要更长时间审查发票，完成支付。

若贵方同意延长付款时间，我方将不甚感激。

保罗·里德 谨上

24. 同意延期付款

Dear Sir,

I refer to your letter of 8 August explaining your need for an extension of time for payment on your account with us due to changed business circumstances.

I'm pleased to inform you this request has been approved on the terms of payment you suggested:

$200 per calendar month (no fixed date per month) commencing June 2010

Note: We appreciate your prompt notification of your need to vary terms of payment, and penalties for current arrears have been waived.

Accordingly, the sum of $325.19 owing for arrears on your previous statement of account is no longer payable.

If you require any further assistance in this matter, please contact me directly on the above phone number or e-mail.

Yours sincerely
Sybil David

敬启者：

兹已查阅你方 8 月 8 日来函，解释由于经营状况的变化，你方需要延期付款。

很高兴通知你方，我方同意按你方提出的付款方式延期付款：

从 2010 年 6 月开始，每公历月（每月无固定日期）支付 200 美元。

注意：若你方需要改变支付方式，请即时通知我方。另外，现有的逾期欠款罚款已免去。

因此，由于欠款，贵方先前账单上未付的 325.19 美元罚款已不需支付。

在此事宜上，如需其他帮助，请直接按以上电话号码或邮箱地址联系我方。

西比尔·大卫 谨上

25. 拒绝延期付款

Dear Sir,

I refer to your phone call concerning a proposal for extension of time for payment of your outstanding account.

This proposal has been considered carefully, and I regret to inform you the proposed terms are not acceptable, due to the four year timeframe.

Please note:

In view of the circumstances you have described, we appreciate that this situation may be very difficult for you to manage.

Accordingly we will grant you a period of one month to make an alternative proposal for terms of payment.

After that period the current terms of payment will be considered to be in force.

Please be advised we will consider any proposal for payment of arrears within a two year timeframe.

If you wish to discuss options in this matter, please contact me directly on the above phone number or e-mail.

Yours sincerely
Toni Clinton

敬启者：

兹确认收到贵方想要延期付款的来电。

经过仔细思考，我方遗憾地通知贵方，贵方的提议未得到采纳，原因是我方无法接受四年的付款时限。

请注意：

鉴于贵方陈述的情况，我方承认贵方难以控制现状的事实。

因此，贵方还有一个月的时间提出另外一种付款方式。

逾期将视为现有付款方式生效。

需告知贵方的是，我方会对付款时限为两年以内的付款方式予以考虑。

如果贵方希望就此事宜进行讨论，请直接按以上电话或邮箱联系我们。

托妮·克林顿 谨上

26. 第一次催款

Dear Sirs,

Reminder of overdue account

If you have already paid this account, please disregard this notice.

This is just a friendly reminder that the following payment is now overdue. Our terms of business require payment of outstanding accounts within 30 days of the date of receipt.

Goods purchased:

1 conditioner	$699.90
1 Persian Rug, Axminster	$150.00
1 Delivery	$ 40.00

Amount due: $889.90

Please arrange for the payment of this amount at your earliest convenience.

Note: Overdue accounts charges are incurred after 60 days from the date of the receipt.

Please contact us if you require further information.

Yours sincerely
Bud Bush

敬启者：

账单超期提醒

若贵方已付款，则忽略此通知。

兹以此函友情提示以下待付款项已超期。你我双方的贸易条款规定账单需在收到之日

30 日内支付。

已购商品：

空调一台	699.90 美元
艾克斯敏斯特波斯地毯一块	150 美元
配送费	40 美元

应付额：889.90 美元

请尽早付款。

注意：账单收到超过 60 天后，将生成超期费用。

如需更多信息，敬请联系。

巴德·布什 谨上

27. 第二次催款

Dear Sirs,

If you have already paid this account, please disregard this notice.

I refer to our previous reminder letter regarding overdue payment on this account:

Goods purchased:

1 conditioner	$699.90
1 Persian Rug, Axminster	$150.00
1 Delivery	$ 40.00
Amount due:	$889.90
Overdue account charges	$133.48 (15% per month)
Total amount payable	**$1023.38**

Please arrange for the payment of this amount at your earliest convenience.

If you are having difficulty paying this account, it may be possible to schedule payments, or arrange a line of credit, or some other method of addressing your needs.

Please contact us on the above phone number or e-mail if you require further information.

Yours sincerely
Bud Bush

敬启者：

若贵方已付款，请忽略此通知。

请查阅我方先前关于迟滞付款提醒的去函。

已购商品：

空调一台	699.90 美元
艾克斯敏斯特波斯地毯一块	150 美元
配送费	40 美元
应付额：	889.90 美元
超期费用：	133.48 美元（每月 15%）
需支付总额	1023.38 美元

请尽早付款。

如果贵方支付有困难，可分期支付，或申请信用额度，或采取其他办法解决贵方困难。

如需更多信息，请根据以上电话号码或邮箱地址联系我们。

巴德·布什 谨上

28. 第二次以后的催款

Dear Sirs,

If you have already paid this account, please disregard this notice.

I refer to our two previous notices regarding overdue account detailed below.

Please note that our policy is to institute collection procedures upon failure to respond to two reminder notices.

As no response has been received to previous notices, collection procedures for the account detailed below, (including overdue account charges), will be instituted if no response to this notice is received within one calendar month of the date of this notice.

Goods purchased:

1 conditioner	$699.90
1 Persian Rug, Axminster	$150.00
1 Delivery	$ 40.00
Amount due:	$889.90
Overdue account charges	$266.96 (15% per month x 2 months)
Total amount payable	**$1156.86**

If you are having difficulty paying this account, it may be possible to schedule payments, or arrange a line of credit, or some other method of addressing your needs.

Please contact us on the above phone number or e-mail if you require further information.

Yours sincerely
Bud Bush

敬启者：

若贵方已付款，请忽略此通知。

请查阅我方先前两次催款通知，账单详见下文：

请注意，若两次催款通知无回复，我方将启动收款程序。

由于未收到先前通知的回复，如果此通知发出后一个公历月内仍未收到回复，我方将启动该账单（包括逾期账罚金）的收款程序。账单细节如下：

已购商品：

空调一台	699.90 美元
艾克斯敏斯特波斯地毯一块	150 美元
配送费	40 美元
应付额：	889.90 美元
超期费用：	266.96 美元（每月 15%*2 个月）
需支付总额	1156.86 美元

如果贵方支付有困难，可按计划支付，或申请信用额度，或采取其他办法解决贵方困难。

如需更多信息，请根据以上电话号码或邮箱地址联系我们。

巴德·布什 谨上

29. 最后一次催款

Dear Sirs,

If you have already paid this account, please disregard this notice.

I refer to our previous notices regarding overdue account detailed below.

Please note that our policy is to institute collection procedures upon failure to respond to two reminder notices.

As no response has been received to previous notices, collection procedures for the account detailed below, (including overdue account charges), have now been commenced.

Goods purchased:

1 conditioner	$699.90
1 Persian Rug, Axminster	$150.00
1 Delivery	$ 40.00
Amount due:	$889.90
Overdue account charges	$400.14 (15% per month x 3 months)
Total amount payable	**$1300.04**

Please contact us on the above phone number or e-mail if you require further information.

Yours sincerely
Bud Bush

敬启者：
　　若贵方已付款，请忽略此通知。
　　请查阅我方先前关于以下逾期账的通知。
　　请注意，我方的政策是，在两次提醒通知未收到回复后启动收款程序。
　　由于之前通知未收到回复，以下账户（包含逾期款罚金）的收款程序现已开始。
　　已购商品：
　　空调一台　　　　　　　　　699.90 美元
　　艾克斯敏斯特波斯地毯一块　　150 美元

配送费	40 美元
应付额：	889.90 美元
超期费用：	400.14 美元（每月 15%*3 个月）
需支付总额	1300.04 美元

如需更多信息，请根据以上电话号码或邮箱地址联系我们。

巴德·布什 谨上

30. 收款代理机构的催款信

Dear Sir,

We are writing to request immediate payment on the amount owed of $164 200, which is more than 180 days past due. This total includes all interest, late fees, and other charges. This amount was originally owed to Acme Financing, Inc., and our company is now handling this account.

Please call (215) 555-1212 immediately to make your payment. If you need to set up a payment plan, inquire about that when you call.

Thank you for your prompt attention to this important matter.

Sincerely,

Dirk Baker

敬启者：

兹以此函要求贵方立即付清所欠 164200 美元，包含所有利息、滞纳金、及其他费用，该款项已拖欠超 180 天。款项归极点金融公司所有，现由我方公司处理该账单。

请立即致电（215）555-1212 完成付款。若贵方需要建立付款计划，亦请致电咨询。

希望贵方从速办理该重要事项，谢谢。

诚挚的 德克·贝克

Unit 5　信用证

Letters of Credit (L/C)

信用证（Letters of Credit 或 L/C）是银行（即开证行）依照买方/进口商（即开证申请人）的要求和指示，对卖方/出口商（即受益人）发出的、授权卖方/出口商签发以银行或买方/进口商为付款人的汇票，保证在交来符合信用证条款规定的汇票和单据时，必定承兑和付款的保证文件。

在国际贸易活动，买卖双方可能互不信任，买方担心预付款后，卖方不按合同要求发货；卖方也担心在发货或提交货运单据后买方不付款。因此需要两家银行做为买卖双方的保证人，代为收款交单，以银行信用代替商业信用。银行在这一活动中所使用的工具就是信用证。

与信用证有关的商务信函主要有要求开证（包括催证）、通知已开证、改证（包括展证）、通知已改证。

要求开证信函书写步骤：首先，告知对方其订单已被确认；其次，简单说明目前订单的状态，要求对方开具信用证。对于信用证的细节要求如种类、期限，必须详尽说明，以免日后改证费时、费钱、费力；最后，保证收到信用证即刻发货。如果对方迟迟未开出信用证，则需要催证，提醒其后果，促使对方尽快开证。

通知已开证信函书写步骤：首先，告知卖家信用证已开具；其次，要求尽快发货，并在发货后及时予以通知。

改证是对已开立的信用证中的某些条款进行修改的行为。**改证信函书写步骤**：首先，确认收到信用证；其次，阐明要求改证（展证）的原因；最后，要求对所列条目进行更改。信用证的修改可以由进口商提出，也可以由出口商提出。如果是由于对方的原因造成必须修改信用证，态度应当强硬；如果是由于己方缘故而提出改证，则态度应当诚恳，并感谢对方的合作。

通知已改证与通知已开证信函的书写步骤类似，不做累述。

❋ 常用句型

1. We have instructed ... to open an irrevocable letter of credit in your favor, covering...

我方已通知……开具一个以你方为受益人的不可撤销信用证，支付……

2. As the goods against your order have been ready for shipment for quite some time, it is imperative that you take in immediate action to have the covering L/C established as soon as possible.

   由于贵方定单已待运相当长时间了，贵方必须立即开出信用证。

3. Please amend the L/C to read partial shipments and transshipment allowed.

   请将信用证改为允许分批装运和转船。

4. Please extend the shipment date of the L/C to… and its valid date to… to allow shipment of said goods.

   请延长信用证的发货日期至……，有效日期至……，以使得上述货物顺利发货。

31. 申请商务信用证

Dear Mr. Sharp,

For the past year, we have been purchasing electronic equipments from your company on a C.O.D. basis. However, we would now like to open a line of credit. Please, let us know your usual credit terms and also what credit references and other business information you require to open such an account.

We hope your company will be willing to comply with our request.

Sincerely,

Michael Well

夏普先生：

过去一年来，我方一直以货到付款方式从贵公司购买电子设备。现在我方希望能申请一个信用额度。请告之你方信用证条款惯例，及开证所需的信用备谘和其他业务信息。

希望贵方愿意满足我方要求。

诚挚的 迈克尔·韦尔

32. 申请具体信用额度

Dear Mr. Wang:

Given our moderate cash reserves, we would like to apply for a $150,000 credit line with your company so as to avoid unnecessary transaction delays.

Over the past several years, we had a number of large deals with you on cash basis, which, we are sure, have adequately established our credit. If you require further credit data, you have our permission to directly contact the Communication and Construction Bank at 8765432 for banking and credit history.

Your early reply will be appreciated.

Sincerely,

Charles Kent

尊敬的王先生：

由于我们的现金储备并非十分充足，因此希望向贵公司申请 150,000 美元的信用额度，以此避免在交易中产生不必要的延误。

过去几年中，我们曾用现金结款的方式与贵公司发生过几宗大型的生意往来。我们相信，这已经为我们建立了良好的信用基础。如你方需要更详细的信用数据，可直接联系交通建设银行查询我公司的信用资料，他们的电话是 8765432。

静候佳音。

查尔斯·坎特 敬启

33. 接受商务信用证的申请

Dear Sir,

Thank you for expressing your confidence and goodwill by requesting a charge account.

Your references have been verified, and we have received satisfactory reviews from your associates. An account has been opened for you, and we trust that you will use it soon and often. You can order conveniently by telephone or on our website.

The terms for your account will be Net 30 Days; our accounting department will print your statement on the last day of each month, and then any credited payment will be due within 30 days.

Now that you are an account holder, we will give you advance notice of any special sales. We will also ensure that your needs are responded to on a VIP basis.

Thank you again for your credit application.

We look forward to working with you in the very near future.

Sincerely yours,
Hugh Wood

敬启者：

您方请求申请赊欠户，感谢您方的信任和诚意。

我方查您方的推荐信属实，也收到来自您方合作伙伴对你们的满意评价。据此为您方开户，相信此账户能很快并经常利用起来。您方可通过电话或我方网站下订单。

您方账户期限为 30 日整，每月最后一日，我方会计部门会打印您方报表，任意信用证付款在 30 日内有效。

由于您方是顾客账户，若有特卖我们有提前通知。我们亦保证您方的需求会得到贵宾级别的回应。

再次感谢您方的信贷申请表。

希望尽快与您合作。

休·伍德 谨上

34. 拒绝商务信用证的申请

Dear Sir,

Thank you for your recent order and your application for a line of credit with our company. When determining customers' eligibility to open charge accounts, we fully investigate each applicant, and we must always follow company policy.

We have reviewed your references and the other information provided on your application. Based on the findings of our credit review process, we cannot justify opening an account for you. If you believe that our decision is unwarranted, then please feel free to contact us so that we may give you further details about our decision. We will still process and deliver your order after payment is received. Your credit application will remain on file, and you may reapply at any time.

Very truly yours,
Dean Hill

敬启者：

感谢贵方近期订单和信用额度申请。我方在判断客户是否适合开立赊欠户前，会以遵守公司制度为基础，详尽调查每个申请者。

我方已评估贵方推荐信及申请书内其他信息。基于信贷审查结果，我方无法为贵方开立账户。如果贵方质疑我方决定，请随时联系索取更详细信息。收到付款后，我方仍会处理并交付贵方订单。而贵方的信贷申请将被保留存档，贵方可随时复申请。

迪安·希尔 敬上

35. 要求对方开证

Dear Sirs,

Thank you for your order No.5631 of July 16. As we have adequate stocks of shoes, your delivery date can be met.

Payment by irrevocable letter of credit is convenient for us, and we shall draw a 60 days' draft on your bank.

We are now awaiting the arrival of your L/C, on receipt of which we shall make the necessary arrangements for the shipment of your order. Your early reply is appreciated.

Yours faithfully
James Mark

敬启者：

感谢你方 7 月 16 日订单，订单号为 5631。我方鞋子现货源充足，因此可按贵方要求的日期发货。

请以不可撤销信用证付款，这将给予我方很大方便。我方将向你方银行开立 60 天后付款的汇票。

期待收到你方信用证，一旦收到，我方将安排订单发货的必要事宜。盼早复函。

詹姆斯·马克 谨上

36. 通知已开证

Dear Sirs,

　　We have instructed the Fujian Branch of the Bank of China to open an irrevocable letter of credit in your favor, covering 10 000 pairs of leather shoes in the amount of US$150,000, valid until 31st July. The Letter of Credit will be confirmed by Bank of China, London Branch, who will accept your 30 days draft on them for the amount of your invoice.

　　The shipping documents required for negotiation are:

　　A full set of clean shipped Bill of Lading;

　　3 Commercial Invoices;

　　1 Insurance Policy.

　　Please advise us by telephone when the shoes have been delivered.

Yours sincerely,
Bill Cotton

敬启者：

　　我方已通知中国银行福建分行开具一个以你方为受益人的不可撤销信用证，支付一万双皮鞋货款总计十五万美元，信用证有效期到 7 月 31 日止。中国银行伦敦分行将对该信用证保兑，并接受你方 30 天后付款的汇票，支付发票金额。

　　议付所需货运单据包括：

　　清洁提单全套单据

　　3 份商业发票

　　1 份保单

　　鞋子发货后，请致电通知我方。

比尔·克林顿 谨上

37. 要求改证和展证

Dear Sirs,

Thanks for your L/C No. 10469, covering your order for 5 metric tons of Shandong Apples, Unfortunately, due to a delay from our suppliers, we are not able to make shipment this month. The delayed consignment will most likely be ready for delivery in early May. We are making arrangements to ship via the S.S. "Star" sailing from Qingdao on about the 12th of May.

Please extend the shipment date of the L/C to May 18th and its valid date to May 30th to allow shipment of said goods.

Thanks a million for your cooperation.

Sincerely,

Tang Hua

敬启者：

感谢贵方支付5公吨山东苹果的信用证，信用证编号为10469。不幸的是，由于供应商延期供货，我方无法在此月发货。延迟的货物预计将于五月准备好等待发货。我方正在安排相关事宜，计划于5月12日左右由"星星"号轮船从青岛港发货。

请延长信用证的发货日期至5月18日，有效日期至5月30日，以使得上述货物顺利发货。

十分感谢贵方的合作。

唐华 谨上

38. 终止赊账权利

Dear Sir,

Over the past two years, you have made six late payments for twenty orders. Because of the significant quantity and delinquency of those payments, we will no longer be able to extend credit to your account. We have endeavored to work with you in the past, and we have discussed these late payments with you on several occasions, but we have seen no changes in your payment behavior. Beginning today, all your orders will require cash or credit card payment before delivery. We also require that you pay your remaining balance before you place any further orders.

We will be happy to continue serving you under these conditions. You can expect the same quality of merchandise and the same fast service in the future.

Sincerely,
Jeremy Green

敬启者：

　　过去两年来，你方的二十笔订单中有六次延期付款。由于这些延期付款的订单数额颇大，违反条约，因此我方将不再对你方账户赊账。过去我们与你方努力合作，并在多个场合与你方讨论过这些延期的付款，然而你方的支付行为并未得到改善。从今日起，你方所有订单需以现金或信用卡结账后才可发货。同时，我方要求你方在继续下订单前付清现有欠款。

　　在此条件下，我方乐意继续为你方服务。未来你可收到同等品质的货物和同样快捷的服务。

诚挚的　杰里米·格林

Unit 6　资信调查　　　　　　　　　　　Credit Inquiries

　　资信调查（Credit Inquiry）指专业机构对企业的注册登记情况、股权结构、人力资源、经营业绩、管理水平、财务状况、行业声誉、以往信用情况等进行调查研究，必要的时候进行实地调查，根据调查结果出具信用报告并对其信用等级给予评定。

　　资信调查中使用最广泛的渠道是银行，此外还可通过商会、相关公司企业、专业信用机构、我国驻外商务机构等渠道进行调查。

　　资信调查的信函除要求被委托方面证实交易对方确系一经贸或企业组织外，更重要的是期望获得对方资本情况、经营能力、信用状况等方面的信息，同时保证对被委托方面所提供的有关信息予以保密。此类信函的语气必须谦恭有礼，忠实诚恳，以取得被委托方面的理解、信任与协助。收到回复的信息后，无论积极还是消极，应当回寄一封感谢信表示信息已收到，这是应有的礼貌。

　　回复这类信函时，应说明此信息须保密。不要提及被查询的公司名称，一般用"该公司"、"有关公司"等安全字眼，尤其是提供消极回复时。除了如实提供情况和提出建议外，回函中还应写明"对所提供情况不负任何责任"这类句子以避免可能的麻烦。

　　资信调查去函写作步骤：1. 选择对方的原因；2. 说明想要调查的细节和原因；3. 保证保守秘密。

　　回函写作步骤：1. 表示收到来信；2. 提供相关信息；3. 希望对方保密。

✷ 常用句型

1. … have given us your name as a credit reference.

   ……指定贵方为其信用证明机构。

2. We should be grateful if you could give us some information about…/ if you would let us know…

   若贵方能提供……信息，我发将不胜感激。

3. Any information we receive from you will be held in strictest confidence.

   我方将严格保密从贵方得到的信息。

4. We are pleased to supply you with the following information.

   我方乐于为贵方提供以下信息。

5. Our relations with them have / have not been satisfactory.

   我们的合作关系融洽 / 不太融洽。

39. 通过银行进行资信调查

Dear Miss Rosa,

  The Alexander Halifax Company, inc. has applied to our company for an open credit account. Ms. Clara Bow, Chief Financial Officer, has given your name as the bank in which her company deposits its funds. In order to determine the company's credit rating, we would like to know your bank's answers to the following questions:

- How long has the Alexander Halifax Company account been with your bank?
- Is its bank balance fairly steady?
- If not, is it subject to drastic fluctuations?
- What credit terms do you extend the company?
- Has the company ever borrowed funds from your bank?
- Has your bank ever denied loans to the company?

All facts and remarks will, of course, be held in strictest confidence.

Thank you very much for your cooperation.

Sincerely,
Jay Hanks

罗莎女士：

  亚历山大哈利法克斯有限公司向我公司申请开账式赊账。从其财务总监克拉拉·鲍女士得知，他们的资金存储在贵行。为了判定该公司的信用等级，我方企盼贵行对以下问题逐一解答。

- 亚历山大哈利法克斯公司在贵行开户多久？

- 其银行结余是否比较稳定？
- 若不稳定，是否大起大落？
- 贵行给予该公司什么信用证条款？
- 该公司曾否向贵行贷款？
- 贵行曾否拒绝向其贷款？

所有事项及评价定将得到最严格的保密。

感谢您的合作。

诚挚的 杰·汉克斯

40. 通过相关公司企业进行资信调查

Dear Mr. Smith,

Mr. Joseph Graph, President of Royal Classic Company, has asked us to extend credit to his company. He has given your name and company as a credit reference.

We would like your opinion of Royal Classic Company's business reputation, promptness of payment, and financial responsibility. Of course, any information you furnish will be treated with the utmost confidence. If we can ever be of similar service to your company, please call on us.

Thank you very much for your cooperation.

Sincerely,
Jay Gray

史密斯先生：

皇家经典公司董事长，约瑟夫·格拉夫先生需要我方为他的公司提供信贷。他提及您的名字，并指定贵公司为其信用证明机构。

我方希望得到贵方对皇家经典公司的信誉、付款及时性和支付能力的评价。当然，贵方提供的任何信息将会得到最严格的保密。如需我们提供类似的服务，请致电。

十分感谢你方的合作。

诚挚的 杰·格雷

41. 通过专业信用机构进行资信调查

Dear Sirs,

Peter & White Co.

  The captioned company is now offering to represent us in the sale of our paint, and has referred us to your agency for detailed information about its credit standing, business capacity and character. We shall appreciate it if you will frankly give us your opinion about these points.

  It goes without saying that any information you may obtain for us will be treated strictly confidential and without any responsibility on your part.

  A thousand thanks.

Sincerely yours,

Sam Lee

敬启者：

彼得怀特公司

  标题项下公司欲代理销售我方油漆产品，告知我方向贵机构索要其信用状况、经营能力和公司特征的详细信息。若贵机构能坦诚相告，我方将不胜感激。

  毋庸置疑，贵机构提供的信息将会得到最严格的保密，贵方无需承担任何责任。

  万分感谢。

山姆·李 谨上

42. 积极的回复

Dear Mr. Colin,

  In reference to your inquiry of May 11, as to the financial standing of XYZ Company in Middletown, South Carolina, we are pleased to inform you that this company enjoys an excellent reputation and has been in business since 1982. We have dealt with Cedexa for the past eight years and they have been very prompt in meeting all their financial obligations during that entire period.

We believe that your company would be justified in working with Cedexa on the credit terms they propose.

                Sincerely,
                Karl Wong

科林先生：

依据贵方 5 月 11 日的询问函，对于南卡罗来纳州米德尔顿市 XYZ 公司的财务状况，我方高兴地告知贵方，该公司从 1982 年便开始经营，一直以来信誉极佳。我方与 Cedexa 做了八年生意，在此期间，他们总能及时偿还债务。

我方相信贵公司完全可以按 Cedexa 提出的信用证条款与之合作。

                诚挚的 卡尔·王

✎ 43. 消极的回复

模板

Dear Sir,

I acknowledge receipt of your letter of November 21. However, I regret that I am unable to give you a satisfactory reference for the Jacques Lamberte Company in Carrollton, Kansas. During the past two years that I have been doing business with Lamberte Company, my experiences have been unsatisfactory. Payments are never made promptly and the company accounts are always in arrears for two or more months.

I trust that this information, which is given to you in strictest confidence, will be helpful to you.

                Sincerely yours,
                Fred Brook

敬启者：

兹确认收到贵方 11 月 21 日来函。遗憾地告知贵方，我方无法为堪萨斯州卡罗顿市的雅克·朗伯特公司提供令人满意的证明。我方与雅克·朗伯特过去两年的合作不尽如人意。该公司从未及时付款，经常欠款两个月或更久。

我方相信此严格保密的信息会对贵方有所帮助。

                弗瑞德·布鲁克 谨上

Unit 7　货运与保险

Shipment & Insurance

贸易的货运方式有很多种：海运、陆运（铁路和公路）、空运，以及联运。最常用的是海运，全世界贸易大约有三分之二是由海运完成的。

装运条件是买卖合同中不可少的一项主要条款，其主要内容包括装运时间、装运港和目的港、装卸时间、装运合同、装运单据等。在FOB、CFR和CIF价格条件下，合同一般规定卖方必须在装船完毕之后向买方发出装船通知（Shipping Advice），内容包括合同号、商品名称、数量、货值、船名及起航日期等，以便买方办理保险（在FOB和CFR条件下），并准备接货。

有关货运的函电包括买方指示装运、卖方通知已装运等。

买方指示装运函件内容写作步骤：1. 确认收到要求开信用证来函，表示感谢；2. 告知信用证已开，要求货物装船；3. 希望继续合作，索要装船通知。

卖方通知已装运函件写作步骤：1. 确认收到来函，告知已完成装运；2. 告知船名、离港和到港日期等信息，随函附上装运单据；3. 对货物的安全到达表示有信心，希望继续合作。

国际贸易运输中，难免会出现货物的损毁、丢失等情况，因此对货物进行投保是一项不可或缺的环节。货物按照FOB（或CFR）条款售出时，保险费用由买方支付。货物按CIF售出时，除非合同另有规定，卖方有责任按行业习惯投保这种货物和航程应予投保的险别，并支付这笔费用。

保险涉及买方、卖方和保险公司这三方，关于保险的函电包括投保询盘、询盘答复、确认投保等。

投保询盘是由投保人向保险公司发出的询问保险率等信息的函电，其写作步骤为：1. 描述待发出货物；2. 询问保率；3. 希望尽快回复。

答复此函写作步骤：1. 确认收到来函，表示感谢；2. 根据保险范围提供保率，若有折扣，亦告知；3. 寄送保单，希望早日回复和继续合作。

确认投保函件的写作步骤：1. 表示感谢，接受保率；2. 重申保险范围、货物价值等信息，告知货物状况；3. 表示感谢，希望合作愉快。

143

✱ 常用句型

1. Please do your best to advance shipment.

   请尽最大努力提前装船。

2. Please advise the name of steamer/ the date of shipment.

   请告知船名/装运日期。

3. Our customers are anxiously awaiting the arrival of the goods.

   我们的客户期待货物的到达。

4. We are now glad to inform you that we have shipped the goods you ordered on board S.S. …

   很高兴通知贵方，你们所定货物已装船于……，将于明日发往贵方港口。

5. Enclosed please find one set of the shipping documents covering this consignment, which comprises...

   随函附上此批货物相关船运单据，包括有……

6. We assume this is merely an oversight on your part; however, we are returning the erroneous shipment.

   我们估计这仅仅是贵方的一个疏忽，不过，我方正准备返还发错的货物。

7. Will you please quote your rate for the cover?

   敬请贵公司把保率报给我们。

8. Please cover for us the following goods with Particular Average for the sum of US$20,000.

   请对下列货物按 20,000 美元保额投保水渍险。

✎ 44. 通知发货情况

Dear Sirs,

Your letter yesterday has been received.

Accordingly, we set out immediately to get in touch with our factories and urged them to hasten their delivery. They have agreed to make early delivery.

    We have already booked the shipping space on S.S "Luna", which is scheduled to sail on the 14th of June. We shall send you an e-mail as soon as the loading is completed.

Yours truly,
Victor Brook

敬启者：

    兹收到贵方昨日来函。

    按来函，我方立即与生产方联系，催促他们提早发货，已得到应允。

    我方已在"月神号"轮船租船订舱，该轮船计划于6月14日启航。装船后我方会速以电邮告知。

维克特·布鲁克 敬上

45. 货运通知

Dear Sirs,

    We are now glad to inform you that we have shipped the goods you ordered on board S.S. "Alexander" which sails for your port tomorrow.

    Enclosed please find one set of the shipping documents covering this consignment, which comprises:

    1. One non-negotiable copy of B/L.

    2. Commercial invoice in duplicate.

    3. One copy of Certificate of Quality.

    4. One copy of Insurance Policy.

    The originals of those are being sent to you through our bankers.

    We are glad to have been able to execute your order as contracted and trust that the goods will reach you in good time to meet your urgent need and that they will turn out to your entire satisfaction.

    We avail ourselves of this opportunity to assure you of our prompt and careful attention in handing your future orders.

Yours faithfully,
Jack Finger

敬启者：

很高兴通知贵方，所定货物已装船于"亚历山大号"，将于明日发往你方港口。

随函附上此批货物相关船运单据，包括有：
1. 非流通提单副本一份
2. 一式两份商业发票
3. 品质证书副本一份
4. 保单副本一份

以上单据原件将由我方银行寄送给贵方。

非常高兴能按合同执行贵方订单，我方相信货物会及时送达，急您所需，令您满意。

借此机会，我方保证以后仍将及时认真地处理你方订单。

杰克·芬格 谨上

46. 通知运输推迟

Dear Sirs,

Just to inform you that your letter of December 3 has been received.

With respect to the remaining 70 tons of apples, as it has been extremely difficult to book a vessel at present, we fail to inform you of the exact departure of a vessel for the time being. If you can book a vessel for us, we can ship the goods at an early date; otherwise we are afraid that we may kindly apply for the extension of your import license.

As soon as we have the opportunity to book a vessel, we will tell you.

Yours sincerely,
John London

敬启者：

兹告知贵方12月3日来函已收到。

由于现在难以租到货船，我方当下无法告知贵方余下70吨苹果的确切发货日期。若贵方能为我方租到货船，我方可早日发货，否则要劳烦贵方延长进口证书的期限。

一旦有可能租到船，将告知。

约翰·伦敦 谨上

47. 通知运货出错

Dear Mr. Oscar,

  Greetings!

  This letter is in regard to your September 20, 2010 shipment to us, which we ordered from you on September 5. If you will recall, the order we made was for 250,000 units of Bosch earphones and 60,000 units of Edifier speakers. However, upon examination at our warehouse, the shipment of earphones was found to be in excess of 50,000 units. The brand of speakers sent to us was also not the brand that we request.

  We assume this is merely an oversight on your part; however, we are returning the erroneous shipment. Please send us the correct brand of speakers we ordered by the soonest time possible, as our client is already waiting for his order. We are also enclosing, for your information, a copy of the original sales invoice showing our correct order.

  We would appreciate receiving the corrected order by September 25 at the latest. If there are any other concerns or clarifications, you may contact John Franken at 010-506-1010.

  Thank you for your prompt action.

Respectfully yours,
Paul Smith

奥斯卡先生：

  您好！

  此函事关贵方2010年9月20发出的货物，我方于9月5日订购该批货物。若您能回忆起，可知我方订单为25万副博世耳机和6万件漫步者音箱。然而，经查验仓库，我方发现该批货物中耳机数量多了5万副，音箱牌子也非我方所订购的。

我们估计这仅仅是贵方的一个疏忽，我方正准备返还发错的货物。而由于我们的客户正需要此单货品，敬请贵方以最快速度发来正确牌子的音箱。兹随函附上一份销售发票副本，上有正确订单，供贵方参考。

请保证我方最迟在 9 月 25 日能收到正确货物，不胜感激。若有其他任何问题或说明，请致电 010-506-1010 与约翰·弗兰肯联系。

感谢您的及时处理。

保罗·史密斯 谨上

48. 回复运输推迟通知

Dear Sirs,

Re: Acknowledgment of delay in delivery of materials

I refer to your letter of February 1 regarding delay in delivery of Order 10/145.

As requested, the circumstances of the delay are acknowledged.

It will be appreciated if the delivery can be made as soon as possible. Please advise new delivery times when known.

Yours sincerely
Jack Brown

敬启者：
回复：原料运送迟滞通知
兹查阅贵方 2 月 1 日关于订单 10/145 推迟运输的来函。
应贵方要求，运输推迟的情况我方已知晓。
希望能尽早发货。获知新的运货日期时请告知我方。

杰克·布朗 谨上

49. 给保险公司的信（询问保险率）

Dear Sirs,

We shall have a consignment of "Siemens" brand, fridge, Model KK28F88TI, value at RMB6 999, to be shipped from Germany to China by S.S. "Prinz".

As shipments are due to begin on August 5, will you please quote your rate for the cover?

Thank you for an early reply.

Very truly yours,
Mark Wood

敬启者：

我们将通过"Prinz"号海伦从德国向中国运送一批西门子牌电冰箱，型号是 KK28F88TI，价值 6 999 元人民币。

由于装船日期定位 8 月 5 日，敬请贵公司把保率报给我们。

望能早日回复。

马克·伍德 谨上

50. 买方请求卖方代为投保

Dear Sirs,

We wish to refer you to our Order No. 101 for 500 cases of Electronic Toys, from which you will see that this order was placed on CFR basis.

As we now desire to have the consignment insured at your end, we shall be much pleased if you will kindly arrange to insure the same on our behalf against All Risks at invoice value plus 10%, i.e. $2,200.00.

We shall of course refund the premium to you upon receipt of your debit note or, if you like, you may draw on us at sight for the same.

We sincerely hope that our request will meet with your approval.

Yours faithfully,
Tom Blair

敬启者：

兹谈及我方第 101 号订单下 500 箱电动玩具，此笔交易按 CFR 成交。

我方希望在当地对此货物投保，如蒙贵方代表我方按发票金额的 110% 投一切保险，即 2 200 美元的价值，我方将十分高兴。

当然，一收到贵方的账单，我方将向贵方付清保费。若贵方愿意，也可向我方按相同金额开立即期汇票。

衷心希望贵方能满足我方的要求。

汤姆·布莱尔 谨上

51. 给保险公司的信（投保）

Dear Sirs,

Please cover for us the following goods with Particular Average for the sum of $20,000:

210 metric tons of pears

150 metric tons of apples

These goods are now lying at No. 2 Dock, Hong Kong waiting to be shipped by S.S. "Victory", due to leave for Spain on 12th January.

We require immediate cover as far as Spain and shall be glad if you let us have the policy as soon as it is ready. In the meantime please confirm that you hold the consignment covered.

Yours faithfully,
James Green

敬启者：
　　请对下列货物按 20 000 美元保额投保水渍险：
210 公吨梨
150 公吨苹果
　　该货现寄存在香港第 2 号码头，等候装在"胜利号"轮于 1 月 12 日启航去西班牙。
　　我们需将该货立即投保到西班牙，保险单准备好后希望您立即交给我们。请确认承保上述货物。

詹姆斯·格林 谨上

Unit 8　投诉、索赔、理赔　Complaints & Claims & Settlements

　　投诉信函通常是买方由于对收到的货物不满而书写的。投诉的原因有送货延误、送错货物、货物不达标、货物损毁等。投诉函应提供准确的订单号或商品型号，详细描述产品出现的问题，表明问题对己方造成的不变，希望对方采取措施尽快解决问题。投诉函的态度应当是坚定、合理和礼貌的，切忌语气嘲讽、粗暴或挖苦，不要使用激怒对方的字眼，否则会使问题不但得不到解决，还影响双方的合作关系。而回复投诉函必须客气、礼貌，需要一定的技巧，用词上要小心、克制。若投诉事出有因，最好真诚地承认问题的存在，并提出解决方案；若投诉无理无据，回复时要使用礼貌而坚定的语气。

　　投诉函的写作步骤：1. 先指明订单号（或货物），再开门见山地提出投诉原因；2. 简要说明具体情况；3. 礼貌地结尾。既可礼貌地提出等待对方及早解决，也可直接建议解决方案。

　　回复投诉函写作步骤：1. 叙述投诉要点；2. 表明己方态度；3. 提出处理意见。

　　索赔函是买卖中的任何一方，以双方签订的合同条款为根据，具体指出对方违反合同的事实，提出要求赔偿损失或其他权利的信函。通常，索赔的起因与投诉起因相似，只是问题更加严重，需要提出索赔。而理赔函是违约的一方受理遭受损失的一方所提出的赔偿要求。简单来说就是对索赔函的回复。对于索理赔函电的拟写，索赔方要实事求是，据理力争；理赔方要澄清事实，分辨是非。这样才有利于纠纷的妥善解决。反之，双方措辞激烈，剑拔弩张，咄咄逼人，或非分奢望，或赖帐狡辩，不仅无益于纠纷的解决，最终很可能会适得其反。

　　索赔函的写作步骤：1. 首先指明订单号或合同交易事项；2. 阐明问题和索赔理由；3. 索赔要求和意见；4. 结语。注意一定要附上对索赔有利的材料。

　　理赔函的写作步骤：1. 引述来函要点；2. 对争议的看法；3. 理赔的意见和办法。在对争议做具体分析的基础上，表明同意赔偿或拒绝赔偿的意见。如拒绝赔偿，要以充分地事实论据驳斥对方的理赔理由。如同意赔偿，要拿出具体的赔偿措施和办法；4. 希望继续合作，赞许对方合作态度。同索赔函一样，理赔函也注意一定要附上相关附件。

✻ 常用句型

1. Would you please correct your shipment by sending the order No. 2530 by the first available vessel?

   请把我方 2530 号订单项下的货物用第一艘可订到仓位的货船运来，以纠正你方发货的错误。

2. We feel it necessary to inform you that your last delivery of our order is not up to the usual standard.

   我们有必要通知你们上次交货达不到正常标准。

3. On comparing the goods received with the sample supplied, we were sorry to notice the great differences in the designs of the machines.

   比较收到的货物和样品后，发现机器在设计上有很大的差异，甚感遗憾。

4. While placing our order we emphasized that any delay in delivery would definitely add to the cost of the goods. That is why we have to raise a claim on refunds for the loss incurred.

   订货时，我们已强调任何交货延迟将无疑增加货物的成本。故此，我们必须索回由此产生的损失费。

5. We've given your claim careful consideration.

   我们已经就你们提出的索赔做了仔细研究。

6. We apologize for the inconvenience it is causing you.

   由此对贵方造成的不便我方表示歉意。

📝 52. 投诉送货延迟

Dear Mr. Jimmy,

　　I with this letter would like to make complaint about the delay of delivery of the material that we ordered you in the last month. This has not only happened for this time itself but there was also delay in many of previous deliveries.

I have already told this fact to your delivery manager but yet there is a problem of delay in delivery. Due to delay in the delivery our production gets delayed because of which our customers are getting delay delivery.

I hope that after this complaint you will take necessary action in this regard and will assure us of timely delivery. If such kind of delay continues in future then we would like to terminate your contract with us.

Thanking you.

Yours sincerely,
Donald Harris

吉米先生：

兹以此函投诉贵方延迟发送我方上月订购的原材料。这类延误并非首次发生，先前就出现过许多次。

在此之前，我方曾向贵方的交付经理反映过情况，但还是出现了延误，从而导致了生产的延误，继而影响我方客户无法及时收到货物。

希望贵方读完这封投诉函后能就该问题采取必要行动，保证我方以后能及时收到货。若再出现延误，我方将终止与你方的合同。

谢谢。

唐纳德·哈里斯 谨上

53. 投诉送错货物

Dear Mr. Forrest,

As a former salesman myself, I dislike to go over the head of the person who is supposedly servicing our account, particularly since your products themselves have been reliable and effective. But now the situation has reached a point where we can no longer abide it. We either resolve it immediately or look for another supplier.

The problem is a dual one. First, on the last ten orders, we received merchandise that we did not request or that has already been shipped to us. Second, the inventory lists and financial statements have been totally different from the actual shipments, making it necessary for our stockroom to double-check every incoming container.

 Since phone calls and correspondence to your regional office here have failed to correct the problem, I would like to find out how we can resolve this to our mutual satisfaction and get on with our business.

Sincerely,
Roy White

福利斯特先生：

 作为一名有经验的销售员，我不愿放弃可能给自己带来利益的合作伙伴，并且贵方的产品的确可靠而实用。然而现在的情况却令我方难以忍受。若无法立刻解决，我方将寻找其他供应商。

 问题有两个方面：首先，过去 10 笔订单中，我方收到的货物或是并非所需的，或是已收到过的；其次，存货清单和财务报表与实际货物毫不相符，使得我方库房必须复核每个入库的集装箱。

 由于致贵方地区办事处的函电均无法解决此问题，我方欲知何以达成双方满意并继续合作的局面。

诚挚的 罗伊·怀特

54. 投诉货物不达标

Dear Sirs,

We have recently received several complaints from customers about your fountain pens. The pens are clearly not giving satisfaction and in some cases we have had to refund the purchase price.

The pens are part of the batch of 500 supplied against our order number 12345 dated 01 June. This order was placed on the basis of a sample pen left by your representative. We have ourselves compared the performance of this sample with that of a number of the pens from this batch, and there is little doubt that many of them are faulty – some of them leak and others blot when writing.

The complaints we have received relate only to pens from the batch mentioned. Pens supplied before these have always been satisfactory.

We therefore wish to return the unsold balance, amounting to 380 pens.

Please replace them with pens of the quality.

Please let us know what arrangements you wish us to make for the return of these unsuitable pens.

Yours faithfully,
Simon Sharp

敬启者：

近日我方收到一些关于你方钢笔质量的客户投诉。这些钢笔的确不尽如人意，我方已向一些顾客退了款。

6月1日的订单，即12345号订单中有一批总数500枝的钢笔，上述钢笔便来自于此。你方代表曾留赠给我方一支样笔，我方照此下了订单。但我们抽取了该批钢笔中的几支与样笔相比后发现许多都是次品——有的会渗漏，有的会在书写时滴墨。

投诉所涉及的钢笔仅来自于上文提及那批，在此之前的钢笔一直都令人满意。因此，我方欲退回未售出的钢笔，共380支。请更换质量过关的产品给我方。

请告知我方退回这些不合格钢笔需要如何安排。

西门·夏普 谨上

55. 投诉货物损坏

Dear Sirs,

We ordered 150 hard drives on 01 June and they were delivered yesterday. I regret that 17 of them were badly scratched.

The package containing these goods appeared to be in perfect condition and I accepted and signed for it without question. It was on unpacking the hard drives when the damage was discovered; I can only assume that this was due to careless handling at some stage prior to packing.

I am enclosing a list of the damaged goods and shall be glad if you will replace them. They have been kept aside in case you need them to support a claim on your suppliers for compensation.

Yours faithfully,
Matthew Young

敬启者：

  我方 6 月 1 日订购的 150 个硬盘已于昨日运达。遗憾的是，其中有 17 个严重刮伤。

  这些货物的包装完好，因此我方签收时未发现问题。在打开包装后才发现了损伤，据此推测，应该是包装前某个步骤的粗心操作所致。

  随函附上受损货物清单，请贵方更换它们。受损货物已留存，以防贵方需要其作为向供应商索赔的证据。

马修·杨 谨上

56. 回复对送货延误的投诉

Dear Ms. Caroline,

  Your letter dated 18 February regarding delays in delivery came as a surprise as the absence of any earlier complaints led us believe that goods supplied to your orders were reaching you promptly.

  It is our usual practice to deliver goods well in advance of the promised delivery dates; the filling cabinets to which you refer left here on 5 February. We are very concerned that our efforts to ensure punctual delivery should be frustrated by delays in transit. It is possible that other customers are also affected and we are taking up this whole question with our forwarders.

  We thank you for drawing our attention to a situation of which had been quite unaware until you wrote to us. Please accept our apologies for the inconvenience you have been caused.

Yours sincerely,
Max Hard

卡洛琳女士：

  贵方 2 月 18 日关于送货延迟的来函使我方始料未及，由于先前从未出现过此类投诉，我方一度相信贵方所订购货物正按时运送于途中。

  我方惯例是提前按照允诺的交付日期送货，贵方来函所指的防火文件柜已于 2 月 5 日发出。我方料想，应是运输途中的延误才不能按时送达。很可能我们的其他客户也受到了影响，因此我方已将整个问题反映给代运人。

  感谢贵方来信使我们了解到情况。给贵方带来不便，请接受我方的道歉。

马克思·哈代 谨上

57. 回复对送错货物的投诉

Dear Ms. Elena,

I was sorry to learn from your letter of 18 August that a mistake occurred in dealing with your order.

This mistake is entirely our own and we apologize for the inconvenience it is causing you. This occurred because of staff shortage during this unusually busy season and also the fact that these 2 books by Lawrence have identical bindings.

12 copies of the correct title have been dispatched by parcel post today.

Your account will be credited with the invoiced value of the books and cost of return postage. Our credit note is enclosed.

We apologize again for this mistake.

Yours sincerely,
Scott Short

埃琳娜女士：
从贵方 8 月 18 日来函得知我方处理订单时出现了错误，非常抱歉。
错误完全是我方责任，因此对贵方造成的不便我方表示歉意。错误的出现一方面是因为旺季员工的短缺，另一方面是因为劳伦斯所著的这两本书装帧完全相同。
12 份正确书籍今天已用包裹派送。
送错书籍的款项和寄回邮费将存入贵方账户。随函附上贷记单。
对此错误我方再次表示歉意。

斯科特·肖特 谨上

58. 回复对货物质量的投诉

Dear Sir,

We are really sorry for the inconvenience you had with the defective computer. We will replace the computer for you if you can please send the computer with the original bill and we will transport the computer you requested. We assure you that you will not face any problem. Last computer was from the lot which was missed out from the stages of testing. It happens very rarely but we apologize for our mistake and assure you that we will be providing you with the new computer as soon as possible.

Please accept the enclosed discount coupon which you can avail on the next purchase. Thank you for your business and we hope you will allow us to serve you in future also.

Sincerely,
Rufus Longman

敬启者：

　　对于电脑质量的不合格而给贵方造成的不便，我方表示诚挚的歉意。我方愿为贵方换货，烦请贵方寄回不合格的电脑及票据原件，我方将按要求寄送所需电脑。我方保证不再出现任何问题。上一台电脑未抽中进行检验，这类事件极少发生，但就此错误我方仍需向贵方道歉，同时保证新的电脑将尽快送达。

　　请查收随函附上的折扣券，贵方可于下次购买时使用。感谢贵方与我方的贸易，希望今后能继续为您服务。

诚挚的　鲁弗斯·朗曼

59. 回复对货物损坏的投诉

【模板】

Dear Mr. Jackson,

I was sorry to learn from your letter of 2 May that some of the hard drives supplied to this order were damaged when they reached you.

Replacements for the damaged goods have been sent by parcel post this morning. It will not be necessary for you to return the damaged goods; they may be destroyed.

Despite the care we take in packing goods there have recently been several reports of damage. To avoid further inconvenience and annoyance to customers, as well as expense to ourselves, we are now seeking the advice of a packaging consultant in the hope of improving our methods of handling.

We regret the need for you to write to us and hope the steps we are taking will ensure the safe arrival of all your orders in future.

Yours sincerely,
Ronald Sterling

杰克逊先生：

  收到贵方 5 月 2 日来函，得知该订单的硬盘送达后发现损坏的情况，我方十分抱歉。

  换货包裹已于今晨发出。损坏货物不需贵方寄回，可摧毁。

  尽管我方小心包装货物，但最近仍受到一些物品损毁报告。为避免造成客户更多不便和困扰，同时也为节省开支，我方打算参考包装顾问的意见，期望能改进我方操作方法。

  很抱歉贵方来函联系此事，希望我方采取的行动能确保贵方今后可以安全地接收到订单货物。

罗纳德·斯特林 谨上

60. 索赔

Dear Mr. Brown,

  As someone who has worked with your company for over 3 years, we were very disappointed to see the documents you produced for our latest publicity campaign.

  As our written agreement stipulated, we expected full color leaflets with explanatory texts, but instead, we found that black and white photos had been included in the prepared leaflets. I think you will agree that a communication problem exists.

  We would like you to send out a photographer to provide us with the promised color coverage, or provide us with a refund.

Yours truly,
Thomas R. Smith,

布朗先生：

  虽与贵公司合作了三年，对于此次贵方制作的最新宣传活动文件，我方非常失望。

  根据我们的书面协议，我方盼望得到的是带有文字解释的全彩传单，但我方发现制出的传单中印有黑白图片。相信贵方也会承认出现了交流问题。

希望贵方能派遣一名摄影师完成预订颜色的传单，或者向我方退款。

托马斯·R·史密斯 谨上

61. 回复索赔

Dear Mrs. Tom,

We were dismayed to receive your letter and the sample computer printout that documented the confusion that has been occurring in your shop as a result of the billing procedures used by our marketing department. I have looked into this situation personally and am convinced that the problem lies in our company's computer programming setup and not in the operations.

Our entire system is being checked and reviewed by an outside consulting firm, and I am confident that we will resolve the problem to your complete satisfaction.

In the meantime, I have submitted a voucher to our accounting department to reimburse you for the costs incurred when you had to crate and return duplicate merchandise.

Thanks for your patience.

Sincerely,
Noel Back

汤姆女士：

  收到贵方来函，并从附寄的计算机打印资料上得知，我方销售部门所使用的开票程序造成了贵店的混乱，我方觉得非常抱歉。从我个人观察来看，问题症结在于我方公司的系统编程安装，而非操作步骤。

  我方的整个系统是由另外的咨询公司检查和评估的。但请相信我方能立即解决问题，使贵方完全满意。

  同时，会计部门已收到我方提交的收据，将赔偿贵方由于不得不用板条箱包装并退回商品而造成的损失。

  感谢您的耐心等待。

诚挚的 诺埃尔·巴克

Unit 9　代理与合作

Agency & Cooperation

　　国际贸易中的代理业务，是指以委托人为一方，委托独立的代理人为另一方，在约定的地区和期限内，代理人以委托人的名义从事代购、代销指定商品的贸易方式。代理商根据推销商品的结果，收取佣金作为报酬。代理商与出口商之间的代理关系有一般代理、独家代理、总代理等几种。

　　与代理相关的信函主要包括请求代理、回复请求代理（包括同意或拒绝）。这类信函目的非常明确,语言尽量简洁,但是该说的话要说清,如证明自己的实力和诚意等。

　　请求代理的信函写作步骤：1. 信函目的；2. 介绍己方公司，突出胜任此代理的能力；3. 期盼对方早日回复。

　　回复请求代理信函写作步骤：1. 确认来信，表示感谢；2. 表明态度（同意或拒绝），说明原因；3. 同意则表示合作，拒绝需表示歉意。

✽ 常用句型

1. We are willing to push the trade in your machines, and hope you will give us the sole agency for our place.

   我们希望为贵公司拓销机械，请将你司在本地的独家代理赋予敝公司为盼。

2. Should I have the honor to be appointed your agent, I shall be prepared to give satisfactory security, either in this province or in England.

   如能成为贵公司的代理，将不胜荣幸。无论在本省还是在英国，本人都能提供满意的服务。

3. We should feel obliged, therefore, by your acquainting us, as early as may be convenient, whether your company either have or are desirous of having an agent here.

   特函查询，贵公司在本地有无代理，有无设立代理的意向，如能早日告知，当不甚感谢。

4. Our bankers, the Yokihama Bank, will give you particulars of our

financial position as an agency, and we shall be pleased to furnish any information which you may require.

本公司作为代理，有关我们的财务情况，请向我们业务往来银行横滨银行查询。若有其他要求，本公司定当尽力满足。

5. We appoint you as our sole agent according to the terms mentioned in your letter of August 8.

   我方现在同意按你方 8 月 8 日来函所提条件，任命你方为我方的独家代理。

6. As we are now only at the get-acquainted stage, we cannot consider your proposal for sole agency.

   由于我们只不过在初交阶段，我们不能考虑你方关于独家代理的提议。

62. 请求代理

Dear Sir,

Please allow us to introduce our company first. We are a family owned business for 30 years. We started with a pharmacy, and now we have 4 pharmacies and a drug store. In the last 10 years we started growing in different fields. We opened a restaurant, and we have 1 under decoration. We invested in retail mobile phones, we already have 4 stores and the 5th store is opening in a couple of months.

Relating fashion business we opened a multi-brand men's fashion store 2 years ago. We would like to grow in the fashion business by becoming an agent for a well known brand CACHAREL. If we reach an agreement we'll open the first shop within 2 months. We already have a 150 m^2 store ready in a large shopping mall. We expect to have at least 5 shops within the next 5 years. You can be sure that we will work hard to give "CACHAREL" brand the appropriate image & marketing strategies.

Your consideration and prompt reply will be appreciated.

Yours faithfully,
Aaron Chan

敬启者：

　　首先请允许我推介一下我公司。我方是一个有着三十年历史的家族企业。最初我们有一家药房，现在发展为四家药房和一家杂货店。过去十年，我们朝不同领域发展：现有一家餐厅，另有一家正在装修；我方在手机零售业也有投资，拥有四个手机卖场，第五个将在几个月内开张。

　　至于时尚行业，两年前我方开始经营一家多品牌男士服装店。我方希望在该行业有所发展，想成为知名品牌"卡夏尔"的代理。我方在一家大型商场内已有一间一百五十平方米的店面，若你我双方达成协议，两个月内第一家商店将会开张。我方计划在五年内开五家商店。贵方可放心，我方会对"卡夏尔"用之以正确的市场营销策略，把其树立成良好的品牌。

　　望贵方认真思考并及早回复。

艾伦·陈 谨上

63. 要求独家代理

Dear Sir,

　　We are a small retail chain with ten sales outlets in the San Diego metropolitan area. Our company specializes in all types of beds (ranging from brass beds, daybeds, French-style and country-style beds, to electric adjustable beds) as well as mattresses (single, twin, queen, and king size and so forth).

　　There is an increasing demand in our sales area for all types of high quality beads and mattresses. For that reason, we are looking for a well-known British manufacturer of these items who is willing to offer us a sole agency to retail their beds and large number of suburbs and other commodities. Our company is already the sole agent for a major French manufacturer of beds and mattresses in the above-mentioned sales territory.

　　Awaiting your answer to this letter with great interest, we remain.

Sincerely yours,
Henry King

敬启者：

　　我们是一家小型零售店，在大圣地亚哥地区有十个销售点。我们公司专门销售各种床（包括黄铜床、法式床、乡村风格床、以及电子调节床）和床垫（单人、双人、大号、特大号等)。

我们的市场对高质量的床和床垫的需求在不断地增加。因此,我们正在寻找一个驰名的英国制造商,指定我公司为大圣地亚哥区唯一代理,其中包括周边的郊区以及社区。我公司现已是法国一家床和床垫的大厂商的唯一代理。

我们怀着浓厚的兴趣,敬候佳音。

亨利·金 敬启

64. 不知对方是否已有代理,请求代理

Dear Sirs,

We write to offer our services as your agents in London. If, however, you are already satisfactorily represented here, please ignore this letter. There is a growing demand here for textiles. As soon as we are in possession of details and samples of your range, we shall be in a position to advise you on their suitability for this particular market, to select qualities that are likely to sell well and then to visit our customers with them.

With regard to references, you may write to any of the major London confirming houses, to our bank, the Union Bank Ltd. , or to any of our customers. We are known throughout the trade as agents of the highest integrity.

We look forward to hearing from you and to the possibility of representing you in London.

Sincerely yours,
John Carter

敬启者:

现去函请求担任贵方在伦敦的代理。倘若贵方已有合适代理请忽略本函。

由于此地对纺织品的需求日增,一旦我们获得你方样品及详细情况,我们便会告知哪些是适销本地市场的,并能选出一些品质适销的商品对客户出售。

关于我们的信用情况,贵方可写信向伦敦主要保兑行,即我们的开户银行"联合银行"或者我们的任何客户询问。在全行业中我们以最诚实的代理而闻名。

不知可否成为伦敦代理,期盼回音。

约翰·卡特 谨上

65. 批发商托销

Dear Sirs,

We're a wholesaler of household porcelain. We handle many major brand names in large volumes, and we can offer excellent discount rates on these products.

Please see our attached list of products. It includes the base and retail prices, and minimum order quantities.

By this offer, we provide:

Set profit margin of 15% for retailers on minimum orders.

Set profit margin of 20% for retailers above minimum orders.

Guaranteed acceptance of returned goods.

Guaranteed refund for defective or damaged goods.

Full 1 year warranty on all products.

If you're interested in our products and our offer, and you'd like more information or have any questions, please contact me directly on the above phone number or e-mail.

Yours sincerely
Leo Hawk

敬启者：

我方是家居瓷器的批发商，不仅能大量提供众多主流品牌的产品，还能对这些产品提供高额折扣。

请收阅附上的产品列表，列表内含底价、零售价以及起订量等信息。

我方提供：

给订购起订量的零售商 15% 利润；

给订购大于起订量的零售商 20% 利润；

保证接受退货；

保证对次货和残货退款；

所有产品一年保修。

如果贵方对我方产品和报盘感兴趣，或需要更多信息，或有其他问题，请按以上电话或邮箱联系我方。

里奥 · 霍克 谨上

Unit 10 合同协议　　　　Contracts & Agreements

66. 买卖合同

PURCHASE CONTRACT

Contract No.:
Date:
Signing Place:
Seller:
Address:
Postal Code:
Tel:
Fax:
Buyer:
Address:
Postal Code:
Tel:
Fax:

The Seller agrees to sell and the Buyer agrees to buy the undermentioned commodity on the terms and conditions stated below:

1. Article No.

2. Name of Commodity and Specification

3. Quantity

4. Unit Price

5. Total Price

Total Amount With _____% more or less both in amount and quantity allowed at the Seller's option.

6. Terms of Delivery

7. Country of Origin and Manufacturer

8. Packing and Standard

The packing of the goods shall be preventive from dampness, rust, moisture, erosion and shock, and shall be suitable for ocean transportation / multiple transportation. The Seller shall be liable for any damage and loss of the goods attributable to the inadequate or improper packing. The measurement, gross weight, net weight and the cautions such as "THIS SIDE UP", "FRAGILE", "HANDLE WITH CARE" shall be stenciled on the surface of each package with fadeless pigment.

9. Shipping Marks

10. Time of Shipment

11. Port of Loading

12. Port of Destination

13. Insurance

Insurance shall be covered by the _____ for 110% of the invoice value against All Risks.

14. Terms of Payment

(1) Letter of Credit: The Buyer shall, _____ days prior to the time of shipment / after this Contract comes into effect, open an irrevocable Letter of Credit in favor of the Seller. The Letter of Credit shall expire _____ days after the completion of loading of the shipment as stipulated. Or

(2) Documents against Payment: After shipment, the Seller shall draw a sight bill of exchange on the Buyer and deliver the documents through Sellers bank and _____ Bank to the Buyer against payment, i.e. D/P. The Buyer shall effect the payment immediately upon the first presentation of the bill (s) of exchange. Or

(3) Documents against Acceptance: After shipment, the Seller shall draw a sight bill of exchange, payable _____ days after the Buyers delivers the document through Sellers, and _____ Bank to the Buyer against

acceptance (D/A _____ days). The Buyer shall make the payment on date of the bill of exchange. Or

(4) Cash on delivery COD: The Buyer shall pay to the Seller total amount within _____ days after the receipt of the goods.

15. Documents Required

The Seller shall present the following documents required to the bank for negotiation / collection:

(1) Full set of clean on board Ocean / Combined Transportation / Land Bills of Lading and blank endorsed marked freight prepaid / to collect;

(2) Signed commercial invoice in _____ copies indicating Contract No., L/C No. (Terms of L/C) and shipping marks;

(3) Packing list / weight memo in _____ copies issued by_____;

(4) Certificate of Quality in _____ copies issued by _____;

(5) Certificate of Quantity in _____ copies issued by _____;

(6) Insurance policy/certificate in _____ copies (Terms of CIF);

(7) Shipping advice: The Seller shall, with-in _____ hours after shipment effected, send by _____ each copy of the above-mentioned documents No. _____ .

16. Terms of Shipment

(1) FOB

The Seller shall, 30 days before the shipment date specified in the Contract, advise the Buyer by _____ of the Contract No., commodity, quantity, amount, packages, gross weight, measurement, and the date of shipment in order that the Buyer can charter a vessel / book ship-ping space. In the event of the Seller's failure to effect loading when the vessel arrives duly at the loading port, all expenses including dead freight and / or demurrage charges thus incurred shall be for the Seller's account.

(2) CIF / CFR

The Seller shall ship the goods duly within the shipping duration from the port of loading to the port of destination. Under CFR terms, the Seller shall advise the Buyer by _____ of the Contract No., commodity, invoice value and the date of dispatch two days before the shipment for the Buyer to arrange insurance in time.

17. Shipping Advice

The Seller shall, immediately upon the completion of the loading of the goods, advise the Buyer of the Contract No., names of commodity, loading quantity, invoice values, gross weight, name of vessel and shipment date by _____ within _____ hours.

18. Quality Guarantee

The Seller shall guarantee that upon Delivery all goods to be delivered by the Seller shall be completely new and shall comply in all material respects with this Contract.

The guarantee period is within _____ days after the date of the completion of unloading of the goods at the port of destination. Within the guarantee period, the Seller shall remove all defects of the goods due to design, workmanship and improper material used either by repairing or by placing the defective parts or the goods on his own account.

19. Inspection

The Seller shall have the goods inspected by _____ days before the shipment and have the Inspection Certificate issued by _____. The Buyer may have the goods reinspected by _____ after the goods' arrival at the destination.

20. Claim

The Buyer shall make a claim against the Seller (including replacement of the goods) by the further inspection certificate and all the expenses incurred therefrom shall be borne by the Seller. The claims mentioned above shall be regarded as being accepted if the Seller fail to reply within _____ days after the Seller received the Buyer's claim.

21. Late Delivery and Penalty

The Buyer shall take all reasonable acts in order to enable the Seller to make delivery and shall take over the goods.

Should the Seller fail to make delivery on time as stipulated in the Contract, with the exception of Force Majeure causes specified in Clause 22 of this Contract, the Buyer shall agree to postpone the delivery on the condition that the Seller agrees to pay a penalty which shall be deducted by the paying bank from the payment under negotiation. The rate of penalty is charged at _____% for every _____ days, odd days less than _____ days should be counted as _____ days. But the penalty, however, shall not exceed _____ % of the total value of the goods involved in the delayed delivery. In case the Seller fail to make delivery _____ days later than the time of shipment stipulated in the Contract, the Buyer shall have the right to cancel the Contract and the Seller, in spite of the cancellation, shall nevertheless pay the aforesaid penalty to the Buyer without delay.

The Buyer shall have the right to lodge a claim against the Seller for the losses sustained if any.

22. Force Majeure

Either party shall not be held responsible for failure or delay to perform all or any part of this agreement due to flood, fire, earthquake, draught, war or any other events which could not be predicted, controlled, avoided or overcome by the relative party. However, the party affected by the event of Force Majeure shall inform the other party of its occurrence in writing as soon as possible and thereafter send a certificate of the event issued by the relevant authorities to the other party within _____ days after its occurrence.

If the Event of Force Majeure last over _____ days, both parties shall negotiate on the performance or the termination of the Contract. However, if the conditions or consequences of Force Majeure which have a material adverse effect on the affected party's ability to perform continue for a period in excess of _____ days and the Parties have been unable to find an equitable solution pursuant to this Clause, the Contract shall terminate automatically.

23. Arbitration

All disputes arising from the execution of this agreement shall be settled through friendly consultations. In case no settlement can be reached, the case in dispute shall then be submitted to _____ arbitration commission in accordance with its Provisional Rules of Procedure. The decision made by this commission shall be regarded as final and binding upon both parties. Arbitration fees shall be borne by the losing party, unless otherwise awarded.

24. Effectiveness

The Contract shall come into effect immediately when it is signed by duly authorized representatives of both parties.

25. Amendment

This Contract shall not be changed verbally, but only by a written instrument signed by the Parties.

Representative of the Buyer:

(Authorized Signature)

Representative of the Seller:

(Authorized Signature)

买卖合同

合同编号：
日期：
签约地点：
卖方：
   地址：
   邮编：
   电话：
   传真：
买方：
   地址：
   邮编：

电话：
传真：
买卖双方同意按下列条款由卖方出售，买方购进下列货物：

1. 货号
2. 商品名称及规格
3. 数量
4. 单价
5. 总值
    数量及总值均有_____%的增减，由卖方决定。
6. 交货条款
7. 生产国和制造厂家
8. 包装及标准
    货物包装应当防潮、防锈蚀、防震并适合于海洋运输，由于货物包装不良而造成的货物残损、丢失应由卖方负责。卖方应在每个包装箱上用不褪色的颜色标明尺码、包装箱号码、毛重、净重及"此端向上"、"易碎"、"小心轻放"等警示标记。
9. 发货标记
10. 装运期限
11. 装运口岸
12. 目的口岸
13. 保险
    由_____按发票金额的110%投一切险。
14. 支付条款
    （1） 信用证：买方应在装运期前/合同生效后_____日，开出以卖方为受益人的不可撤销的议付信用证，信用证在装船完毕后_____日内到期。或
    （2） 付款交单：货物发出后，卖方出具以买方为付款人的付款跟单汇票，按即期付款交单（D/P）方式，通过卖方银行及_____银行向买方转交单证，换取货物。或
    （3） 承兑交单：货物发运后，卖方出具以买方为付款人的付款跟单汇票，付款期限为_____后_____日，按即期承兑交单（D/A_____日）方式，通过卖方银行及_____行，经买方承兑后，向买方转交单证，买方在汇票期限到期时支付货款。或
    （4） 货到付款：买方在收到货物后_____天内将全部货物支付卖方。
15. 单据
    卖方应将下列单据提交银行议付/托收：

（1） 标明通知收货人/收货代理人的全套清洁的、已装船的、空白抬头、空白背书、并注明运费已付/到付的海运/联运/陆运提单；
（2） 标有合同编号、信用证号（信用证支付条件下）及装运唛头的商业发票一式 _____ 份；
（3） 由 _____ 出具的装箱或重量单一式 _____ 份；
（4） 由 _____ 出具的质量证明书一式 _____ 份；
（5） 由 _____ 出具的数量证明书一式 _____ 份；
（6） 保险单正本一式 _____ 份（CIF 交货条件）；
（7） 装运通知：卖方应在交运后 _____ 小时内以 _____ 方式邮寄给买主上述第 _____ 项单据副本一式一套。

16. 装运条款

（1） FOB

卖方应在合同规定的装运日期前 30 天，以 _____ 方式通知买方合同号、品名、数量、金额、包装件、毛重、尺码及装运港可装日期，以便买方租船订舱。装运船只到达装运港后，如卖方不能按时装船，发生的空船费或滞期费由卖方负担。在货物越过船舷并脱离吊钩以前一切费用和风险由卖方负担。

（2） CIF 或 CFR

卖方须按时在装运期限内将货物由装运港装船至目的港。在 CFR 条件下，卖方应在装船前两天以 _____ 方式通知买方合同号、品名、发票价值及开船日期，以便买方安排保险。

17. 装运通知

装载完毕，卖方应在 _____ 小时内以 _____ 方式通知买方合同编号、品名、已发运数量、发票总金额、毛重、船名/车/机号及启程日期等。

18. 质量保证

卖方保证其所交付的货物在交货时是全新的，并且在所有实质方面符合本合同规定。

货物的质量保证期为自货物在目的港卸货完毕之日起 _____ 天。在质量保证期内，凡因设计、制造工艺和所用材料不符合合同规定而产生的缺陷，卖方应自负费用进行修理或更换货物或部件。

19. 检验

卖方须在装运前 _____ 日委托 _____ 检验机构对本合同之货物进行检验并出具检验证书，货到目的港后，由买方委托 _____ 检验机构进行检验。

20. 索赔

买方凭其委托的检验机构出具的检验证明书向卖方提出索赔（包括

换货），由此引起的全部费用应由卖方负担。若卖方收到上述索赔后_____天未予答复，则认为卖方已接受买方索赔。

21. 迟交货与罚款

    买方应采取一切理应采取的行动以便卖方交付货物，且买方应接收货物。除合同第二十二条不可抗力原因外，如卖方不能按合同规定的时间交货的，买方应同意在卖方支付罚款的条件下延期交货。罚款可由议付银行在议付货款时扣除，罚款率按每_____天收_____%，不足_____天时以_____天计算。但罚款不得超过迟交货物总价的_____%。如卖方延期交货超过合同规定_____天时，买方有权撤销合同，此时，卖方仍应按时按上述规定向买方支付罚款。

    买方有权对因此遭受的其他损失向卖方提出索赔。

22. 不可抗力

    由于水灾、火灾、地震、干旱、战争或协议一方无法预见、控制、避免和克服的其他事件导致不能或暂时不能全部或部分履行本协议，该方不负责任。但是，受不可抗力事件影响的一方须尽快将发生的事件书面通知另一方，并在不可抗力事件发生_____日内将有关机构出具的不可抗力事件的证明文件寄交对方。

    如果不可抗力事件持续_____日以上，双方应就继续履行或终止合同事宜进行协商。如不可抗力事件或其影响持续超过_____天，且双方无法按照本条的约定达成一项公正的解决方案，则本合同自动终止。

23. 仲裁

    在履行协议过程中，如产生争议，双方应友好协商解决。若通过友好协商未能达成协议，则提交_____仲裁委员会，根据该会仲裁程序现行规定进行仲裁。该委员会裁定是终局的，对双方均有约束力。除另有规定外，仲裁费用由败诉一方负担。

24. 合同生效

    本合同自双方授权代表签字之日起生效。

25. 合同修改

    本合同不得以口头方式修改，而须经双方签署书面文件后方可修改。

    买方代表（签字）：   卖方代表（签字）：

67. 经销协议

DISTRIBUTE AGREEMENT

This contract is made as of the _____ day of _____, by and between (Supplier), a _____ organized and existing under the laws of _____, with its principal place of business at _____, and _____ (Distributor), a organized and existing under the laws of _____, with its principal place of business at _____.

Contract No.:

Party A:

Party B:

1. Definition

There are the following terms in this contract:

(1) "Accessories"

Accessories may be deleted from or added to Attachment _____ and Supplier may change the contents of the contract, by mailing written notice of such changes to Distributor. Each change shall become effective within _____ days following the date notice thereof is mailed to Distributor.

(2) "Goods"

Which means those items described in Attachment _____. Goods may be deleted from or added to Attachment _____, which may be changed by Supplier at its sole discretion at any time by mailing written notice of such changes to Distributor. Each change shall become effective within _____ days following the date notice thereof is mailed to Distributor.

(3) "Spare Parts"

Which means all parts and components of the Goods and/or any special devices used in connection with the maintenance or servicing of the Goods. Supplier declares that a complete list of Spare Parts is set forth in Attachment _____. Spare parts may be deleted from or added to Attachment _____ and their specifications and design may be changed by Supplier at its sole discretion at any time by mailing written notice of such changes to Distributor. Each change shall become effective within _____ days following the date notice thereof is mailed to Distributor.

(4) "Trademark"

Which means any trademark, logo, or service mark, whether or not registered, used to represent or describe the Products of Supplier, as set forth in Attachment_____.

2. Appointment of Distributor

Supplier hereby appoints Distributor as Supplier's Exclusive Distributor of Products in the Territory. It is understood that Supplier can law-fully prevent its distributors located elsewhere from supplying Products for sale or use within the Territory and that it has no obligation to do so.

3. Relationship between Both Parties

Distributor is an independent contractor and is not the legal representative or agent of Supplier for any purpose and shall have no right or authority (except as expressly provided in this Agreement) to incur, assume or create in writing or otherwise, any warranty on the part of Supplier. Supplier shall not exercise any control over any of Distributor's employees, all of who are entirely under the control of Distributor. Distributor shall be responsible for the acts and omissions of Distributor's employees.

Distributor shall, at its own expense, during the term of this Agreement and any extension thereof, maintain full insurance under any Labor Laws effective in the state or other applicable jurisdiction covering all persons employed by and working for it in connection with the performance of this Agreement, and upon request shall furnish Supplier with satisfactory evidence of the maintenance of such insurance.

4. Sale of Products

Distributor shall use its best efforts to distribute the Products and to fully develop the market for the Products within the Territory. The parties have consulted together and now agree that if Distributor's best efforts are used as provided in this Section, a minimum of _____ Products (Annual Market Potential) will be purchased and distributed in the Territory during the first year of this Agreement. At the beginning of each sub-sequent year the parties will consult together in good faith and agree on the Annual Market Potential applicable to that year; provided, however, that if they cannot agree, the Annual Market Potential for the immediately Preceding year will apply to the current year.

5. Advertisement

Distributor shall be entitled, during the term of the distributorship created by this Agreement and any extension thereof, to advertise and hold itself out as an authorized Distributor of the Products. At all times during the term of the distributorship created by this Agreement and any extension thereof, Distributor shall use the Trade-marks in all advertisements and other activities conducted by Distributor to promote the sale of the Products. Distributor shall submit samples of all proposed advertisements and other promotional materials for the Products to Supplier for approval and Distributor shall not use any such advertisements or promotional materials without having received the prior written consent of Supplier to do so. Distributor shall not, pursuant to this Agreement or otherwise, have or acquire any right, title or interest in or to Supplier's Trade-marks.

6. Distributor Sales, Service and Storage Facilities

Distributor shall, at its expense, engage and maintain a sales, service and parts handling organization in the Territory, staffed with such experienced personnel as are necessary to enable distributor to perform its obligations under this Agreement.

Distributor shall, at its expense, maintain facilities and personnel in the Territory that will enable it promptly and satisfactorily to perform, at a reasonable price, all inspection, maintenance and other necessary servicing of Products sold by Distributor. To assist Distributor in the discharge of this service and maintenance function, Supplier shall provide service and maintenance training, without charge, to any reasonable number of Distributor's personnel as Distributor shall designate.

Distributor shall, at its expense, at all times store and maintain its inventory of Products in accordance with current, applicable instructions issued by Supplier from time to time. Distributor shall, at its expense, deliver one copy of Supplier's current, applicable operation and maintenance manual to each Customer at the time of sale and, at that time, Distributor shall, at its expense, fully explain and demonstrate to the customer the proper method of operating and maintaining the Products.

Distributor shall mail to Supplier, during the term of the distributorship created by this Agreement and any extension thereof, prompt written notice of the address of each location at which products are stored, and the address of each facility established by Distributor to sell and service the Products. Supplier may, through its designated agent, inspect all such locations and facilities and the operations conducted therein at any time during normal business hours.

7. Spare Parts and Accessories

Distributor shall keep in stock an adequate supply of Spare Parts and Accessories for the servicing of Goods. No Spare Parts or Accessories not manufactured by Supplier shall be used in connection with the Goods unless they have been approved in writing by Supplier.

8. Confidential Information

Written Technical data, drawings, plans and engineering in technical instructions pertaining to the Products are recognized by Distributor to be secret and confidential and to be the property of Supplier. Those items shall at all times and for all purposes be held by Distributor in a confidential capacity and shall not, without the prior written consent of Supplier, (i) be disclosed by Distributor to any person, firm or corporation, excepting those salaried employees of Distributor who are required to utilize such items in connection with the sale, inspection, repair or servicing of Products during the term of the distributorship created by this Agreement or any extension thereof, or (ii) be copied or used by Distributor, its employees or agents at any time following the expiration or termination of this Agreement or any extension thereof. Supplier may require as a condition to any disclosure by

Distributor pursuant to this Section that any salaried employee to whom disclosure is to be made sign a confidentiality agreement, enforceable by Supplier, containing terms satisfactory to Supplier.

9. Purchasing Product

Distributor shall purchase its requirements for the Products from Supplier. Such requirements shall include purchasing and maintaining an inventory of Products that is sufficient to enable Distributor to perform its obligations here-under, and at least _____ demonstration model of the Goods and Accessories.

Supplier shall supply to Distributor sufficient Products to enable Distributor to meet the full demand for Products in the Territory. All orders for Products transmitted by Distributor to Supplier shall be deemed to be accepted by Supplier at the time such orders are received by Supplier to the extent that they are in compliance with the terms of this Agreement and Supplier shall perform in accordance with all accepted orders. Supplier shall confirm its receipt and acceptance of each order within _____ days of receipt of the order.

10. Business Procedure

Each order for Products issued by Distributor to Supplier under this Agreement shall identify that it is an order and shall further set forth the delivery date or dates and the description and quantity of Products which are to be delivered on each of such dates. An order for Products shall not provide a delivery date less than _____ days after the date that order is delivered to Supplier.

11. Termination

Any party wants to terminate the relationship, or any cancellation of orders by Distributor shall be in writing. If Distributor cancels an order, which has been accepted by Supplier, Distributor shall reimburse Supplier for any cost incident to such order incurred by Supplier prior to the time it was informed of the cancellation.

12. Purchase Price

The prices for Goods, and any discounts applicable thereto, are set forth in Attachment _____. The prices for Accessories, together with any discounts applicable thereto, are set forth in Attachment _____. The prices for Spare Parts, together with any discounts applicable thereto, are set forth in Attachment _____. All prices are FOB (the Delivery Point). If the price for any Product is not set forth on Attachment and Distributor nevertheless orders such a Product from Supplier, the parties hereby evidence their intention thereby to conclude a contract for the sale of that Product at a reasonable price to be determined by the Parties mutually negotiating in good faith.

13. Price Changes

Supplier reserves the right, in its sole discretion, to change prices or discounts applicable to the Products. Supplier shall give written notice to Distributor of any price change at least _____ days prior to the effective date thereof. The price in effect as of the date of Distributor's receipt of notice of such price change shall remain applicable to all orders received by Supplier prior to that effective date.

14. Packing

Supplier shall, at its expense, pack all Products in accordance with Supplier's standard packing procedure, which shall be suitable to permit shipment of the Products to the Territory; provided, however, that if Distributor requests a modification of those procedures, Supplier shall make the requested modification and Distributor shall bear any reasonable expenses incurred by Supplier in complying with such modified procedures which are in excess of the expenses which Supplier would have incurred in following its standard procedures.

15. Delivery

The title to and risk of loss of Products shall pass from Supplier to Distributor at the Delivery Point.

Supplier shall be responsible for arranging all transportation of

Products, but if requested by Supplier, Distributor shall, at Supplier's expense, assist Distributor in making such arrangements.

16. Inspection and Acceptance

Promptly upon the receipt of a shipment of Products, Distributor shall examine the shipment to determine whether any item or items included in the shipment are in short supply, defective or damaged. Within _____ days of receipt of the shipment. Distributor shall notify Supplier in writing of any shortages, defects or damage, which Distributor claims existed at the time of delivery. Within _____ days after the receipt of such notice, Supplier will investigate the claim of shortages, defects or damage, inform Distributor of its findings, and deliver to Distributor Products to replace any which Supplier determines, were in short supply, defective or damaged at the time of delivery.

17. Payment

Upon delivery and acceptance of Products, Supplier may submit to Distributor the invoice for those Products. Distributor shall pay each such proper invoice within _____ days after Distributor's receipt of that invoice. Payment shall be made in _____ to a bank account to be notified in writing by Supplier to Distributor.

18. Arbitration

All disputes arising from the execution of this Agreement shall be settled through friendly consultations. In case no settlement can be reached, the case in dispute shall then be submitted to _____ for arbitration in accordance with its provisional rules of procedure. The decision made by this Commission shall be regarded as final and binding upon both parties. Arbitration fees shall be borne by the losing party, unless otherwise awarded.

Representative of the Supplier:

(Authorized Signature)

Representative of the Distributor:

(Authorized Signature)

Date:

Place:

经销协议

　　本协议由_____（供应商），根据_____法律成立和存在的（主要经营场所_____），和_____（经销商），根据_____法律成立和存在的_____（主要经营场所）于_____年_____月_____日在_____签订。

合同号：

供应商：

经销商：

1. 定义

　　本协议中有以下术语：

　　（1）"附件"

　　　　供应商有权在附件_____中随时增减部分协议内容，但应通过信函方式书面告知经销商。

　　（2）"货物"

　　　　指在本协议附件_____中所描述的物品。供应商有权在附件_____删除或增加部分货物，但应通过信函方式书面告知经销商。这种变更在信函寄出后_____日内生效。

　　（3）"零配件"

　　　　指货物和（或）维护、服务货物所用的特殊装置中所包含的所有配件和零件。供应商声明完整的零配件清单在本协议附件_____中列明。供应商有权在附件_____删除或增加部分零配件，也有权改变零配件的规格和设计，但应通过信函方式书面告知经销商。这种变更在信函寄出后_____日内生效。

　　（4）"商标"

　　　　指在本协议附件_____中列明的、在供应商产品上使用或描述的任何商标、标识和服务标记，不论其是否注册。

2. 指定经销商

　　供应商在此指定经销商为本区域内的独家经销商。供应商有权阻止位于其他区域的经销商在本区域内，销售和使用供应商提供的产品。

3. 双方关系

　　经销商是独立的合同当事人，不是供应商法律上的代表人或代理人，没有权利以书面或其他形式代表供应商承担任何保证（除非有明确的约定）。经销商的员工应由经销商控制，供应商无权使用、控制。经销商应对其员工的行为或过失负责。

　　在本协议生效或续展期间，经销商应根据当地生效的劳动法规为从事本协议项下工作或与本协议有关的员工购买充分的保险，并在供应商的要求下提供足够的证据证明已购买保险。

4. 产品销售

　　经销商应在本区域内尽力销售产品和充分扩大市场。双方协商并同意经销商应尽力在本协议的第一年在本区域内购买和销售最少＿＿＿＿＿产品（年市场潜力）。在此后每年的年初，双方将友好协商并确定当年适用的年市场潜力，但如双方意见无法统一，则继续适用上一年的年市场潜力。

5. 广告

　　经销商有权在本协议有效期或续展期内进行广告宣传或表明自己授权经销商的身份，有权在广告或推广活动中使用供应商的商标。经销商应事先将广告或宣传资料的样稿提交供应商批准，经销商不得未经供应商书面同意进行广告宣传。除非本协议另有约定，经销商不得主张或享有供应商商标的任何权益。

6. 经销商销售、服务及库储设备

　　经销商应在本区域内雇佣或运营一个销售、服务、处理其他事务的组织，并配备能从事本协议项下工作的有经验的销售人员。

　　经销商应在本区域内以合理的价格保持设备运行和人员匹配，完成所售产品的检验、维护和其他必要的服务。为帮助经销商承担服务和维护职责，供应商应在合理的限度内，免费对经销商指定的人员提供服务和维护培训。

　　经销商应根据供应商随时签发的现行适用的清单来保持一定的库存储备量，并自行承担费用。经销商应在销售时向客户提供现行适用的操作维持手册，并向客户充分解释和演示操作及维护的适当方法，费用由经销商承担。

　　在本协议有效期和续展期内，经销商应向供应商及时报告库储货物数量和为保证销售、服务所配备的设备的地点。供应商可以指定代表人在营业时间测查上述地点、设备和操作方式。

7. 零配件及附件

　　经销商应保证货物足够的零配件及附件的库存。非供应商生产的零配件及附件不得在货物上使用，除非获得供应商的书面同意。

8. 保密信息

　　经销商获得的有关产品的技术数据、图纸、计划和工程技术指导是保密的，所有权归属于供应商。无论什么时候、出于任何目的，经销商仅能秘密地持有这些资料，未经供应商书面同意不得：（1）向任何人、商行、公司披露，除非经销商员工在本协议有效期或续展期内为了销售、检验、修理、服务产品的需要而使用。（2）在本协议或续展期终止后，经销商的员工复制、使用。供应商根据本款可以要求经销商与接触保密信息的员工签订可执行的保密协议，其内容须满足供应商的要求。

9. 产品采购

    经销商应向供应商购买必备产品，包括采购、维持经销商能履行本协议义务的一定量的产品的库存，和至少_____（套）产品和附件的展示模型。

    供应商应提供充足的产品以满足本区域产品需求。经销商向供应商下的符合协议条款要求的订单到达供应商则视为供应商接受该订单，供应商应按接受的订单履行义务。供应商应在收到订单后_____天内确认收到和接受订单。

10. 业务程序

    经销商下的每张订单都应明示订单性质，并进一步明确交付日期、货物规格和不同日期应发的数量。交付日期不得早于供应商收到订单后_____天。

11. 业务终止

    双方中任何一方要终止业务关系或经销商想取消订单应采用书面形式，如供应商接受经销商取消订单，经销商应赔偿供应商因此所产生的截止到通知取消前的所有费用。

12. 购买价格

    货物的价格和折扣、货物附件的价格和折扣、零配件的价格和折扣分别在本合同附件_____上列明。所有价格为交付点离岸价。如经销商向供应商订购附件上没有价格的产品，则双方应通过友好协商确定一个合理的价格并订立合同。

13. 价格变化

    供应商有权改变货物的价格或折扣。供应商应最迟在价格生效前_____天书面通知经销商价格变化。在收到价格变化通知之日起，经销商在价格变化生效前收到的订单执行变化后的价格。

14. 包装

    供应商按适合运输的包装标准对产品进行包装，费用自行承担。但如果经销商要求改变包装模式，供应商应按要求改变包装，而由此产生的额外费用由经销商承担。

15. 交货

    货物的所有权和货损风险从交付时起转移给经销商。

    供应商应负责安排运输，但如果供应商要求，经销商应予以安排，费用由供应商承担。

16. 检验和收货

    在收到货物后，经销商应及时检查货物，确定是否有货物短缺、瑕疵和损坏。如有上述情况，经销商应在收到货物后_____天内书面通知供应商。在收到通知后_____天内，供应商应调查货物短缺、瑕疵和损坏情况，并通知经销商结果。如确认货物在交付时存在短缺、瑕疵和损坏，供应商应予以更换。

17. 付款

    在交付和接收产品后，供应商向经销商提交该批货的发票。经销商将在收到发票后_____天按发票金额支付货款，用_____支付到供应商书面提供的银行账户。

18. 仲裁

    在履行协议过程中，如产生争议，双方应友好协商解决。若通过友好协商达不成协议，则提交_____仲裁，根据该会仲裁程序现行规定进行仲裁。该委员会的决定是终局性的，对双方均具有约束力。除另有规定外，仲裁费用由败诉方负担。

供应商代表（签字）：　　　　　　经销商代表（签字）：

时间：

地点：

68. 销售代理协议

SALES AGENCY AGREEMENT

Contract No.:

Date:

This Agreement is entered into by and between the parties concerned on _____ in _____, on the basis of equality and mutual benefit to develop business on terms and conditions mutually agreed upon as follows:

1. Contracting Parties

Supplier (hereinafter called "party A"):

Agent (hereinafter called "party B"):

2. Appointment of Agency

Party A hereby appoints Party B to act as his selling agent to sell the commodity mentioned below.

3. Name of Commodity

4. Territory

In _____ only.

5. Minimum Turnover

It is mutually agreed that Party B shall under-take to sell not less than _____ of the aforesaid commodity in the duration of this Agreement.

6. Confirmation of Orders

The quantities, prices and shipments of the commodities stated in this Agreement shall be confirmed in each transaction, the particulars of which are to be specified in the Sales Confirmation signed by the two parties hereto.

7. Price and Payment

After confirmation of the order, Party B shall arrange to open a irrevocable L/C available by draft at sight in favour of Party A within the time stipulated in the relevant S/C. Party B shall also notify Party A immediately after L/C is opened so that Party A can get prepared for delivery.

8. Exclusive Right

In consideration of the exclusive rights granted herein, Party A shall not, directly or indirectly, sell or export the commodity stipulated in Article 3 to customers in _____ through channels other than Party B; Party B shall not sell, distribute or promote the sales of any products competitive with or similar to the above commodity in _____ and shall not solicit or accept orders for the purpose of selling them outside _____ . Party A shall refer to Party B any enquiries or orders for the commodity in question received by Party A from other firms in _____ during the validity of this agreement.

9. Commission

Upon the expiration of the Agreement and Party B's fulfillment of the total turnover mentioned in Article 2, Party A shall pay to Party B _____ % commission on the basis of the aggregate amount of the invoice value against the shipments effected.

10. Market Report

Party B shall forward once every three months to Party A detailed reports on current market conditions and of consumers' comments. Meanwhile, Party B shall, from time to time, send to party A samples of similar commodities offered by other suppliers, together with their prices, sales information and advertising materials.

11. Advertising and Expenses

Party A shall bear all expenses for advertising and publicity within the aforementioned territory in the duration of this Agreement and submit to Party A all patterns and/or drawings and description for prior approval.

12. Validity of Agreement

This Agreement, after its being signed by the parties concerned, shall remain in force for _____ days from _____ to _____. If either party wishes to extend this Agreement, he shall notice, in writing, the other party one month prior to its expiration. The matter shall be decided by the agreement and by the consent of the parties hereto. Should either party fail to implement the terms and conditions herein, the other party is entitled to terminate this Agreement.

13. Force Majeure

Either party shall not be held responsible for failure or delay to perform all or any part of this Agreement due to flood, fire, earthquake, drought, war or any other events which could not be predicted, controlled, avoided or overcome by the relative party. However, the party affected by the event of Force Majeure shall inform the other party of its occurrence in writing as soon as pos-sible and thereafter sends a certificate of the event issued by the relevant authorities to the other party within 10 days after its occurrence.

14. Arbitration

All disputes arising from the execution of this Agreement shall be settled through friendly consultations. In case no settlement can be reached, the case in dispute shall then be submitted to _____ for arbitration in accordance with its provisional rules of procedure. The decision made by this Commission shall be regarded as final and binding upon both parties. Arbitration fees shall be borne by the losing party, unless otherwise awarded.

15. Other Terms & Conditions

(1) Party A shall not supply the contracted commodity to any other buyer(s) in the above mentioned territory. Direct enquiries, if any, will be referred to Party B. However, should any other buyers wish to deal with Party A directly, Party A may do so. But Party A shall send to Party B a copy of sales confirmation and give Party B _____% commission on the basis of the net invoice value of the transaction(s) concluded.

(2) Should Party B fail to pass on his orders to Party A in a period of _____ days for a minimum of _____, Party A shall not bind himself to this Agreement.

(3) For any business transacted between governments or other official departments of both parties, Party A may handle such direct dealings as authorized by Party A's government without binding himself to this Agreement. Party B shall not interfere in such direct dealings nor shall Party B bring forward any demand for compensation therefrom.

(4) Without other oppositional regulations, this Agreement shall be subject to the terms and conditions in the sales confirmation signed by both parties hereto.

Party A: _____ **Corporation**

Party B: _____ **Corporation**

销售代理协议

合同号：

日期：

本协议于_____年_____月_____日在_____由双方在平等互利基础上达成，按双方同意的下列条件发展业务关系：

1. 协议双方

    供货人（以下称"甲方"）：

    _____

    销售代理人（以下称"乙方"）：

    _____

2. 代理委托

    甲方委托乙方为销售代理人，代为推销下列商品。

3. 代理商品名称

4. 代理区域

    只限在_____。

5. 最低业务量

    双方约定，乙方在协议有效期内，销售不少于_____的商品。

6. 订单确认

    本协议所规定商品的数量、价格及装运条件等，应在每笔交易中确认，其细目应在双方签订的销售协议书中做出规定。

7. 价格与支付

    订单确认之后，乙方须按照有关确认书所规定的时间开立以甲方为受益人的不可撤销的即期信用证。乙方开出信用证后，应立即通知甲方，以便甲方准备交货。

8. 独家代理权

    基于本协议授予的独家代理权，甲方不得直接或间接地通过乙方以外的渠道向_____顾客销售或者出口第三条所列商品；乙方不得在_____经销、分销或促销与上述商品相竞争或类似产品，也不得招揽或接受以到_____以外地区销售为目的的订单。在本协议有效期内，甲方应将其收到的来自_____其他商家的有关代理产品的询价或订单转交给乙方。

9. 佣金

    在本协议期满时，若乙方完成了第五条所规定的数额，甲方应按装运货物所收到的发票累计总金额付给乙方_____%的佣金。

10. 市场商情报告

    乙方每三个月向甲方提供一次有关当地市场情况和用户意见的详细报告。同时，乙方应随时向甲方提供其他供应商类似的商品样品及其价格、销售情况和广告资料。
11. 广告及费用

    在本协议有效期内,乙方在上述代理区域所做广告宣传的一切费用,由甲方承担。乙方须事先向甲方提供宣传广告的图案及文字说明,由甲方审阅同意。

12. 协议有效期

    本协议经双方签字后生效,有效期为_____ 天,自_____ 至_____ 。若一方希望延长本协议,则须在本协议期满前一个月书面通知另一方,经双方协商后决定。若协议一方未履行协议条款,另一方有权终止协议。

13. 不可抗力

    由于水灾、火灾、地震、旱灾、战争或协议一方无法预见、控制、避免和克服的其他事件导致不能或暂时不能全部或部分履行本协议,该方不负责任。但是,受不可抗力事件影响的一方须尽快将发生的事件以书面的形式通知另一方,并在不可抗力事件发生后十天内将有关机构出具的不可抗力事件的证明寄交对方。

14. 仲裁

    在履行协议过程中,如产生争议,双方应友好协商解决。若通过友好协商达不成协议,则提交_____ 仲裁,根据该会仲裁程序现行规定进行仲裁。该委员会的决定是终局性的,对双方均具有约束力。除另有规定外,仲裁费用由败诉方负担。

15. 其他

    (1) 甲方不得在上述销售代理区域,向其他买主供应本协议所规定的商品。如有询价,当转达给乙方洽办。若有买主希望从甲方直接订购,甲方可以供货,但甲方须将有关销售确认书副本寄给乙方,并按此次交易的净发票金额给予乙方_____ % 的佣金。

    (2) 若乙方在_____ 天内未能向甲方提供至少_____ 订货,甲方将不承担本协议的义务。

    (3) 对双方政府间或其他官方间的贸易,甲方有权按其政府的授权进行有关的直接贸易,而不受本协议约束。乙方不得干涉此种直接贸易,也无权向甲方提出任何补偿或佣金要求。

    (4) 如果没有相反约定,本协议受签约双方所签订的销售确认条款的制约。

    甲方: _____ 公司   乙方: _____ 公司

Unit 11　感谢函及其他　　Letters of Thanks & Others

　　贸易中也要注重礼尚往来，受人恩惠后送上一片感激之情，是对对方劳动的尊重。

　　感谢函是表达感激之情的常用方式之一。感谢函既体现出一个人或一个公司的交往能力，同时也有助于维系和睦友好的关系。

　　国际贸易中的感谢函涉及各种主题，主要有感谢购买产品、感谢合作机会等等。此类信函中要洋溢着感激之情。在叙述事实的过程中，除了要突出对方的好和表示谢意外，行文要始终饱含着感情。这种感情要真挚、热烈，使所有看到信的人都受到感染。此外，切不可不着边际地大发议论。

　　感谢函的写作步骤：1. 表示感谢；2. 说明感谢事由；3. 希望继续合作或再次表示感谢。

　　国际商务操作中大部分细节都需要使用信函，涉及广泛。

✻ 常用句型

1. We would like to take this chance to extend our thanks to you.

   我们希望借此机会对贵方表示感谢。

2. I would like to express my appreciation for…

   非常感激您……

3. Thank you again for…

   对……再次表示感谢。

✎ 69. 感谢给予合作机会

Dear Owens,

　　We are glad that you choose our firm to organize a farewell party for your company's 25th year celebration on 20th December. We guarantee you that we will take good care of the entire event as well as your clients. You will face no problems from our side and we promise you to make it a grand successful event so that your clients and business partners will remember the event for years.

It is a matter of pride for us to serve such a big company. We will serve to our level best.

Wish to look forward for more such opportunities.

Thank You.

Sincerely,
Kate R. Riddle

尊敬的欧文斯：

很高兴您选择我方来组织于 12 月 20 日的贵公司 25 周年庆典宴会。我们向您保证，我们会认真对待整个宴会并招待好您的顾客。我方将克服所有困难，并承诺打造一次盛大成功的宴会，让您的顾客以及商业合作伙伴数年后仍旧对此记忆犹新。

能为如此大的公司服务是我方的荣幸，我们将为您竭诚服务。

期待更多这样的机会。

谢谢！

诚挚的 凯特·R·瑞德

70. 感谢购买产品

Dear Sir/ Madam;

We at PQC Software Solutions Ltd, feel privileged to find an excellent opportunity to thank our esteemed customers for being an integral part of our organization and allowing us to serve you better.

Further we desire to extend our earnest thanks for the purchase of assembled software package from our company. We will strive to maintain a harmonious cooperation with you.

We would also like to take this chance to extend our support in case of any problems or replacements related with the product. We are looking forward for your continuous business dealing with us in the future.

Thank you.

Sincerely,
Ray Kent

敬启者：

　　PQC 软件解决方案有限公司倍感荣幸能有这样一个绝佳的机会，来表达我们对尊敬的客户的谢意，感谢你们成为我公司不可缺少的部分，以及给我们机会让我们为您服务。

　　此外，我方非常感谢您购买我们的组装软件包。我方将竭尽全力为您服务。

　　我方还想借此机会表明，如有任何与产品有关的问题，我们都将全力支持。期待与您继续合作。

　　谢谢！

诚挚的　雷·肯特

71. 感谢安排见面

Dear Ms. Bowman,

　　Greetings!

　　I would just like to express my appreciation for giving me so much of your precious time during our appointment last Jan 5 to discuss the possibility of my company doing business with yours. It was a very fruitful discussion, and I'm glad we were able to come to terms on the Bakersfield building project.

　　In line with what we discussed, our in-house attorney, Mr. Clark George, will be in touch with your office to set a follow-up appointment in order to thresh out the details of our agreement. We are also sending over the relevant paperwork for you to look over before the meeting.

　　Thank you again for the very informative meeting, and please feel free to contact my office at 060-1007604 if you have any further concerns. I look forward to working with you on this and other projects.

Respectfully yours,
Daniel Fredricksen
President, LXS Company

尊敬的鲍曼女士：

　　您好！

　　非常感谢您在去年1月5日抽出大量宝贵的时间，与我方讨论双方合作事宜。那次讨论卓有成效，很高兴我们能够就贝克斯菲尔德建设项目达成协议。

　　按照上次的讨论，我方内部委托律师克拉克乔治先生将会与您办公室联系预约，以讨论我们协议的细节。我方也将寄给您相关的书面材料，供您会前浏览。

　　再次感谢这次内容丰富的会议，如若有什么疑问，请随时与我办公室联系，联系电话是060-1007604。期待与您在此次项目的合作。

LXS 公司董事长 丹尼尔·弗雷德里克森 敬上

72. 告知对方其提议已得到通过

Dear Mr. Mitchell,

We are very happy to inform you that the board of directors has selected your proposal during the general meeting held on 12th September 2010. We are satisfied with all the aspects mentioned therein and would like to give you the contract for the 50 slab casting machines.

We would send our representative to your office for the remaining paperwork and the token amount. All this machines should be completed within 18months as per your proposal latter. The payment for the same will be done in three installments first on the date of contract, second on the date of completion on 25 machines and third on the date of completion of the contract. Your organization is known organization for the production of the slab casting machines hence we would love to have cordial relationship between two companies.

Yours Truly,
Hayden K. Stephens

尊敬的米切尔先生：

　　很高兴告诉您，董事会在2010年9月12日的全体会议上最终选择了您的提案。我们对您提案中所涉及的各个方面都很满意，想与您签订50台板坯连铸机的购买合同。

　　我们将派代表去您办公室，签署一些遗留的书面材料并支付象征性的金额。按照您后来的提案，所有的机器将在18个月内完成。付款分三次完成，第一次是签订合同之日,第二次是完成 25 台机器之日,第三次是合同完成之日。贵公司在板坯连铸机制造方面十分有名,我方希望这次的合作愉快。

海·K·史蒂芬斯 敬上

73. 邀请捐款

Dear Mr. Mike,

  I am writing this letter to you for a purpose. I want to tell you that we are organizing a programme on the awareness of HIV AIDS. The show will consist of a play and many speeches which will create awareness among the people. This dangerous disease is spreading very rapidly nowadays.

  It is a need of the hour to save the people from this disease and create awareness among them regarding this. Thus we request you to sponsor our show. We are doing this for a good purpose and due to this we need your active participation.

  I hope you will consider this letter.

Yours sincerely,
David Dave

尊敬的迈克先生:

  我写这封信给您是为了一个目的。我想告诉您我们正在组织一个预防艾滋病的活动。活动内容包括一场话剧和几个演讲,为的是让公众意识到,这一危险的疾病正在快速传播。

  目前我们十分需要预防人们不感染艾滋病,树立这方面的防护意识。因此,我们请求您资助此次活动。我们做的是公益事业,因此十分需要您的积极参与。

  希望您能考虑。

大卫·戴夫 谨上

74. 捐款函

Dear Sir,

  I am writing this letter on behalf our official members and take pleasure to inform you that we decided donate a sum of $10,000 to your organization.

Recently we came to know about your organization and various social welfare activities carried out by your organization. So, we wanted to join hands with you and help the needy people in time.

You can use this money for all your social welfare events and programs. You can also use our banner to advertise your event, which may give you an upper edge in reaching common people.

Waiting to hear your reply!!

Thanks and regards.

Sincerely,
Toby Mill

敬启者：
　　我代表公司成员写这封信，很高兴告知您我们决定给您的组织捐赠一万美元。
　　近来，我们了解到您的组织举办过各种社会福利活动，因此，我们渴望与您携手，提供及时的帮助给需要的人。
　　您可以将这笔钱用于您所有的社会福利活动。您还可以使用我们的标语为您的活动做广告，这可能会有利于打动大众。
　　等待您的回复！
　　谢谢。

诚挚的 托比·米尔

75. 回复捐款函

Dear Mr. Anthony,

We are writing this letter to you from the bottom of our heart. Two months before we wrote a letter to you for a request to give donation to us. You immediately considered our request and you did the needful. It was a great help from your side. We were really in need of funds and donations.

We wanted to conduct a medical camp for our members but were unable to conduct due to low funds. But now from your help we will be able to do so. We really thank you for helping us. We assure you that your money will be used for a good purpose. We will also like to call you to attend various our functions. Your donation of Rs.500,000 will really help us for our development purposes.

Thank you.

Yours sincerely,
Robin Marshalls.

尊敬的安东尼先生：

  谨写此信，表达我们对您真诚的谢意。两个月前，我们写信给您，希望能得到您的捐款。您立即考虑了我们的请求，真是雪中送炭。您给了我们巨大的帮助，我们真的十分需要资金和捐款。

  之前我们想为成员建立一个医疗所，可是由于缺少资金而不能实现。但是，现在有了您的帮助，我们就能够完成医疗所的建立。真心地感谢您的帮助。我们向您保证，您的捐款都将用于做好事。我们还想请您参加我们的各种活动。您 50 万卢比的捐款将会有利于我们的发展。

  谢谢！

罗宾·马歇尔 谨上

76. 表示终止业务往来

Dear Sir,

  I am writing you this letter to terminate our deal with you as our official marketing client. This is a decision that the board has come up and it will take effect immediately and cannot be subjected to an appeal. We have come up with this decision because our quality assurance department found out that the services that you render are of low quality and that it has not affected our sales at all.

  We hope that this will serve as a call for you to improve your services. If in the future we see that you have grown to be a better marketing services provider, then we will be very happy to be in a marketing deal with you again.

Yours faithfully,
Patrick Mores,
Executive Director,
Roadway Products Inc.

敬启者：

　　我写这封信是要终止您作为我们官方营销客户的合作。这是董事会的决定，即刻生效，不容改变。作此决定是因为我们的质量保证部门认为，您提供的服务令人不满，并未对我们的销售起到什么好的影响。

　　我们希望这次事情对您是个警钟，让您提高自己的服务质量。如果将来我们看到您能提供出色的营销服务，我们很乐意与您再次合作。

诚挚的 Roadway 产品有限公司执行董事
帕特里克·莫里斯

特别奉献

一　外贸术语中英对照

All Water 全水路
Bill of Lading 海运提单
Buying Rate 买价
Bunker Adjustment Factor 燃油附加费
COST AND FREIGHT 成本加海运费
Collect 运费到付
Container Service Charge 货柜服务费
Container Yard 货柜场
Consignee 收货人
Certificate of Origin 产地证
Currency Adjustment Factor 货币汇率附加费
Container Freight Station 集装箱集散站/货运站
CFS/CFS 散装交货（起点/终点）
Customs House Broker 报关行
Carriage and Insurance Paid To 运费、保险费付至目的地
Commodity 商品
Carriage Paid To... 运费付至目的地……
Container 柜子
Document Against Acceptance 承兑交单
Delivery Order 到港通知
Document Against Payment 付款交单
Delivered At Frontier 边境交货
Destination Delivery Charge 目的港码头费
Delivered Duty Paid 完税后交货
Delivered Duty Unpaid 未完税交货
Delivered Ex Quay 目的港码头交货
Delivered Ex Ship 目的港船上交货
Document Number 文件号码
Work/Ex Factory 工厂交货
Freight Forwarder 货运代理

Fuel Adjustment Factor 燃料附加费
Freight All Kind 各种货品
Free Alongside Ship 装运港船边交货
Free Carrier 货交承运人
Full Container Load 整柜
Federal Maritime Commission 联邦海事委员会
Free On Board 船上交货
General Rate Increase 全面涨价
Handling Charge 代理费
Inside Sales 内销售
Independent Action 各别调价
Letter of Credit 信用证
Land Bridge 陆桥
Less Than Container Load 拼柜
Measurement Ton 尺码吨（即货物收费以尺码计费）
Master Bill Of Loading 主提单
Mini Land Bridge 小陆桥，自一港到另一港口
Mother Vessel 主线船
Multimodal Transport Document 多式联运单据
Notify 通知人
Ocean Freight 海运费
Overland Continental Point 货主自行安排运到内陆点
Operation 操作
Origen Receive Charges 本地收货费用（广东省收取）
Prepaid 预付
Port Congestion Surcharge 港口拥挤附加费
Port Of Destination 目地港
Port Of Loading 装运港
Shipper 发货人
Sales Contract 售货合同
Shipping Order 装货指示书
Selling Rate 卖价
Service Contract 服务合同
Steam Ship Line 船公司

Terminal Receiving Charge 码头收柜费
Trans-Ship 转船，转运
Transit Time 航程
Terminal Handling Charges 码头操作费（香港收取）
Total 总共
Time Volume Contract/ Rate 定期定量合同
Vessel Operating Common Carrier 船公司
Weight or Measurement ton 即以重量吨或者尺码吨中从高收费
Weight Ton 重量吨 (即货物收费以重量计费)
Yard Surcharges 码头附加费

特别奉献

二　金融术语中英对照

issue IOU 打白条
certificate of deposit（CD）大额存单
withdraw deposits in large amounts 大额提现
wide-spread decline 大面积滑坡
(all-in-one) mono-bank system 大一统的银行体制
loan loss reserves (provisions) 呆账准备金
idle loans 呆滞贷款
non-performing loans 贷款沉淀
loan classification 贷款分类
credit control;to impose credit ceiling 贷款限额管理
credit disciplinary (constrain) mechanism 贷款约束机制
to act as fiscal agent 代理国库
make loans on behalf of other institution 代理金融机构贷款
ear-marked loans 戴帽贷款
reversed transmission of the pressure for easing monetary condition 倒逼机制

moral hazard 道德风险
regional disparity 地区差别
the primary industry 第一产业
the secondary industry 第二产业
the service industry; the tertiary industry 第三产业
deferrable assets 递延资产
insufficient orders 订货不足
time deposits 定期存款
raising funds from targeted sources 定向募集
host country 东道国（请见"母国"）
independent accounting 独立核算
treasury bills 短期国债
treasury bills 对冲操作
claims on non-financial sector 对非金融部门债权
diversified ownership 多种所有制形式
independent accounting 独立核算
treasury bills 短期国债
sterilization operation 对冲操作
claims on non-financial sector 对非金融部门债权
claims on non-financial sector 多种所有制形式
hyperinflation 恶性通货膨胀
secondary market 二级市场
to issue currency 发行货币
total stock issue 发行总股本
required reserves; reserve requirement 法定准备金
institutional shares 法人股
institutional shareholders 法人股东
institutional shareholders 法治
real estate investment 房地产投资
to ease monetary policy 放松银根
off-site surveillance (or monitoring) 非现场稽核
non-bank financial institutions 非银行金融机构
non-profit organizations 非赢利性机构
assignment of central and local taxes; tax assignment system 分税制

segregation of financial business (services) 分业经营
risk exposure 风险暴露（风险敞口）
risk management 风险管理
risk management 风险意识
risk-weighted capital ratios 风险资本比例
risk-based capital standard 风险资本标准
public service charges;user's charges 服务事业收入
poverty alleviation 扶贫
negative growth 负增长
double-entry budgeting; capital and current budgetary account 复式预算制
reform experimentation 改革试点
leverage ratio 杠杆率
leveraged buyout 杠杆收购
to raise funds by offering high interest 高息集资
non-institutional shares 个人股
non-institutional shares 根本扭转
open market operations 公开市场操作
deposit public funds in personal accounts 公款私存
public utilities 公用事业
public utilities 公有经济
public ownership 公有制
profit-to-cost ratio 工业成本利润率
industrial value added 工业增加值
supply exceeding demand;excessive supply 供大于求
supply exceeding demand;excessive supply 鼓励措施
joint-equity cooperative enterprises 股份合作企业
joint-equity enterprises 股份制企业
joint-equity enterprises 股份制银行
fixed asset loans 固定资产贷款
tariff reduction and exemption 关税减免
tariff concessions 关税减让
tariff incentives;preferential tariff treatment 关税优惠
to regularize (or standardize)…behavior 规范行为

economies of scale 规模效益
national interest and people's livelihood 国计民生
other government outlays to individuals 国家对个人其他支出
country risk 国家风险
international division of labor 国际分工
balance of payments 国际收支
wholly state-owned commercial banks 国有独资商业银行
the state-owned (or public) sector 国有经济（部门）
state-owned enterprises (SOEs) 国有企业
state-ownership 国有制
erosion of state assets 国有资产流失
government securities repurchase 国债回购
primary underwriters of government securities 国债一级自营商
excessive competition 过度竞争
excessive expansion 过度膨胀
rational expectation 合理预期
core capital 核心资本
joint-venture enterprises 合资企业
dividend 红利
sound macroeconomic performance 宏观经济运营良好
macroeconomic fundamentals 宏观经济基本状况
macroeconomic management (or adjustment) 宏观调控
macroeconomic objectives (or targets) 宏观调控目标
bad debt 坏账
debt service 还本付息
unit export cost; local currency cost of export earnings 换汇成本
funds in float 汇兑在途
advance payment of remittance by the beneficiary's bank 汇兑支出
unification of exchange rates 汇率并轨
demand deposits 活期存款
exchange rate misalignment 汇率失调
Diversified (mixed) ownership 混合所有制
monetary policy stance 货币政策态势
overdue obligations 过热贷款拖欠

特别奉献

三 中国主要银行名称中英对照

THE PEOPLE'S BANK OF CHINA 中国人民银行
INDUSTRIAL AND COMMERCIAL BANK OF CHINA 中国工商银行
CHINA CONSTRUCTION BANK 中国建设银行
AGRICULTURAL BANK OF CHINA 中国农业银行
BANK OF CHINA 中国银行
BANK OF COMMUNICATIONS 交通银行
CHINA MENCHANTS BANK 招商银行
CHINA CITIC BANK 中信银行
CHINA DEVELOPMENT BANK 国家开发银行
AGRICULTURE DEVELOPMENT BANK OF CHINA 中国农业发展银行
THE EXPORT-IMPORT BANK OF CHINA 中国进出口银行

Chapter 03

跨洋求学

  随着改革开放的深入、国民文化和经济水平的提高以及人们对知识的渴求，越来越多的学生和在职人员选择出国深造。

  远跨重洋求学，所要付出的不仅仅是金钱、时间，还有更多的艰辛、智慧，同时也要面临更大的压力和挑战。在申请出国的过程中，令许多中国学生头疼的一个问题就是语言。别说到了国外，即便还没踏出国门半步，国外校方就会和你用各种英文信件进行交流，让你准备各种英文材料。有时候，即便是英文功底较好的同学或是上班族都会感到束手无策，不知如何面对各种文体的留学材料，最终不得不一掷千金，把麻烦事儿交给中介公司，回来长叹一声："这么多年的英语白学了。"

  其实，要准备好各种留学英文材料并不困难。留学所要准备的材料就那么几种，文体也都相对固定，有中上英文水平的同学或是上班族都可以自己完成这方面的写作。当然，各种文件的写作是有格式、规范和套路的，我们所要做的，就是多看例文，研究别人是如何写的，并将其灵活地运用。逐渐地大家就会发现，只要认真模仿、虚心学习，请人翻译的钱还是可以省下来的。本章就将较为全面地介绍在留学申请过程中各种文件的写作方法。

Unit 1　求学简历

CVs

　　个人简历（CV 或 Resume）是个人经历的概述。简历用得最多的情况一般有两种，一个是求职，另一个就是求学了。本章专门讲求学简历。

　　许多读者朋友都知道，在英文中，简历既可以说是 CV (curriculum vitae)，也可以说是 resume。那么，这两词有什么细微的区别？二者在长度、内容和应用范围上都有所不同。现在常常有人把 CV 和 Resume 混起来称为"简历"，其实精确而言，CV 应该是"履历"，Resume 才是简历。Resume 概述了与求职有关的教育准备和经历，是对经验技能的摘要，其主要目的在于说服用人单位老板雇佣自己；Curriculum Vitae 则集中说明学术工作，不重视与文化程度和学习成绩无直接关系的资料。

　　CV 的长度由其内容确定，有时可长达十页，年轻人的履历一般长度都在二至四页，而老资历的通常也在六至八页。内容应包括：姓名、地址、电话号码及电子邮件地址；文化程度；受何奖励和大学奖学金；教学相关经历；有何论著发表；语言或其他技能，课外活动及个人爱好。

　　Resume 大多只需一页大小，而有两页的是具有广泛工作经验的人才。内容应包括：姓名、地址、电子信箱（可选）和电话号码（当地和固定的）；工作岗位（可选）；教育；获何荣誉奖励；有关功课（可选）；经历——应列出组织、地址、日期、工作名称、成绩和职责的简述。

　　综上，可见求学简历叫 CV 似乎更为准确一些。

　　申请国外院校入学或是奖学金资助，提交个人简历时应说明申请人具备了相应的教育背景、技能和工作经历。如果申请人是申请研究生及以上的学历，那么简历中还需要包括相关教学和研究经历、出版的论文或专著、获得的研究资助、加入的专业团体、获奖情况等信息。这些内容能够大大增加被录取的可能性，因为这些充分证明了申请人的学术能力。留学简历一般包括以下内容：

1. 申请人基本信息（包括姓名、联系方式等）；
2. 教育背景；
3. 专业经历（即和本专业直接或间接相关的学术活动、工作、实习等）；

4. 社会活动（如志愿者等）；
5. 个人爱好；
6. 其他技能（语言、计算机、乐器等）。

简历的写作需要注意：
1. 语言简练，一般省略主语；
2. 排版清晰，重点突出，可适当运用大写、加粗、下划线等方式标出重要信息，以便校方审阅者一目了然；
3. 学术著作、出版物的表达方式以及相关元素（如作者、发表时间、标题、出版刊物等）的顺序要体现专业性，按照国际惯例来，不能乱排。注意标题和刊物名称要斜体。
4. 简历重点是体现学术能力部分，如出版物等，内容尽量丰富，越多越好，若能举出长长的一列，将无疑能给自己加分很多。当然，切忌无中生有，一定要实事求是。

1. 本科生简历

PERSONAL INFORMATION

Name: *Wang Li*
Gender: Female
Date of Birth: 29/03/1986
Telephone: +86-13986258000, +86-27-87669000
E-mail: yuchen@yahoo.cn
Address: XXXXX
Citizenship: People's Republic of China

EDUCATIONAL BACKGROUND

Bachelor of Science in Financial Engineering
Economics and Management School, Wuhan University, expected 2008.
General GPA: 3.74 Major GPA: 3.78 Ranking: 2/66
Core Courses: Financial Engineering, Financial Economics, Corporate Finance, Securities Investment Analysis, Derivative security, Fixed Income of Securities, Dynamic Optimization, Time Series Analysis.

RECORDS OF STANDARD TESTS

TOEFL 102 (Reading 29, Listening 28, Speaking 20, Writing 25) Sep. 2007.

GRE 1290 (V 520, 65%, Q 770, 88%) AW 4.5, 54% Jun. 2007.

IELTS 7 (Listening 7.5, Reading 7.5, Writing 6, Speaking 7) May. 2007.

WORKING EXPERIENCES

China Construction Bank, Hubei Branch, Wuhan, China July. 2007 - Aug. 2007

Summer Intern, Personal Financial Department
- ♣ Assisted with service of personal credit card.
- ♣ Participated in the bank's strategic transformation and training program of customer service quality.

Bank of China, Hubei Branch, Wuhan, China July. 2006 - Aug. 2006

Summer Intern, Personal Consumption and Loan Department
- ♣ Assisted in Housing Mortgage Loans and Auto Loans transactions.
- ♣ Helped arrange official files.
- ♣ Participated in the market investigation of Auto Loans which covered more than 90% staff in the bank and obtained more than 100 pieces of useful information.

IMPORTANT PROJECTS

Program of Chinese National Natural Science Foundation
Prof. Assistant and Asset Pricing 2007 - 2008
- ♣ Collecting relevant materials and papers.
- ♣ Data Analysis and Processing.
- ♣ Assisting with constructing and consummating the pricing model.

PUBLICATIONS

- ♣ *Relationship between interest rate and stock price index in China, X monthly*, Oct, 2007

- Empirical Research on Return Volatility of Aluminum Futures Market in China, ***Communication in Finance and Accounting, (to be published)***

ACADEMIC HONORS

- *Second-class scholarship and "Excellent Student"*, Wuhan University Sep. 2007
- *Second Prize of the "National Case Study Competition"* Dec. 2006
- *First Prize of the "Competition of economic cases of Industries"* Dec. 2006
- *Second-class scholarship and "Excellent Student"*, Wuhan University Sep.2006
- *Second-class scholarship and "Excellent Student"*, Wuhan University Sep.2005
- *Third-class scholarship and "Excellent Freshman"*, Wuhan University Sep.2004

SKILLS

- Computer skills: Proficient in Microsoft Word, PowerPoint, Access, Excel and Eviews
- Other skills: Passed the Highest Level (Level 10) of National Piano Amateur Grade Testing.
- Detail-oriented, team-spirited, responsible and motivated

个人信息

姓名：王丽
性别：女
生日：1986 年 3 月 29 日
电话：+86-13986258000，+86-27-87669000
邮件：yuchen@yahoo.cn
地址：XXXXX
国籍：中华人民共和国

教育背景
金融工程学学士
武汉大学经管学院，2008年毕业。
全科 GPA：3.74 专业课程 GPA：3.78 排名：2/66
主要课程：金融工程学、金融经济学、公司理财、证券投资分析、衍生证券、固定收益债券、动态优化、时间序数分析。

标准测试成绩
托福：102（阅读29，听力28，口语20，写作25）；测试时间：2007年9月
GRE: 1290（V520,65%,Q770,88%）AW4.5,54%；测试时间：2007年6月
雅思：7（听力7.5，阅读7.5，写作6，口语7）；测试时间：2007年5月

工作经历
2007.7-2007.8 中国建设银行湖北分行 中国武汉
暑期实习 私人金融部
- 协助私人信用卡业务
- 参与该行的战略转型以及客服质量的培训项目

2006.7-2006.8 中国银行湖北分行 中国武汉
暑期实习 私人消费信贷部
- 协助房贷、车贷业务
- 协助安排办公档案
- 参与车贷市场调查，该调查覆盖该行90%以上的员工，获得100多份有用信息。

重要项目
中国国家自然科学基金
2007-2008 教授助理，资产定价
- 收集相关资料和论文
- 数据分析和加工
- 协助建立健全定价模型

出版论文
《中国利率和股价指数之间的关系》，《X月刊》，2007.10
《中国铝期货回报波幅实证研究》，《金融会计通讯》，（将要付梓）

学术荣誉

2007.9 武汉大学二等奖学金和"优秀学生"称号
2006.12 "国家案例研究竞赛"第二名
2006.12 "行业经济案例竞赛"第一名
2006.9 武汉大学二等奖学金和"优秀学生"称号
2005.9 武汉大学二等奖学金和"优秀学生"称号
2004.9 武汉大学三等奖学金和"优秀新生"称号

技能

计算机：熟练掌握 MS Word, PowerPoint, Access, Excel 和 Eviews.
其他技能：通过国家业余钢琴十级（最高级）
个人描述：注重细节，团队合作，有责任心，富有激情

2. 硕士简历

Kelly Bryant

bryantkelly@gmail.com
Address: XXXXX

Education

University of California, Berkeley - School of Information
- ♣ Masters of Information Management and Systems, May 2006
- ♣ Concentration in Human-Computer Interaction, User Interface Design, Information

Visualization and Database Management
- ♣ 3.79 GPA

Keene State College
- ♣ Bachelor of Arts, Mathematics, Minor: Art, May 1998
- ♣ Member of Kappa Mu Epsilon, Mathematics Honor Society
- ♣ 3.53 GPA cum laude

Experience

Interaction Designer - Educational Technology Services - UC Berkeley October 2005 - present

- ♣ Designed user interaction for an online equipment reservation system
- ♣ Performed heuristic evaluation and provided design recommendations for open source

course management system

Helpdesk Administrator - Sapient - TEK Systems

November 2000 - February 2001

- ♣ Provided first level technical support to advanced users
- ♣ Participated in support team, 70% field support 30% call tracking in Remedy Help Desk

Helpdesk Technician - Keene State College - Campus Technology Services

October 1998 - September 2000

- ♣ Managed daily activities of a technical support center in an academic setting including

seven technicians

- ♣ Provided first line technical support for over 550 faculty and staff members
- ♣ Created and maintained documentation related to technical policies and procedures

Projects

iBuyRight

www.projectibuyright.com

- ♣ Served as Project Manager for Masters final project team to set project goals and

milestones as well as to communicate progress with stakeholders

- ♣ Played a key role in the visual and interaction design of mobile prototypes
- ♣ Performed needs and usability analysis using interview, surveys and comparative analysis

Empty Orchestra

<http://dream.sims.berkeley.edu/~kbryant/emptyorchestra.php>

- ♣ Designed and implemented a database of karaoke studios and songs

that alleviates
search and browse problems with current karaoke systems
- ♣ Implemented design using MySQL and PHP and documented system design in a written

report

UFOVis

<http://www.sims.berkeley.edu:8000/academics/courses/is247/f05/projects/ufovis/>

- ♣ Created a visualization of UFO sighting data to facilitate potential spatial and temporal

pattern recognition for information visualization course
- ♣ Implemented design using Yahoo! Maps API

Skills

- ♣ Very familiar with principals of graphic design and visual communication
- ♣ Strong logical and analytical approach to problem solving
- ♣ Experience with the following software:

Photoshop, Illustrator, Indesign, GoLive, Flash including ActionScript, Flash Lite,

Dreamweaver, Fireworks, Omnigraffle, Microsoft Office products, MS Project, Visio

- ♣ Knowledge of HTML, CSS, Javascript, PHP, mySQL, Java, XML

克里　布莱恩
邮箱：bryantkelly@gmail.com
地址：XXXXX

教育背景
伯克利大学信息学院
- 2006.5 信息管理和信息系统硕士

- 主攻人机互动、用户界面设计、信息可视化和数据库管理
- GPA：3.79

基恩州立学院
- 1998.5 文学士学位，数学 辅修：艺术
- 数学荣誉协会 Kappa Mu Epsilon 成员
- GPA：3.53（优等）

工作经历

2005.10- 今 伯克利大学教育科技服务 互动设计师
- 为一家在线设备预订系统设计用户界面
- 进行启发性评估，并为开放课程管理系统提供设计建议

2000.11-2001.2 TEK 系统 Sapient 服务 服务台管理员
- 为高级用户提供一流技术支持
- 参与支持团队，在客服部门 70% 外场支援，30% 客户电话跟踪

1998.10-2000.9 肯恩州立学院校园技术服务部 服务台技术员
- 在一个学术团队的技术支持中心处理日常事务，该团队包括七名技术员
- 为 550 多名教师和员工提供一流技术支持
- 制定并维护与技术政策和程序相关的文件编制

参与项目

iBuyRight 项目

相关网址：www.projectibuyright.com
- 在硕士结业项目组中担任项目经理，制定项目目标、项目重点，与相关方交流项目进展
- 在动态原型的视觉和互动设计中扮演重要角色
- 通过走访、调查和比较分析来进行需求和可用性分析

Empty Orchestra 项目

相关网址：<http://dream.sims.berkeley.edu/~kbryant/emptyorchestra.php>
- 设计并使用了一种卡拉 OK 录音棚和歌曲数据库，缓解了当前卡拉 OK 系统在搜索和浏览方面的问题
- 用 MySQL 和 PHP 将设计付诸实践，在一份文件报告中记录系统设计

UFOVis 项目

相关网址：<http://www.sims.berkeley.edu:8000/academics/courses/is247/f05/projects/ufovis/>
- 将 UFO 视觉数据可视化，给信息可视化课程的潜在时空模型认知提供了便利

- 用 Yahoo! Maps API 演示了设计

技能
- 熟知图形设计和视觉交流原则
- 在解决问题过程中具有较强的逻辑和分析能力
- 熟悉以下软件：Photoshop, Illustrator, Indesign, GoLive, Flash including ActionScript, Flash Lite, Dreamweaver, Fireworks, Omnigraffle, Microsoft Office products, MS Project, Visio
- 对 Knowledge of HTML, CSS, Javascript, PHP, mySQL, Java, XML 等也有一定的掌握

3. 博士简历

Jinying Chen

University of Pennsylvania
Department of Computer and Information Science
Cell phone: (732) 668-7728
Office: (215) 573-7736

Home Address:
XXXXX

jinying@cis.upenn.edu

Education

University of Pennsylvania, Philadelphia, PA, USA Ph.D. candidate 2001 - Pres.

Department of Computer and Information Science

Dissertation: Towards High-performance Word Sense Disambiguation by Combining Rich Linguistic Knowledge and Machine Learning Approaches (to be defended in July, 2006)

Advisor: Martha S. Palmer

Committee Members: Joshi K. Aravind, Claire Cardie, (external examiner), Mitch P. Marcus (chair), Lyle H. Ungar

University of Pennsylvania, Philadelphia, PA, USA M.S. 2000 - 2001

Department of Computer and Information Science

Tsinghua University, Beijing, China M.E. 1998 - 2000, B.S. 1994 -

1998
   Department of Computer Science and Technology

Research Experience

   Department of Computer and Information Science, University of Pennsylvania
   Ph.D. Candidate 2001 - 2006
   ......
   Department of Computer Science & Technology, Tsinghua University, Beijing, China
   Master Student, Senior College Student 1997 - 2000
   ......

Honors and Awards

- ♣ Graudate student research fellowship from the Department of Computer and Information Science, University of Pennsylvania. Sept. 2000 - pres.
- ♣ Tsinghua-Motorola Outstanding Student Scholarship, top 3 among over 50 graduate students in the Department of Computer Science and Technology, Tsinghua University. Oct. 1999
- ♣ Honor of Excellent Student of Tsinghua University, top 10 among over 150 undergraduate students in the Department of Computer Science and Technology, Tsinghua University. Nov. 1997
- ♣ Honor of Excellent Student of Tsinghua University, top 10 among over 150 undergraduate students in the Department of Computer Science and Technology, Tsinghua University. Nov. 1995
- ♣ First Prize in the Tenth National High School Student Contest in Physics in Tianjin, sponsored by Chinese Physical Society and Tianjin Physical Society. Top 10 among over 1,000 competition participants in Tianjin area. Nov. 1993.

Publications

- Jinying Chen and Martha Palmer. Clustering-based Feature Selection for Verb Sense Disambiguation. In Proceedings of the 2005 IEEE International Conference on Natural Language Processing and Knowledge Engineering (IEEE NLP-KE 2005), pp. 36-41. Oct. 30- Nov. 1, Wuhan, China, 2005.
......

Oral Presentations (2001-2006)

- "Towards Robust High Performance Word Sense Disambiguation by Combining Rich Linguistic Knowledge and Machine Learning Methods", in the 7th Penn Engineering Graduate Research Symposium, Feb. 15, 2006.
......

Other Professional Activities

- Organizer of the weekly seminar, the Computational Linguists' Lunch (CLUNCH), attended by about 30 faculty members and students mainly from the Department of Computer Science and Information and the Department of Linguistics, University of Pennsylvania. Spring, 2003
- Teaching assistant for the graduate-level course CIT594 II - Programming Languages and Techniques, which is oriented to master students in the Department of Computer and Information Science, University of Pennsylvania. Spring, 2002
......

Reference

Joshi K. Aravind, PhD (joshi@linc.cis.upenn.edu, 215-898-8540)

Martha S. Palmer, PhD (Martha.Palmer@colorado.edu, 303-492-1300)

Lyle H. Ungar, PhD (ungar@cis.upenn.edu, 215-898-7449)

陈金英

宾夕法尼亚大学计算机与信息科学系 学校地址：XXXXX

手机：(732) 668-7728

办公室电话：(215) 573-7736

家庭住址：XXXXX

邮箱：jinying@cis.upenn.edu

个人网址：<http://www.cis.upenn.edu/~jinying>

教育背景

2001- 今 宾夕法尼亚大学 美国宾夕法尼亚州费城 博士在读

计算机与信息科学系

论文：《通过结合丰富的语言知识和机器学习方法达到高性能词义消歧》，（答辩时间 2006 年 7 月）

指导老师：玛莎·S·帕莫

委员会成员：霍什·K·阿瑞文，克莱尔·卡尔迪（校外监考员），米奇·P·马尔卡斯（主席），莱尔·H·恩格

2000-2001 宾夕法尼亚大学 美国宾夕法尼亚州费城 理科硕士

计算机与信息科学系

1998-2000 清华大学 中国北京 教育学硕士

计算机系

1994-1998 清华大学 中国北京 理学士

计算机系

研究经历

宾夕法尼亚大学计算机与信息科学系 博士生在读 2001-2006

……（从略）

中国北京 清华大学计算机系 研究生、大四本科生 1997-2000

……（从略）

荣誉和奖励

2000.9- 今 宾夕法尼亚大学计算机与信息科学系研究生研究员

1999.10 清华大学计算机系"清华 - 摩托罗拉优秀学生奖学金"，50 名研究生中前 3 名

1997.11 清华大学计算机系"清华优秀学生"荣誉称号，在 150 名本科生中前 10 名

1995.11 清华大学计算机系"清华优秀学生"荣誉称号，在 150 名本科生

中前 10 名

1993.11 第十届全国高中生物理竞赛天津赛区一等奖，成绩位列天津赛区 1 000 多名参赛者的前 10 名。该竞赛由中国物理协会和天津物理协会主办。

出版论文

陈金英，玛莎·帕莫，《在动词语义消歧上以聚类为基础的特征选择》。2005 年电气与电子工程师协会自然语言处理和知识工程学国际会议论文集（IEEE NLP-KE 2005），pp. 36-41. 10. 30- 11. 1，中国武汉，2005。

……（从略）

口头报告（2001-2006)

"通过结合丰富的语言知识和机器学习方法达到强大而高性能的语义消歧"，第七届宾夕法尼亚工程学研究生研究专题报告会，2006 年 2 月 15 日。

……（从略）

其他专业活动

- 2003 年春 每周研讨会"计算机语言午餐"（CLUNCH）的组织者。该研讨会由约 30 位宾夕法尼亚大学计算机系和语言学系的教师和学生参加。
- 2002 年春 研究生课程 CIT594 II - 编程语言和技术的助教。该课程针对宾大计算机系的研究生开设。

……（从略）

推荐人

霍什·K·阿瑞文，博士，（joshi@linc.cis.upenn.edu, 215-898-8540）
玛莎·S·帕莫，博士，（Martha.Palmer@colorado.edu, 303-492-1300）
莱尔·H·恩格，博士，（ungar@cis.upenn.edu, 215-898-7449）

Unit 2　申请出国个人陈述

Personal Statements

　　个人陈述（Personal Statement）可以缩写为 PS，是申请材料中最重要的文件之一。通过个人陈述，你可以告诉申请学校的相关人员你的个人情况、学术能力以及学术或人生愿望。通常，**个人陈述需要具备以下六个内容：**

1. 你的个人简介，包括出生环境等，只要你觉得有助于你展现自我；
2. 你想要学习的课程或者主攻的方向是什么；
3. 你为何选择这一领域（往往可以联系到自己小时候的某某兴趣，这时候前面的铺垫就派上用场了）；
4. 你在这个领域的学术基础如何；
5. 你为什么选择该校；
6. 你对自己人生的规划。

个人陈述写作需要注意以下几点：

1. 下笔前一定要构思好，最好写好提纲；
2. 要查阅相关学校相关专业的资料，尤其是去学校官网查最新信息。了解这些信息，可以让自己的写作更有方向性、针对性，切忌乱开枪；
3. 好好展示自己的英语水平，让对方相信你的英文能力能够胜任他们的学术任务。当然，语言方面不要刻意追求华丽，给人做作之感，而要力求朴实，以情动人，以理服人。
4. 写完后自己先检查一遍，再让其他两个英文较好的人检查一遍。千万不能有拼错单词、错误的语法出现；尤其是单词的拼写，拼错会给对方留下粗心的印象。在整体布局上，也要让其他人看看是否合理。

4. 文科生

Personal Statement

Nine years ago, I was luckily chosen to be an announcer and reporter for my junior high school's broadcasting station. Since then, I have been dreaming to be a professional media worker.

In 2008, I was admitted to ABC University by majoring in radio and television journalism, an interdisciplinary science. Courses like Communication Research Methods, Mass Media and Journalism Theory help me make acquaintance with media research direction and basis research methods; News Interview and Writing and Monographic Direction teach me to combine theory with practice; Study Guides of Literature and Selective Reading of News Works let me fully perceive cultural qualities required to be a distinguished media worker. Meanwhile, I have immersed myself in some famous works so as to widen my scope of vision. "Inquisitive" and "diligent in mind" are words my teachers often use to describe me. For the past undergraduate years, I have achieved an average score of 86.16/100, ranked the fourth in my grade of 56 students, bringing home annual scholarships. My review article titled "Ant Tribe: We Don't Want Special Treatment" has won the Fujian Journalism Award (2010). Honors and awards spur a more intensive love for media industry and boost my confidence to continue what I am doing.

As for a to-be media worker, being concentrated on people's livelihood counts much. In 2009, "ant tribe" received wide attention in China. Superficially, the social phenomenon reflects impoverished lives Chinese undergraduates are suffering from. It actually mirrors a widening economic gap among urban and rural people. The red-hot topic easily attracted my attention and relevant reports were collected. In order to dig into this phenomenon, I carefully studied books or reports written by William, the first scholar who started the topic. After one-year hard work, I compiled the mentioned thesis in which I tried to view this social problem from a particular angle. It is my belief that the society should respect the tribe and encourage them to pursue their own dreams by leaving them enough time and space. They should never be treated specially. My article was later published at *fjsen.com* and granted FJSEN Annual Top Ten Reviews Award, FJSEN Q3 Top Ten Reviews Award and Fujian Journalism Award (Fujian's highest prize for news writing), which were great honors for an undergraduate. This experience made me realize that as long as one holds keen observation, he or she would find good topics ubiquitous in our daily life. I am currently focusing on microblog, a rising power in mainland which indicates China's media has been gradually moving towards democratization. Meanwhile, it also reminds me of different ways young people in mainland, Hong Kong and Taiwan use to gather information. In my view, hidden information behind the heat is of high research value.

News is always waiting to be discovered through practice. For the past years, I have taken an active part in social practice so as to acquaint myself with social trends and make clear of my vocational plans. In the summer holiday of sophomore year, I was honorably offered a chance to serve as a journalist in the 26th Summer Universiade after a round of selection. The great event allowed me to personally experience the busy life of media workers: having meetings to select topics, writing manuscripts and preparing for interviews. Sometimes, I was working hard until two or three o'clock in the morning. No matter how late I got to sleep, I had to get up at 8 a.m. and then headed to specific locations for interviews. During the internship, I wrote 150 microblogs and three articles. Two of my microblogs were later found at China Youth Daily and the article "How Kids Watch Games without Knowing Rules" got published in the newspaper "Universiade Together" and cyol.net. At the completion of this activity, I became goal-oriented.

In my junior year, I went to study as an exchange student at Shih Hsin University enjoying a high reputation in Taiwan's media circle for its eminent researches on journalism. I was like a sponge tirelessly absorbing advanced thoughts from knowledgeable and veteran teachers. The one-year study facilitated my knowledge in news and broadcasting and television journalism. Due to my brilliant academic records, I was granted the access to Fun Taiwan program. Delightedly, I was lucky enough to join its television game show-Fun Taiwan Challenge gathering over 50 senior producers and cameramen. In this internship, I studied revised scripts for a hundred of times and carefully observed how to organize a big team and turn scripts into real scenes. What worthy of mention are its production strategies. The team would like to spend a long period of time in making Production Bible episode by episode, containing detailed information and creative ideas through exchange. The internship was quite different from what I served in the mainland. It is my firm belief that Taiwan's production strategies are more effective and adjustable to modern media industry than those of the mainland. On the other hand, I am convinced that media production companies will gradually dominate the mainland's media industry in the coming future. After completing this internship, I have generated the idea of further exploring media in Hong Kong, an internationalized metropolis known for open atmosphere, updated philosophies and advanced managerial systems.

One of my teachers ever said to me, "Success is interest plus endeavor". To my firm belief, my intense interest in media, extensive knowledge, diligent mind, prudent attitude and strong communication skills will assist me in accomplishing my postgraduate studies and promoting my future success. I have the confidence that to study at your famous university will be an unforgettable experience in my life.

Thank you in advance for your time and favorable consideration.

Applicant: Zhang Yan
December 1, 2011

个人陈述

九年传媒缘，一生传媒路。从初中一次偶然的选拔机会成为了校广播电台的播音员兼记者后，我便爱上了传媒。

带着对传媒的热爱，我于2008年考入ABC大学广播电视新闻学专业。这是一门知识涵盖面十分广阔的交叉学科。四年里，通过《传播研究方法》《大众传播》《新闻学理论》等传播专业理论课程，我了解了媒体传播的研究方向和基本的分析研究方法；通过学习《新闻采访与写作》《专题片编导》等实践课程，我学习了如何将理论融会贯通与实际；通过《文学作品导读》《中外新闻作品选读》等中西文化课程，我更好地理解了一个优秀的媒体人所应具备的文化底蕴。此外，为了扩展专业知识面，我还常常阅读许多传媒界知名作品，让在自己接受更多元的传播文化观点。勤奋好学、善于思考是大学老师对我的一致评价,优异的学习成绩以及深入的学术专研能力是我四年努力学习的最大收获。四年中,我的平均成绩接近86.5分,年级排名保持在4/56,连年获得优秀学生奖学金,还凭借评论文章《不要把蚁族群体特殊化》获得了2010年福建省新闻奖……这一系列的肯定,使我对传媒的兴趣更加浓厚,并对自己能在这个领域做出成绩充满了信心。

作为一名准传媒人,我认为最重要的是要有一颗关注社会民生的心。2009年,"蚁族"这一话题铺天盖地,从表面上看这是大学毕业生的生活写照,但从深层次上却反映了我国城乡间的巨大差异。因此,这一话题引发了我浓厚的兴趣和密切关注。每次看到有关蚁族的报道或者文章,我都会收集起来。为了了解这个话题更深入的背后,我特别找来第一个调查研究"蚁族"现象的学者威廉写的《蚁族》等相关的调查报告书籍,认真地研究和分析蚁族现象的背后。经过近一年的累积研究,我完成了评论文章《不要把蚁族群体特殊化》。在这篇文章中,我尝试从另一个角度去看待这一社会话题。因为同样作为一名大学生的我,对于蚁族内心的想法深有同感。所以,我提出了社会应该尊重这些有梦想的"蚁族",给他们足够的空间和时间去实现自己的理想生活,而不要将他们特殊化。这篇文章最终发表在福建东南网,在连获了东南网年度和季度奖的同时还让我成为大学生中少有的福建新闻奖获得者(福建新闻作品类最高奖)。这是对我尝试做一个有思想的媒体人的肯定,也让我深刻地体会到好的选题就在身边,只要用心观察全心投入。正如,最近大陆兴起的微博成为了我新的关注话题,我认为微博给民众提供了一个自由发声的平台,这种强大的微博力量预示着中国的媒体已在逐步迈向民主化。同时也让我联想到了大陆的年轻人与香港、台湾地区的年轻人接受传播资讯的途径不一样。我认为,这些现象的背后都有非常高的研究价值。

一直以来,我都坚持"新闻永远在路上",因此,我不仅从理论方面学习,也积极地参与社会实践,去了解业界的发展现状,寻找自身的未来方向。大二的暑假,我通过层层选拔,成为了第26届世界大学生运动会的一名记者。在此期间,我真正体会到了什么是忙碌的媒体人生活:每天除了开选题会、写稿,还要准备第二天的采访资料,一忙就是凌晨两三点。而第二天早上八点又得准时出发到各个采访点。期间,完成150条微博、3篇稿件。两条微博发表于《中国青年报》、《不懂比赛规则的小朋友如何看比赛》发表于中青在线、《一起大运报》。当我回到课堂时,我的学习变得更有目标了。

大三,我来到台湾世新大学进行交流学习。在这所以传媒专业闻名台湾业界的大学里,我就像一块大海绵,在世新的汪洋里不停地吸收着那些来自有着渊博知识的理论老师和丰富经验的业界资深老师们的精华。这一年的学习,我对新闻、广电的理论知识有了更深刻的理解。同时,我还凭借优异的成绩申请到了 Discovery 的《疯台湾》节目实习，从中对台湾媒体制作公司为主的体制有了深入的了解。提起这次实习，我心中充满了兴奋。因为幸运的我正好赶上了《疯台湾》节目组正在筹备拍摄一季的大型节目《疯台湾大挑战》。这个节目聚集了台湾业界在这类节目上最资深的制作人和摄影师近 50 人。实习中，我除了协助研究制作 team 修改过上百遍的脚本外，还特别观察了统筹制作人如何管理规划一个如此盘大的团队，以及如何把简单的脚本化成象的执行。让我收获最大的是节目制作方式，他们用了非常长的时间制作每一集的 Production Bible，里面涵盖了节目制作会涉及的每一个细节需要的信息，那些有趣的创意就是在一次次正向思维与逆向思维的撞击中产生的。这与我在大陆的实习有很大的区别，我认为在以创意和思想为主导的媒体领域，台湾的制作方式更为高效。因此，我相信，在不久的将来，传媒制作公司也会成为大陆媒体行业的主体。这也直接激发了我到有着同样媒体氛围的香港学习媒体相关专业的想法。

香港是一个国际化的大都市，不仅具有开放的新闻言论氛围，而且在传媒理念和体制方面也比大陆走得更远。因此，我做出了到贵校学习的决定。我记得一句老话曾说过：兴趣加努力等于成功。我相信凭借浓厚的兴趣、热情、扎实的理论基础，以及勤学好问的学习态度和爱思考、爱交流的性格特点，我一定可以顺利完成学业，并取得预期的优异成绩；我也相信在贵校的学习将会是我人生中最受益的经历。

感谢您在百忙之中考虑我的申请，谢谢！

学生：张燕
2011 年 12 月 1 日

5. 理工科生

模板

Personal Statement

Studying life processes in molecular terms deeply appeals to me. I was fascinated by the importance of simple molecules, such as water molecule; playing its role as a biological solvent, reactant molecule and temperature regulator. Studying Biochemistry will enhance my interest in the structure and the functions of biological molecules. I enjoy the fact that it uses the principles and techniques of chemistry to understand basic biological process in living things. I am interested in both the practical and theoretical study of biochemistry, in this area of study I believe that I have the motivation, commitment and determination to succeed.

I am looking forward to studying Biochemistry, in particular genetics, pharmacology and neurology because I find them very fascinating and exciting. I enjoyed studying A-level chemistry, especially the biological aspect of the subject. Studying mathematics and physics at A-level allowed me to think clearly and logically, providing me with the ability to work accurately, and hence increasing my problem solving skills.

My first schooling was in 2003. I had no formal education for the first 14 years of my life due to some family reasons. Considering the disadvantages I have faced I believe that I have made huge progress, not only in the acquisition of the English language but also academically. This meant working harder than my contemporaries and I was fully prepared to do that, by working independently and teaching myself. In my gap year I want to develop myself in order to build up my self-esteem and gain self-confidence. I want to focus on the skills I wish to develop in order to contribute to a more sustainable future.

I find volunteering at Cancer Research very rewarding; allowing me to use my personal qualities to help the community and to contribute to the world and its worthy causes. It also gives me the opportunity to learn new skills and gain much needed experience, hence increasing my confidence. It is hugely fulfilling as I'm doing it out of passion and interest. I undertook a 5-week work experience at *** Hospital; spending my time at different departments, including pathology, hematology, and imaging. My duties included taking measurements, carrying out Statistical analysis using my Mathematical skills and observing the staffs performing their duties. The hematology and nuclear imaging departments were very exciting as they involve diagnosing any disease through different methods. Combining this experience with the knowledge I have gained helped me appreciate and understand not only what biochemistry is about, but also the reasons I am doing it for.

I enjoy craft work, including sewing and knitting, which increases my ability to be more creative and I'm willing to extend it to a more advanced level in my gap year. I have also enrolled in Arabic classes as my ambitions include becoming multi-lingual and broadening my horizons and interests.

I am certain that biochemistry is the right course for me because not only will it fulfill my interest in science, but also help me achieve my long term goal of becoming a Biochemist. I am looking forward to extending my knowledge and developing my analytical and research skills in order to reach my full potential.

Thank you for your time and attention. Your kind consideration will be highly appreciated.

Zhou Kang
Dec. 19th, 2011

个人陈述

　　从分子的角度来研究生命过程，这深深地吸引了我。简单分子让我着迷，他们至关重要，像水分子，既可以做生物溶剂，又可以做反应物，还可以起到温度调节器的作用。研究生物化学将会增进我对生物分子结构和功能的兴趣。这门学科利用化学的原理和技术来理解万物基本的生物学过程，这让我很感兴趣。我对生化专业的实践和理论研究都感兴趣，我相信，在生化领域的研究上，我有取得成功的动力、意志和决心。

　　我期待着研究生化学，尤其是遗传学、药理学和神经病学，因为我认为他们非常迷人，非常刺激。我喜欢学习高级化学，尤其是其中有关生物学的部分。学习高级数学和物理使我的思路清晰、有逻辑，也使我能够一丝不苟地工作，因而提高了我解决问题的能力。

　　我从 2003 年才开始受学校教育。出于一些家庭原因，我在我人生中的前 14 年都没有接受过正式教育。考虑到我曾经面临的劣势，我认为我取得了巨大的进步，不仅仅是在英语方面，在学术方面亦是如此。这意味着我比同辈人付出了更多的努力，当时通过独立工作和自学，我也为这场硬仗做好了充分准备。在毕业后，我希望继续深造，以获得自尊和自信。我想专注于自己希望提升的技能，使未来的发展更有后劲。

　　我发现在癌症研究所做志愿者大有裨益，这份工作使我能够利用自己的才能服务社区，为这个世界及慈善事业添砖加瓦。通过志愿者活动，我还学习了新的技能，获得了宝贵的经验，也增加了我的自信。因为是出于热情和兴趣，这份工作让我很充实。我在 *** 医院实习了五个星期，在病理、血液和放射等不同科工作。我在医院的职责包括：测量、利用数学知识进行数据分析，以及协助其他工作人员。血液科和放射科非常令人兴奋，因为它们通过不同的方法进行诊断。知行结合使我不仅知道了什么是生物化学，还知道了我为什么要研究它。

我喜欢做手工,包括缝纫和编织。这使我更加富有创造力,我也希望在毕业之后将其延伸到一个更高的水平。我还报班学习了阿拉伯语,因为我希望成为多语言人才,并开拓自己的眼界,发展自己的兴趣。

　　我坚信,生物化学是我正确的选择,因为它不仅能够满足我对科学的兴趣,还能够帮助我实现成为生物化学家的远期目标。我期待着自己能够博学多闻,提高自己的分析和研究能力,充分挖掘自己的潜能。

周康
2011 年 12 月 19 日

Unit 3　推荐信　　Letters of Recommendation

推荐信（Recommendation Letter）在申请材料中也占有重要的分量。它从一个第三者的角度对申请人的才能和资格做一个评价。可以说，有推荐信和没有推荐信，差别是很大的；有好的推荐信和只有一般的推荐信，差别也是很大的。申请学校时，学校一般都会要求申请者提供两到三封推荐信。

写作要素：
1. 推荐人的身份，在何种身份下认识该申请人，认识多长时间或何时认识该申请人，曾在何课程上教过该申请人。
2. 申请人的表现、学习能力、论文、成绩、全班人数和该申请人排名。
3. 申请人的工作能力和领导能力，团队合作能力等。
4. 申请人是否适合在该企业工作或在该校学习。

写作结构：
1. 推荐人与申请人的关系。推荐人是在什么环境下认识申请人，以及相识多久。申请人希望申请的哪一个学期和科系。
2. 推荐人对申请人资格评估。推荐人初识申请人时，对他有何特别的印象。举例证实推荐人对于申请人的评估结果。
3. 对于申请人个人特质的评估（如：沟通能力、成熟度、抱负、领导能力、团队工作能力，以及正直等），或是有哪些需要改进的地方。
4. 结论：推荐人对于申请人的整体评估。评估申请人完成学业以后，未来在个人和专业上的发展。申请人会为这个科系及团体带来什么贡献。

注意： 欧美文化及其重视个人信誉，因此可以说，推荐人以自己的信用向国外教授所作的推荐，是整个申请中的一个很大的变数。一些人认为写推荐信的人官衔或者行政职位越高越好，所以，他们通常都去找系主任、院长甚至校长。其实，相对来说，美国教授更注重写推荐信人的研究业绩和学术地位。如果你申请的学校正好是推荐人的母校，那么这种推荐往往会起到意想不到的良好效果。

此外，推荐信的内容应涉及自己的课外活动和社会实践活动，但建议，不要写太多的课外活动、社会实践活动以及个人性格和爱好，毕竟到美国是以做学问为主，也许美国教授更希望在信中看到你有没有搞研究的能力。如果你曾参与了某位教授的研究项目，写过不错的论文或参与过研究计划、担任过研究助理，则一定要在信中讲清。

6. 老师为学生写的推荐信（理工类）

To whom it may concern,

  This letter is to recommend Pearson Knowall for higher studies in you esteemed university. I have known Pearson for the last three years when I taught Electro mechanics to his class during his study.

  He has amicable relationship with all his peer groups. His communication skill is very effective and I consider him a person with a lot of self-confidence.

  He is very dedicated to his studies. In a class of 75 students he has been able to maintain his ranking amongst the top 5% in the class.

  With all the above points in him, I would strongly recommend him for higher studies at your esteemed university. In this connection I would even recommend his name for any scholarships that you University consider he deserves.

  If you need any further clarification, please feel free to contact me any time.

Sincerely,
Thomas Recomanda

敬启者：
  本人推荐皮尔森·诺沃同学进入贵校深造。本人教授他们班的机电科目，到现在认识皮尔森已经有三年了。
  他团结同学，善于交际，由此可见他充满了自信。
  他学习起来也非常投入。在一个有 75 名学生的班级里，他的排名能够保持在前 5%。
  综合以上各点，我强烈推荐皮尔森进入贵校深造。根据他的情况，我甚至愿意推荐他成为贵校奖学金候选人，获得任何与他的能力相当的奖学金。

如果您需要进一步的证明，请随时联系我。

诚挚的 托马斯·瑞克曼达

7. 老师为学生写的推荐信（文科类）

To Whom It May Concern,

This letter is to recommend Ms Catherine Lee to take up her Doctoral Studies in psychology in you esteemed university. During my tenure in the department of psychology in this institution I have had the opportunity to guide and assess quite a number of students who have passed with flying colors, and she is one of them.

Ms Lee has been known to me since she joined her Masters in Psychology three years back. I have found her intelligent and very sincere in her studies. She is self-motivated and always keeps ahead of her peers. With her effort and sincerity she has been able to remain at the top 5% of her class.

Ms Lee also devote some of her time to extra-curricular activities in between her studies. She is a member of the Dramatics Club and is a very good swimmer. Due to her wit and sense of humor she is very popular amongst her classmates.

Therefore I find it a pleasant duty to recommend Ms Lee for pursing her Doctoral Studies and I am confident she will excel in her studies.

I am sure you are going to consider the recommendation favorably.

Sincerely,
Jamuna Salanki
Head of Department of Psychology
*** Universtiy

敬启者：

　　本人推荐凯瑟琳·李女士到贵校进行心理学博士的深造。在担任我校心理学系教师期间，本人有幸指导并评价了颇多以优异成绩通过测试的学生，李女士就是其中之一。

　　我第一次见李女士是在三年前，当时她开始了心理学研究生的学习。我发现了她的聪颖和好学。她学习动力足，在同龄人中一直遥遥领先。由于勤奋刻苦、虚心好学，她的成绩保持在班上前5%的水平。

　　李女士在学习的空隙还会花些时间参加课外活动。她是校戏剧社社员，还是个游泳健将。幽默诙谐的她深受同学们的喜爱。

　　综上，我很高兴地推荐李女士到贵校读博。我相信，她在学习上将会出类拔萃。

　　同时我也相信，您会积极考虑本人的推荐。

诚挚的 贾木娜·沙兰吉
*** 大学心理系主任

8. 管理人员为员工深造写的推荐信

To Whom it May Concern,

　　It is my honor to recommend John Doe for matriculation into the Graduate program at your esteemed Institute. I have had the pleasure to know and work with John for the last six years. He first worked with me as an intern in the software development organization at XYZ in Syracuse, NY. Following his graduation from R Institute, I was fortunate enough to keep track of his career so that when the opportunity arose, I was able to recruit him to his current position at ABCD. The characteristics of John that attracted my attention then, and led me to hire him out of Company B last year, make it easy for me to give him an unqualified endorsement for graduate study.

　　John brings to all of his activities energy, enthusiasm, and commitment. This is to be expected in any successful member of an entrepreneurial organization, and in this regard John fits in well. Be it in the parsing of intricate algorithms in a billing system, or the establishment of best practices with an emerging technology, John consistently delivers high-quality software for our organization. This speaks to his overall intellect and ability to learn, attributes that will serve him well in graduate study.

　　While John is a relatively junior member of our organization as measured by tenure, he quickly established himself as a go-to person in the product domains in which he has worked. He has been ever-willing to work with members of our organization to share his knowledge and expertise, most notably as a presenter for presentations on product functions. He has a deep-rooted spirit of helpfulness that coupled with his quick grasp of subject matter speaks well to his potential as a teaching assistant or instructor.

What I find most engaging in John's character are his wide-ranging interests outside of software. Two of his abiding interests are game theory and economics. He can be quickly engaged in an in depth discussion, for instance, of the rationale behind EZ-Pass, or the lack-of-rationality of the financial markets. John's broad range of interests speaks well to his potential as researcher, both in bringing a wide range of theory to the research at hand, as well as carrying forward new hypotheses of interest to researchers.

John Doe is a valued member of our organization whom we have learned we can rely on, regardless of the difficulty of the task at hand or the novelty of the challenge. His combination of intelligence, commitment, perseverance, creativity, and compassionate character will certainly make him a valuable member of any academic program. I encourage you to look favorably upon his application.

Sincerely,
George Smith
(Title)
(Company)
(Address)
(Phone)
(E-mail)

敬启者：

我很荣幸推荐约翰·多尔到贵校读研。我很高兴在过去的六年里与约翰相识并共事。我们第一次共事是在纽约州希拉克斯市XYZ地区的一个软件开发机构，他当时是个实习生。他从R大学毕业后，我有幸一直关注他的就业情况，当机会成熟，我就将他聘用到了他现在ABCD的职位。约翰的品格不仅吸引了我的注意力，让我去年从B公司将他挖至我们公司，而且让我毫不犹豫地做出了无条件支持他读研的决定。

约翰给他参与的所有活动带来了活力、热情和保证。这是一个企业单位员工所要具备的，而在这点上约翰表现甚佳。无论是在开票系统中复杂算法的语法分析上，还是在某种新兴科技最佳操作模式的建立上，约翰持续不断地给我们单位带来高品质的软件。这一切证明了他的智慧和学习能力，也为他的研究生学习提供了保证。

虽然从工龄上说，约翰还是我们单位较为年轻的成员，但他很快就在其工作的产品部成为了一个不可或缺的专家。他一直乐意与同事合作，分享自己的知识和专业技能。最值得一提的是，他在众多产品讨论会上担任陈述人。他不仅具有乐于助人的精神，还能够快速抓住重点，这说明他具备了成为助教或指导员的潜力。

我认为约翰最吸引人的地方，当属他在软件开发之外还有广泛的兴趣爱好。其中两个由来已久的爱好便是游戏理论和经济学。他可以很快融入一场有深度的讨论，比如EZ-Pass背后的原理，或是金融市场的无序。约翰的广泛爱好说明了他的研究潜力，他既可以将大量的理论引入手头上的研究活动，也可以提出能够使研究者们感兴趣的新猜想。

约翰·多尔是我单位的一位重要成员，无论眼前的工作有多困难，面临的挑战如何陌生，他都是我们值得信赖的同事。他集智慧、诚信、坚毅、创新和爱心于一身，必将成为任何一个学术项目的重要成员。我希望贵处积极考虑他的申请。

诚挚的 乔治·史密斯
（头衔）
（单位）
（地址）
（电话）
（电邮）

9. 邀请推荐人写推荐信

Dear Mrs. Rebecca,

I would be really grateful to you if you can provide me a recommendation for me from your side. This letter will help me to get admission in a reputed college for my higher studies. I have written this letter to give you more information about my achievements and my life to aid you writing a recommendation letter for me.

I'd like you to focus on the various aspects of my schooling including character, academics, and activities so the University will get a broad sense of my talents.

Could you please comment on a few of these below-mentioned points in your letter?

1. My consistently good grades in the school in all the standards
2. My participation in and beyond the class.
3. My involvement in helping other students with their academics.
4. My science fair project: Evolution of Man, that was selected the Best in State.

Please inform me in case you need any other information. Your support means a lot!

Thank you.

Yours Truly,
Christian Bennington

亲爱的热贝卡女士:

倘若您能帮我写一封推荐信,我将不胜感激。希望您能帮助我进入一所著名的高校深造。随信附上关于我学业成绩和个人生活的更多信息,以帮助您撰写这封推荐信。

希望您的信中能够包括我在校的各方面表现,包括性格、学习和活动,这样一来,我所申请的大学就能对我有全面的了解。

您可否就下列的一些方面进行评价?
1. 我在各方面优异的成绩。
2. 我对课内外活动的积极参与。
3. 我对其他同学学业的热情帮助。
4. 我的科技会项目:"人类的进化"。该项目被评选为全州第一。

若有任何需要进一步了解的问题,请告诉我。您的支持意义重大!

非常感谢。

克里斯蒂安·本宁顿 谨上

10. 感谢老师写的推荐信

Dear Mrs. Smith,

I can't thank you enough for the letters of recommendation you wrote. I know you put a lot of time and effort into them and hope you know how much I appreciate it. I hope I can do the same for someone else someday.

I will keep you posted on any responses I get.

Thanks again!

            Sincerely,
            Martin

亲爱的史密斯女士：

  千言万语都道不尽我对您推荐信的感谢之情。我知道您一定在上面花费了不少的时间和精力，我希望您知道我对此的感激。愿日后我也能为他人提供同样的帮助。

  但凡校方有回函，我一定告知。

  再次谢过！

                马丁 敬启

Unit 4 申请过程中与大学的各种联络信件
Application Correspondences

申请留学是个比较复杂的过程，申请信在其中则显得格外重要，可以说是申请成功的关键。申请留学大致分为三个阶段：申请阶段、接到录取通知阶段以及动身出国阶段。由于来回往复的各种信件较多，我们在此暂且介绍几个关键步骤。

1. 索取入学申请表。这是第一步。你可以采用信函或填写索取表格的方式向所申请学校的招生办索取入学申请表以及简章等。有些申请表格可以直接到相关学校的网站上下载。填写申请表时，要写清个人信息、学习的专业、中学或大学学习的课程、其他学术背景、工作经历、英语水平等。有些大学还要求填写附表，证明经济能力。

2. 告知校方已经寄出相关材料。填写好表格后，往往可以把自己的简历、个人陈述、推荐信等材料一并寄去，同时，还需要缴纳申请费。之后申请人和校方之间往往还会展开一系列关于申请材料的信件往来，这部分经常是通过电邮完成的，既高效又经济。

3. 通知录取阶段。如果收到学校录取通知书，则需要先对校方表示感谢，然后继续询问后面的事宜，如住宿等。如果校方拒绝录取，有些同学选择就此罢休，一句话也不回复，其实我们建议还是礼貌性地回复一封。当然，如果对校方的拒绝理由不满意（往往这类同学是比较铁了心想进入那个学校的），那么还可以进行申诉（Appeal），说不定还有峰回路转的可能。

11. 索取入学申请表

Dear Sir/Madam,

I am a senior student in Xiamen University, China and I am very much interested in the Modern Languages MA Program of your university and plan to apply for admission for the Fall of 2012. I would appreciate it very much if you would send me the application forms and further information about the program. My mailing address is shown on the top of this letter.

Thank you for your kind help.

Sincerely yours,
Li Ming

敬启者：

  本人是中国厦门大学的一名大四学生，对贵校现代语言学的研究生项目颇感兴趣，希望申请 2012 年秋季入学。倘贵处能回寄入学申请表以及关于该项目的详细信息，本人将不胜感激。本人通信地址见此信上方。

  感谢您的帮助。

李明 谨上

12. 校方对索取信息的回复

Dear Mr. Chen,

  Thank you for your inquiry concerning our graduate program. I enclose an application form for financial aids and a brochure describing research activities in the Department of Computer Science. I am also enclosing a document about the general information of this department.

  Please feel free to write if you have any questions.

Very truly yours,
Ethan Miller

亲爱的陈同学：

  感谢您询问我校的研究生项目。随信附上一份资助申请表和一份介绍计算机系研究活动的手册。同时寄上一份介绍计算机系概况的文件。

  有问题请来信。

诚挚的 伊森·米勒

13. 告知校方已填好入学申请表

Dear Sir,

  Thank you very much for the information you sent me about your financial aids and the application form, which I am returning herewith, duly filled in. Also enclosed is a money order from the Bank of China of 40 U.S. dollars for the application fee.

I look forward to hearing good news from you.

Sincerely yours,
Li Ming

尊敬的先生：

十分感谢您为我寄来贵校的相关资助信息和申请表。现将正式填好的申请表，连同一张支付申请费的中国银行开具的 40 美元汇票一同寄上。

期待着您的好消息。

李明 谨上

14. 告知校方各项材料正分别寄出

模板

To whom it may concern,

Enclosed you will find my application materials for admission to Stanford for the Fall of 2012. I have included completed application forms, financial statement, academic statement and application fee.

As for other materials, I have requested ETS to send you the official reports of my TOEFL and GRE scores and my university to send the official records of my performances in the undergraduate studies. Three letters of recommendation will be mailed to you by suitable references of mine.

I would appreciate it if you could process these materials as expediently as possible. Please contact me at (+86)135 0000 0000 if there are any problems or questions. I look forward to hearing from you, and to attending Stanford.

Thank you for your time and attention.

Regards,
Li Ming

敬启者：

随函附上我申请 2012 年秋季入斯坦福大学学习的材料。其中包括填好的申请表、财力证明、读书计划和申请费。

至于其他材料，我已经请求 ETS 寄去我的 TOEFL 和 GRE 成绩正式通知单，也已请求原来大学寄去本科成绩单。三封推荐信也将由适当的推荐人寄去。

倘您能尽快处理这些材料，我将不胜感激。若出现任何困难或疑问，请通过电话(+86)135 0000 0000 联系我。期待您的来信，也期待进入斯坦福大学学习。

感谢拨冗阅信。

李明 敬启

15. 询问申请材料是否收到

To whom it may concern,

    I am a Chinese applicant to your university's Linguistics MA Program. I am writing to confirm whether you have received my application package via mail to the graduate admissions office about three weeks ago. Please let me know if anything is missing.

    Thank you for your assistance with this matter and I look forward to hearing from you.

Sincerely yours,
Li Ming

敬启者：

    本人是贵校语言学研究生项目的一名中国申请者。来函确认贵处可否收到三周前本人通过邮局寄去的申请材料。若有任何遗漏，烦请告知。

    感谢帮助。静候佳音。

李明 谨上

16. 告知校方 TOEFL 和 GRE 成绩已寄出

Dear Sir,

    Thank you for your letter regarding my TOEFL and GRE scores.

    I took the TOEFL and GRE examinations at the beginning of this year. I have written to the ETS and received a reply. They have agreed to send my scores to you as soon as possible.

To my knowledge, all my credentials have been sent to you or requested to send to you till now. Your kind attention to my application is much appreciated.

              Faithfully yours,
              Li Ming

敬启者：

  感谢您来信询问我的 TOEFL 和 GRE 成绩。

  我今年年初参加了这两项考试。我已给 ETS 去函，并已收到回函。他们已同意尽快将我的材料寄往你处。

  据我所知，到目前为止，我的所有证明材料都已被寄往或是要求被寄往你处。谢谢您对我申请的关注。

              诚挚的 李明

17. 告知已按要求补寄经济资助证明和成绩单等

Dear Sir,

Thank you for your message dated November 4th, 2011, with reference to my application materials.

As requested, I have enclosed a completed financial certificate and score reports from my current university, and hope that they can reach you in good condition.

If you need any further information concerning my application, please let me know.

Thank you for your time and attention.

              Sincerely yours,
              Li Ming

敬启者：

  感谢贵处 2011 年 11 月 4 日关于本人申请材料的来信。

  本人现已按要求附上一份本人当前就读大学开具的完整经济证明和成绩单，望贵处悉数收毕。

  若在申请问题上还需任何材料，烦请告知。

劳烦览信，本人不胜感激。

李明 敬启

18. 询问申请进展情况

Dear Sir/Madam,

  I am writing to inquire into the status of my application. I applied for admission into Law School at your university, and my application number is 00000. Can I check my application status on line now? When can I find out about the admission results?

  I look forward to hearing from you regarding my application status.

  Thank you!

Sincerely,
Li Ming

敬启者：
  本人望询问申请贵校的进展情况。本人申请进入贵校的法律系学习，申请号为00000。请问现在我可以在网上查看申请状态吗？我何时才能查出申请结果？
  敬候佳音。
  谢谢！

李明 谨上

19. 录取通知书

Dear Mr. Sun,

  It is my pleasure to inform you, on behalf of the economics department, of your admission to the Ph. D. program at X University beginning September, 2012. The size and strength of our applicant pool is such that only the strongest candidates can be admitted, and our offer of admission to you reflects our great confidence in your potential as an economist. The quality of the faculty and graduate students, combined with an outstanding academic atmosphere, makes the Economics Department a unique place to pursue graduate study. We hope that you will join the department in September.

The X Economics Department is committed to continuing financial support of all graduate students in the department. Students in good standing will receive full tuition plus stipend in the form of Teaching and Research Assistantships for the duration of their graduate studies towards the Ph.D. degree. The University has not yet set the stipends for the 2012-2013 academic year. However, last year the stipend from Teaching and Research assistantships was $15,000, and we expect a modest increase for the 2012-2013 academic year.

Successful applicants ordinarily have a number of offers from which they must choose. In reaching a decision, you may find it helpful to communicate directly with our faculty members or graduate students whose interests parallel your own. Please feel free to call our student services officers, Katherine Lee at (000) 0000000, if you need assistance in obtaining names or phone numbers of people to talk to.

The high quality of our students is a distinguishing feature of our program. To facilitate planning and arrangement, we would like to hear your response to this offer as soon as you have made a decision, but in any case, no later than the formal deadline of April 30, 2012.

Sincerely yours,
Joseph R. Flood
Professor of Economics
Chair, Graduate Admissions Committee

亲爱的孙先生：

我谨代表经济学系，很高兴地通知您，您已经获得了X大学2012年九月博士生入学资格。此次申请者人数众多，实力强劲，因此只有最强的申请者才有资格被录取。而这份录取通知书正反映出了我们坚信您有成为一名经济学家的潜质。经济学系师资雄厚，生源一流，加之学术氛围浓厚，这些都使其成为不可多得的研习之地。我们期待您在九月份的加入。

X大学的经济学院一直致力于给所有研究生提供经济资助。优秀学生将获得学费全免外加薪金，薪金即学生在研究生到博士生的学习过程中担任助教或是科研助理所获得的报酬。我校暂时还没有定下2012-2013学年的薪金数额。但去年的助教助理薪金水平是15 000美元,预计今年会有适度的增加。

成功的申请者一般都会有众多学校供其选择。为了帮助自己决策,您可以直接与我校的教师或是兴趣一致的研究生进行交流。如果您需要获得咨询人的姓名或手机号,请随时拨打我们学生处老师凯瑟琳·李的电话(000)0000000。

一流的生源是我系研究生部的特点。为方便筹划和安排,我们希望您做出决定后尽快回复此函,但无论如何,请最迟于2012年4月30日前给予答复。

诚挚的 约瑟夫·R·弗拉德
经济学教授
研究生招录委员会主席

20. 拒绝通知书

Dear Sir,

Your application for admission to Cambridge has been reviewed. It is my unpleasant duty to inform you that we are unable to approve your admission.

The volume of application for admission received by Cambridge far exceeds the number of students we are able to accommodate and, as a result, admission is a selective process and highly competitive, for this reason we are able to accept only a limited number of undergraduate international students who present outstanding records of previous academic achievement. Your application was considered in competition with those of other undergraduate international applicants. Unfortunately, we were not able to select you for admission.

We appreciate your interest in Cambridge and your understanding of the circumstances which place a limit on the number of students that we are able to accept. Our decision on your application does not in any way reflect on your ability to continue your education and we hope that you will not be discouraged form investigating the many opportunities that may be available to you at other institutions of higher education.

Sincerely yours,
David J. Smith

尊敬的先生：

我们审核了您给剑桥大学的申请书。但是，遗憾地告知您我们不能接受您的申请。

本校所收到的申请人数大大超过了我们可以招收的学生人数，竞争非常激烈，我们只能从中有选择地录取。因此，我们只招收了海外有限数目的成绩优异的大学本科毕业生。我们将您的成绩与别人的作了比较，但没能选择您。

非常感谢您对剑桥大学的兴趣和您对我们限制人数的理解。我们的决定丝毫不能说明您不能继续深造。希望您不要灰心，继续去其他高校寻找机会。

大卫·J·史密斯 谨上

21. 申请者表示同意入学

Dear Sir,

Thank you very much for your letter, stating that my application for admission to the undergraduate program at the University of Northern Plains has been accepted and approved. It is an honor to notify you that I intend to enroll as an undergraduate, with my coursework beginning as of the fall semester of this year.

Please let me know what the next steps are, and I will be pleased to proceed with planning. I look forward to being a student at your fine university. Thank you again.

Sincerely,
Li Ming

敬启者：

非常感谢您来信告知北部平原大学研究生院已经接受并通过了我的入学申请。很荣幸地通知您，我愿意成为贵校的研究生，于今年秋季入学。

请告知接下来我需要做的事，我希望有计划地完成整个过程。期待成为贵校的学生。再次致谢。

李明 谨上

22. 申请者谢绝入学

Dear Sir,

Thank you very much for admitting me to your prestigious university. But I regret to inform you that before your letter arrived, I had accepted an offer of admission from another institution.

Your assistance to my application, however, is appreciated and I will never forget it. Thank you again for admitting me to your university.

Sincerely yours,
Li Ming

敬启者：

非常感谢贵校录取。但是我很遗憾地告诉您，在您的信到来之前，我已然接受了另外一所学校的录取。

然而，我仍然非常感谢您在我申请过程中的帮助，对此我将永远铭记。再次感谢贵校的录取。

李明 谨上

23. 询问住宿问题

To whom it may concern,

I am already recruited by your esteemed university, and I have several questions about your housing situation.

Is on-campus housing available? If so, what does it cost and how do I apply? If on-campus housing is not available, is there off-campus housing in close proximity to the campus? What are my best resources for finding such housing?

Please contact me with any housing information you may have available, or please direct me to someone who can provide such information, such as a local real estate agent. I look forward to your reply.

Thank you very much for your time.

Regards,

Jim Karter

敬启者：

  本人已被贵校录取，现有几个关于住宿的问题。

  请问可以住校吗？如果可以，费用如何，怎样申请？如果不可，请问校外有邻近学校的住宿吗？要获得这样的住宿，最好查看什么信息？

  若您有任何关于住宿的信息，烦请联系我，或者将拥有这类信息的联系人的联系方式告知，比如当地的房地产中介。敬候佳音。

  感谢拨冗阅信。

吉米·卡尔特 敬启

24. 申请住校

To whom it may concern,

  I accept your kind offer of a full-time scholarship with deep appreciation. This is to inform you that I wish to enroll in September. I am preparing for the enrollment now. I wish to live on campus.

  If possible, would you please book me a two-bedroom apartment shared with an American boy student?

  Thank you very much for your assistance.

Sincerely yours,
Li Ming

敬启者：

  非常感谢贵校给我的全额奖学金。我写此信是告知您我决定9月份到贵校报到。现在正为报到做准备，并希望能够住校。

  如果可能，您能否帮我订一间和美国男学生合住的双人房间？

  多谢您的帮助。

李明 谨上

25. 申请延期入学

To whom it may concern,

  I am writing to apply for a three-month deferment of my enrollment at your university as my grandfather is sick and I have to take care of him for several months. I was raised up by him and I just can't leave him here and go to the US.

Would you please let me know your acceptance of the deferment as soon as possible?

Should it require a fee or deposit to hold my place, please do not hesitate to contact me. Thank you in advance for your assistance. I look forward to attending your university then.

Thanks for your time and consideration.

Very truly yours,
Li Ming

敬启者：

由于本人祖父生病，需要本人照料数月，因此本人希望申请延期三个月入学。本人从小由祖父带大，断不可前去美国而置其不顾。

请问可否尽快告知这份申请的通过情况？

倘若保留本人的入学资格需要额外的费用或是定金，请随时联系我。提前感谢您的帮助。期待进入贵校学习。

对您付出的宝贵时间和慎重考量，本人不胜感激。

李明 谨上

26. 通知校方已获得护照和签证

Dear Sir,

This is to inform you that I am going well with the preparation for the forthcoming trip to the United States. I have obtained my passport and visa. The travel agency is arranging my journey. As soon as my travel plan comes out, I will notify you of the time of my arrival.

Looking forward to meeting you in Yale.

Yours sincerely,
Li Ming

尊敬的先生：

　　写此信是通知您我的赴美准备工作一切顺利。我已经拿到了护照和签证，旅行社正在安排我的行程。一旦行程敲定，我会马上告知您我到达的时间。

　　期待早日在耶鲁见到您。

李明 谨上

Unit 5　申请奖学金　　　　Scholarship

奖学金是大家都非常关心的问题。奖学金有以下几种（这所有奖学金都可以统称为 Scholarship）：

1. Fellowship：这是大家最喜欢的一种奖学金，不干活白拿钱，而且不用缴税；即使缴的话，税率还比 TA 或者 RA 低。
2. Tuition Scholarship：帮你出全部或者部分学费。
3. Teaching Assistantship（TA）：助教，一般是 1/2 的助教，教课、改作业、批卷子、组织本科学生讨论，一周一般干 20 小时的活，任务比较固定。1/2 的意思是一周只需要工作 20 小时（全职工作是每周 40 个小时，20 个小时正好是 1/2）。去当 TA，但是没有考过 TSE 的，一般学校会提前给你 TA 培训，这一般会要求你要比其他的人提前入学，不过这个培训也是学校出钱，所以不必担心。
4. Research Assistantship（RA）：助研，一般就是帮忙在实验里打工，这个工作的辛苦程度就要看你老板要你去干什么了，可能没什么活干，那将非常轻松；也可能有很多活，比较累。这个和教授有关。

申请奖学金的态度要诚恳，说清为什么申请，并且展示自己申请的资质（尤其在学术方面的）。

27. 提出奖学金申请

Dear Mr. Hall,

　　Your prominent school has the reputation of producing great nurses. A while ago, I heard the news that your school is giving out hundreds of scholarship to those who are commendable and wanted to become a professional nurse.

　　I want to grab this chance and apply for scholarship. I am a caregiver graduate and wanted to learn more on how to become a full pledge nurse. I would be truly delighted if you can check out and view my scholarship application.

 I want to be a part of your great college and learn more about nursing. Please do find my profile, essay and other qualifications that are attached here with my application letter. Hope that you will call me back soon.

Sincerely Yours,
Douglas A. York

尊敬的霍尔先生：

 贵校盛产护士，声名远播。不久前，本人听说贵校发放了数百个奖学金名额，奖励那些优秀而有志成为专业护士的学生。

 本人希望争取这次申请奖学金的机会。本人是一名护理研究生，希望进一步学习如何成为一名真正的护士。倘若贵校能检查并审核我的奖学金申请，本人将非常高兴。

 本人希望成为贵校的一员，学习更多护理知识。请接收本人的简历、论文和其他随函附上的资质证明。期待早日回复。

道格拉斯·A·约克 谨上

28. 索取奖学金申请表

Dear Sir,

 I should like to apply for one of the scholarships that your department may be offering to students from other countries. Would you please send me the necessary application forms and any further details about the scholarships?

 I am a postgraduate student of University of Science and Technology Beijing. I major in microelectronics engineering, and do some research work during my study years. I hope to have a further study and continue to do my research work if I succeed in obtaining the engineering scholarship.

 Enclosed please find two letters of recommendation and my score report card. Thank you for your consideration. I look forward to your reply.

Respectfully yours,
Li Ming

敬启者：

　　本人有意申请贵系的外国留学生奖学金。请问可否寄来必要的申请表和任何有关奖学金的更多细节？

　　我是一名北京科技大学的学生。我的专业是微电子工程，在学习期间还做一些研究工作。如果我成功获得工程奖学金，我希望进行更深入的学习，并继续我的研究工作。

　　随函附上我的两封推荐信以及成绩单。感谢您的工作。静候佳音。

李明 敬启

29. 寄回填好的奖学金申请表

Dear Sir,

　　I am returning herewith, duly completed, the application form for scholarship which you have kindly sent me. Thank you again for your time and assistance.

Sincerely yours,
Li Ming

敬启者：

　　承蒙您的好意，寄给我奖学金申请表格。现已按要求填好，随函寄回给您。再次感谢您百忙之中的帮助。

诚挚的 李明

30. 感谢给予奖学金

Dear Mr. Alexander,

　　I wanted to show my great appreciation for awarding me the Civil Engineering Scholarship for two years. I want to thank you for providing the opportunity to continue my studies in your college. I am very grateful that with the entire applicants that applied for the scholarship, I was chosen to be one of those recipients.

　　I also want to pledge, that I will do my very best in my studies in order to get high grades every semester and graduate with flying colors from your university.

Once again, thank you so much for granting me the scholarship and for giving me the opportunity to let my dreams come true.

            Yours Truly,
            Kimberly C. Gregory

尊敬的亚历山大先生：

  我要对您给予我为期两年的土木工程奖学金表示深深的感谢。要感谢您给我机会在贵校继续深造。能在众多申请者中被选中，我深表感激。

  同时，我保证将会尽全力学习深造，争取每个学期都拿到好成绩，以优异的成绩毕业。

  再次感谢颁发奖学金，也感谢您给我实现梦想的机会。

            金伯利·C·格雷戈里 谨上

Unit 6　经济资助（助学金）及资助证明
Financial Aid & Certificates

校方提供的经济资助（Financial Aid），从某种程度上来说，也可以看成是奖学金，有些地方就把它归类为奖学金，这类资助有我们中国大学的"勤工俭学"的意思。有时经济资助不仅仅是校方提供的，还有家长、国家、公司单位等等，这类一般就是真正意义上的"资助"了。

经济资助证明对于申请人的成功申请有着至关重要的作用，若在这一关卡住，那么前面的一切努力都化为乌有。资助证明由资助人开具，说明申请人有足够的经济能力支付学习、访问以及在外生活的一切费用。以下几点需要注意：

1. 对于格式，每个学校没有统一标准。有些学校有一封写好的证明书，只需资助人或担保人填写。
2. 财力表现方式不限，可以是定期存款、活期存款、支票存款或是有价证券、国库公债、股票等形式。只要能显示其票额足够即可。
3. 开户人不一定是本人，可以是申请人的家人、亲戚、朋友，但要写清与申请人的关系。
4. 证明具有法律效力，一定要慎重填写。

31. 递交申请材料

To whom it may concern,

Enclosed you will find my completed financial aid application and all necessary information. Please examine the enclosed material to ensure that it has been filled out correctly and that no crucial information is missing.

If there is anything else you require to make your decision, please do not hesitate to contact me. I look forward to hearing from you soon.

Thank you.

　　　　　　　　　　　　　　　　　　　　　　Regards,
　　　　　　　　　　　　　　　　　　　　　　Jim Karter

敬启者：

随函附上本人填好的经济资助申请表和所有必要的信息。请检查附件中的材料，确保其填写正确，并且没有重要信息遗漏。

如果您在做出决定前还需要其他材料，请随时联系我。静候佳音。

谢谢。

吉米·卡尔特 谨上

32. 询问申请进展

To whom it may concern,

On February 8th I mailed you my completed application and additional information to be considered as a candidate for the X financial aid program. To date, I have not received any word from you regarding the results of that submission.

Please contact me at your earliest convenience and let me know whether or not I have been selected to receive financial aid, or whether you are still making your decisions. The information will help me make some of my plans for the coming year. You may reach me at 000 0000.

Thank you very much.

Regards,
Jim Karter

敬启者：

2月8日，本人向您寄去了填讫的 X 经济资助项目申请表以及其他信息。到目前为止，本人尚未收到贵处关于那份申请的任何回复。

烦请尽快告知本人是否已获得经济资助，或者是否贵处依然处于决定阶段。申请结果将影响到我来年的计划。您可以致电 000 0000 联系本人。

非常感谢。

吉米·卡尔特 谨上

33. 学校通知获得经济资助

Dear Mr. Maniscalco,

It is our pleasure to inform you that our college, Fulton Institute, has selected you to be this year's sponsorship recipient. As you know, Fulton Institute has been existed for 35 years, being renowned for its high achievers annually.

We are happy to inform you that your application for a tuition fee waver has been approved for the first year of your college studies, with possible sponsorship in the following year depending on your first year results. The Institute's board of trustees is proud to finance $1,500 towards your education to cultivate the potential we believe, is in you for excellence.

Please respond to this scholarship offer before the end of this month to facilitate the sponsorship progress.

We hope to hear from you soon.

Ms. Jenny Baker
Fulton Institute
Scholarship Department

亲爱的玛尼思卡尔克：

非常高兴地通知您，富尔顿学院已经将您选为经济资助受益人。如您所知，富尔顿学院建院35年，以每年送出成功的毕业生闻名遐迩。

很高兴地告诉您，您关于减免学费的申请已经获得通过，您入学第一年的学费将被减免，若第一年成绩优异，次年也可能获得减免待遇。院董事会很荣幸资助您1 500美元教育费用，我们相信您有出类拔萃的潜质，而这笔资金将助您将这种潜力开发出来。

请在月底前回复此函，推进申请进程。

静候佳音。

杰尼·贝克
富尔顿学院奖学金部

34. 感谢提供经济资助

To whom it may concern,

I just wanted to write a brief note to express my sincere thanks and great pleasure at having been selected to receive financial aid from the X program. This will go a long way toward helping reach my educational and career goals.

    Thank you again for selecting me.

Regards,

Jim Karter

敬启者：

    短短此函谨向贵校给予本人 X 项目经济资助表示诚挚的感谢，本人非常高兴。这对本人实现学术和职业目标将大有裨益。

    再表谢意。

吉米·卡尔特 谨上

35. 国家留学基金管理委员会出具的公派资助证明

China Scholarship Council

March 5, 2011

To whom it may concern,

    This is to certify that Mr. Lai Jinde has been awarded a scholarship under the State Scholarship Fund to pursue his research in the United States as a visiting scholar. The awardee was selected through a rigid academia evaluating process organized by China Scholarship Council (CSC) in 2010. The scholarship totals $17,000 (covering the international airfare, stipend, and other necessary allowances) for a period of 12 months. The Education Section of the Chinese Embassy for the Chinese Consulate General in your country is entrusted by CSC to look after the welfare of the awardee and make the payment to the individual.

    CSC is a non-profit institution affiliated with the Ministry of Education of the P.R. China. It is entrusted by the Chinese Government with the responsibilities of managing the State Scholarship Fund and other related affairs. It sponsors Chinese citizens to study abroad and international students to study in China.

    In accordance with the laws and regulations and related policies, the awardee has signed CSC an "Agreement for Study Abroad for CSC Sponsored

Chinese Citizens". In this notarized Agreement, the awardee promises to return to China upon completion of his research within the set time.

中国国家留学基金管理委员会

敬启者：

兹证明赖金德先生获得中国国家奖学金基金下的奖学金，以此帮助其完成访学研究的工作。该获奖人在 2010 年由中国国家留学基金管理委员会（CSC）组织的一个严格的学术评价体系中脱颖而出。该奖学金共计 17 000 美元（包括国际航班、薪金和其他必要的津贴），期限是 12 个月。中国驻贵国总领事馆的中国使馆教育部门受 CSC 委托，负责关照获奖人福利并为其颁发奖金。

CSC 是中华人民共和国教育部下属的一个非营利性的机构。它受中国政府委托，负责管理国家留学基金以及其他相关事务。CSC 支持中国公民赴境外留学，也支持外国来华留学生。

根据法律法规和相关政策，获奖人与 CSC 签署了《中国国家留学基金管理委员会资助中国公民留学协议》。协议中，获奖人保证在规定时间内完成研究后返回中国。该协议已经公证。

2011 年 3 月 5 日

36. 单位出具的公派资助证明

To whom it may concern,

This is to certify that Li Ming has received the financial support from ABC Company to pursue a one-year study abroad. Li Ming has received a financial support totaling $12,000 covering international airfares, stipend and other allowances. Li Ming is now a promising employee in our company, and is permitted to study at Oxford University form September 1, 2012 to August 20, 2013.

Yours faithfully,
Zhang Wei

敬启者：

兹证明李明获得 ABC 公司的经济资助，进行一年的出国学习。李明获得了共计 12 000 美元的经济资助，其中包括国际航班、薪金和其他津贴。李明现为我公司一位很有潜力的员工，并被牛津大学录取，上课时间是 2012 年 9 月 1

日至 2013 年 8 月 20 日。

张伟 谨上

37. 家长资助证明

To whom it may concern,

I, Mr. Li Jianguo, will support my son, Mr. Li Ming, during his 24 months study at Cambridge University.

I have attached bank statement of RMB 400,000, which amounts to USD 63,000 in total and assure that I can support his study with the money shown here and other funds not indicated here.

If you need any further information, please do not hesitate to contact me.

Sincerely yours,
Li Jianguo

敬启者:

  本人李建国将为儿子李明在剑桥大学为期 24 个月的学习进行经济资助。

  随函附上一份共计 40 万元人民币，约合 6.3 万美元的银行对账单，并保证本人可以用此单上显示以及未有显示的资金对其学习进行资助。

  若您还需要任何其他信息，请随时联系本人。

李建国 谨上

38. 家长担保函

Letter of Supporting

(time)

To: British Embassy

Dear Sir or Madam:

  I am the applicant Li Ming's father and guarantor for his study in Britain, Li Jianguo. I have been working as the sales manager in ABC Co. Ltd. since 2001 with annual income RMB 180,000 (excluding year-end bonus) after tax. For better development in the future, my son, Li Ming decided to go to Britain for further study. I am willing to provide my savings RMB 550,000 to support my son. I guarantee that my son Li Ming will have no economic difficulties in Britain and obey the laws and regulations. I am willing to bear all the responsibility if any problems happen.

　　Please give kind consideration to my son Li Ming's visa application. Thanks a lot!

　　I hereby to guarantee.

Li Jianguo
Signature: _____

担保信

致：英国大使馆：
尊敬的签证官先生/女士：

　　我是申请人李明的父亲兼其在英国留学的担保人——李建国，2001年至今工作于ABC有限公司，任销售部经理一职，年薪为人民币18万元（税后，不含年终奖金）。我儿李明为了将来能有更广阔的就业前景，计划赴英国学习，我愿意提供我的积蓄55万人民币的银行存款作为他赴英国留学的费用。我保证我儿子李明在英国期间不会在经济方面遇到任何困难，并保证他不会触犯任何法律，若有任何问题，我愿意承担一切责任！

　　希望签证官对我儿子李明的签证申请给予善意的考虑，谢谢！
　　特此担保！

李建国
签名：_____
（时间）

39. 资助人的单位收入证明

Certificate of Employment

To whom it may concern,

　　This is to certify that Mr. Li Ming, an interpreter of ABC Company, has worked in this company since the year 2005. He has an annual income (before tax) of RMB 120,000, including salary, rewards, and year-end bonus (His personal income tax is deducted by relevant department automatically).

Sincerely yours,
Zheng Qingyuan

单位收入证明

敬启者:

  兹证明李明先生是 ABC 公司的口译员,自 2005 年起在我公司工作。李先生税前年薪为人民币 120,000 元,其中包括薪水、奖励和年终奖金(其个人收入所得税已由有关部门自动扣除)。

郑清远 谨上

Unit 7　学历、学位、奖励、工作经历证明
Relevant Certificates

无论是申请学校还是签证，学历证明、成绩单等都是非常必要的证明材料。这些文件都是校方和签证官做出决定的重要依据，用以判断申请人是否有能力完成学习和是否有资格得到签证。这些材料都需要有申请人就读学校的印章。一般来说，申请人都会有一份中文的证明和成绩单。但在申请出国留学时，往往要先翻译成英文。一般来说，翻译稿的格式要尽量靠近原稿，然后再在适当的地方标注此为"the translation of the original piece"字样，翻译件同样要盖上学校公章。

成绩单也是如此，翻译件格式要尽量接近原件格式，也需要盖上学校的公章。由于成绩单往往是一个巨大的表格，而且比较复杂，因此本单元暂不举例。

同时，在申请过程中由于提到了自己的一些奖励情况、工作经历，因此有时有必要向校方提供这方面的证明。这就需要找奖状颁发单位以及工作单位的相关部门索取证明了。如果证明是中文，需将其翻译为英文，同时注上此为翻译件。原件和翻译件都需盖上相关部门的公章。证明的信件一般言简意赅，用语正式严肃。工作证明可以适当写长一些，加上一些对申请人的评价等。

40. 本科学历证明

Education Certification

This is to certify that student ***(name), ***(gender), born in *** (Month), *** (Year), studied a *** -year undergraduate course at *** University from *** (Month), *** (Year) to *** (Month). *** (Year), majoring in ***. Having passed all courses stipulated in the teaching program, the above student received a graduation certificate in *** (Month), ***(Year)

(certificate serial number: ***)

Academic Affairs Office
*** University
Dare: Year-Month-Day

学 历 证 明 书

　　同学，（性别），***年***月***日生。***年***月至***年***月在我校***专业完成了***年制本科教学计划规定的全部课程，成绩合格，于***年***月取得毕业证书。

　　（证书编号：***）

*** 大学教务处（盖章）
*** 年 *** 月 *** 日

41. 硕士学历证明

Education Certification

　　This is to certify that student ***(name), ***(gender), born in *** (Month), *** (Year), studied a *** -year postgraduate course at *** University from ***(Month), *** (Year) to *** (Month). *** (Year), majoring in ***. Having passed all courses stipulated in the teaching program, the above student received a graduation certificate in *** (Month), *** (Year).

　　(certificate serial number: ***)

Academic Affairs Office
*** University
Dare: Year-Month-Day

学 历 证 明 书

　　同学，（性别），***年***月生。***年***月至***年***月在我校***专业完成了***年制研究生教学计划规定的全部课程，成绩合格，于***年***月取得毕业证书。

　　（证书编号：***）

*** 大学教务处（盖章）
*** 年 *** 月 *** 日

42. 本科学位证明

Academic Degree Certification

　　This is to certify that student *** (name), ***(gender), born in ***

(Month), ***(Year), studied a ***-year undergraduate course at Soochow University from*** (Month), *** (Year) to *** (Month), *** (Year), majoring in *** The student has duly completed the program and graduated. a Bachelor Degree of *** is hereby conferred on the student in *** (Month), *** (Year) through verification in accordance with the requirement of PRC Regulations of Academic Degrees.

(certificate serial number:***)

Academic Affairs Office
Soochow University
Date:

学 位 证 明

学生 ***(姓名)，***（性别），*** 年 *** 月生。自 *** 年 *** 月至 *** 年 *** 月在我校 *** 专业完成了 *** 年制本科学习计划，现已毕业。经审核符合《中华人民共和国学位条例》的规定，*** 年 *** 月授予学士学位证书。

（证书编号：***）

苏州大学教务处（盖章）
*** 年 *** 月 *** 日

43. 硕士学位证明

Academic Degree Certification

This is to certify that student *** (name), ***(gender), born in *** (Month), ***(Year), studied a ***-year postgraduate course at Soochow University from*** (Month), *** (Year) to *** (Month), *** (Year), majoring in *** The student has duly completed the program and graduated. a Master Degree of *** is hereby conferred on the student in *** (Month), ***(Year) through verification in accordance with the requirement of PRC Regulations of Academic Degrees.

(certificate serial number:***)

Academic Affairs Office
Soochow University
Date:

学位证明

　　学生 ***(姓名)，***（性别），*** 年 *** 月生。自 *** 年 *** 月至 *** 年 *** 月在我校 *** 专业完成了 *** 年制研究生学习计划，现已毕业。经审核符合《中华人民共和国学位条例》的规定，*** 年 *** 月授予硕士学位证书。

　　（证书编号：***）

苏州大学教务处（盖章）

*** 年 *** 月 *** 日

44. 奖励证明

To whom it may concern,

　　This is to certify that Miss Han Can, a senior student in the English Department of China Foreign Affairs University, received three *** Awards, which only students among the top 5 percent are entitled.

China Foreign Affairs University

Nov. 12, 2011

敬启者：

　　兹证明韩灿，外交学院英语系大四学生，曾三度荣获 *** 奖学金，此项殊荣仅排名前 5% 的优等生才有资格获得。

外交学院

2011 年 11 月 12 日

45. 工作经历证明

Working Certificate

21/12/2011

To British Embassy

Whom It May Concern,

　　ABC Development Co. Ltd. was founded in 1995 with the registered capital of RMB20,000,000. We mainly deal with X.

　　Mr. Li Ming has been working in our company since 1995. Due to his outstanding working behavior, Mr. Li was promoted to the sales manager.

Mr. Li worked hard and had opening up wide market for our company, which made our company has a stable position in the keener competition. His yearly salary is RMB 48,000 and his personal income tax has been deducted and paid by our company.

For better development in the future, Mr. Li decided to go to Britain for further study. Our company needs high-qualified manager, so we totally agree with his study plan and sincerely hope that Mr. Li can come back to our company for further work after finishing his study.

Please do not hesitate to contact us if you require any further information!

Hereby certified!

Liao Kaige
General Manager
ABC Co. Ltd.
Dec. 12. 2011

工作证明

ABC 有限公司成立于 1995 年，注册资金为人民币贰仟万元。公司的经营范围主要包括 X。

李明先生于 1995 年加入我公司，后因工作业绩突出，被提升为销售部经理。李先生工作认真负责，为我公司开发了广阔的市场，使公司在竞争激烈的市场中占据了一席之地。公司给予李明的年薪为人民币 4.8 万元，其个人所得税由我公司代扣代缴。

李先生为了将来在国内有更好的发展，决定赴英国留学深造，我公司也十分需要高素质的管理人才，所以我们十分赞同其留学计划并真诚欢迎李明先生学成回国后能继续在我公司从事工作。如有进一步需要，欢迎与我公司取得联系！

特此证明！

总经理．廖凯歌
ABC 有限公司
2011 年 12 月 21 日

特别奉献

一 世界著名高校名称中英对照

1. Harvard University US
   哈佛大学 美国
2. Massachusetts Institute of Technology US
   麻省理工学院 美国
3. University of Cambridge UK
   剑桥大学 英国
4. University of California Berkeley US
   加州大学伯克利分校 美国
5. Stanford University US
   斯坦福大学 美国
6. University of Oxford UK
   牛津大学 英国
7. Princeton University US
   普林斯顿大学 美国
8. University of Tokyo Japan
   东京大学 日本
9. Yale University US
   耶鲁大学 美国
10. California Institute of Technology US
    加州理工学院 美国

特别奉献

二 世界名校校训中英文对照

1. Oxford University: The lord is my illumination.
   牛津大学：上帝赐予我们知识。

2. Cambridge University: Here is light and sacred draughts. (Hinc lucem et pocula sacra.)

   剑桥大学：求知学习的理想之地。

3. University of Edinburgh: The learned can see twice.

   爱丁堡大学：智者能看到表象，也能发现内涵。

4. Harvard University: Let Plato be your friend, and Aristotle, but more let your friend be truth.

   哈佛大学：以柏拉图为友，以亚里士多德为友，更要以真理为友。

5. Yale University: Truth and light.

   耶鲁大学：真理、光明。

6. Princeton University: In the Nation's service and in the service of all nations.

   普林斯顿大学：为国家服务，为世界服务。

7. Columbia University: In the light shall we see light.

   哥伦比亚大学：在上帝的启示下我们寻找知识。

8. Dartmouth College: A voice crying in the wilderness.

   达特茅斯学院：广漠大地上（对知识）的呼唤。

9. United States Millitary Academy at West Point: Duty, Honor, Country.

   西点军校：职责、荣誉、国家。

10. University of Michigan: Art, Science, Truth.

    密歇根大学：艺术、科学、真理。

11. Toronto University: As a tree with the passage of time.

    多伦多大学：像大树一样茁壮成长。

12. London University: Let everyone come to the university and merit the first prize.

    伦敦大学：我们为至高荣誉齐聚于此。

13. University of Cape Town: Good hope.

    开普敦大学：美好的希望。

14. University of Sydney: Although the stars are changed, our spirit is same.

    悉尼大学：繁星纵变，智慧永恒。

特别奉献

三 美国各州州名中英对照

Alabama 亚拉巴马州 –AL
Alaska 阿拉斯加州 –AK
Arizona 亚利桑那州 –AZ
Arkansas 阿肯色州 –AR
California 加利福尼亚州 –CA
Colorado 科罗拉多州 –CO
Connecticut 康涅狄格州 –CT
Delaware 特拉华州 –DE
Florida 佛罗里达州 –FL
Georgia 佐治亚州 –GA
Hawaii 夏威夷 –HI
Idaho 爱达荷州 –ID
Illinois 伊利诺伊州 –IL
Indiana 印第安纳州 –IN
Iowa 艾奥瓦（衣阿华）州 –IA
Kansas 堪萨斯州 –KS
Louisiana 路易斯安那州 –LA
Maine 缅因州 –ME
Massachusetts 马萨诸塞州（麻省）-MA
Maryland 马里兰州 –MD
Michigan 密歇根（密执安）州 –MI
Minnesota 明尼苏达州 –MN
Mississippi 密西西比州 –MS
Missouri 密苏里州 –MO
Montana 蒙大拿州 –MT
Nevada 内华达州 –NV
New Hampshire 新罕布什尔州 –NH
New Jersey 新泽西州 –NJ
New Mexico 新墨西哥州 –NM

New York 纽约州 –NY
North Carolina 北卡罗来州 –NC
North Dakota 北达科他州 –ND
Ohio 俄亥俄州 –OH
Oklahoma 俄克拉荷马州 –OK
Oregon 俄勒冈州 –OR
Pennsylvania 宾夕法尼亚州 –PA
Rhode Island 罗得岛 –RI
South Carolina 南卡罗来州 –SC
South Dakota 南达科他州 –SD
Tennessee 田纳西州 –TN
Texas 得克萨斯州 –TX
Utah 犹他州 –UT
Vermont 佛蒙特州 –VT
Virginia 弗吉尼亚州 –VA
Washington 华盛顿州 –WA
West Virginia 西弗吉尼亚州 –WV
Wisconsin 威斯康星州 –WI
Wyoming 怀俄明州 –WY

Chapter 04

人力资源管理文书

　　人力资源管理文书一般在企事业单位使用,主要是用于人员的招录、调动、奖惩、辞退等事宜。企业的用人是一门学问,很大程度上,这门学问都从这些人事文书上体现出来了。写好人力资源管理文书,既对企业和人才的发展起到推动促进的作用,又是写作者职业修养的体现。人力资源管理方面的文书很多,如招聘广告、求职信、简历、面试通知、录用通知、培训计划、绩效考核方案、人事申请和批复、人事通知、辞职信、辞退信等等。由于是公文,因此写作时要注意使用正式语言,言词简练,直达主题。本章选取了人力资源管理领域的主要几种文书形式,并进行了较为详细的介绍。

Unit 1　招聘广告
　　　　　　　　　　　　　　　　　　　Recruitment Advertising

　　招聘广告（Recruitment Advertising）是用来公布招聘信息的广告，也是对招聘方的一种宣传。同时，招聘广告有一定固定的内容，例如招怎么样的人、具体的要求是什么等等。

　　让我们设想一下，企业最缺什么，人才！人才选拔决定着企业的生产力。人才竞争的激烈程度，也让企业更重视自身的人才选拔工作。作为人力资源部门的重要工作，招聘广告的设计影响着它的宣传效果。一份优秀的招聘广告要充分显示出企业对人才的吸引和企业自然的魅力。那么招聘广告要怎么写才最有效果、最吸引人呢？

　　首先，从了解招聘广告的定义开始，即企业招聘人才时在相关的招聘媒体（含网络招聘、报纸招聘、现场招聘、店面招聘）发布企业的招聘信息，也是对招聘方的一种宣传。

　　其次，明白招聘广告的主要组成部分。一般来讲，招聘广告是写给求职者看的，主要包括：公司名称、企业简介、岗位名称、招聘名额、职位描述、职位要求、职位待遇、联系方式等几个环节组成。当然，有时限于篇幅和突出重点的不同，个别环节可以适当省略，如公司简介等。

　　那么，招聘广告写作中，有什么需要注意的呢？

1. 先要弄明白招聘广告写给谁看的及对方看后是否能心动。
2. 要弄明白招聘广告发布的媒体是什么，这点也很关键。切忌繁文缛节没完没了，既占篇幅又没说到重点，避免求职人群走马观花遗漏招聘岗位。
3. 招聘广告也可以加上企业对人才如何重视、如何培训、如何晋升等关键点突出来。
4. 避免不必要的争议，广告招聘的内容不能有对种族、性别、年龄的偏见。

　　一份好的招聘广告对企业很重要，招聘广告怎么写，除了要做到以上所说的内容外，还要在整体上把握招聘广告语的设计效果。注意，一个优秀的招聘广告一定要做到如下要求：使人过目不忘的广告词，讲明所要招聘的职位、交代好申请方式，使用鼓励性、刺激性用语；应说明招聘的岗位、人数、所需的资格条件，并注明待遇。

现在，大多数企业都接受电子邮件投简历的方式，因此求职者除通过附件发送简历、求职信以及推荐信之外，或许还需在必要的时候将身份证、学位证、毕业证、健康证等相关证件的照片或扫描件通过电邮发送到用人单位邮箱。

1. 生产部门

ELECTRONIC ASSEMBLERS NEEDED!
$12 PER HOUR WITH BENEFITS.
40 HRS PER WEEK,
PAID VACATION AND HOLIDAYS.
LOOKING TO HIRE 7 PEOPLE IMMEDIATELY!
Apply in person at or send your resume to:
ABC Company
Address: XXX
Phone Number: 111111
E-mail your resume to: hr@abccompany.com
Fax your resume to: (555) 555-5555

诚聘电子装配工！
每小时 12 美元外加津贴
每周 40 小时
带薪休假
急招 7 人！
现场申请或是将简历投至
ABC 公司
地址：XXX
电话：111111
电邮：hr@abccompany.com
传真：（555）555-5555

2. 行政部门

Candidate,

Because of continued success and growth, we have an administrative assistant position available!

XYZ Company is a large, diverse pharmaceutical company with 40,000 employees nationwide and $200 million in revenues. Our mission is to improve medicine by developing the most cost-effective medicine with few side effects for patients worldwide. Founded in 1973, XYZ Company employs a diverse team of individuals dedicated to our mission by offering an excellent salary and benefit package, such as health, dental and vision insurance and gym membership reimbursement. We offer a casual work environment and a flexible schedule because we understand your personal life is as important as your professional life. If you're dedicated and ready to work for an organization that cares about you, we have an opening for an administrative assistant.

Responsibilities include:

(List responsibilities of the position.)

Educational Requirements:

(List education requirements.)

Please send your resume and cover letter to: fancy@XYZcompanyemail.com to be considered for this unique opportunity.

求职者:
由于我公司不断成功和成长，现需要一名行政助理!
XYZ 公司是一个大型、多样化的医药公司，在全国各地有员工 40 000 人，年收入 2 亿美元。我们的使命是通过为全世界的患者开发性价比最高、副作用最小的药品来改善医药行业。XYZ 公司创办于 1973 年，汇聚各方面人才，雇员敬业奉献，拥有高额薪水和良好的福利待遇，比如医保、牙眼保险以及健身房会员卡补助。我们提供舒适的工作环境和灵活的考勤制度，因为我们理解，员工的个人生活和职业生活一样重要。如果你爱岗敬业，愿意为一家关心你的公司工作，我们这里就有一份行政助理的职位等着你。
岗位职责:
（列举岗位职责）
教育程度要求:
（列举教育程度要求）

欲求此职位者，请将简历和求职信发至 fancy@XYZcompanyemail.com。

3. 销售部门

Job Announcement

Dear Candidate,

This letter is to grab your attention about the job openings in our company. Our company is regarded as a best company in the sales field in the whole England. We need ambitious and sincere people. The applicant must have a minimum of 6 years of job experience in sales department. Applicants will be given positions as per their qualification. Applicants need to fulfil our prescribed requirements and attachments. We give free medical facilities, good working environment, and try to bring out the best in our employees.

As soon as possible send your application on robin.rob@tel.com. The candidates have to go for an interview when they get selected. If there is any doubt regarding the working pattern of our company, you can contact our person from 8.00a.m. to 5.00p.m. Monday to Friday on our address which is displayed below.

With regards,
Robin M Rob,
Senior sales manager,
*** Inc
****

诚聘

亲爱的求职者：

敬请关注我公司的求职信息。我公司被认为是全英格兰销售领域最好的公司之一。我们诚聘具有远大抱负而又心地诚恳的人员。应聘者需具备至少六年以上的销售部门工作经验。申请者将依据其资质被分配到相应岗位。申请者需要满足规定的要求和条件。我们将提供免费的医疗设施与良好的工作环境，并将竭力发挥雇员的潜能。

请尽快将申请发至邮箱 robin.rob@tel.com。在聘用之前，申请者需经过一轮面试。若对我公司的工作模式有任何疑问，您可以根据下方显示的我公司地址，在周一至周五早八点至晚五点之间联系我公司的工作人员。

诚挚的 罗宾·M·洛玻
*** 公司高级销售经理
地址：********

4. 实习生招聘

X Co. Internship

Title: Department: Finance & Controlling

Duration of internship: 6 months (full-time, 5 days per week).

Preferred starting date: ASAP

Salary: RMB 3,000 per month

Note: Please keep studentship during the whole internship period

Brief Description of Assignment:

Responsibilities and essential works include but are not limited to the following:

- Support team in the area of Risk Management to discuss & report project progress, decisions and activities;
- Support team in the area of Process Management to continuously update business processes to ensure them truly reflect company's operations;
- Support team in the areas of Internal Control System, and support coordination with outsourced consultants activities.

Qualification Requirements:

1. Excellent written and spoken English skills;
2. At least Bachelor Degree in Business related majors;
3. Advanced IT/Computer skills (MS Office, especially PPT and Excel);
4. Intercultural experience and flexibility on adapting to Chinese culture;
5. Experience in project management/administration;
6. Specialize in information management.

The Application:

Please send your resume in both Chinese and English forms to 1234@gmail.com. And do remember to make the subject of your e-mail in the pattern of "Name-School-Grade-Major" and please tell us your possible time for this internship.

X 公司实习生招聘

职位：财务和控制部门
实习期：6 个月（全职，每周 5 天）
开始日期：越快越好
薪水：3 000 元 / 月
注意：请确保实习期间始终保持学生身份

任务简介：
至少要承担以下职责，完成以下工作：
1. 在风险管理中协助团队，讨论和报告项目进程、决策以及活动；
2. 在进程管理中协助团队，实时更新业务进程，确保其真实反映公司运作；
3. 在内部控制制度上协助团队，支持团队与外包顾问活动间的合作。

申请条件：
1. 英语口语、写作俱佳；
2. 商务相关专业，至少本科学历；
3. 高级 IT/ 计算机技术（微软 Office 软件，尤其是 PPT 和 Excel）；
4. 具有跨文化交流经验，在适应中国文化上具有灵活性；
5. 在项目管理和行政上有一定经验；
6. 熟悉信息管理。

申请方式：
请将中英文简历投至 1234@gmail.com。务必将邮件主题格式设为"姓名 – 学校 – 年级 – 专业"，并请告诉我们您可以实习的时间。

Unit 2　求职简历

Resumes

求职简历（Resumes）又称求职资历、个人履历等，是求职者将自己与所申请职位紧密相关的个人信息分析整理并清晰简要地表述出来的书面求职资料，属于一种应用写作文体。在这里求职者用真实准确的事实向招聘者明示自己的经历、经验、技能、成果等内容。求职简历是招聘者在阅读求职者求职申请后对其产生兴趣进而进一步决定是否给予面试机会的极重要的依据性材料。

一般的求职简历需要包含以下几个基本结构：

1. 个人信息（Personal Information）：指姓名、地址、邮编、电话、电子信箱等内容。这项内容放在简历第一页的上部，以方便招聘者与自己联系。
2. 求职目标（Career Goal）：即求职者所希望从事的职位。此项可放置在第一项，也可放置在第二项。
3. 教育背景（Educational Background）：即求职者的接受教育情况，如何时何校获何学历或者学位，把最高的学历或者学位放在最前面，然后依次往前推导。
4. 工作经历（Work Experience）：求职者的工作资历经验，应该是与此申请职位相关的内容，可采取由近及远的顺序安排，也可采取将与所申请职位最相关的内容置前的顺序安排。

上述四大项内容是必须具备的，其他内容如知识储备、具体技能、获得荣誉等均可酌情写入简历。

在中文实践中，我们常常会看到各种不同的简历类型，比如时序型、功能型、综合型、履历型、图谱型等格式。而在英文中，人们比较偏向于版面清晰的分项式简历（Item Pattern）和表格式简历（Form Pattern）。本单元中介绍的例子都为分项式，因其最为常见。大家通过例子可以发现，西方人对个人信息的要求没有中国人那么复杂，比如一般不会要求写婚姻状况、政治倾向等，有时候简洁到只有基本的联系方式。同时还可以发现，英文工作简历的重头戏是工作经历部分，而学历部分往往放置在最后写，而且非常简约，只说明就读学校、就读年份、所学专业以及学位。

写工作简历时应注意：
1. 针对职位。可能求职者的资历非常丰富，但不要因此模糊个性和长处，如有必要可分别写作针对不同职位的求职简历。要充分结合意向职位的要求来撰写自己的工作经历，你的简历上体现的优势刚好符合企业的要求。
2. 突出优势。要通过突出自己的优势来推销自己，最好把最能展示自己优势的内容放在首页，以求醒目。要在自我评价中言简意赅地突出自己的优势，让企业 HR 看到你的价值。
3. 客观真实。求职简历所列内容务必实事求是，不能无中生有，任何虚假的内容都不要怀着侥幸心理写入求职简历。但是，求职者可以在语言描述上下些功夫，美化一下工作，这就看诸位功夫如何了。比如许多学生在实习期间其实只是做些端茶送水的工作，他们会写成 administrative assistant；或者有些人曾经发过传单，他们会写 responsible for marketing；还有些人参加过一些项目组，其实干的都是边边角角的活，但在简历上也可以放心地写上参与了某某项目的开发。这样写既没有违背事实，又"抬高了身价"。
4. 简洁表述。避免使用第一人称，要采用简洁的无主句式表达，尽量使用行为动词，少用形容词等修饰性语言。
5. 注重格式。不要把求职简历写成繁琐保守的自传书信体或者封闭表格式，宜按内容采用清晰有序的板块列项式，另外也不要装订成有封面、目录、封底等项目的书册式。

5. 会计求职简历

（模板）

Jim Feyol

576, Division Street
Chicago, Illinois-05778
(342) 465-886

OBJECTIVE:

An accountant position that helps in utilizing my professional experiences, and capability to communicate with managers and administrative heads.

QUALIFICATIONS:

- Worked as Administrative Accountant in a small sized motor works manufacturing company serving overall national market.
- maintained accounts, journal entries and recording auditors statements and documents.
- Two years experience with Certified Public Accountants.

EXPERIENCE:

Discover Financial Company, Illinois. 2000 ~ Present.

Accountant:

- Developed, and maintained all aspects of business accountancy, marketing, and data processing of company.
- Worked on financial budgeting, capital expenditure, cash flow and foreign-exchange dealings.
- Established close relations between bank executives and auditors.

Tribune Company. 1998 ~ 1999.

Accounts Payable Clerk:

- Applied a new software program which helped in increasing department productivity and reduce errors by 15%.
- Providing excellent customer service on a consistent basis which ensures customer value.

Auditor: 1996 ~ 1998.

- One year experience in auditing private, public holding, and government companies.
- Prepared financial statements, profit and loss accounts, balance-sheets and schedules.

EDUCATION:

UNIVERSITY OF ILLINOIS.

Bachelor's Degree, with major in Accountancy, Masters in Banking and Finance, 1997.

吉米·费耶

伊利诺斯州（05778）芝加哥底维逊街 576 号
电话：（342）465886

求职目标：

会计职位，能够用上我的专业经验，锻炼与管理人员和领导的沟通能力。

个人资质：

- 在一家小型汽车制造公司担任管理会计，服务全国市场。
- 保管账目、分类账，记录审计员的报表和文件。
- 两年注会经验。

工作经历：

发现财务公司 伊利诺斯州 2000~ 今

会计师：

- 开发和维护公司的各类商业会计、市场营销和数据处理。
- 参与财政预算、资本支出、现金流动和外汇交易。
- 在银行主管和审计员间建立密切联系。

特里布恩公司 1998~1999

应付账款办事员：

- 运用了一个新的软件项目，提高了部门生产力，将错误率降低 15%。
- 持续提供良好的客户服务，确保了客户价值。

审计员：1996~1998

- 一年审计公私股份和国企的经历。
- 撰写财务报表、损益表、资产负债表和日程安排。

教育背景：

伊利诺斯大学

学士学位，会计专业，精通银行和金融业务，1997 年。

6. 金融分析师求职简历

Carl Furman

123, Ellis Street

Boston, MA, 01234

(123) 456 789

Academic Background

University of California, San Diego, CA
- ♣ Achieved Bachelor of Science Degree in Finance (1994)

Computer Programming Skills
- ♣ Operating Systems: Windows2000, Windows9X, Windows XP, Windows ME, and Windows Vista.
- ♣ Office Package: Microsoft Excel, Microsoft Word, Microsoft PowerPoint, Microsoft Access, and Microsoft Outlook Express.
- ♣ Knowledge of Lotus 1-2-3, IBM PC, WordStar, MS-Dos, and Lotus Macros.

Professional Excellence Summary
- ♣ More than 5 years of broad experience in the financial market.
- ♣ Ability to deal with various customers, employees and staff members.
- ♣ Excellent communication skills both verbal and written.
- ♣ Able to set up priorities and take quick decisions and apply them to meet the deadline.
- ♣ Self motivated.
- ♣ Easily adjustable to innovative tasks and concepts.

Professional Background

Global Trust Bank Ltd, St. Helena, CA
Corporate Accounting Analyst (2004 ~ Present)
- ♣ Accountable for analyzing and preparing fund and income statements, salary schedules, and balance sheets.
- ♣ Examine balance sheets, fund and income statement key ratios by making use of trend reports and prepare gap details as well.

Pioneer Bank & Trust, San Carlos, CA
Intern (2000~2003)
- ♣ Carefully managed the servicing of depositor's accounts having amount exceeding $50,000.
- ♣ Maintain customer care relations, book keeping, and verification of checks.

Corn Belt Bank, San Jose, CA
Relationship Analyst (1995~1999)
- ♣ In charge of managing documents, researched papers and financial reports for helping quantitative analysis and estimation of the bank's association with international contacts.

卡尔·福尔曼
马萨诸塞州（01234）波士顿伊利斯街 123 号
电话：（123）456 789

学术背景

加利福尼亚大学 加利福尼亚州 圣地亚哥
- 金融学士学位（1994）

计算机编程

- 操作系统：Windows 2000, Windows9X, Windows XP, Windows ME, and Windows Vista.
- 办公软件：Microsoft Excel, Microsoft Word, Microsoft PowerPoint, Microsoft Access, and Microsoft Outlook Express.
- 其他：Lotus 1-2-3, IBM PC, WordStar, MS-Dos, and Lotus Macros.

优秀专业素质总括

- 在金融市场 5 年的广泛经历
- 与各类顾客、雇员和工作人员沟通良好
- 良好的口头和书面交流能力
- 能抓住重点，果断决策，迅速实施，按期完工
- 充满热情
- 对于新任务、新概念有较好的适应能力

从业经历

全球信托银行有限公司 圣赫勒拿 加利福尼亚
企业会计分析师（2004~ 今）
- 负责分析和准备基金表、损益表、工资单和资产负债表
- 通过利用趋势报告、研究差距细节来检查资产负债表、基金和损益表中的重要比率

先驱银行和信托公司 圣卡洛斯 加利福尼亚州

实习生（2000~2003）
- 对储户超过 50 000 美元的账户进行了认真管理服务
- 维系客户纽带、记账、审核支票

玉米带银行 圣何塞 加利福尼亚

关系分析师（1995~1999）
- 负责管理文件，研究文献和财政报告以帮助进行定量分析和评估银行与国际客户间的关系

7. 计算机行业求职简历

Carl Furman
123, Ellis Street
Boston, MA, 01234
(123) 456 789

OBJECTIVE

Seeking for a position as Computer Programmer or Software Engineer to contribute relevant experience and education background.

SUMMARY OF QUALIFICATIONS

- Established capability in the provision of customer support services.
- Capable in the execution and design of program development, database restore/trouble-shooting utilities as well as release system to update clients on the modern version of software, including an On-line message system.

EXPERIENCE

PETERSON BECKER INDUSTRIES, Huston, TX

(1990 ~ Present) Senior Programmer

- Planned file arrangement and perform actual coding based on functional plan necessities. Individual development of new generator product.
- Execution and design of latest system enhancement.
- A privately owned software company focused on the requirements

of the health care industry.

(1989 ~ 1990)Programmer/Analyst
- ♣ Maintained presented clients and determined serious issue in a suitable fashion.
- ♣ Gave on-site support as well as installed software for new patrons.
- ♣ Created on-line message format for associates of the programming group.

EDUCATION

(1994~Present)BRIGHAM YOUNG UNIVERSITY, Provo, UT
Enrolled in Graduate Mathematics program
(1986~1990)NORTHFACE UNIVERSITY, Salt Lake City, UT
Bachelor of Science Degree: Computer Science Engineering

COMPUTERS

Programming Languages:
- ♣ C,
- ♣ C++,
- ♣ Pascal,
- ♣ LISP,
- ♣ IBM,
- ♣ PL/1

Databases:
- ♣ SQL/DS

Oracle Hardware:
- ♣ IBM 3090,
- ♣ HP 9000

卡尔·福尔曼
马萨诸塞州（01234）波士顿伊利斯街 123 号
电话：（123）456 789

求职目标

寻求计算机程序员或软件工程师的职位，以利用相关经验和教育背景。

个人能力总括
- 具备提供用户支持服务的能力
- 能够执行和设计程序开发、数据库恢复/故障排除工具,能够缓释系统,告知用户软件更新,包括在线留言系统

工作经历

皮特森·贝克实业公司 休斯顿 得克萨斯州

(1990~今)高级程序员
- 设计文档排列,在单项规划需要的基础上进行实际编码。新型发生器产品的个体开发。
- 系统更新的执行和设计。
- 一家向医保产业需求倾斜的私人软件公司。

(1989~1990)程序员/分析师
- 维持公司与现有顾客的联系,适当决定重大事项
- 为新客户提供现场支持及软件安装服务
- 为编程小组的同事创建在线留言模式

教育背景

(1994~今)杨柏翰大学 普罗沃 犹他州
数学专业研究生
(1986~1990)北面大学 盐湖城 犹他州
理学士学位,计算机工程

计算机技能

编程语言:
- C,
- C++,
- Pascal,
- LISP,
- IBM,
- PL/1

数据库:
- SQL/DS

Oracle 硬件:
- IBM 3090,
- HP 9000

8. 市场营销求职简历

Victor Smith

68, Pride Street

Clinton, NY, 0618

(0978) 491 0315

Objective

Looking for an entry-level position in the advertising field.

Skills

- Excellent command over sales management, mass communication and advertisement.
- In-depth knowledge of brochure, video and documentary film production and marketing support.
- Experience of 2 years part time employment as a supervisor.
- Comfortable working on computer.
- Proven ability to manage and organize the things well.
- Excellent communication skills both verbally and written.

Education

- Achieved bachelor's degree in Advertisement from the New York University in the year 2005.
- Done diploma in advanced mass media and video, writing for film, radio or TV
- Worked in a documentary film "New Horizon" and worked as assistant director, script advisor and sound assistant.

Professional Experience

Assistant Manager

Waren Pictures Inc., Los Angeles, CA

2005~present

- Responsibilities include provide assistance to manager of operations, analysis of accounts and ensure the costs.
- Ensure the warehouse inventory distribution to branch offices.

♣ Prepare documents for posting and billing of the union labor.
♣ Plan the sheets of daily cut.
♣ Operated instrument computer system.

维克多·史密斯

纽约州（0618）克林顿市骄傲大街 68 号

电话：（0978）491 0315

求职目标

寻求广告领域初级岗位

个人能力

- 熟悉销售管理、大众传媒和广告
- 深入了解宣传册、视频和纪录片产品以及营销支持
- 2 年的兼职销售监督员经验
- 熟悉计算机工作环境
- 有管理和组织实战能力
- 良好的口头和书面沟通能力

教育背景

- 2005 年获得纽约大学广告专业学士学位
- 完成高级大众传媒、影视、电影脚本、广播、电视台词写作等课程
- 参与纪录片《新的地平线》的拍摄过程，期间担任导演助理、脚本顾问以及音效顾问

职业经历

沃伦影像公司 洛杉矶 加利福尼亚州

2005~今

- 负责为业务经理提供帮助、分析账目、控制开支
- 监督仓库存货分配到分支机构
- 准备工会工人的账单文件
- 制定每日开支削减计划
- 操作计算机系统

9. 人力资源职位求职简历

Carl Furman

123, Ellis Street

Boston, MA, 01234

(123) 456 789

PROFESSIONAL BACKGROUND

Personal Manager

Mahad construction, Juneau, Alaska

April 2006 to Present

- ♣ Responsible for human resources goals & objective expansion.
- ♣ Co-ordinate with employees & build strong relationship.
- ♣ Adjust human resources to financial plan.
- ♣ Helped in expansion of Guidance Program.
- ♣ Manage company profit & recompense.
- ♣ Collect figures for workers Profit Booklet

Personnel Administrator

Royal Management, Juneau, Alaska

December 2004 to April 2006

- ♣ Produce advertisements for Movement Employment Program.
- ♣ Managed extra costs i.e. training recompense as well as member of staff appointment plan.

Manager of Personnel/payroll

Oxford universities, in U.S.A.

January 2003 to December 2004

- ♣ Monitored technological and clerical workers.
- ♣ Interviewed, trained and ended recruits.
- ♣ Discussed budget, salary, & company plan.
- ♣ Found & resolve recruits grievance.

Assistant Manager

At Excel Industries in Trenton, New Jersey

July 2001 to December 2003

- Appointed & terminated recruiters.
- Analyzed & resolved recruits grievance.
- Acted as a mediator among home office, East Coast office, and client companies.

EDUCATION

Bachelor of Arts Degree in English, 2000, Juneau College, Juneau, Alaska

卡尔·福尔曼
马萨诸塞州（01234）波士顿伊利斯街 123 号
电话：（123）456 789

个人背景

人事部经理
马哈建筑公司 朱诺市 阿拉斯加
2006.4~今
- 负责人力资源部门目标拓展
- 与员工协作并建立密切关系
- 使人力资源适应财政计划安排
- 协助完善指导纲要
- 管理公司收益和补偿事宜
- 为员工盈利手册收集数据

人事主管
皇家管理公司 朱诺市 阿拉斯加州
2004.12~2006.4
- 为"流动招聘计划"制作广告
- 管理额外费用，如培训补贴和员工任命计划

人事部经理
牛津大学（美国）
2003.1~2004.12
- 监督技术工人和文职人员
- 负责新雇员的面试、培训和解雇
- 讨论预算、薪酬和公司规划
- 发现和解决新雇员的不满

副经理
超越实业 特伦顿 新泽西州

2001.7~2003.12
- 负责新雇员的任命和解雇
- 分析和解决新雇员的不满
- 在总公司、东海岸分公司和客户公司间进行协调

教育背景

2000 年获得朱诺大学英语专业学士学位 朱诺市 阿拉斯加

10. 行政助理求职简历

Nickey Boye

288, Park Avenue

Grand Rapids, MI 07306

(201) 555 2938

Objective

To show my skills, ability and experience in a progressive company by applying for the post of Administrative Assistant.

Profile

Can execute numbers of projects simultaneously.

Specialized in office and administrative procedure.

Can handle computer and numerous software application.

Excellent communication skills.

Experience

1990~Present

ANASTASIA INSTITUTE, Grand Rapids, Ml

Administrative Assistant

- ♣ Office management, word processing, spreadsheet, and billing.
- ♣ Coordinate assignment of students for their academic counselor.
- ♣ Handle student complaints and problem such as racism etc.

1987~1990

DIABETES CENTER, Holland, MI

Administrative Secretary

- ♣ Planned and executed weekend patient conferences.

- Coordinated finance.
- Coordinated refreshments for special events.
- Budgeted professional seminars.

Education

BACHELOR OF ARTS/COMMUNICATION STUDIES
1983
Kramer College, Kalamazoo, Ml
G.P.A. 3.25; Graduated Cum Laude
CERTIFICATION IN MEETING MANAGEMENTS
1989
Landsend College, Holland, Ml

Software Skills

- ♣ Proficient in WordPerfect 5.1.
- ♣ MultiMate; Lotus 1-2-3; Q A; Professional Write.
- ♣ Wang Working Knowledge - dBase III+.
- ♣ CRT IMS System, Microsoft Word 4.
- ♣ Microsoft Office.
- ♣ Pro-Cite 2.0.
- ♣ Display Write.

尼奇·博艺

密西根州（07306）激流市公园大街 288 号

电话：（201）555 2938

求职目标

通过申请行政助理一职，在一家成长型的公司展示我的技术、能力和经验。

个人能力

能够同时处理多个项目

熟悉办公室和行政程序

掌握计算机操作和大量软件

良好的沟通能力

从业经历

1990~今

安娜斯塔西娅学院 大激流市 密歇根州

行政助理
- 办公室管理，文字处理，数据表处理，账单管理
- 为辅导员协调学生作业
- 处理学生的意见和问题，如种族主义

1987~1990

糖尿病中心 荷兰市 密歇根州

行政秘书
- 计划并开展周末病人会议
- 协调财政事务
- 为特殊会议置办茶点
- 负责专业研讨会的预算

教育背景

传播学研究专业学士学位

1983

克莱默学院 卡拉马祖市 密歇根州

GPA：3.25 优秀毕业生称号

会议管理学位

1989

朗森学院 荷兰市 密歇根州

计算机能力

- 熟练掌握 WordPerfect 5.1.
- MultiMate; Lotus 1-2-3; Q A; Professional Write.
- Wang Working Knowledge - dBase III+.
- CRT IMS System, Microsoft Word 4.
- Microsoft Office.
- Pro-Cite 2.0.
- Display Write.

Unit 3　求职信

Cover Letters

　　求职信（Cover Letters）是求职者写给招聘单位的信函，是写信人就某一职位向收信人提出请求，属申请信的一种。求职信起到毛遂自荐的作用，好的求职信可以拉近求职者与人事主管（负责人）之间的距离，获得面试机会多一些。求职信一般包括以下几个方面的内容：首先要阐述清楚招聘信息的来源以及所申请的职位；其次简述个人信息；然后进一步强调自己的能力，表达抱负，并请求给予面试机会；最后提出自己的希望，希望得到面试的机会，并且告诉对方你的联系方式。

写作注意事项：
1. 充分收集目标公司的信息，了解该公司主要从事的领域以及需要的人才类型。
2. 认真分析自己的能力，确定该公司是否适合自己，以及什么岗位适合自己。
3. 求职信的语言属于正式用语，在写作过程中一定要注意用词简洁准确，语气礼貌自信，态度不卑不亢，所给信息具有一定的可信度。尤其是在强调自身经历和优点的时候，更应把握尺度。
4. 由于篇幅较短，而申请者需要尽可能地向用人单位推销自己，所以在求职信中宜笼统概说自己的求学和工作经历，突出一至两个吸引眼球的闪光点即可。
5. 强调自己的加入能为对方带来什么利益，淡化自己想要从对方处得到的好处，尤其是金钱方面的，当然，提倡写自己希望得到锻炼和提升。
6. 语言生动丰富，不千篇一律。最好控制在一页纸以内。纸张最好是白色的。写好后一定要有自己的亲笔签名以显示诚意（电子邮件另当别论）。
7. 要站在用人单位的角度查看自己的求职信，不当处及时修改。

11. 应届毕业生的求职信

Dear Mr. Smith,

I saw the position of financial analyst posted in the career center of Community University. As a recent college graduate my studies and internship experience well qualify me for this position.

The ad. mentions that you are looking for someone who can lead, who can do excellent quantitative analyses and who can work well with others.

Last summer I did my internship with Thomas Zinn Real Estate Development. It was my responsibility to rectify errors in rent calculations and in schedules. Using the skills I had gained in my courses, especially those related to my business degree, I was able to assist in correcting these problems that the group was facing.

As a recent college graduate I can also point to the skills I used as part of a student organization helped me to work with the team and become an active member and a person sought out by others for assistance.

If given the chance, I believe I can assist your company as a financial analyst, and can bring to the table all of the knowledge I have gained in both the classroom and during my internship. If you find that a recent college graduates with my skills match your needs for this position, I hope that you will contact me soon about an interview so we can further discuss this opportunity.

Thank you for your consideration.

Sincerely,
Carrie Hand

亲爱的史密斯先生：

我在社区大学的招聘信息中心看到您发布的招聘金融分析师的信息。作为一名应届大学毕业生，我所学的知识和实习经验使我能够胜任这份工作。

广告中提到，您要寻找一位有领导力、擅长做定量分析、有团队精神的人。

去年夏天，我在托马斯·新房地产开发公司实习，负责纠正近期计算和日程安排中的错误。通过将大学的知识学以致用，尤其是和我商科学历相关的知识，我成功协助纠正了我们团队面临的各种问题。

　　作为一名应届毕业生，我在学校社团的工作经验也值得一提。在社团中，我与整个团队共事，成为了一名积极成员和他人的好帮手。

　　倘若有幸得到聘用，我相信我可以作为金融分析师为贵公司献上绵薄之力，并将在课内外的一切所学付诸实践。如果您认为具备这样条件的应届毕业生符合您对这一岗位的要求，我希望您可以尽快联系我进行面试，以便进一步讨论这一机遇。

　　请考虑这一申请，谢谢。

卡里·韩德 谨上

12. 略有经历的求职者的求职信

Dear Mr. Koch,

　　I found your advertisement in "Daily Times" dated 23rd June, 2010 for the position of Zoology Teacher and it sparked my interest. So I would like to request you to accept this letter and the enclosed resume as my application for the same.

　　I am a zoology post graduate from the University of Boston. I have also taken a bachelor's degree in education. After the completion of my studies, I joined St. Marry's Convent as a junior science teacher. I make sure that I will produce an energizing and creative learning environment that will bring out the best qualities in students. I have the required credentials, patients and positive attitude that is required for this post.

　　I hope my application will be considered and I am looking for a kind response.

　　Thank You.

Sincerely,
James Codie

亲爱的科奇先生：

　　我在 2010 年 6 月 23 日的《每日时代》上看到您招聘动物学老师的广告，这激起了我的兴趣。在此请您接受这封求职信以及随信附上的一份个人简历，这都是我的申请材料。

我是波士顿大学的一名动物学研究生，之前还得到过一个教育学学士学位。毕业后，我在圣玛丽修道院担任低年级自然老师。我相信我能够创造出一个充满活力和创造力的学习环境，充分激发学生的潜能。我具备了这一职位所要求的资历、耐心以及积极态度。

望能考虑我的申请，静候佳音。

谢谢。

詹姆斯 · 科迪 谨上

13. 职场老手求职信

Dear Sir,

This is in reference to the advertisement given in Deccan Herald about the vacancy of science teacher in your school. I wish to apply for the same position.

I am a post graduate in mathematics and also hold the B.E. degree and have almost 7 years of experience in teaching mathematics in senior section. I have handled both CBSE and state curriculum. Presently I am working as the Mathematics teacher in *** and I am taking classes for 8th and 9th grade. I wish to join your school as one of my cousin is working here and she always talks about the high standards of teaching that are maintained in your school and how the teachers have the scope to learn new concepts and teach it to the students in a better way. I also know that the relationship between a teacher and students in your school is more like friends. I have always wanted to work in such an environment.

I am enclosing my resume for your review and look forward to a positive reply from you.

Thank you.

Sincerely,
Joy Baker

敬启者：

　　此信是应聘贵校发布在《德干先驱》上的科学教师一职。本人希望获得该职位。

本人是数学专业研究生，同时还有教育学士学位，在高年级数学教学岗位有近 7 年从业经历。本人既教过中学教育中央委员会制定的课程内容，也教过州立的课程内容。目前，本人在 *** 学校担任八年级和九年级的数学教师。我希望加入贵校的教师队伍，因为我的一个表姐正在贵校任教，她经常提及贵校一贯保持的高水准的教学质量，以及贵校给予教师学习新知并以更好的方式将其教授给学生的机会。我还知道贵校的师生关系犹如朋友之间的关系。我一直期望能够在这样的环境下工作。

随信附上本人的简历。静候佳音。

谢谢。

乔伊·贝克 谨上

14. 在校生实习求职信

Gentlemen,

I am in my first year of Law School at *** University and I am seeking a summer internship. Professor John Smith, my academic advisor, recommended I apply to your firm.

I have maintained a consistent 3.6 GPA through my first year and am very interested in Disability Law which you specialize in. This will fit well with my undergraduate degree in Business Management. I plan to gain experience throughout my legal studies so that I may enter the legal profession well prepared.

I am looking forward to your positive response at your earliest convenience.

Sincerely
Mathew Holgreen

敬启者：

本人现为 *** 大学法学院一年级学生，欲寻求一份暑假实习工作。我的导师约翰·史密斯教授推荐我申请贵公司职位。

我在法学院一年级保持了 GPA3.6 的成绩，对《残疾人保障法》兴趣浓厚，而该法正是贵公司的长项。这份实习还与我本科的企业管理专业对口。我打算在研究法律的过程中获得经验，为今后进入法律行业铺路。

若方便，请尽早恢复。静候佳音。

马修·霍尔格林 谨上

Unit 4　推荐信和工作证明　Recommendations & References

　　推荐信（Recommendation Letters）是一个人为推荐另一个人去接受某个职位或参与某项工作而写的信件，是一种应用写作文体。推荐信用可以来证明你个人的技能和特点，一般在特殊情况下才需要，最好能留一份在手边，以便于你急于找工作、申请奖学金或者其他任何需要介绍信的情况下备用。工作证明（Reference）其实也可以翻译成介绍信。其实在功能上与推荐信是差不多的，许多外国人常常将其混为一谈。如果非要分一分 recommendation 和 reference 的区别，那么后者通常更为概括性，书写时并不需要有特定的对象，然而前者更为明确，它是针对特定的某个人而书写的。推荐信往往都是对被推荐者的各种赞扬，也都是求职者邀请推荐者写。而工作证明则有可能是对求职者的不做评价甚至是否定，且要求写工作证明的可能是求职者，也可能是用人单位。

　　由于我们姑且可以将推荐信和工作证明当作一种文体（事实上它们确实几乎没有太大差别），因此本单元且将二者的写作要领一并介绍。首先，这类问题的称呼一般都是 To whom it may concern（"敬启者"或是"致相关人"），因为不知对方是谁。这类文体的其他写作要素包括：

1. 推荐人的身份，在何种身份下认识该申请人、认识多长时间或何时认识该申请人。
2. 申请人的工作能力、领导能力、团队合作能力等。
3. 申请人的态度和表现，包括工作态度、为人处世技巧等。
4. 申请人是否适合在该企业工作。

写作结构：
1. 推荐人与申请人的关系。推荐人是在什么环境下认识申请人，以及相识多久。要说明申请人希望申请的是什么职位；或者有时也可以不写，因为往往一封推荐信是写好后留给求职者的，写时往往不知以后的情况，因此我们常常可以看到诸如"因此，我想张三将成为任何用人单位的一笔宝贵财富"或是"因此，我毫无保留地推荐李四就职任何相关岗位"这样的语句。
2. 推荐人对申请人资格评估。推荐人初识申请人时，对他有何特别的印象；或是开始印象不是很深刻，但是工作中的某种品质深深打动了推荐人。举例证实推荐人对于申请人的评估结果。
3. 对于申请人个人特质的评估（如：沟通能力、成熟度、抱负、领导能力、团队工作能力，以及正直等），或是有哪些需要改进的地方。
4. 结论：推荐人对于申请人的整体评估。评估申请人一旦被录用后，会为这个公司及团体带来什么贡献。
5. 记住留下自己的联系方式（虽然用人单位往往已经从申请人的资料中了解到），并告知若有疑问，欢迎随时联系本人。

15. 求职者要求提供推荐

Dear Mr. Bush,

My contact to you today is regarding a recommendation I am seeking from you to write on my behalf. Since we worked together for many years, I feel you are the person best qualified to offer this information.

My interests in the position I am seeking with ABC Company are in line, yet slightly heightened, with the roles and duties I carried out while employed at XYZ Company. It is a career goal of mine to expand to the highest possible potential I can and a solid recommendation would help me get there.

If you would be so gracious as to submit a recommendation to:

John Smith

Human Resources Department

ABC Company

9874 Right Way

Atlanta, GA 88888

Your aid in this request would greatly be appreciated. If you have any questions or concerns, you can contact me through e-mail: e-mail@email.com, or by phone: 123-456-7891.

Sincerely,

Jack Lee

尊敬的布什先生：

今天写信给您，是希望您能为我写一封推荐信。由于我们共事了多年，我认为您是写推荐信的不二人选。

我对 ABC 公司这一职位的兴趣与我对 XYZ 公司的职位和职责的兴趣相似，也许还要大一些。我的职业生涯目标就是要充分挖掘自己的潜能，而您的一封推荐信将会助我抵达成功的彼岸。

若您不吝帮忙，请将推荐信寄至：

约翰·史密斯

ABC 公司人力资源部

佐治亚州（88888）亚特兰大怀特街 9874 号

若承蒙帮助，我将不胜感激。若您有任何疑问或是担忧，请通过邮箱 emial@email.com 联系我，或是拨打电话 123-456-7891。

诚挚的 杰克·李

16. 原工作单位领导推荐

Dear Mr. Sinn,

As the manager of the Global Commercial Bank, I worked with John Sean for the last three years. John started out in the company as cashier and he has been well so he was promoted in the level of Clerk B2.

John has been very professional, responsible and dependable. There's a rotation policy in the bank where employees are allowed to work on various departments and John has fully took advantage of this. He is presently one of the employees in his grade with the largest knowledge and very eager to learn everything. John is very flexible and he learns quickly. He is one of the favorite employees of the manager and most of the employees like him.

I recommend John because of his dedication, knowledge and skills. Given the opportunity, he will be a great asset to any employer. I am very pleased to refer John and you can contact me easily concerning John's competence.

Truly yours,

Mark Rowling

亲爱的辛先生：

　　作为国际商业银行的经理，我与约翰·肖恩在过去的三年一起工作。约翰初来公司的时候只是个出纳，由于表现出色，他被提升为 B2 级职员。

　　约翰非常专业、负责、可靠。我行有一种岗位轮换制度，即员工可以在各种部门工作。约翰充分利用了这一制度。目前，约翰是他所在级别的员工中知识最丰富、求知欲最强的人之一。约翰很灵活，学习快。他是经理最中意的员工之一，受到了大多数员工的欢迎。

　　我推荐约翰是因为他的奉献精神、丰富知识和娴熟技能。如果给他一个机会，他将成为任何公司的一份宝贵财富。我很高兴能够给约翰写推荐信。若您还想对约翰的能力有所了解，您可以很方便地联系到我。

马克·洛林 谨上

17. 原雇主推荐

To whom it may concern,

　　Mr. Kirkpatrick was employed for nine years as the Business Manager at this firm, having begun his career here in administration. He is currently employed as a business consultant on an ongoing basis.

　　I have known Mr. Kirkpatrick for a number of years both as a personal and professional acquaintance. I have deeply respect his character and abilities.

　　He is very highly regarded by both management and staff of this organization for his knowledge and professionalism. He is the person to whom staff and management turn for advice and guidance across a wide range of business issues.

　　Mr. Kirkpatrick is a hard working, very reliable person with a strong work ethic. The primary features of Mr. Kirkpatrick's work are great productivity and extremely high quality standards of performance. He progressed rapidly up the ladder of responsibility from his beginning as an administration clerk to becoming our business manager, in five years.

　　After his departure to start a business consultancy, Mr. Kirkpatrick was immediately re-hired as a business consultant by management. He has since been working with our company regularly in this capacity. During this period he has successfully negotiated several contracts for the firm. He has shown himself to be particularly able to deal with very sensitive clients and difficult business situations.

I have no hesitation in recommending Mr. Kirkpatrick for any business management or consultancy role.

Sincerely,
Robert Stock

敬启者：

克里克帕特里克先生在我公司担任了九年的业务经理，刚来时负责管理工作。现在，他还在担任业务顾问一职。

不管在工作方面还是在个人方面，我都和克里克帕特里克先生是多年的熟人了。我深深敬佩他的人格和能力。

由于知识渊博、工作专业，我公司从管理层到员工都对他持有高度评价。在众多业务问题上，员工和管理层都会向他寻求建议和指导。

克里克帕特里克先生是个勤奋、可靠的人，具有良好的职业操守。他的主要特点就是工作高产优质。他晋升神速，从一开始的行政文员到现在的业务经理，仅用了五年时间。

离开我公司而开始业务顾问的工作之后，克里克帕特里克先生很快又被我公司管理层返聘为业务顾问。从那以后，他定期为我公司服务。在此期间，他成功地为公司谈成了几份合同。他特别能够与非常敏感的客户交流，也很会处理业务困境，这点已显而易见。

我毫无保留地推荐克里克帕特里克先生担任任何业务经理或是顾问的职位。

罗伯特·斯托克 谨上

18. 同事推荐

Dear Mr. Oregon,

Maria has been working with me in the position of the insurance sales agent in the past one and half years. I have worked with Maria for long and I believe that I am suited to talk about and comment with regard to her performance and skills.

Maria was responsible for marketing various insurance products that our company produced which comprises both personal and corporate packages. She sought for some new clients, distinguished the features of every product and then assisted them in filling of the applications. Maria was also responsible of ensuring that the payments are received and the reimbursements are all paid.

Maria is a very knowledgeable sales agent in terms of marketing and she has exhibited the skill to influence potential clients to purchase a product and promote the company products in the corporate level. I am always impressed by Maria's work and I would say that she is a hard working and creative sales person.

I believe that Maria will be very valuable to any employer. If you have more questions about her skills and abilities, you can contact me.

Sincerely yours,
Clint Redford

亲爱的奥兰格先生：

在过去的一年半里，玛利亚作为保险销售代理，一直与我共事。我与玛利亚长期共事，相信有这个资格谈论和评价他的表现和技能。

玛利亚负责推销我公司推出的各类保险产品，其中既有个人产品，也有企业套装。她寻找了一些新的客户，将每种产品分门别类，然后帮助客户填写保险申请单。玛丽还要保证公司收到付款以及赔款悉数交付。

玛利亚在营销方面是个见多识广的销售代理，她显示出自己有能力影响潜在客户购买某一产品，也有能力向公司级别的客户推销我们的产品。我一直对玛利亚的工作表现印象深刻。我要说，她是一个勤快而有创造力的销售人员。

我相信，玛利亚对于任何雇主来说，都是一笔宝贵的财富。若您对她的技术和能力还有什么疑问，可以联系我。

克林特·瑞德佛 谨上

19. 朋友推荐

To whom it may concern,

I prove that I know Samantha Brady and she's been my friend for over 4 years. Samantha has been my coworker at work and this is the reason why we're really close. She's responsible and reliable individual. She always volunteers to arrange events and often assures they're successful. Samantha is accommodative and nice and tries to let new coworkers feel at ease by helping them and assisting them. Though she's the department head, she is not domineering and can convince the team to attain company objectives. Thus, Samantha really made it to maximize the potential of the team. She's a faithful friend and often eager to aid me when I am in need.

For other things you want to know about her, I will be glad to provide you further information.

Sincerely,

Laura Hilton

敬启者：

我证明我与萨曼达认识，我们交上朋友已经有四年了。萨曼达也是我的同事，这就是我们为什么如此亲密。她是一个负责、可靠的人。她总是志愿安排活动，并且往往能够保证活动的成功。萨曼达性格随和，对人友善，并通过帮助新的同事来使他们消除紧张。虽然她是部门经理，但她却从不盛气凌人，而是能够以理服人，让团队达到公司的目标。这样，萨曼达成功地将团队的潜力最大化了。作为朋友，她也十分可靠。每当我有需要，她都热情相助。

若还有任何信息未有告知，本人非常愿意提供给您。

劳拉·希尔顿 谨上

20. 老师推荐

Dear Ms. Jones,

I am writing this recommendation letter at the request of Katie Kingston who is applying for Student Volunteer Program at St. Francis Hospital this summer.

I have known Katie for two years in my capacity as a teacher at Smithtown Middle School School. Katie took English and Spanish from me and earned superior grades in those classes. Based on Katie's grades, attendance and class participation, I'd rate Katie's academic performance in my class as superior.

Katie has a number of strengths to offer an employer. Katie is always interested in supporting others. For example, this year when we worked on our class community service project, Katie was helpful to me in collecting and organizing the food for the food pantry here in Smithtown.

In conclusion, I would highly recommend Katie Kingston. If her performance in my class is any indication of how she'd perform in your position, Katie will be a positive addition to your organization. If you should ever need any additional information, you can feel free to contact me at 555-5555 or by e-mail at e-mail@email.com anytime.

           Sincerely,
           Susan Samuels
           Teacher, Smithtown Middle School

尊敬的琼斯女士：

  我写这封推荐信，是应凯蒂·金森的要求，推荐她申请今年夏天圣弗朗西斯医院的学生志愿者项目。

  作为史密斯郡中学的一名教师，我认识凯蒂已经有两年了。凯蒂是我英语课和西班牙语课的学生，这两门课程，她都取得了优异的成绩。根据凯蒂的成绩、出勤和课堂表现，我给凯蒂的成绩在班上是遥遥领先的。

  作为一名员工，凯蒂有许多方面的才能。凯蒂一向乐于助人。比如，今年我们班进行社区服务的时候，我要为史密斯郡的食品站收集和管理食物，而凯蒂帮了我的大忙。

  总而言之，我强烈推荐凯蒂·金森同学。如果她在我课堂上的表现能够多多少少反映出她在工作岗位上的表现，那么凯蒂将不辱使命。如果您需要任何其他信息，请随时联系我。我的电话是555-5555，电子邮件地址是e-mail@email.com。

           诚挚的 苏珊·萨缪尔
           史密斯郡中学教师

21. 求职者要求提供工作证明

Dear Mr. Doe,

  I am writing to ask whether it would be possible for you to provide a reference for me?

  If you were able to attest to my qualifications for employment, and the skills I attained during my tenure at ABC Company, I would sincerely appreciate it.

I am in the process of seeking employment and a positive reference from you would enhance my prospects of achieving my career goals.

Please let me know if there is any information I can provide regarding my experience to assist you in giving me a reference. I can be reached at 123@abcd.com or (111) 111-1111.

Thank you for your consideration.

Sincerely,
John Smith

尊敬的多尔先生：

  我写此信，是想请问您可否帮我写一份工作证明？

  若您能够证明我的工作资质以及我在 ABC 公司任职期间学到的技术，我将不胜感激。

  我此刻正在求职阶段，而您的一封工作证明会增强我实现职业目标的可能性。

  为帮助您完成这份证明，若您需要提供关于我工作经历的任何信息，只要是我能提供的，请联系我。我的邮箱是 123@abcd.com，电话是（111）111-1111。

  烦请考虑，谢谢。

约翰·史密斯 敬启

22. 用人单位要求提供工作证明

【模板】

Dear Mr. Fisherman

Peter Paul has applied to our company, Acme Container Company, for the position of shipping supervisor. He would be assisting the Warehouse Manager in overseeing both incoming and outgoing shipments of our materials. This would involve managing inventories which amount to thousands of dollars each day.

Mr. Paul has given us your name to contact as a reference. I understand that he has worked for the Good Deal Manufacturing Company for a number of years doing similar work.

Would you be willing to provide some insight as to his work ability and habits? We would also be looking for information about his work history and overall record.

Thank you for your time.

Sincerely

Mark Allen, Human Resources

Acme Container Company

尊敬的菲舍蒙先生：

皮特·保罗先生申请了我公司——极点集装箱公司的装运监督员一职。若得到该职位，他将协助仓库管理人员监督我公司材料的进出口装运。这一职位涉及管理库存，而我们的库存量每天都会达到成千上万美元之多。

保罗先生将您作为他的工作证明人。我了解到，他在贵公司——好交易制造公司做了多年类似的工作。

您是否愿意就他的工作能力和行为习惯提供一些见解？我们还将查看他的工作经历和总体工作记录。

感谢百忙之中抽出时间览信。

诚挚的 马克·艾伦

极点集装箱公司人力资源部

23. 工作证明（好评）

Dear Mr. Thomson,

I have known Mr. James for the past four years that he worked in my company. I know him to be a hardworking and efficient worker. I have to add that I have the utmost confidence in him. When Mr. James is on duty I know that the safety of my workers are in good hands, for Mr. James is one person who is genuinely concerned for the workers and with his vast knowledge and experience in handling industrial accidents, I can rest assured that everything is running in order.

Mr. James gets along well with his co-workers. They too have the utmost confidence in him. I am sure they, like me, would hate to see him leave the company. We would surely lose an excellent worker and a good friend. However, I cannot stop him from wanting to return to his home town to work. He has mentioned to me on several occasions that he has to return home to look after his aged parents. That, indeed, is very commendable.

             Yours sincerely,
             David A. Flood

尊敬的汤姆森先生：

  我和詹姆斯先生认识有四年了，过去这四年他在我的公司工作。在我眼里，他是一个勤快而高效的工人。我必须要说，对于他，我有百分之百的信心。每当詹姆斯先生值班的时候，我就知道我其他工人的生命安全有保障，因为詹姆斯先生是真正地关心工人。由于他在处理工业事故方面拥有丰富的知识和实战经验，我可以确定一切都井然有序，因而也就高枕无忧。

  詹姆斯先生与他的工友们相处融洽。大家对他也有百分之百的信心。我相信他们和我一样，也不愿意看到詹姆斯先生离开我们的公司。失去了他，我们不仅失去了一个优秀的工人，还失去了一个很好的朋友。然而，他本人想回老家工作，这是我无法阻挡的。他曾在多个场合向我提到过，他必须回家照看年迈的双亲，而这样的孝心也着实难得。

             大卫·A·弗拉德 敬启

24. 工作证明（中评）

Dear Mr. Thomson,

  With regards to your letter asking for a reference for Mr. James, I can only say that I do not know him well enough to give a fair assessment of his ability, character, etc.. Actually I was surprised that he gave my name as a reference at all. I was not informed of it.

  Still I asked his immediate supervisor, Mr. Ken, and he said that Mr. James work is satisfactory. Mr. James works best if given proper supervision. In that capacity he should perform up to expectations.

             Yours sincerely,
             David A Flood

尊敬的汤姆森先生：

  您希望我写一份詹姆斯先生的工作证明，我只能说，根据我对他的了解程度，还不足以对他的能力、性格等方面做出一个公正的评价。事实上，他将我作为证明人，我颇为吃惊。他没有将此事告诉我。

尽管这样，我还是询问了他的顶头上司肯先生。肯先生说，詹姆斯先生的工作令人满意。若要詹姆斯先生拿出最佳表现，最好是予以适当监督。在那种情况下，他的表现会超出人们的期待。

大卫·A·弗拉德 敬启

25. 工作证明（差评）

Dear Mr. Thompson,

Concerning your request for a reference for Mr. James, I am afraid I cannot help you. Mr. James worked here for only two weeks before suddenly disappearing without notice. I do not know him well enough to give any sort of comment.

Yours sincerely,
David A Smith

尊敬的汤姆森先生：

您希望我为詹姆斯先生写一份工作证明，对此我可能无法帮上忙。詹姆斯先生只在我们单位工作了两周，随后便一声不吭地走了。我对他了解有限，难以做出任何评价。

大卫·A·史密斯 敬启

Unit 5　工作岗位的申请和回复 Employment Correspondences

有了申请者的求职信,基本就会有接下来的用人单位和申请者之间的各种往来函件。其中包括用人单位告知收到申请、通知面试、确定面试、面试感谢信、通知面试结果、接受或拒绝职位等一系列过程。这类信件一般都比较正式,因为双方基本都不甚了解对方,因此不会在用语上过于随意。求职者本人要通过礼貌的用语博得用人单位的好感,而用人单位也可以通过礼貌用语来树立自己的威严或是体现自己的人性化。

通知收到申请材料的信一般比较简洁,有时只是三两句话。明确表示收到,以使申请人安心。然后表示有众多信件,处理需要一定时间,会在多少工作日后给予回复。最后感谢申请人对公司的关注。

有时,若用人单位信件不是很多,也往往省略上一步,直接通知申请人面试,或是通知不能面试。**通知面试的信,一般步骤以及必备元素包括**:1. 恭喜申请材料通过,欢迎面试;2. 面试时间、地点以及其他需要注意或携带的东西,如是否正装,带上身份证、证书原件等;3. 有时可将面试的大致内容透露给申请人,方便其准备;4. 表示期待申请人的到来。

而**通知不能来面试的信**,则要说清不能来的理由,往往都是因为简历不符合要求或是其他申请者的条件更好。当然,还要给足申请者台阶下,不能一棍子打死。**具体内容大致是**:"1. 简历已经收到,对你印象深刻;2. 但是,由于某某原因(申请人太多,竞争激烈,或是你的经历不是我们最需要的),我们没有通过你的简历,无法邀请你参加面试;3. 安慰的话,如这不是因为您不好,而是因为竞争激烈;或是您可以关注某某岗位,您的经验申请那个岗位也许机会更大;或是您的材料已经被收入我们的人才库,我们以后一旦有需要,会及时通知您来面试,等等;4. 感谢对我公司的关注。"

面试结束后,用心的申请人都会写一封**面试感谢信**给用人单位,首先是表示态度诚恳,其次可以给自己的成功求职增加筹码。一般面试感谢信都在面试后的两天内寄出,趁热打铁,越快越好。一般步骤包括:1. 感谢对自己的关注和给予面试机会,稍微提示自己是谁(面试人员太多了);2. 重申对该职位的兴趣;3. 如果面试中有什么漏掉的信息，或是很想展示的方面，利用此信补充；4. 简要重述或提醒面试官自己的良好技能，说明自己可能给公司带来什么利益，顺便提及面试过程中的精彩难忘片段；5. 若在面试中，用人单位有要求提供什么进一步的信息资料，在这封信中补充完整。

聘用信（就是我们常说的 Offer）是通知录用的信件，是求职者忙活了半天最希望见到的。由于面试中一般都会口头协商好聘用后的各种要求和待遇等，因此此信往往是对口头协商的一次书面确定。它一般要包括：表示恭喜；正式聘用的日期；被聘用的职位；工作职责；工作地址；工资起薪；相关福利等等。

有了聘用信，当然就会有通知未能聘用的信。这类信件和上述拒绝面试的信基本是相同的思路。即感谢对公司的关注和前来面试，赞扬申请人的表现。接着，话锋一转，说明因为什么而不能录用。再说些鼓励的话和祝福早日找到合适工作的话。

收到聘用信后，于情于理，申请人都要表示感谢。这样的感谢信不需要太长，将自己的感谢之情表达清楚即可，以示礼貌。

当然，并非所有的聘用信都会收到"好脸色"的，有时申请人也会把用人单位"炒"了。原因很多，比如生活地点的突然变化、家庭原因等等，当然最多的还是在别处另有高就。**拒纳信的步骤一般包括：** 1. 向用人单位问好，感谢录用；2. 礼貌地拒绝录用，说明拒绝原因；3. 结尾语气要积极，赞扬对方公司，祝愿找到合适的雇员。

26. 用人单位收到简历后的初步回复

Dear applicant,

　　We have received your application for the above position. Due to overwhelming response, we are still in the process of selecting suitable candidates for interview. You will be informed of our selection in due course.

Yours sincerely,
Hiring manager

亲爱的申请者：
　　我们已经收到了您对上述职位的申请材料。由于申请者较多，我们仍在选择适合面试的申请人。您会在一定的时间内收到我们的通知。

人事部经理 谨上

27. 用人单位审阅求职信后的面试邀请

Dear Ms Josephine,

With regards to your application for the position of Assistant Editor in our company, we would like you to come to our office for an interview on 25 May, 2011 at 9:30 a.m.

Please bring along the original copies of your certificates and other relevant documents. We look forward to meeting you. Thank you.

Yours sincerely,
Li Hua

尊敬的乔瑟芬女士：

您申请了我公司的助理编辑一职，我们希望您于 2011 年 5 月 25 日早 9:30 来办公室面试。

请带上您的证书原件和其他相关文件。我们期待与您见面。谢谢。

李华 谨上

28. 用人单位审阅求职信后的回绝

Dear Ms Josephine,

I refer to your e-mail of 20 May, 2011. We appreciate your interest in our company. I regret to inform you that at the present time we have no vacancies.

We would, however, encourage you to regularly check our website www.123.com for future job and career opportunities. Your personal interest has been noted and will receive due consideration in your future applications.

Yours sincerely
Hiring manager

尊敬的乔瑟芬女士：

我们收到了您于 2011 年 5 月 20 日发来的求职邮件。我们对您对我公司的关注表示赞赏。但遗憾地告诉您，公司目前还没有空余的职位。

然而，我们鼓励您经常查阅公司网站 www.123.com，以获取日后的工作机会。您对我公司的兴趣得到了我们的关注，若日后您还来我公司申请职位，您将得到适当的考虑。

人事部经理 敬启

29. 求职者对面试邀请的拒绝

To Whom It May Concern,

　　I am very pleased to belong to the applicants that you have requested for a final job interview. With all the things that I have heard about your company, everyone that will be qualified to work are so proud of your company because it is very prestigious and it's a big opportunity to be a part of it. However, I need to decline your invitation for an interview because I already have a job in a certain company and I just have signed a contract to them.

　　I am so regretful to decline this interview but I have no choice but to do it because of my existing contract to the company where I am presently working. I hope this is not the last time that you will contact me for an interview. Thank you very much for your appreciation of my application.

Sincerely yours,
Christy Jeffers

敬启者：

　　非常高兴能够成为贵处选择的进入最后一轮面试的申请者。据我所知，每位有资格在贵公司工作的人都非常自豪，因为贵公司闻名遐迩，能成为你们的一员是一个绝佳的机遇。然而，由于我已经在某公司找到了一份工作，并且刚刚与他们签订了合同，因此我不得不拒绝贵处的面试邀请。

　　对于这次拒绝我本人表示非常遗憾，但是我别无选择，因为现在已经有合同在身，并且已开始工作。我希望这不是贵公司最后一次通知我面试。非常感谢贵公司对我申请材料的认可。

克里斯蒂·杰夫斯 谨上

30. 用人单位面试后的回绝

Dear Ms Josephine,

I want to thank you for speaking with me yesterday concerning ABC Company's employment opening. I have reviewed your work history, educational background, and goals.

I appreciate your honesty and openness during our conversation, but I feel that your credentials are not the best match for our current open position. Many applications have been reviewed, and another applicant has been selected for this position.

Your application will be placed on file for 90 days. If you would like to apply for another open position within the company, please feel free to do so at any time.

Thank you for considering us, and please accept my best wishes for your future.

Sincerely,
Hiring manager

尊敬的乔瑟夫女士:

非常感谢昨天您在 ABC 公司的面试中与我交流。我重新看了一遍您的工作简历、教育背景和求职目标。

我对您在谈话中开诚布公的态度表示赞赏,但我认为就您的资历来看,您并非当前空缺职位的最佳人选。我们审阅了众多求职者的材料,有一位求职者被选中。

您的申请材料将被存档 90 天。如果您有意申请我公司的其他空缺职位,请随时向我们申请。

感谢您考虑我公司。请接受我对您未来最美好的祝愿。

人事部经理 敬启

31. 求职者面试后的感谢信(争取工作机会)

Dear Sir,

I was fortunate to have attended the interview held on the 18th of this month. The interview was for the post of ***.

The job, as you presented it, seems to be of my interests. I will bring to the position strength, assertiveness and the ability to encourage others to work cooperatively with the department. Since I have a long experience of working with the nursing staff, I shall try to prove to be an asset to your college.

I also have a wide administrative experience and also understand your need for administrative support. My detail orientation and organizational skills will help to free you to deal with larger issues. I appreciate the time you took to interview me. I am very interested in working for you and look forward to hearing from you about this position.

Thank You.

Yours Sincerely,
David Ronaldson

敬启者：

能够参加本月 18 日的面试，我感到很幸运。我申请的是 *** 一职。

根据贵处的岗位描述，这份工作恰好与我的兴趣相符。若蒙聘用，我将发挥自己的能力与自信，鼓励他人与本部门合作。由于我有长期与护士共事的经历，因此我会尽我所能，证明自己是贵院的一笔财富。

我还有较多的管理经验，也知道贵处需要行政管理支持。我对细节的把握和在组织方面的能力将使你们能够放下心来处理更重要的事务。非常感谢贵处在百忙之中对我进行面试。我对贵处的职位甚是有意。期待贵处的通知。

非常感谢。

大卫·罗纳尔森 谨上

32. 录用通知（正式职位）

Dear Mr. Charles,

We are pleased to inform you that our Board of Directors have agreed to offer you a job as Biology Teacher in our school. This appointment begins on 1 Jan, 2011.

The appointment is subject to probation period of three months and entitles you to a monthly starting salary of USD 3,000. On confirmation you will be entitled to medical benefits and an annual salary increment of USD100 subject to approval by the Board of Directors.

If you decide to accept our offer, please fill in and return the enclosed form to us as soon as possible. Thank you.

Yours sincerely,
Henry Brown

尊敬的查尔斯先生：

非常高兴地通知您，我校校董会已经同意邀请您担任我校生物老师。该任命于 2011 年 1 月 1 日起生效。

该任命包含三个月的试用期，您的基本工资是每月 3 000 美元。一旦校董会同意正式录用您，您将获得医疗补助，每年的薪酬增幅是 100 美元。

如果您决定接受我们的职位，请尽快填好附表并寄回给我们。谢谢。

亨利·布朗 谨上

33. 申请人接受工作岗位

Dear Mr. Brown,

It was wonderful meeting you and your two colleagues at my job interview with your company on the 5th. Thank you so much for taking the time to tell me more about the position and your company.

Thanks also for extending to me an offer to join your company in the position of senior manager of marketing. I am pleased to notify you that I intend to accept this offer. I look forward to receiving the documents that I will need to sign in order to formally accept the job offer.

Thank you again. I am eager to make a lasting contribution to your company's success in the near future.

Best regards,
John Smith

尊敬的布朗先生：

本月 5 号在面试中见到您和您的两位同事使我非常高兴。非常感谢您花时间告诉我关于该职位和贵公司的更多信息。

　　对您提供的贵公司市场部高级经理一职，我同样表示感谢。很高兴地告诉您，我愿意接受这一职位。我期待贵处寄来的合同文件，签约后，本人将正式接受该职位。

　　再次感谢。我迫切希望为贵公司不久后的成功做出源源不断的贡献。

约翰·史密斯 敬启

34. 申请人拒绝工作岗位

Dear Mr. Brown,

　　Thank you very much for considering me for the position of senior manager of marketing with your company. However I would like to withdraw my application for the job. I am unable to accept this position as I have accepted a similar position with other company.

　　I truly appreciate your taking time to interview me and share information on the opportunity and your company.

　　Best wishes for your company's continued success.

Best Regards,
John Smith

尊敬的布朗先生：

　　非常感谢您对本人申请贵公司市场部高级经理一职的考虑。然而，本人希望撤销这一申请。由于本人已接受另一家公司的相似职位，故不能再接受该职。

　　对您拨冗对本人进行面试，并与我分享该职位以及贵公司的信息，本人表示由衷的感谢。

　　祝贵公司的事业不断取得成功。

约翰·史密斯 谨上

Unit 6　申请和批复

Applications & Replies

　　申请（Application）是个人或集体向组织、机关、企事业单位或社会团体表述愿望、提出请求时使用的一种文书。申请书的使用范围广泛，同一般书信一样，也是表情达意的工具。申请书要求一事一议，内容要单纯。在人事方面，申请的内容一般有请假、加薪、晋升、调动等。申请通常是下级向上级传达的文书，因此语气要诚恳、谦逊、朴素，切忌随意和平起平坐；理由要充分、明确、清晰。在申请书的最后，要表达对通过申请的期待。中文的申请中，往往在后面需要加上日期，英文则可加可不加。建议读者朋友们在实践中加上，以便单位备份。注意，中文的日期往往在署名的下方，而英文则一般是在信的上方，下方也可。

　　批复（Reply）是用于答复下级机关请示事项的公文，它是机关应用写作活动中的一种常用公务文书。这里的"请示"，即我们所说的申请，是我国官方对这一文体的正式叫法。批复是上级向下级发送的文书，因此语气中一般要带着威严，较为正式。然而和中文的批复不同，英文的批复往往在亲和力方面更胜一筹，也不一定要有中文中的标题之类的格式；而且相较于中文批复的极端简洁，英文的往往字数会多一些。批复中一般包括：1. 批复引语：一般称收到某文，或某文收悉。要写明是对于何时、何日、关于何事的请示的答复，时间和文号可省略；2. 批复意见：即针对请示中提出的问题所作的答复和指示，意思要明确，语气要适当，什么同意，什么不同意，为什么某些条款不同意，注意事项等都要写清楚；3. 批复要求（其实可以单独算作结尾），是从上级机关的角度提出的一些补充性意见，或是表明希望、提出号召。如果同意，可写要求；不同意，亦可提供其他解决办法。至于落款，英文的批复则往往非常简单，和其他类型的信件无异。

35. 病假申请

模板

Dear Mr. Michael,

　　I am writing to confirm that I shall not be in the office for a period of one week and shall be on a leave of absence starting 30th July, 2009. As you are already aware, I will be undergoing a minor surgery on 30th July, 2009, which will require one week of complete rest.

I am involved in two major projects at present with Fairfield technologies and Bluestar Enterprises. I have handed over my responsibilities to my colleague Sarah Parker, who is well versed with the projects and will handle the same without any problem.

I shall rejoin and resume work on 6th August, 2009, as agreed.

Thank you.

Yours sincerely,
Jonas Mathews

尊敬的迈克尔先生：

此信是要向您确认我将离岗一周时间，我的请假从 2009 年 7 月 30 日开始。正如您所知，我在 2009 年 7 月 30 日要做一次小手术，而这次手术需要一周的调养时间。

目前我手上有两个项目，分别是与公平领地技术公司和蓝星公司的工程。我已经将我的责任移交给我的同事莎拉·帕克，她对这两项工程业务熟悉，要她来接手不会有任何问题。

如您之前所同意，我将于 2009 年 8 月 6 日重返工作岗位。

谢谢。

乔纳斯·马修斯 谨上

36. 产假申请

Dear Diana,

I wish to apply for maternity leave from 31st July, 2009 and have attached the relevant form of application. As you are aware, I am pregnant and the baby is due on the 20th of August, 2009. I wish to apply for full maternity benefit for the period of maternity leave beginning 31st July, 2009 up to 20th June, 2010. I shall intimate any delay, if any, in my resuming duties and similarly, will notify if I am to join earlier than 20th August.

I have not taken any annual leave for this year and wish to combine it with the maternity leave and request that I may be allowed to do so. I request you to kindly confirm the dates of relieving and resuming.

Awaiting your response at the earliest and thanking you for your consideration.

Yours sincerely,
Amanda Morgan

亲爱的戴安娜：

我想申请从 2009 年 7 月 31 日起开始产假，并附上了相关的申请表。如您所见，我怀孕了，预产期就在 2009 年的 8 月 20 日。同时，在 2009 年 7 月 31 日至 2010 年 6 月 20 日我的孕产假期间，我想申请全额孕产福利。如果产期延后，我将告诉您我延迟回岗；同样，如果我会在 8 月 20 日之前复岗，到时我也将通知您。

今年我尚未申请任何年假，希望年假和产假能够合并，望得到批准。请您确定我的放假日期和复岗日期。

希望早日收到您的批复，并对您的考虑表示感谢。

阿曼达·摩根 谨上

37. 事假申请

Dear Sir,

I wish you to be informed that I will not be available for a period of two days starting from 6th August, 2010 to 7th August, 2010. I have purchased some property in the suburbs and during these two days I shall be finalizing the legal details of the same and taking possession of the house. I shall also be shifting into the new residence immediately and as a result I shall not be able to attend office on those two days.

I shall be available on phone, however, for any problems that may occur. In addition, I have instructed my colleague John as to the details of the projects I have been handling and he is well aware of the situation and can handle the same for two days. I kindly request you to grant me a leave for two days.

Thank you.

Yours Sincerely,
Brian Paulson

尊敬的先生：

特此告知，2010年8月6日和7日我将无法前来上班。我在郊区购买了一些房产，在请假的两天中，我需要完成这些房产的法律程序并接手它们。同时我还要马上搬到新家。因此，在那两天我可能无法到岗。

然而，若有任何情况发生，可以通过电话联系我。我已就手上项目的具体细节对同事约翰进行了指导，他已经了解了情况，有能力在这两天接受这个项目。恳请您批准我两天的事假。

谢谢。

布莱恩·保罗森 谨上

38. 休假申请

Dear Mr. Veron,

  I am writing this letter in order to ask for the leave from work for one week for Christmas holiday. I wish to ask for the specific days since my family will be visiting me from December 22 until December 28. I am writing you earlier in order to have more chances to get the positive answer. Please, note that this leave will not affect on my work since I will make assure that everything is in the order before I leave. My contact number will be at your disposal as well if you need something urgently.

  I will really appreciate if you can give me this chance to meet my family since I haven't seen them from last year. I would like to see you personally and discuss the details. I am always available for the additional questions in case you have them.

  Thank you very much and hope for your soon answer.

  Thanking in advance.

Sincerely Yours,
Richard Brown

尊敬的维纶先生：

我想向您申请一周的休假时间过圣诞节。由于我的家人会在12月22日至28日期间来看我，因此我希望能将假期安排在这一特定时间段内。我提前向您递交申请，希望得到肯定答复的可能性会更大些。请放心，放假之前我会确保一切工作井井有条，因此这次休假不会影响我的工作。同时，如果您有急事需要联系我，也请随时打电话给我。

如果您能给我这次与家人相见的机会，我将不胜感激，因为自去年以来，我们一直都没有见过面。我希望能和您面谈细节。若您还有什么别的问题，我随时愿意回答。

非常感谢，静候佳音。

再次提前感谢您。

理查德·布朗 谨上

39. 加薪申请

Dear Mrs. Smith,

I am working within your company during last two years as a sales executive. I enjoy the work and thank you for the opportunity provided. I remember the day I entered your company as a trainee and now I am experienced sales executive and thankful for that. I would like to ask for the personal meeting with you since I would like to discuss the pay rise in my salary.

I demonstrated good work, the company's sales increased twice during the past two years. I am loyal to the company and love my work. My salary, however, is still on the same level since my first day of work. I strongly believe that after two years I deserve a rise in my salary. My contribution and qualifications give me a right to ask for it.

I kindly ask you to arrange the meeting in order to discuss this matter and my performance.

Hope for your prompt answer.

Thank you in advance.

Sincerely,
Tony Verner

尊敬的史密斯夫人：

我在过去的两年中一直担任您公司的销售主管一职。我很喜欢我的工作，也很感谢您将这个机会提供给我。我记得我刚进入您公司的时候还是个实习生，而现在却成为了一名经验丰富的销售主管。对此我深怀感激。我希望能和您见个面，因为我想和您讨论一下我的加薪问题。

我工作业绩优异。在过去的两年中，公司的销售额增加了两倍。我对公司忠心耿耿，也对我的工作充满热爱。然而，我的薪水与我刚开始工作的第一天相比却丝毫不见增加。我相信，两年之后，我应当得到更多的薪水。出于我的贡献和资质，我申请加薪。

烦请您对我们的面谈做出安排，以便我们商讨加薪申请以及我的工作表现。期待您的早日回复。

提前感谢您。

托尼·维纳 谨上

40. 晋升申请

Dear Mr. Zachary,

  I am writing this letter to request your kind attention on my career. First of all I would like to take this opportunity to say thanks for accommodating me as a member of the Synergy Project team. I have been working with the team for the last five years and during this tenure I have learnt extensively and gained lots of experience.

  After acquiring enough knowledge, I consider that the time has come when I need to move upwards in position. This movement will implement my learning to the advantage of our company. At this stage of my career, a promotion would be very motivating for me and will encourage me to do more toward the prosperity of the company.

  I vow my dedication and sincerity to the company and remain optimistic that the company will offer me a break in serving the company in a better position.

  Thank you for your time and consideration.

Yours Sincerely,
Phineas Ridley

尊敬的扎查理先生：

  我写此信，希望您能对我的工作情况给予适当的关注。首先，我想借此机会感谢您让我加入协同项目组。过去五年,我一直在项目组中工作,在这五年间,我广泛地学习,获得了许多经验。

在学到了许多知识后,我想我应该得到提升了。我的晋升将是对公司有益的。在我职业生涯的这个阶段,一次晋升将会是对我积极性的极大促进,将会鼓励我为公司的繁荣壮大付出更多。

我发誓,我将尽最大的诚意奉献公司。同时我也相信,公司会给我的职业生涯一个突破,让我在一个更高点为公司服务。

您在百忙之中看信和考虑这一申请,对此我非常感激。

菲利斯·瑞德里 谨上

41. 调动工作申请

Dear Mr. Michael,

I am writing this letter in order to request you to transfer me to New York office of our company. The reason of such request is that I have to move to New York in the end of this month due to some very important family circumstances. I enjoy working in our company and don't want to quit and search another job in New York. Therefore, I kindly ask you to consider my transfer to New York. I am looking forward to staying in the company and using my skills and potential to the benefit of our firm even being far away from London.

In case you wish me to train somebody for replacing me in the company's office here, I would love to do that. I really hope for the positive answer from you since I want to continue work in our firm.

Looking forward to hearing from you soon.

Sincerely,
Jack Brown

尊敬的迈克尔先生:

我申请被调动到我公司的纽约办事处工作。我提交这份申请是由于一些非常重要的家庭环境因素,我不得不在本月底搬到纽约居住。我非常喜欢在我公司工作,不想辞掉工作而在纽约另寻他职。鉴于此,我恳请您对我的调动申请予以考虑。我期待着继续留在公司,并凭借自己的技术和潜力为公司服务,即便是远离伦敦。

如果您需要我培训哪位员工，以让他/她接替我在这里的工作，我将非常乐意。我真心地期待能够得到肯定的答复，因为我真的希望继续在我公司工作。

静候佳音。

杰克·布朗 谨上

42. 事假批复

Dear Mr. Goldsborough,

  Greetings!

  We have considered your request for a leave of absence to deal with certain personal matters, and we are pleased to inform you that it has been approved. Your leave is set to begin on March 15 and you are expected to return to the office by April 1. During the period in question, you will continue to receive your regular salary through direct deposit and be covered by the company health plan, subject to the terms and conditions set forth by our provider.

  Please coordinate with your immediate supervisor regarding any pending work which has yet to be completed, as well as the handling of your regular responsibilities.

  Best wishes for the speedy resolution of your family problems.

Sincerely yours,
Robert McNeill
Personnel Manager, Fisher Company

亲爱的格斯布朗先生：

  您好！

  我们考虑了您关于请假解决一些个人事务的申请，我们很高兴地通知您，您的申请已经得到了同意。您的事假开始于3月15日，4月1日前，您就需要回到工作岗位上。请假期间，您将继续得到常规工资，我们会直接打到您的工资账户上。您也将根据我们的保险公司制定的条款和条件，继续享受公司的医疗保险。

  关于尚未完成的工作和您的日常职责，请与您的上司进行协商。

  祝您尽快解决您的家庭问题。

43. 休假批复

Dear Mr Jesse,

This letter is in regards to the application for leave of absence submitted by you at the beginning of the year. You will be glad to know that management has approved your leave of absence for 50 days as requested by you and thus officially, you will be on leave from 1st march, 2011 to 20th April, 2011. We have informed all the relevant departments and units about your period of leave.

Please be informed that the accounts department is informed about your sanctioned leave period and it is ensured that your salary and other entitlements are correctly credited to your account.

On behalf of all the management team, I would like to extend best wishes for your leave. Hope you will have great time.

Yours faithfully,
Thomas D Moody
HR Manager
Moody Corporation

亲爱的杰西先生：

本信是对您于年初提交的休假申请的批复。恭喜您，管理层已经批准了您所要求的 50 天的休假申请。这样，您的正式休假时间将是从 2011 年 3 月 1 日至 2011 年 4 月 20 日。我们已将您的休假时间段告知了所有相关部门和单位。

财务科已经了解到您得到批准的休假时间，他们会确保您的薪水和其他福利准确无误地打到您的账户上。

我谨代表所有管理人员，祝您度过一个美好的假期。假期愉快！

诚挚的 托马斯·D·穆迪
穆迪公司人事部经理

44. 加薪批复

Dear Mr Jesse,

This letter is to inform you that HR team has evaluated your application of revised remuneration and approved it. Thus, your revised remuneration will be $90,000 and will be effective from 5th Feb, 2011.

Old Salary: $75,000 per annum

Revised Salary: $90,000 per annum

Effective Date: 5th Feb 2011

You will be required to sign the attached documents and return one copy to HR Departments for our records. Please read the terms and conditions thoroughly and sign it saying that you agree with the revised remuneration package.

In addition to increased salary, you will also be entitled for performance bonus and various other incentives.

Please feel free to contact HR department for any clarifications required.

Respectfully yours,
Thomas D Moody
HR Manager
Moody Corporations

尊敬的杰西先生：

此信特来告知，人事小组已经评估了您的加薪申请，并予以通过。这样，您变更后的工资为每年 9 万美元，自 2011 年 2 月 5 日起生效。

原有工资：75 000 美元 / 年

改后工资：90 000 美元 / 年

生效日期：2011 年 2 月 5 日

请在附属的文件上签字，并将其中一份寄回给人事部门，以便我们存档。请读完所有的条款和条件，并签字说明您同意修改后的工资。

在您增加的薪酬之外，您还将得到业务分红和各种激励奖金。

若还有任何问题需要澄清，请随时联系人事部门。

恭敬的
托马斯·D·穆迪
穆迪公司人事部经理

45. 晋升批复

Dear Mr. Cash,

Greetings!

We are pleased to inform you that due to your exemplary performance, your application of being promoted to the rank of Senior Supervisor in your department has been approved. This means that you will now be supervising staff members working in one of the department's sub-divisions, and will be reporting directly to the head of the department. You have also been promoted two additional salary tiers and will now be receiving a salary of $5,240 a month, as well as other benefits with your new position.

Please consult with your immediate supervisor regarding the turnover of your duties to other staff and schedule a meeting with the department head before the end of the week regarding your new responsibilities.

Congratulations on your new position and we hope that you will continue performing at the same exemplary level that you have demonstrated in the past.

Sincerely yours,
Christopher Jennings

亲爱的卡什先生：

您好！

非常高兴地告诉您，由于您的带头模范表现，您关于晋升本部门高级管理员的申请已经得到了批准。这意味着，您将监督您所在部门其中一个分支的所有员工，并直接向部门经理报告。同时，您的薪资水平也将晋升两级，现在您的薪水是每月 5240 美元，同时，您还将得到与您现在地位相符的其他福利。

请与您的上司商讨您的职责交接问题，并于本周末之前与部门经理安排一次约见，讨论您新的职责。

祝贺您升迁！我们希望您能和往常一样，继续发挥带头模范作用。

克里斯多分·杰尼斯 谨上

Unit 7　企业各类人事通知　Notices & Announcements

通知（Notice & Announcement）是我们经常可以看到的，在学校、单位、还有公共场所都可以看到。通知的类型也很多，上级对下级的某项工作的要求和安排叫指示性通知。这种通知要注意把要求和措施部分交待清楚，可以分条也可用小标题的形式，这样才能便于下级执行。会议性的通知大家都见过，一般就是目的、会议的名称、内容、参加人员、会议时间、地点等，要注意的是要把这些写正确，通知错时间地点就是你的失职了。通知还有批转性通知、转发性通知，这类的通知就是有话则长，无话则短，也就是要简明扼要，直接陈述事宜即可。

按照发布的方式分，通知可以被分为两种，一种以布告（Bulletin）的形式发送，一种以信件（Letter）的形式发送。布告形式的目标群体往往较大，而信件一般只针对当事人而发。

写通知前要明确：通知的受众是谁；为何要写这份通知；发布形式；以何语气写这份通知。通知的语言要简易、简洁、直接、流畅。

通知主要包括这些部分：

1. 标题（Title）：对公众的通知可用"Notice"，也可用具体通知事由作为标题，而对私人的信件类通知则可不写标题。
2. 正文（Body）：包括通知对象、事由、理由、时间、地点、注意事项等，具体的人事方面的通知需简洁明了，适当的时候要体现出人情味儿。
3. 发布者（Sender）：放在正文后，右下角处，可加上发布者的职位。
4. 发布日期（Date）：这个可有可无，一般信件类的没有，而布告类的往往需要添加；尤其在中文写作习惯中，几乎是都会添加。

46. 晋升通知

Dear Mr. Chen,

We are writing to let you know that you have been selected to be promoted from position A to position B, effective immediately. During the past two years with our company, you have consistently demonstrated your work ethic, creative ideas, and your superb qualifications. We know you will excel in your new position.

We will also be making a formal announcement to the entire staff about your promotion this week, so be on the lookout for that.

Congratulations on this promotion, and we look forward to your contributions as our new marketing manager. Thank you for being such a valuable asset to our company and for your loyal service.

Sincerely yours,
Tom White

尊敬的陈先生：

我们通知您，您将从 A 职位晋升到 B 职位，立即执行。在为我公司工作的过去两年里，您不断展示出自己的职业操守、创新能力和卓越资质。我们相信您在新的岗位上也将出类拔萃。

本周，我们也将向全体员工发布一份正式的关于您晋升的通知，敬请期待。

我们对您的晋升表示祝贺。我们期待您在市场部经理的岗位上为公司再做贡献。您是我们公司的一笔宝贵财富，对公司一向忠心耿耿，对此我们深怀感激。

汤姆·怀特 谨上

47. 年终奖通知

Dear All,

As a way to thank employees for dedicated efforts in the past year, we will be distributing year-end bonuses to all employees on December 21. Each employee will receive a separate letter stating the amount of the bonus, which will be included along with the direct deposit for the December 21 paycheck.

If you have questions, please contact Human Resources. We thank you for your hard work this year and look forward to continued success and prosperity as we begin another year together.

Best regards,
Tom White

President
ABC Company

亲爱的员工们：

  为答谢大家在过去一年里的辛勤努力，我们将在 12 月 21 日对所有雇员颁发年终奖金。每位员工将分别收到一封通知信，信上会说明各自得到的奖金数额。奖金将随同 12 月 21 日发出的工资，一并打入诸位的工资账户。

  若有问题，请联系人力资源部。我们对大家今年的努力工作表示感谢，并期待我们明年携手，再创成功与辉煌。

诚挚的 汤姆·怀特
ABC 公司总经理

48. 警告通知

Dear Mr. Lee,

  This is in regards to your poor attendance; I have noticed that during the past three months you have been taking unplanned leaves. Well once in a while it's understood that that could be some personal reason. But you have been missing from work from past one week and you come back saying your sister was not well and was hospitalized. It's really annoying that you didn't even bother to inform or pick up the call when called. I have checked your leaves and you have used all your leaves and not left with any more. Also you already have taken 10 unplanned leaves. You know, as a company policy, a person cannot avail more than 2 unplanned leaves in a month. It's only allowed in emergency cases, but as my records you have been taking leaves every month and this is effecting your production which in turn effects the team.

  I have been questioned by the seniors. Please take it seriously or you will have to face the consequences.

  I hope you understand the effect of such warning and will be regular going forward.

Sincerely yours,
Noah Miller

尊敬的李先生：

  此信意在提醒你注意自己糟糕的出勤情况。我注意到，在过去的三个月里，你有数次都擅自离开岗位。当然，若是一次两次的离开，还可以说是你确有一些私人原因。但是从上周开始，你就不在工作岗位上，回来时你声称自己的妹妹病了，还被送医院了。让我们恼怒的是，你甚至懒得把情况告诉我们，给你电话也不接。我已经检查了你的请假情况，发现你已经用完了你所有的请假权利，一次也不剩。同时，你已经有十次的擅离职守记录。你知道公司有规定，员工每月擅自离开工作岗位的次数不得超过两次。除非发生紧急情况，否则不得擅自离开工作岗位。但根据我的记录，你每个月都曾擅离职守，这影响到了你的业绩，更影响到了整个团队。

  上级已经就此对我进行了询问。请严肃对待，否则后果严重。

  我希望你明白这一警告的作用，并且在日后能够正常出勤。

诚挚的 诺亚·米勒

✏️ 49. 辞退通知

模板

Dear Miss. Liu,

  We have frequently asked you to demonstrate greater effort and greater commitment to your work. We gave you numerous chances to improve your performance and to meet the company's required standards. Your recent work has not been complete or accurate, however, and it is unacceptable.

  Because of your poor performance, our company has decided to remove you from your position as a sales person. If you feel that we have made this decision based on insufficient knowledge, then please feel free to speak with me immediately. I will review any personal information that you provide as I deem necessary.

  I wish you luck in your future endeavors.

Sincerely yours,
Noah Miller

尊敬的刘女士：

  我们时常要求你在工作上显示出更大的努力和更多的责任心。我们给了你无数次的机会，让你改善自己的工作表现，达到公司规定的标准。然而，你最近的工作不仅没有做完，而且做得粗枝大叶，这是令人无法接受的。

由于你的拙劣表现，公司已经决定不再聘用你为销售人员。如果你认为我们是因为得到的信息不足而做出了这样的决定，请随时找我谈话。如果认为有必要，我将复查你所提供的一切信息。

祝你今后一路顺风。

诺亚·米勒 谨上

50. 裁员通知

Dear All,

As you undoubtedly know, our company has faced some serious challenges in recent years. We have made numerous critical changes in our efforts to weather these times. Despite that, we find it necessary to take some drastic measures. One of these involves personnel, and more specifically, we will be reducing our staff and laying off 50 employees within the next month. Individual employees affected by this change will receive notification directly from their managers.

Thank you for your efforts toward helping our company face these severe challenges. If you have questions or need further details, please do not hesitate to contact Human Resources.

Sincerely yours,
Noah Miller

亲爱的员工们：

你们一定知道，近年来，我公司遇到了一些严重的挑战。为了渡过难关，我们做出了许多重大改变。除了已经做出的变革，我们认为还有必要采取一些严厉的措施。其中一项措施是人事方面的，具体地说，就是在下个月之内，我们将裁去50名员工。受这一措施影响的员工将会直接从他们的经理处得到通知。

感谢大家努力帮助公司面对这些严峻的挑战。若大家有问题，或是希望得到更多的细节信息，请随时联系人力资源部。

诺亚·米勒 谨上

51. 职务空缺通知

Dear All,

Sunrise Investments announces a job opening for a human resources assistant within the Human Resources department. This position is available immediately, and the HR managers will begin conducting interviews on Monday, February 10th.

Please contact Human Resources at 555-1212 for further details on the position and on required job qualifications.

Sincerely yours,
Noah Miller

亲爱的员工们：

　　日出投资公司宣布，人力资源部现有人力资源助理一职空缺。该职位现在就可申请，人力资源部管理人员将于2月10日（周一）开始面试。
　　请拨打555-1212联系人力资源部，以获得该职位及其要求资质的详细信息。

诺亚·米勒 敬上

52. 介绍新员工

Dear All,

Sunrise Investments is excited to announce the newest member of our company's dynamic team. On October 16, Debra Jones joined the technical support department as technical manager. In her new position, Debra oversees a staff of 15 company associates. She brings 17 years of experience in various technical support capacities.

We are eager to see Debra's positive contributions to our company and enthusiastically welcome her to our organization.

Sincerely yours,
Noah Miller

亲爱的员工们：

　　日出投资公司激动地宣布，我们活力四射的团队又增添了一名新成员！10

月 16 日，德博拉·琼斯作为技术经理，加入了技术支持部门。在她的新岗位上，德博拉要监管 15 名员工。她在各种技术支持岗位上获得了 17 年的工作经验。

我们热切期待德博拉为公司做出的积极贡献，并热烈欢迎她加入我们公司。

诺亚·米勒 谨上

53. 员工辞职通知

Dear All,

After 20 years of service with Allied Constructions, Bill Dodds is resigning from his position as executive vice president, effective May 6th. We are extremely grateful for Bill's contributions to the company and wish him the very best in his future endeavors.

We will provide further details on this transition as the information becomes available.

Sincerely yours,
Ethan Carter

亲爱的员工们：

在为联合建筑公司服务了 20 年之后，比尔·多斯先生将辞去他现在执行副总裁的职务，自 5 月 6 日起生效。比尔为公司做出了巨大贡献，对此我们无比感激。祝愿他今后的事业一切顺利。

关于这一事件的详细信息确定之后，我们将向大家提供。

伊森·卡特 谨上

54. 员工退休通知

Dear All,

With mixed feelings, we announce that two of our company's longtime employees are retiring in June. Jack Wills has worked in the accounting department as manager for 23 years, and Ellen Silver has been an assistant with the IT department for 17 years.

In honor of their service and friendship, we will be holding a retirement party for Jack and Ellen in the cafeteria on September 18 from 2 p.m. to 3 p.m.

Please join us for this celebration as we thank Jack and Ellen and wish them the very best.

Best regards,
Noah Miller

亲爱的员工们：

  我们带着复杂的心情宣布，公司的两位长老级员工将于六月份退休。杰克·威尔斯在会计部门担任了 23 年的经理，艾伦·西尔维作为 IT 部门的助理工作了 17 年。

  为向他们的付出和友谊致敬，我们准备于 9 月 18 日下午 2 点到 3 点在自助餐厅为杰克和艾伦举办退休派对。

  请届时参加这一庆祝活动。我们对杰克和艾伦表示感谢，祝他们万事如意。

诺亚·米勒 谨上

55. 员工死亡通知

Dear All,

  It is with heavy hearts that we inform you of the death of our longtime employee, George Gerard, on October 20th. As you know, George had suffered with a prolonged illness in recent years. Needless to say, we will all miss him more than words can express. He was not just our co-worker but our good friend as well.

  We will announce details regarding the memorial service as we hear more from George's family.

Sincerely yours,
Noah Miller

亲爱的员工们：

  我们带着沉重的心情通知大家，我们的长期雇员乔治·格拉德先生于 10 月 20 日与世长辞了。众所周知，乔治在近些年一直受到疾病的长期困扰。无需多言，我们对他的思念之情难以言表。他不仅是我们的同事，还是我们的朋友。

  一旦从乔治家人处得到关于追悼会的详细信息，我们将通知大家。

诺亚·米勒 谨上

56. 假期安排通知

Dear All,

All offices and locations of our company will be closed for the holidays from December 25, 2011 through January 1, 2012. During this time, all facilities will be locked and inaccessible. All locations will reopen for business at 8:30 a.m. on January 2, 2012.

Please contact Human Resources if you have questions about the holiday closing. We wish you and your family a relaxing and safe holiday season.

Sincerely yours,
Noah Miller

亲爱的员工们：

从 2011 年 12 月 25 日至 2012 年 1 月 1 日，我们公司的所有办公室和厂址都将闭门放假。放假期间，所有场所将被关闭，不准进入。所有办公场所将于 2012 年 1 月 2 日早上 8:30 起重新开放。

若对假期关闭办公场所有任何疑问，请联系人力资源部。我们祝您和您的家人度过一个放松而安全的假期。

诺亚·米勒 谨上

57. 开会通知

Dear All,

Sunrise Investments will hold a special all-employee meeting in the auditorium of Building B on Friday, January 21 at 3 p.m. Key personnel will discuss some changes in the company's organization. After a presentation at the beginning of the meeting, there will be an opportunity for employees to ask questions.

All employees are required to attend this meeting. We look forward to seeing you there.

Best regards,
Noah Miller

亲爱的员工们：

　　日出投资公司将于 1 月 21 日（周五）下午 3 点在 B 楼礼堂召开特殊全体员工大会。重要员工将讨论公司在组织上的一些变化。会前的报告结束后，员工们将有机会提出问题。

　　所有员工必须参加这次会议。期待在会场见到大家。

诺亚·米勒 谨上

Unit 8　辞职信

Letters of Resignation

员工提出辞职，一般情况下，是需要向单位递交正式的辞职信（Letter of Resignation）的。辞职信本身，作为员工的一种结束与单位之间劳动关系的意思表示，具有法律效力，并且会对劳动关系结束的性质、双方责任的划分产生最有决定性的影响。因此，员工在写辞职信时，是需要慎重思考的。

辞职信正文应具备以下要素：1. 受理者恰当的称呼；2. 辞职决定及其理由（如：未受公司重用或尊重，健康、家庭或个人原因，另觅一份更适合自己的工作等）；2. 缓和气氛的语句，如对原单位所给予工作机会以及提供的工作经历表示感谢，对因自己辞职而给对方带来的不便表示歉意，表达对原单位的良好祝愿等等。同时，有时还可以简要加上自己给公司做过的好事，或是赞扬领导和同事，以给对方留下积极印象。

写辞职信的时候要注意：

1. 作为一名员工，在写辞职信之前，不要仓促行动，也不要意气用事。想辞职时，就先要想清楚，你想行使的是哪一种辞职的权利，这种性质的判断，是需要一定的法律基础的。
2. 在想清楚辞职权利的前提下，员工需要确定自己选择哪一种性质的辞职，并且在确定之后，寻找合适的辞职理由。
3. 措词温和，不可激化矛盾。找到合适的理由之后，在具体行文时，不可语气过于生硬，不可因辞职信本身而与单位激化矛盾。但是更不可过于委曲求全，不敢宣告理由而使自己被动。
4. 顺利取得相应的证据；员工对于自己辞职的行为本身、辞职的理由负有举证责任。因此员工在辞职前、辞职时就应当有意识地保留相应的证据。比如领导签过字的辞职申请、自己写的辞职信、单位发的工资条等各种证据，切记，证据需要是原件。
5. 千万要注意：避免负面评论。不论什么原因，不要对你的公司政策、老板、管理人员、同事做任何负面评价。不要认为人走了就可以得罪所有的人，破罐子破摔。为他人，是积口德；为自己，是体现素质，也是给自己留条后路，以免日后若需要原工作单位写工作证明或是推荐信时，遭到拒绝或是恶评。

58. 由于找到其他工作而辞职

Dear Mr. Smith:

In accordance with the terms of my written contract, I hereby give you three weeks notice of my intention to leave. My last day will be March 29, 2009.

I have been offered employment with another organization and have accepted the new post. I apologize for any disruption this will cause but assure you that I will assist with the transfer of duties and responsibilities before leaving.

I would like to thank you for the opportunity to be a part of your team and wish you and your colleagues all the very best for the future.

Yours sincerely
Jean James

尊敬的史密斯先生：

　　根据合同条款，我在此提前三周递交辞职意向书。我在公司最后的日期是2009年3月29日。

　　我得到并接受了另一家公司的职位邀请。我对这一变化可能产生的影响表示歉意，但我向您保证将在离职之前协助责任的转交工作。

　　感谢您给我这次机会，让我成为您团队的一员。祝您和您的同事们今后万事顺意。

锦·詹姆斯 敬启

59. 由于身体原因而辞职

Dear Mr. Smith:

In accordance with the terms of my written contract, I hereby give you two weeks notice of my intention to leave. My last day will be March 29, 2009.

As you are aware I have been unwell for some time and due to the ongoing nature of my illness, I do not feel able to continue in my present role. I apologize for any disruption this will cause but assure you that I will assist with the transfer of duties and responsibilities before leaving.

I would like to thank you for the opportunity to be a part of your team and wish you and your colleagues all the very best for the future.

Yours sincerely
Jean James

尊敬的史密斯先生：

根据合同条款，我在此提前两周递交我的辞职意向书。我在公司最后的日期是 2009 年 3 月 29 日。

正如您所见，我生病已经有一段时间了，由于病情持续，我认为自己已无力继续留在现在的岗位了。我对这一变化可能产生的影响表示歉意，但我向您保证将在离职之前协助责任的转交工作。

感谢您给我这次机会，让我成为您团队的一员。祝您和您的同事们今后万事顺意。

锦·詹姆斯 敬启

60. 由于搬家而辞职

Dear Mr. Smith,

The purpose of this letter is to inform you of my resignation from my current position as Junior Auditor with Acme Wholesale Distributors, Inc. My last day of work will be Friday, March 10, 2009. As you know, my family will move to Illinois, where I was born and raised, and for that reason I have to tear away from my current job here.

I would like to take this opportunity to express my sincere appreciation for your guidance and counsel during the three years that I have worked under your supervision at Acme. I have learned a great deal about computerized auditing procedures and I am certain that the skills I have acquired will be of value throughout my career.

I know that I have been fortunate to have been associated with Acme Wholesale Distributors because I have learned so much about how important providing outstanding customer service is in today's business environment.

Please use the address on this letter to send my final paycheck and any other official communications that may be necessary.

Sincerely,
Jean James

尊敬的史密斯先生：

　　我写此信的目的是告诉您我将辞去现在担任的极点批发经销公司初级审计员一职，我在公司工作的最后一天将是 2009 年 3 月 10 日（周五）。如您所知，我将举家迁往伊利诺斯州，我就是在那儿出生和长大的。正因为如此，我不得不忍痛辞去现在的工作。

　　我想借此机会感谢您在过去的三年里给我的指导和建议，我在极点公司的工作都是在您的监督下完成的。我学到了很多关于审计电算化程序的知识，我相信这些技术对我的整个职业生涯都将大有裨益。

　　我深知，能够成为极点公司的一员是我的幸运。因为在这里，我认识到了提供杰出的客户服务在今天的商业环境下是多么的重要。

　　请将最后一份薪水寄到这封信上的地址，若需要投寄其他正式书信，也请寄到这里。

锦·詹姆斯 敬启

61. 由于与公司人员意见不合而辞职

【模板】

Dear Mr. Smith,

　　Please accept my letter of resignation. I am giving the company two weeks notice, and my last day of employment will be March 22,'2009. Although you and I have had our differences of opinions, I would like to express my appreciation to you and the company for the learning experience I have had here.

　　If there is anything I can do to ease the transition of my responsibilities, please let me know. Once again, thank you for the opportunity to contribute to your team.

Sincerely,
Jean James

尊敬的史密斯先生：

　　请接受我的辞职信。我提前两周通知公司我的辞职消息。我在公司工作的最后一天将是 2009 年 3 月 22 日。虽然你我意见不合，但我对你和公司给我的这次学习机会表示感激。

若在我的责任转交上有什么可以帮上忙的，请告诉我。再次感谢你给我机会，让我为团队做贡献。

锦·詹姆斯 谨上

62. 接受辞职

Dear Ms Miles,

I write with reference to your resignation letter dated 29th October, 2010. We hereby accept your resignation and the company will release you by 15th November, 2010.

Your resignation has been intimated to the Accounts Department who will process your dues and clear them on your last working day.

I'd like to take the opportunity to thank you for your service and high standards of performance of your duties. We have appreciated your work greatly, and your departure is regretted.

On behalf of the company I wish you all the best for your future.

With best wishes,
Sincerely,
Rictor Stone

亲爱的迈尔斯女士：

此信是对您 2010 年 10 月 29 日的辞职信的回复。我们在此接受您的辞职，公司将在 2010 年 11 月 15 日之前批准您离开。

我们已将您辞职的信息告知会计部门，他们将处理您应得的薪水，并在您的最后一个工作日结清。

我想借此机会感谢您的付出以及您高水准的工作。我们对您的工作深为赞赏，您的离去令人惋惜。

我谨代表公司祝您万事顺利。

里克特·斯通 敬上

特别奉献

一　世界著名企业名称中英对照

1. Exxon Mobil 埃克森美孚 美国 炼油
2. Wal-Mart Stores 沃尔玛商店 美国 零售
3. General Motors 通用汽车 美国 汽车
4. Ford Motor 福特汽车 美国 汽车
5. DaimlerChrysler 戴姆勒克莱斯勒 德国 汽车
6. Royal Dutch/Shell Group 皇家荷兰壳牌集团 荷兰/英国 炼油
7. BP 英国石油 英国 炼油
8. General Electric 通用电气 美国 电子电气
9. Mitsubishi 三菱商事 日本 多样化
10. Toyota Motor 丰田汽车 日本 汽车
11. Mitsui 三井物产 日本 多样化
12. Citigroup 花旗集团 美国 金融
13. Itochu 伊藤忠商事 日本 多样化
14. Total Fina Elf 道达尔菲纳埃尔夫 法国 炼油
15. Nippon Telegraph & Telephone 日本电报电话 日本 电信
16. Enron 安然 美国 能源
17. AXA 安盛 法国 保险
18. Sumitomo 住友商事 日本 多样化
19. Intl. Business Machines 国际商用机器 美国 计算机
20. Marubeni 丸红商事 日本 多样化
21. Volkswagen 大众 德国 汽车
22. Hitachi 日立 日本 电子电气
23. Siemens 西门子 德国 电子电气
24. Ing Group 荷兰国际集团 荷兰 保险
25. Allianz 安联 德国 保险
26. Matsushita Electric Industrial 松下电器 日本 电子电气
27. E. ON 费巴 德国 多样化
28. Nippon Life Insurance 日本生命 日本 保险
29. Deutsche Bank 德意志银行 德国 银行

30　Sony 索尼 日本 电子电气
31　AT&T 美国电话电报 美国 电信
32　Verizon Communications 弗莱森电讯 美国 电信
33　U.S. Postal Service 美国邮政总局 美国 邮递包裹
34　Philip Morris 菲利普莫里斯 美国 食品烟草
35　CGNU 商联保险 英国 保险
36　J.P. Morgan Chase 摩根大通银行 美国 银行
37　Carrefour 家乐福 法国 零售
38　Credit Suisse 瑞士信贷集团 瑞士 银行
39　Nissho Iwai 日商岩井 日本 多样化
40　Honda Motor 本田汽车 日本 汽车
41　Bank of America Corp. 美洲银行 美国 银行
42　BNP Paribas 法国巴黎银行 法国 银行
43　Nissan Motor 日产汽车 日本 汽车
44　Toshiba 东芝 日本 电子电气
45　PDVSA 委内瑞拉石油 委内瑞拉 炼油
46　Assicurazioni Generali 忠利保险 意大利 保险
47　Fiat 菲亚特 意大利 汽车
48　Mizuho Holdings 瑞穗控股 日本 银行
49　SBC Communications 西南贝尔 美国 电信
50　Boeing 波音 美国 航空航天
51　Texaco 德士古 美国 炼油
52　Fujitsu 富士通 日本 计算机
53　Duke Energy 杜克能源 美国 电力煤气
54　Kroger 克罗格 美国 零售
55　NEC 日本电气公司 日本 电子电气
56　Hewlett-Packard 惠普 美国 计算机
57　HSBC Holdings 汇丰控股 英国 银行
58　Koninklijke Ahold 的 荷兰 零售
59　Nestle 雀巢 瑞士 食品

二 企业部门及职位中英对照

Marketing and Sales （市场与销售部分）
Vice-President of Sales 销售副总裁
Senior Customer Manager 高级客户经理
Sales Manager 销售经理
Regional Sales Manager 地区销售经理
Merchandising Manager 采购经理
Sales Assistant 销售助理
Wholesale Buyer 批发采购员
Tele-Interviewer 电话调查员
Real Estate Appraiser 房地产评估师
Marketing Consultant 市场顾问
Marketing and Sales Director 市场与销售总监
Market Research Analyst 市场调查分析员
Manufacturer\'s Representative 厂家代表
Director of Subsidiary Rights 分公司权利总监
Sales Representative 销售代表
Assistant Customer Executive 客户管理助理
Marketing Intern 市场实习
Marketing Director 市场总监
Insurance Agent 保险代理人
Customer Manager 客户经理
Vice-President of Marketing 市场副总裁
Regional Customer Manager 地区客户经理
Sales Administrator 销售主管
Telemarketing Director 电话销售总监
Advertising Manager 广告经理
Travel Agent 旅行代办员
Salesperson 销售员
Telemarketer 电话销售员

Sales Executive 销售执行者
Marketing Assistant 市场助理
Retail Buyer 零售采购员
Real Estate Manager 房地产经理
Real Estate Broker 房地产经纪人
Purchasing Agent 采购代理
Product Developer 产品开发员
Marketing Manager 市场经理
Advertising Coordinator 广告协调员
Advertising Assistant 广告助理
Ad Copywriter(Direct Mail) 广告文撰写人
Customer Representative 客户代表

Computers and Mathematics （计算机部分）
Manager of Network Administration 网络管理经理
MIS Manager 电脑部经理
Project Manager 项目经理
Technical Engineer 技术工程师
Developmental Engineer 开发工程师
Systems Programmer 系统程序员
Administrator 局域网管理员
Operations Analyst 操作分析员
Computer Operator 电脑操作员
Product Support Manager 产品支持经理
Computer Operations Supervisor 电脑操作主管
Director of Information Services 信息服务主管
Systems Engineer 系统工程师
Hardware Engineer 硬件工程师
Applications Programmer 应用软件程序员
Information Analyst 信息分析员
LAN Systems Analyst 系统分析
Statistician 统计员

Human Resources （人力资源部分）

Director of Human Resources 人力资源总监
Assistant Personnel Officer 人事助理
Compensation Manager 薪酬经理
Employment Consultant 招募顾问
Facility Manager 后勤经理
Job Placement Officer 人员配置专员
Labor Relations Specialist 劳动关系专员 Recruiter 招聘人员
Training Specialist 培训专员
Vice-President of Human Resources 人力资源副总裁
Assistant Vice-President of Human Resources 人力资源副总裁助理
Personnel Manager 职员经理
Benefits Coordinator 员工福利协调员
Employer Relations Representative 员工关系代表
Personnel Consultant 员工顾问
Training Coordinator 培训协调员

Executive and Managerial （管理部分）

Chief Executive Officer (CEO) 首席执行官
Director of Operations 运营总监
Vice-President 副总裁
Branch Manager 部门经理
Retail Store Manager 零售店经理
HMO Product Manager 产品经理
Operations Manager 操作经理
Assistant Vice-President 副总裁助理
Field Assurance Coordinator 土地担保协调员
Management Consultant 管理顾问
District Manager 市区经理
Hospital Administrator 医院管理
Import/Export Manager 进出口经理
Insurance Claims Controller 保险认领管理员
Program Manager 程序管理经理

Insurance Coordinator 保险协调员
Project Manager 项目经理
Inventory Control Manager 库存管理经理
Regional Manager 区域经理
Chief Operations Officer (COO) 首席运营官
General Manager 总经理
Executive Marketing Director 市场行政总监
Controller (International) 国际监管
Food Service Manager 食品服务经理
Production Manager 生产经理
Administrator 医疗保险管理
Property Manager 房地产经理
Claims Examiner 主考官
Controller (General) 管理员
Service Manager 服务经理
Manufacturing Manager 制造业经理
Vending Manager 售买经理
Telecommunications Manager 电信业经理
Transportation Manager 运输经理
Warehouse Manager 仓库经理
Assistant Store Manager 商店经理助理

特别奉献

三 形容个人品质的词汇中英对照

able 有才干的，能干的
adaptable 适应性强的
active 主动的，活跃的
aggressive 有进取心的
ambitious 有雄心壮志的
amiable 和蔼可亲的
amicable 友好的
analytical 善于分析的
apprehensive 有理解力的
aspiring 有志气的，有抱负的
audacious 有冒险精神的
capable 有能力的，有才能
careful 办理仔细的
candid 正直的
competent 能胜任的
constructive 建设性的
cooperative 有合作精神的
creative 富创造力的
dedicated 有奉献精神的
dependable 可靠的
diplomatic 老练的
disciplined 守纪律的
dutiful 尽职的
well-educated 受过良好教育的
efficient 有效率的
energetic 精力充沛的
expressivity 善于表达
faithful 守信的，忠诚的

frank 直率的，真诚的
generous 宽宏大量的
genteel 有教养的
gentle 有礼貌的
humorous 有幽默
impartial 公正的
independent 有主见的
industrious 勤奋的
ingenious 有独创性的
motivated 目的明确的
intelligent 理解力强的
learned 精通某门学问的
logical 条理分明的
methodical 有方法的
modest 谦虚的
objective 客观的
precise 一丝不苟的
punctual 严守时刻的
elastic 实事求是的
responsible 负责的
sensible (advisable) 明白事理的
sporting 光明正大的
steady 踏实的
systematic 有系统的
purposeful 意志坚强的
sweet-tempered 性情温和的
temperate 稳健的
tireless 孜孜不倦的

Chapter 05

行政文书

　　行政文书涵盖方方面面，种类繁多，是国家机关、企事业单位内部以及单位之间交流的文书形式。作为公文，它们基本都非常正式，以体现其严肃性和执行力。这类文书的英文写作不仅仅需要有基本的英文书信写作常识，还需要对正式英文文体有较好的把握能力，其中包括选词、句式、称呼等。因此，能否写好行政文书，是英语学习者、文秘工作者英文水平的重要体现，没有良好的英语功底做支撑，一般是很难做到的。

　　在我国，国家对公文的种类进行了非常明确的规定，包括命令、决定、报告等。但在英语实践中，国外往往没有相对应的文体，或是对这样的文体没有如我们这般强烈的意识。因此，在与外国友人交流的过程中，需要酌情对行文的格式、措辞、逻辑等进行相应调整，使其以西方人便于理解和接受的形式呈现出来；当然，中文原文的翻译除外，因为译文是要忠实于原文的。

　　本章中选取的例文类型，许多都不是我国规定的公文类型，但不管在国家机关还是企事业单位，这些文种几乎都是最常见的，因而也是最实用的。它们包括：证明、奖状、通知、报告、备忘录、会议议程、会议纪要、新闻稿、致辞等等。希望能给读者朋友们的写作实践提供一些有益的参考。

Unit 1　证明

Certificates

　　证明（Certificate）是以机关、团体、单位或个人证明一个人的身份经历或一件事情的真实情况，供接受单位作为处理和解决某人某事的根据的书信。

　　书写证明时要慎重，除了所证明的事情一定要实事求是、准确无误外，还应注意用语明确、肯定，不得涂改。为便于查考，证明应留底稿，并进行登记。

　　证明的分类有很多种，依据不同，分类也不同。比如从证明的内容来看，我们可以将证明分为证明某人身份、证明某人某一时期的工作经历和证明某件事情真相的证明等。

　　从证明具体的存在方式上来划分的话，我们还可以将证明分为公文式、书信式、便条式三种格式。证明还可以因开据证明之人的不同而分为以组织的名义所发的证明和以个人的名义所发的证明两种。

　　证明的格式：不论是哪种形式的证明，其结构都大致相同，一般都由标题、称呼、正文、署名和日期等构成。

　　1. 标题

　　证明的标题通常就是在第一行中间冠以"证明（Certificate）"字样，英文可以大写，中文可以加粗。

　　2. 称呼

　　通俗地说，要证明给谁看，就写谁。

　　3. 正文

　　正文要在称呼写完后另起一行，空两格书写。要针对对方所要求的要点写，要你证明什么问题就证明什么问题，其他无关的不写。如证明的是某人的历史问题，则应写清人名、何时、何地及所经历的事情；若要证明某一事件，则要写清参与者的姓名、身份及其在此事件的地位、作用和事件本身的前因后果。也就是要写清人物、事件的本来面目。英文证明中的最常用句式为：It's hereby certified that…

　　4. 落款

　　落款即署名和写明成文日期。要在正文的右下方写上证明单位或个人的姓名称呼，成文日期写在署名下另起一行，然后由证明单位或证明人加盖公章或签名、盖私章，否则证明将是无效的。

证明的注意事项：
1. 以个人名义所发的证明。要写明写证明者本人的政治面貌、工作情况等，以便审阅证明的人了解证明人的情况，从而鉴别证明材料的真伪与可信程度。
2. 个人所写的证明的内容如果本人不太熟悉，应写"仅供参考"的提示性语言。因为证明有时是作为结论性证据的，所以要实事求是、严肃认真、要尽量言之有据。
3. 对于随身携带的证明，一般要求在证明信的结尾注明有效时间、过期无效的期限。
4. 证明的语言要十分准确，不可含糊其辞。证明不能用铅笔、红色笔书写，若有涂改，必须在涂改处加盖公章。

本书为读者朋友们列举了几类常用的证明，有身份证明、简历证明、在读证明、工作证明、离职证明、收入证明、夫妻关系证明。

身份证明是对一个人的身份给出书面证实。要求明确写出被证实者姓名、性别、年龄和职务。最后是证人署名。

简历证明是对一个人的简历给出书面证实。除了交代被证人身份外，还需简述被证人的相关学习、工作经历，获过荣誉奖项等。最后是证人署名。

在读证明只需证明某人为某学校几年级在读学生，最后证人署名即可。

工作证明是用于证实某人的工作经历。

离职证明是用于证实某人在某单位的离职。一般应声明其在职所担任职务，必要时说明离职原因。

收入证明是对某人于某企业单位的收入情况的书面证实。

夫妻关系证明是对某夫妇的夫妻关系给予书面证实，需要给出他们成为夫妻的时间。

1. 身份证明

INDENTITY CERTIFICATE

This is to certify that Mr. Cai Kaijian, male, aged 28, is an expert in electronics invited from the People's Republic of China by this Institution.

ABC Institution

(Time)

身份证明

兹证明，蔡凯建，男，28岁，是由我院从中华人民共和国派出的电子学专家。
ABC 机构　　　　　　　　　　　　　　　　　　　（盖章）
　　　　　　　　　　　　　　　　　　　　　　　（时间）

2. 简历证明

RESUME CERTIFICATE

It is hereby certified that Mr. Tao Jiang, male, born in Shanghai city, in February, 1958, is now a professor in the Physiology Department of Beijing Medical University.

Mr. Tao graduated from Xi'an Medical College in 1980 with a Bachelor of Science degree and completed his postgraduate course in Beijing Medical College in July, 1983 for the degree of Master of Science. He received his Doctor of Philosophy degree from University of Pennsyvania in the United States of America in 1987.

From 1987 to now, he has been the professor in Beijing Medical University.

　　　　　　　　　　　　　　Li Feng
　　　　　　　　　　　　　　(Signature)
　　　　　　　　　　　　　　Public Notary
　　　　　　　　　　　　　　Beijing Notary Public Office,
　　　　　　　　　　　　　　The People's Republic of China

简历证明

兹证明，陶江，男，出生地上海，出生时间1958年2月，现为北京医科大学生理学系教授。

陶先生于1980年毕业于西安医科大学，获得理学士学位，并于1983年7月完成北京医科大学研究生课程，获得理科硕士学位。他于1987年在美国宾夕法尼亚大学获得生理学博士学位。

自1987年至今，他一直担任北京医科大学的教授。

　　　　　　　　　　　　　　李峰
　　　　　　　　　　　　　（签名）
　　　　　　　　　　中华人民共和国北京市公证处公证员

3. 在读证明

CERTIFICATE

To whom it may concern,

This is to certify that Mr. Xie Ming is currently a senior student in the English Department of China Foreign Affairs University.

(signature)
English Department,
China Foreign Affairs University
(Time)

在读证明

相关单位：

兹证明，谢明现为外交学院英语系大四年级的一名在读学生。

（签名）
外交学院英语系
（时间）

4. 工作证明

CERTIFICATE

To whom it may concern,

This is to certify that Ms. Lorraine Gonzales was a bona fide Instructor of this college.

This further certifies that Ms. Gonzales was employed and taught in this school from June 2000 up to March 2005.

This certification is issued to Ms. Gonzales upon her request for whatever legal purposes it may serve.

Issued this 26th of May 2005 at *** University.

Allan Rodrigo
College Administrator
(Time)

工作证明

相关单位：

兹证明，罗拉恩·工扎勒斯女士的确曾任本学院教师。

工扎勒斯女士从 2000 年 6 月至 2005 年 3 月受聘任教于本校。

本证明应工扎勒斯女士要求开具，可服务于任何适当的法律用途。

本证明开于 2005 年 5 月 26 日，开具单位为 *** 大学。

阿兰·罗德里格

行政处

（时间）

5. 离职证明

CERTIFICATE OF LEAVING OFFICE

To whom it may concern,

  This is to certify that Miss Li Bing was employed in the General Manager's Office as English secretary for the period from October, 2004 to May, 2009.

  During that time she proved herself to be industrious and capable. She left us of her own accord.

Kang Yijun

General Manager

ABC Company

(Time)

离职证明

相关单位：

兹证明，李冰小姐自 2004 年 10 月至 2009 年 5 月在本公司任总经理办公室英文秘书。

此间她工作勤奋，能干。此次离职，纯属自愿。

ABC 公司

康伊均

（时间）

6. 收入证明

CERTIFICATE OF INCOME

To whom it may concern,

  I certify that the annual income of Mr. Zhang Qingjun, an employee of ABC Company, is RMB 80,000, with a monthly income of RMB 6,600.

            Chen Ming
            President
            ABC Company
            (Time)

收入证明

相关单位：

  本人证明ABC公司员工张清军先生的年收入为80,000（八万）元人民币，每月工资为6600（六千六百）元人民币。

            陈铭
            ABC公司总裁
            （时间）

7. 夫妻关系证明

CERTIFICATE OF MARRIAGE

To whom it may concern,

  This is to certify that Mr. Zhang Yihong and Mrs. Jin Hui are husband and wife. They went into marriage in July, 1994.

            *** Committee
            (Time)

夫妻关系证明

相关单位：

兹证明张毅宏先生和金惠女士为夫妻。他们于1994年7月结婚。

            *** 居委会
            （时间）

Unit 2　奖状

Certificates of Merit

奖状（Certificates of Merit）是授予获奖单位或个人的奖励证明书，用来表示对单位或者个人获得成绩的一种认可和表扬。奖状是授予获奖单位或个人的奖励证明书，以表示对单位或者个人获得成绩的一种认可和表扬。奖状多种多样，最普遍的是学习成绩的奖状，还有三好学生、优秀学生等等。除此，社会中还有各式各样的奖状，总之，名目繁多。

一张奖状一般应该包括以下几个方面的内容：获奖人姓名（或获奖单位名称）、获奖时间、获得何种奖项（或获得何种荣誉称号）、颁奖单位名称、颁奖单位公章、颁奖时间等。

最后署下立办单位（时间）。下面列出了几种典型的奖状类型，如优秀学生奖状、学科竞赛奖状、杰出市民奖状、模范领导组织奖、杰出教练奖状、季度优秀员工奖。

提示：中英文的奖状是有颇有不同的，这点大家在下面的例子中也可见一斑。很多情况下，英文的奖状往往写成竖排居中的形式，乍一看有点像诗歌，学习时需注意观察，英文的奖状上，各种元素（获奖人、奖项、颁奖单位等）出现的顺序。

8. 优秀学生奖状

模板

Sophomore of the Year

Awarded to

Sharon Johnson

In commendation of

An outstanding academic standing

And perfect attendance record

From

The Staff and Faculty

ABC University

May 2009

奖　状

莎朗·约翰森同学：

　　为表彰你优秀的学习成绩和良好的出勤表现，ABC 大学将你评为优秀大二学生。

ABC 大学全体教职员工
2009 年 5 月

9. 学科竞赛奖状

Jones Middle School
Honors
Peter King
For your outstanding performance in the
ABC County Science Fair
"Environmental Management
in an Orbital Space Station"
FIRST PLACE
PHYSICAL SCIENCE DIVISION
Physics Staff Room
2009

奖　状

皮特·金同学：

　　你的作品"轨道空间站的环境管理"在 ABC 县的科学竞赛中表现优异，荣获第一名，琼斯中学特颁此证，以资奖励。

物理教研室
2009 年

10. 杰出市民奖状

ALL COUNTY
ACHIEVERS AWARD
2009
Presented to
James Ross

In appreciation for
outstanding and dedicated
service to our community
Jefferson County
Board of County Commissioners

奖 状

詹姆斯·罗斯同志:

　　为感谢你在社区服务方面的杰出表现和倾心奉献,杰弗森县授予你 2009 年杰出市民奖。

杰弗森县县委会
2009 年

11. 模范领导组织奖

Exemplary Leadership Award
Presented to Joseph Karter
under whose 5 years of leadership
the GizmoGadget development team
won five patents and two "Product of the Year" awards.
Bill Smith,
Chairman & CEO, XYZ Corporation

奖 状

约瑟夫·卡尔特先生:

　　在您过去 5 年的领导下,机子模咔叽特研发团队荣获五项专利和两项"年度产品奖",公司特将模范领导组织奖授予您。

比尔·史密斯
XYZ 公司董事长兼 CEO

12. 杰出教练奖状

Coach's Award
Presented to David Smith

for outstanding character, leadership
and athletic performance
during the 2010~2011 basketball season
with the Smithville Tigers
of the Smithville Varsity League
***

奖 状

大卫·史密斯先生:

　　由于您在 2010~2011 篮球赛季中带领史密斯威尔大学联盟的史密斯威尔老虎队，展示出了您杰出的个人品质、领导水平和运动表现，特授予您杰出教练奖。

***（颁奖单位）

13. 季度优秀员工奖

EMPLOYEE
OF THE SEASON
Jan.~Mar. 2009
Presented to
William Foster
Without you
we would not be!
Thanks for your
hard work
ABC Corporation

奖 状

威廉·佛罗斯特:

　　没有你的付出，就没有我们的成就！感谢你的辛勤工作！特授予你 2009 年 1 月至 3 月季度优秀员工奖。

ABC 公司

Unit 3　通知

Notices & Announcements

通知是上级对下级、组织对成员或平行单位之间部署工作、传达事情或召开会议等所使用的应用文。通知的写法有两种：一种是以布告形式（NOTICE）贴出，把事情通知有关人员，如学生、观众等，通常不用称呼；另一种是以书信的形式，发给有关人员，这种通知写作形式同普通书信，只要写明通知的具体内容即可。通知要求言简意赅、措辞得当、时间及时。

通知的格式包括标题、称呼、正文、落款。

1. 标题：往往是"NOTICE"，有时可以根据具体通知内容具体写，如 LECTURE，ACQUISITION，JOB OPENING 等；当然，也可以不写。
2. 称呼：写被通知者的姓名或职称或单位名称。在第二行顶格写。有时，因通知事项简短，内容单一，书写时略去称呼，直起正文。
3. 正文：另起一行，空两格写正文。正文因内容而异。开会的通知要写清开会的时间、地点、参加会议的对象以及开什么会，还要写清要求。布置工作的通知，要写清所通知事件的目的、意义以及具体要求和作法。切记，通知一定要言简意赅，一目了然，一般来说，少用修饰性的词语。
4. 落款：分两行写在正文右下方，一行署名，一行写日期（英文里有时略去）。

14. 搬迁通知

Dear All,

After 15 years of operation, our company's South Side location will be closing as of Friday, March 12. This location has served us well, and based on our future plans, consolidating into our main location is appropriate. Therefore, all equipment and personnel at the South Side location will begin the transition to our main location on Monday, March 8.

If you have questions about this transition or how it might affect you, please contact Human Resources at extension 7843. Thank you for your patience as we move through the process of closing the South Side location.

Best regards,
Joseph King

各位同事：

　　在 15 年的经营之后，我公司的南部办公地点将在 3 月 12 日（周五）关闭。这个办公地点是个很好的环境，但根据我们未来的计划，将其与我们的总部合并更为合适。因此，南部办公地点的所有设备和人员将从 3 月 8 日（周一）开始进行搬迁。

　　如果您对这次搬迁以及搬迁对您可能产生的影响有任何疑问，请拨打分机号 7843 联系人力资源部。在我们关闭南部办公地点的过程中，感谢您的耐心配合。

约瑟夫·金 谨上

15. 设立分支办公地点通知

Dear Friends,

　　It is with great anticipation and excitement that we announce the opening of Mountain Technologies' second location, in Highlands, Arizona. This satellite location will be at 395 Sage Street, and its functions will include customer service and technical support.

　　Our headquarters and main offices will continue to be in Phoenix. We plan to hold a grand opening and tour of our new Highlands location this summer, so stay tuned for further details.

　　Thank you, as always, for your continued support. We attribute our success to people like you.

Sincerely yours,
Emily Juan
President of Mountain Technologies

亲爱的朋友们：

　　带着满心期待和激动之情，我们宣布山峦科技公司位于亚利桑那州高地市的第二个办公场所开始运作。这个分支办公处将坐落在智者大街 395 号，其业务范围将包括客户服务和技术支持。

我们的总部和主要办公地点依然在凤凰城。我们计划在今年夏天为高地市的新址举办盛大的开业仪式和旅行活动，关于具体细节，敬请期待。

再次感谢各位长期以来的支持。我们的成功归功于诸位朋友。

诚挚的 艾米丽·胡安
山峦科技公司董事长

16. 拓展业务通知

Respected Sir

This letter is on behalf of Friends & Company and we are hereby pleased to inform you that we are expanding our business to its 3rd phase as planned with the assistance & backup of very trustworthy associates like you, who have supported us from the start & in all the odds for which we are very gratified & seek the same in the near future.

As far as for the expansion plans, in the 3rd phase we will be able to reach out for new so as to serve you in a more convenient method. The 3rd phase will help us in serving you with the most modern techniques & packages which will aid you accomplish your tasks even more swiftly and precisely.

Hence to conclude with saying that we will be serving you with the best of our available resources & present in a better modern way.

Thank you.

Mr. Sudesh Bhise.

尊敬的先生：

我们谨代表诸位朋友和公司非常高兴地告诉您，我们将要根据计划，把业务拓展到第三阶段了。这些进步都是在像您这样非常值得信赖的伙伴帮助和支持下实现的。您从一开始便支持我们，风雨无阻，对此我们感激不尽，并希望在不久的将来得到同样的支持。

根据扩张计划，在第三阶段，我们将能够接触新鲜资源，这样便能为您提供更为便捷的服务。第三阶段中，我们将利用最现代化的技术和资源套装为您服务，这些技术将更为快速和准确地完成你们的任务。

信末，我们重申，我们将用手中最好的资源为您服务，并让我们的服务更好、更现代化。

谢谢。

苏德什·比瑟

17. 收购通知

Dear Customers,

We are pleased to announce that we have recently acquired the business assets of ABC Corp. based in New York.

ABC Corp. is a leader in the automobile windshield repair and replacement business in New York State.

The joining of forces with ABC Corp. will give us a strong presence in the Northeast and which will further strengthen our mission to be a truly national organization.

We look forward to serving you better as a result of the acquisition.

Sincerely,
Jill Jones

亲爱的顾客：
  我们很高兴地宣布，近日我们收购了纽约州 ABC 公司的商业资产。
  ABC 公司是纽约州自动挡风玻璃维修和更换服务业的领头羊。
  吸收 ABC 公司的业务实力，将提高我公司在东北地区的地位，并进一步完成我公司成为一家真正的全国性公司的使命。
  我们期待此次的收购能够让我们为您提供更好的服务。

吉尔·琼斯 谨上

18. 公司周年庆祝通知

To all staff members of Generic Company,

Ten years ago I, along with my partners, founded Generic. When we started, we had only four workers and a single delivery van. Today, we have already established factories in five states and are marketing our products abroad.

We are also providing over 5,000 jobs in the local community. These are not inconsiderable achievements at a time when the majority of companies fail within their first year. To mark this very special occasion, we are holding a company barbecue at the Hot Steers Grill on 21st Avenue starting at 4 pm on September 21. There will also be a live band performing starting at 8pm for those who would like to go dancing after dinner.

Attire is semi-formal and friends and family are welcome. If possible, however, please inform your supervisors beforehand of how many guests you intend to invite.

We hope to see you all there.

Sincerely yours,

John Smith

President, Generic Company

聚能公司的全体员工:

十年前，我和我的同伴创立了聚能。公司刚成立的时候，我们只有四个工人和一辆货车。而如今，我们已经在五个州建立了工厂，还将自己的产品远销海外。

同时，我们给当地创造了 5 000 多个就业岗位。在许多公司都止于创业第一年的背景下，这些都是巨大的成就。为了纪念这一特殊场合，我们将于 9 月 21 日下午 4 点在 21 大街的热舵烧烤店举办公司的烧烤聚会。对于晚餐后还想跳舞的同仁，晚 8 点后还将有一支乐队进行现场表演。

聚会衣着不必太正式，欢迎邀请朋友和家人参加。但如果可以，请提前告知你们的工长各自期望邀请人员的数目。

期待届时见到诸位。

聚能公司总裁 约翰·史密斯 谨上

19. 公司更名通知

ANNOUNCEMENT

Dear clients,

Please be informed that from 25th October, 2011, ABC Co. Ltd. will be replaced by XYZ Co. Ltd.

October 1, 2011

通知

敬告顾客，从 2011 年 8 月 25 日起，ABC 公司将更名为 XYZ 公司。

2011 年 8 月 1 日

20. 开会通知

NOTICE OF MEETING

There will be a scheduled staff meeting at 3:00 p.m. on Monday, 16 January, 2012, in the Conference Room at the department. All the staff members are expected at the meeting.

General Office
12 January, 2012

开会通知

2012 年 1 月 16 日（周一）下午 3 点将会按计划召开员工大会，开会地点位于我部的会议室。全体员工都需参加。

总务处
2012 年 1 月 12 日

Unit 4 报告

Reports

报告（Reports）是向上级机关汇报工作、反映情况、提出意见或者建议，答复上级机关的询问时使用的公文。报告既可以采用书信形式或是备忘录形式书写，也可采用叙述文体书写。报告中往往插入图片、表格、图表等辅助说明材料。

在各行各业的实际操作中，报告的种类和写法很多，如市场调查报告（Marketing Report）、可行性研究报告（Feasibility Report）、调查分析报告（Investigation Report）等。报告的长度也悬殊巨大，有的较短，一页则止，而有的却可以出成一本书，这要根据上级具体要求以及报告对象复杂程度来定夺。

报告的格式和写法：正文，结构与一般公文相同。从内容方面看，报情况的，应有情况、说明、结论三部分，其中情况不能省略；报意见的，应有依据、说明、设想三部分，其中意见设想不能省去。从形式上看，复杂一点的要分开头、主体、结尾。开头使用多的是导语式、提问式给个总概念或引起注意。主体可分部分加二级标题或分条加序码。结尾可展望、预测，亦可省略，但结语不能省。具体说来，可以分为以下步骤：

1. 写报告的目的。
2. 项目的目的。
3. 工作日程、地点，若是定期报告或是相关类型，则需稍微总结上次报告。
4. 主要活动或经历。调查过程要客观、公正，列举要详尽，由此得出的结论要正反两面都分析。报告是上级决策的关键依据，如果丧失了客观性，可能会造成决策失误。
5. 调查结果或收获。列出客观事实，不带主观描述。
6. 结论与建议。提出一些建设性的意见，或是进行总结。
7. 下一步行动。

打报告要注意做到：情况确凿，观点鲜明，想法明确，语气得体，不要夹带请示事项。

21. 市场调查报告

（说明：一般来说，报告是一个很系统、详细的工程，因此许多报告篇幅较长，甚至可以单独成一本书。限于篇幅，这里将以一篇市场调查报告的目录为例，向读者们展示这种报告的宏观轮廓。）

China Early Education Market Report, 2008~2009

1. Overview of China Early Education Market

1.1 Definition

1.2 Overview

1.3 Policies

1.4 Developments

2. Analysis of China Early Education Market

2.1 Overview Analysis

2.2 Kindergarten Teachers

2.3 Supply and Demand

2.4 Chain Operations

3. Online Early Education

3.1 Characteristics

3.2 Industry Chain

3.3 Market Size

4. Regional Developments

5. Major Schools

5.1 Juren

5.1.1 Profile

5.1.2 Characteristics

5.1.3 Development

5.2 Babycare

5.2.1 Profile

5.2.2 Characteristics

5.2.3 Development

5.3 R.Y.B. Education Institution

5.4 Huijia Kindergarten

5.5 Babyblossom

5.6 Gymboree

5.7 Baby Art

5.8 Golden Cradle Kindergarten

6. Investment Risks and Opportunities Analysis

Relevant Materials

Selected Charts Classification of Early Education in China

The Number of Kindergarten Students in China, 2005~2007

The Number of Kindergarten Teachers in China, 2005~2007

The Number of Newborns and Birth Rate in China, 1993~2007

Industry Chain of Pre-school Online Education

The Number of Online-Education Candidate and Growth Rate in China, 2004~2010

Babycares Branches in Beijing and Shanghai

Profits of Babycare

Demographic Structure of China in 2007

The Number of Private Kindergartens, 2006~2007

Educational Laws and Regulations in China

Education Background of the Schoolmaster and Full-time Teachers, 2007

Academic Title of the Schoolmaster and Full-time Teachers, 2007

Franchising of Baby Art in China

中国早教市场报告 2008~2009

1. 中国早教市场概述
    1.1 定义
    1.2 概述
    1.3 政策
    1.4 发展
2. 中国早教市场分析
    2.1 整体分析
    2.2 幼儿园教师
    2.3 供求关系
    2.4 中国运作实践
3. 网上早教
    3.1 特点

3.2 产业链
　　3.3 市场规模
4. **区域发展情况**
5. **重点学校案例分析**
　　5.1 巨人
　　5.1.1 学校简介
　　5.1.2 学校特点
　　5.1.3 学校发展
　　5.2 东方爱婴早教学校
　　5.2.1 学校简介
　　5.2.2 学校特点
　　5.2.3 学校发展
　　5.3 红黄蓝教育机构
　　5.4 汇佳幼儿园
　　5.5 启稚摇篮早教中心
　　5.6 金宝贝
　　5.7 创意宝贝
　　5.8 金色摇篮幼儿园
6. **投资风险和机遇分析**

相关资料
　　中国早教分类图表精选
　　2005~2007 中国幼儿园学生人数
　　2005~2007 中国幼儿园教师人数
　　1993~2007 中国新生人口数量和出生率
　　网络学前教育产业链
　　2004~2010 中国在线教育机构数量和增长率
　　东方爱婴早教学校北京、上海分校
　　东方爱婴早教学校盈利情况
　　2007 年中国人口结构
　　2006~2007 私人幼儿园数量
　　中国教育相关法律法规
　　2007 年校长和全职教师教育背景报告
　　2007 年校长和全职教师学术职称报告
　　创意宝贝在中国的特权

22. 可行性报告

FEASIBILITY REPORT

MEMORANDUM

TO: Golden Lakes Condominium Association
FROM: Robert Fields, Grounds Committee Chair
DATE: 1 October, 2011
SUBJECT: Recreation Building Grounds Resodding

Because the remodeling of the Golden Lakers Condominium recreation building has resulted in grass damage to the surrounding common area, I have investigated the feasibility of resodding these areas.

The criteria for the project include:
1. adequate sod for a twenty-square-foot area
2. a price within the $4 500.00 budget
3. a guarantee

Four landscape companies have estimated the project. The table shows the company, price, project length, and guarantee details of each:

Comparative Bids for Recreation Grounds
Resodding Project

Company	Price ($)	Length (days)	Guarantee
Green Company	3 707	3	None
Landscape Professionals	3 984	2	6 inspections in 6 mos. Replacements at no cost.
K-Mart Professional Crew	4 000	3	6 inspections in 12 mos. Replacements at no cost.
Luxury Landscape	4 439	3	6 inspections in 4 mos. Replacements at no extra cost.

Conclusion

While all four prices are within our budget, the K-Mart Professional Crew offers the best guarantee at a price comfortably below our budget for the resodding.

I recommend we contract the K-Mart Professional Crew inasmuch as the guarantee offers six inspections over a full year with sod replacement as necessary within that period at no extra cost. Further, the contract should be awarded contingent that the work can be completed before November 20, when the northern owners return south for the winter.

Joseph Carter

可行性报告

备忘录
收件人：金湖公寓协会
发件人：路面委员会主席：罗伯特·菲尔德
日期：2011 年 10 月 1 日
事由：娱乐大厦路面重铺草皮事宜

由于金湖公寓娱乐大厦翻新工程导致了周边路面草坪的损坏，本人调查了在该区域重铺草皮的可行性。

该项工程的标准包括：
1. 足够铺设 20 平方英尺区域的草皮
2. 预算在 4 500.00 美元之内
3. 质量担保

四家绿化公司评估了该项目。下表显示了公司名、要价、耗时和各自的担保细节：

娱乐大厦周围路面草皮重铺工程相关公司出价比较

公司名称出价（$）工期（日）担保细节	价格	时长（天）	保修
绿色公司	3 707	3	无
景观专家	3 984	2	6 个月 6 次检查，免费更换损坏草皮。
K 市专业队	4 000	3	12 个月 6 次检查，免费更换损坏草皮。
奢华景观	4 439	3	4 个月 6 次检查，免费更换损坏草皮。

总结

虽然四家公司的出价均在我方预算内，但是 K 市专业队公司在稍低于我方预算的价格基础上提供了最好的质量担保。

由于 K 市专业队公司在全年内提供 6 次检查，且在承诺期范围内免费更换受损草皮，本人建议我方与 K 市专业队公司签订合同。同时，为迎接北方居民南下过冬，该合同应规定该工程在 11 月 20 日之前竣工。

约瑟夫·卡特

23. 进度报告

PROGRESS REPORT

TO: David Williams
FROM: Team #3 (Carol Jones, Jack Yates, Joan Brown, Karen Smith)
DATE: February 13, 2012
SUBJECT: Progress On Informational Report

This memo describes the progress our team has made since our last progress report on February 6, 2012.

Background: Our team is researching desktop video conferencing technology for Company A. Our informational report to the company's CIO is due March 20, 2012.

Action Items Completed: In preparation for this assignment, each member of our team was assigned particular tasks and discussed findings on Sunday, February 12. Each member completed research on specific areas of this technology and completed two pages of the rough draft.

- Carol: Surveyed users via the Internet, worked on introduction for rough draft.
- Jack: Completed research on desktop cameras and wrote two pages of rough draft.
- Joan: Completed research on software, wrote two pages of rough draft, and took rough draft to writing center with Jack.
- Karen: Completed research on microphones, wrote two pages of rough draft, and contacted Robin with Arrow Electronics for more

information and suggestions.
- ♣ All members: Held meeting on Sunday, February 12, reviewed each member's two pages, brought all pages together in a rough draft, reviewed report guidelines and identified pieces of the report that are still missing.

Action Items To Be Completed: Each member has now been assigned these tasks:

Karen	Interview software users	March 1st
Carol	Get product specifications from vendors	March 1st
Jack	Add info from Karen & Carol, then take paper to writing center	March 1st
Joan	Fine-tune the rough draft for final printing	March 1st

Anticipated Problems: Our progress is still on schedule. However, we anticipate difficulty in cohesively bringing together the two pages each team member has written for the rough draft. We will overcome this problem through careful proofreading, revising and editing along with help from the writing center.

By February 20, you will have another updated progress report from our team. If you would like further information, please contact us via e-mail.

进度报告

收件人： 大卫·威廉姆斯
发件人： 第三分队（卡罗·琼斯、杰克·叶芝、琼·布朗、卡伦·史密斯）
日期： 2012年2月13日
事由： 信息报告进展情况

本备忘录记录了自2012年2月6日上一份进展报告递交以来，我组取得的新进展。

背景：我组正为A公司引用计算机视频会议技术一事进行研究。我们对该公司的信息总管的信息报告截止日期为2012年3月20日。

已完成的行动项目：在准备这项工作的过程中，我组每位成员都接受了特殊任务，并于2月12日（周日）讨论了各自的研究成果。每位成员都完成了这项技术具体层面的研究活动，并形成了两页长的草稿。

- 卡罗：通过互联网调查了该技术的用户，负责草稿的简介部分。
- 杰克：完成了对计算机摄像头的研究，并完成了两页的报告草稿。
- 琼：完成了对软件的研究，完成了两页的报告草稿，并与杰克一道将草稿递交编辑中心。
- 卡伦：完成了对麦克风的研究，完成了两页的报告草稿，并联系到箭头电子公司的罗宾先生，询问其他的信息和建议。
- 所有成员：于2月12日（周日）开会，审阅了每个成员的两页报告草稿，将其汇总为一份草稿；审阅了报告纲要并指出了报告中的遗漏点。

尚待完成的行动项：目前各成员的任务：

卡伦	调查软件用户	3月1日前完成
卡罗	向卖主调查产品详细信息	3月1日前完成
杰克	汇总凯伦和卡罗的资料，将报告递交编辑中心	3月1日前完成
琼	润色报告草稿，打印最终报告	3月1日前完成

可能出现的问题：我组工作仍然按计划进行。然而我们预计，在将每位组员的两页报告草稿有机结合的过程中可能会遇到困难。为应对这一困难，我们会在编辑中心的协助下进行仔细校对、修订和编辑。

2月20日之前，我组将向您递交新的进度报告。如果您需要更多信息，请通过电子邮件联系我们。

24. 年度报告

Annual Report

ABC Organization　　　Address: XXX　　　Phone: XXX
Fax: XXX　　　　　　　Website: XXX　　　E-mail: XXX

ABC Organization's mission is to assist in the protection and recovery of missing, abused, and neglected children.

Dear Friends,

One of the joys of preparing an annual report is that it gives us the opportunity to look back and be thankful for all that has been accomplished.

The past fiscal year was filled with wonderful opportunities and many challenges. Some of the highlights were:

- ♣ Assisted in recovery of 250 children
- ♣ Strengthened our ID Child program to benefit both current missing children and prevent further child kidnappings through the sale of a child identification bracelet
- ♣ Created new after-school programs at local community center to help neglected and abused children
- ♣ Produced a public service announcement with the assistance of a local sports hero

The following is an overview of ABC Organization's income and expenses for the fiscal year ended June 30, XXXX.

<u>Total Support & Revenue:</u>	$XXX,XXX
Program Expenses:	
♣ Child ID Program	$XXX,XXX
♣ Recovery and After School Program	$XXX,XXX
♣ Total Program Expense	$XXX,XXX
Management & General Expenses:	$XXX,XXX
Fundraising Expenses:	$XXX,XXX
Total Expenses:	$XXX,XXX
Total Assets*:	$XXX,XXX
Total Liabilities*:	$XXX,XXX
Net Asset Balance:	$XXX,XXX

<u>Board of Directors</u>
Charles Johnson, Chairman
Maria Ibarra, Treasurer
Peter Williams, Secretary
Calvin Johnson, Trustee
Roger Kingston, Trustee

Inez Martinez, Trustee
Janie Piermont, Trustee
Nicolas Vanderbilt, Trustee
Joel W. Mehl, Executive Director

年度报告

ABC 组织	地址：XXX	电话：XXX
传真：XXX	网站：XXX	电邮：XXX

ABC 组织的使命是协助保护失踪、受虐和被忽视的儿童，慰抚他们的创伤。
亲爱的朋友们：

撰写一份年度报告的快乐之一，就是这一过程能够让我们回顾过去，对一切成就满怀感激。过去的一个财政年充满了美妙的机遇和诸多挑战。其中的一些亮点是：

- 参与了 250 名儿童的康复过程
- 强化了儿童身份认证项目，通过销售儿童身份认证手镯，我们不仅可以使已经失踪的孩子获益，还可以防止更多的儿童绑架事件
- 在当地社区中心开设了新的课外活动，帮助被忽视和虐待的儿童
- 在当地的一名体育明星的协助下，制作了一个公益广告

以下是 ABC 组织在截至 XXXX 年 6 月 30 日的财政年之内的收支概览。

总收入：	$XXX,XXX
项目经费：	
• 儿童身份认证项目 *	$XXX,XXX
• 儿童康复和课外项目 *	$XXX,XXX
• 总项目开销	$XXX,XXX
管理经费和总体经费：	$XXX,XXX
赞助经费：	$XXX,XXX
总开销：	$XXX,XXX
总资产：	$XXX,XXX
总债务：	$XXX,XXX
净资产负债：	$XXX,XXX

董事会成员名单
主席：查尔斯·约翰逊

财务主管：玛利亚·伊巴拉
秘书：皮特·威廉姆斯
理事：卡尔文·约翰森
理事：罗格·金斯顿
理事：伊内兹·马定内兹
理事：杰尼·皮埃尔蒙
理事：尼古拉斯·范德比尔特
执行董事：乔尔·W·梅尔

25. 故障调查报告

Investigation Report

Dec. 16

Dear Mr. President,

  Upon the request of our Worker's Union, the inspection group of our company conducted an on-the-spot observation in the dormitories of the workers on Dec. 15, 2011. The inspection proved that the heating system didn't work well. The room temperature was as low as 2℃. It's hereby recommended that the heating system should be repaired as early as possible.

Zhang Wei

调查报告

尊敬的董事长先生：

  根据公司工会的请求，检查小组于 2011 年 12 月 15 日对职工宿舍进行了实地考察，考察结果表明暖气效果不佳，室温低达 2℃。鉴于此，建议尽快修理暖气以解决该问题。

张伟
12 月 16 日

Unit 5　备忘录　　　　　　　　　Memorandum (Memo)

备忘录（Memorandum 或其缩写 Memo）是指公司内部用来传递信息的文本，类似留言条。它一般局限于公司或部门内部的交流，本公司或部门之外的人一般看不到。其主要功能包括：1. 提供会议摘要；2. 为主管人员与职员之间的交流提供更便捷的渠道；3. 确认电话交谈或会面的内容。

备忘录一般使用非正式文体，但也可以根据内容及收件人与发文人之间关系而具体决定，例如向上级报道重要事情就需要使用正式文体。如果备忘录内容不止一个，则可以采取分段的形式，也可采用数字编号。

写备忘录前要考虑以下几点：
- 这份备忘录是写给谁的；
- 出于什么原因而写这份备忘录；
- 用什么语气和措辞更为恰当。

备忘录的结构形式一般包括以下几个部分：

1. 信头(Heading)：包括To(收件人), From(发件人), Subject(主题)和 Date（日期）等要素。To 后面接收件人姓名、职务等；From 后面接备忘录写作者的姓名（注意作者姓名前面不用 Dr., Miss, Mr., Ms 之类的称呼）；Subject 后是备忘录主要内容的概括性小标题；Date 后写日期。几项要竖着写下来，顶格写。

"主题"往往是很短的一句话，甚至是一个单词，旨在提醒收件人是何事由，切忌画蛇添足，给收件人获取信息带来麻烦。

2. 正文段落：正文部分包括开头语（简述情况）、正文（提出要对方做什么或注意什么等，要言简意赅）和结束语（表示礼貌，力求简洁）。

3. 附件（Enclosure）：若有附件，则附上；若无，则免。

注意：1. 由于备忘录相对于其他文体较为随意，尤其是公司内部日常交往中经常使用，因此在实际运用中会被省略一些内容，或是不按照正规内容来写。比如，有些人会把自己（即发送人）写在末尾。2. 有时为了慎重起见，撰写者还需在正文后签名。

26. 交代员工做事的备忘录

To: Joan Smith
From: John Smith
Date: 13 January, 2009
Subject: Alpha Systems request for revised quote on system upgrade

Verbal advice from Alpha Systems management indicates they need a complete new quote for their upgrade by 21 January, 2009.

Alpha Systems will be sending us new information by e-mail today, regarding specifications for their servers, which will now include standard Linux and Apple capabilities, not just Windows as previously advised. The intention is that they will run a full suite of server capabilities.

This information will be forwarded to you directly this afternoon by Alpha Systems IT manager.

Please cease work on other projects and have this new quote drafted by 16 January, so we can consult with Alpha in advance, and review and redraft if required.

收件人：琼·史密斯
发件人：约翰·史密斯
日期：2009 年 1 月 13 日
事由：阿尔法系统索要修订版的系统升级要价

阿尔法系统管理人员的口头建议表明，2009 年 1 月 21 日之前，他们需要对系统升级进行全新报价。

阿尔法系统今天将会通过电邮给我们传来新的信息，介绍他们服务器的详细情况。这次将不仅仅是之前提到的 Windows 系统，还包括 Linux 和 Apple 系统。他们的想法是要运作一整套的服务器。

这一消息将于今天下午由阿尔法系统的 IT 经理直接传达给你。

请停止其他项目的工作，在 1 月 16 日之前安排完成这份新的报价，以便我们提前与阿尔法方面协商，并在必要的情况下审阅和改写材料。

27. 要求提供进度报告的备忘录

To: Mr. Rhey Santos
Subject: Progress Report on Lending Operations

In connection with the preparation of our annual report on loans, may we request for a copy of the progress report on lending operations as of January 2006 to enable us to get certain data on said report needed for our annual report.

Mr. Henry Tan
Director

收件人：雷·桑通斯
事由：贷款操作进度报告

由于要准备我们的年度借贷报告，烦请您提供一份 2006 年 1 月起的《贷款操作进度报告》复印件，以便我们在年度报告中引用上述报告中的数据。

亨利·唐
董事

28. 公司规定变更备忘录

Subject: Cost Saving Measures
To all Concerned Employees,

As you know, the country has been undergoing an economic recession that has also affected our company's financial performance. In light of this, we are constrained to implement the following cost-cutting measures in order to reduce our operating costs.

1. Air conditioners must only be operated from nine to five, after which they must be shut down. It is the responsibility of sub-department heads to ensure that this procedure is followed strictly.

2. Except in cases where there is urgent work to be completed, all workers must be out of the office by nine at the latest. If they need to stay beyond this time, they must inform their immediate supervisors.

3. The use of office supplies is also to be restricted. Employees must

inform their supervisors if they need to avail of any new supplies and sign in the logbook for monitoring purposes.

We hope that all employees appreciate the need for these and any other cost-cutting measures the company deems necessary, and will cooperate fully with company officials in helping to implement them.

Respectfully yours,
Ted Farmer
President, Sigma Corporation

事由：缩减开支措施
全体相关员工：

  如诸位所知，我国正在经历一场经济衰退，这场衰退也影响到了我公司的盈利情况。鉴于此，我们不得不贯彻以下缩减开支方案，以减少公司的运营成本。

  1. 空调使用时间限制在上午9点到下午5点之间，其他时间必须关闭。各部门领导负责保证严格执行此项规定。

  2. 若无遇到紧急任务，所有员工最迟需在晚9点前离开办公室。若任何人需要超时留在办公室，则需告知本人的上级领导。

  3. 办公室用品的使用也需得到限制。若员工需要使用任何新的办公用品，均需报告上级领导，并在记录册中签字，以作监督。

  我们希望所有员工理解这些规定以及公司认为必要的其他节俭措施，并充分配合公司管理人员，将其落实。

恭敬的 特德·法尔摩尔
西格玛公司董事长

29. 公司更名备忘录

To: All Employees
From: The Executive Director
Re: Company X Branding

  Many of you have been involved in our most recent campaign to create a new, fresh, and modern logo for our organization that reflects the direction that we are taking in the next 10 years. We are looking forward to taking this giant leap with you as we venture forward into the future of Company X!

  As part of the new direction that the company is taking, we are also bidding farewell to our previous company name, Company X. We have launched several successful and ground breaking projects as Company X, but alongside our effort to move forward is to move away from our traditional brand, and giving way to the modern and innovative products of Company Y!

Effective 01 July, 2010, we shall change to the name "Company Y". You will be briefed by Human Resources and your immediate superiors as to the department-level changes that need to be immediately implemented.

Also, all employees are invited to join the launch of Company Y on July 1, 2010 . Let us join hands and be together as we move forward to our company's success!

收件人：全体员工
发件人：执行董事
事由：公司 X 商标

你们中的许多人都参与了近期开展的为公司创造商标的活动，使之新颖、鲜活、时尚，同时能够反映公司未来十年的发展方向。在我们向 X 公司的未来挺进的同时，我们期待着与诸位共同飞跃！

作为公司新方向的一个部分，我们要对过去的公司名称"X 公司"说再见了。我们在公司 X 的历史中曾成功地完成了数个重大项目，但若我们要继续前行，就需要摒弃过去的叫法，采用更富有现代感和创造力的产品商标：Y 公司！

从 2010 年 7 月 1 日起，我公司将正式更名为 "Y 公司"。至于部门方面急需实行的变动，人力资源部和你们的上级领导将会简要向你们介绍。

同时，欢迎全体员工参加于 2010 年 7 月 1 日举办的 Y 公司更名仪式。让我们携手共创公司成功的未来！

30. 会议通知备忘录

Memorandum on Sales Department's Participation at ABC World Congress

TO : Mr. Lim Meng Wee
FROM : Mr. Victor Wong
DATE : 18 June, 2010
SUBJECT: ABC World Congress

The ABC is staging the ABC World Congress on July 19~July 23, 2010 in Beijing, China. Kindly inform every member of the sales force to mark the date, since we have signed up as one of the participating firms. I would appreciate it if you would encourage everyone to go, and provide me with the names of those who will be attending no later than the 30th of June. We will, of course, pay the entrance fees for all those attending.

In connection with said event, please handle the following:

- ♣ Set up reception table with brochures at the Congress venue
- ♣ Coordinate with advertising agency and reserve for advertising space in two major daily newspapers; include an advertorial about our company participation at the National Advertising Congress
- ♣ Order new banners for the aforementioned event

If you have any questions, please don't hesitate to call me up or bring it up at the next management meeting.

Thank you for your prompt attention to this matter.

销售部参加 ABC 国际代表大会备忘录

收件人：林蒙伟
发件人：维克多·王
日期：2010 年 6 月 18 日
事由：ABC 国际代表大会

ABC 将于 2010 年 7 月 19 日~7 月 23 日在中国北京举办 ABC 世界代表大会。烦请销售部各位成员到期与会，因为我公司也已签名表示参与。如果你部门鼓励所有成员参加，并在 6 月 30 日前将与会人员名单提供到我处，本人将不胜感激。当然，我们将支付所有与会者的入场费用。

关于上述会议，请做好以下工作：

- 在会场设立接待处，摆放宣传册。
- 与广告宣传机构合作，在两家主要日报上预留广告位，包括一篇宣传我公司参与全国广告代表大会的文章。
- 为上述大会订购新的横幅。

若有任何问题，请随时给本人电话，或是在下次管理会议中提出。

感谢及时关注此事。

Unit 6　会议议程和会议纪要 Meeting Agendas & Minutes

首先，我们来谈谈会议议程（Meeting Agenda）。

会议议程（Meeting Agenda）是指在会议上各项内容的安排，会议议程有助于与会者做好开会的各项准备，有点像给会议做计划。要使会议顺利进行，必须有明确的会议进行时间、地点、议项、出席人员等一切有关事项，并在会议召开前以书面形式告知有关人员，以便其为开会做好准备。

会议议程有的简约，有的复杂，主要看主办方的要求。简约的可以简单列出事项就好，而复杂的则会细分到具体几点到几点进行大会的哪项，一目了然。

一般来说，一次会议要包括以下几个方面：
1. 宣布会议开始；
2. 点名；
3. 宣布会议法定人数（有的小会、非正式会议以及对与会人员法律要求不高的大会没有此项）；
4. 宣读上次会议记录；
5. 通过上次会议记录；
6. 主席发言；
7. 与会者发言；
8. 讨论未完成的事项；
9. 讨论新的事项；
10. 宣布下次会议日期；
11. 宣布会议结束。

写会议议程需要注意以下几点：
1. 严格按照上级要求，将需要讨论的问题和事项全部包括在议程里，合理安排时间，分清主次；
2. 考虑每个议项的排列顺序；
3. 安排时间需要合理，重要议题不能给少量时间，而次要问题也不可耗时太多。

下面来谈谈会议纪要。

会议纪要（Minutes）是用于记载、传达会议情况和议定事项的公文。它用于党政机关、社会团体、企事业单位召开的工作会议、座谈会、研讨会等重要会议。会议纪要通过记载会议基本情况、会议成果、会议议定事项，综合概括地反映会议精神，以便与会者统一认识，会后全面如实地进行传达组织落实开展工作的依据。会议纪要通常情况只印发到会的单位，视情况抄送有关的单位。为便于上级了解工作开展情况，也要抄报上级主管部门。

在各种会议纪要中，陈述记录（Minutes of Narration）最为常见。所谓陈述记录，就是对会上的讨论和达成的协议、结论等作简要的叙述。

会议纪要主要由以下三部分构成：

1. 会议的基本情况（Basic Information）：包括会议名称（要写全称）、开会时间、地点、会议性质、与会人员等。一般都是在开会之前写好。同时，还要记下开会当天的情况。如会议主持人、出席会议应到和实到人数，缺席、迟到或早退人数及其姓名、职务等。如果是群众性大会，只要记参加的对象和总人数，以及出席会议的较重要的领导成员即可。如果某些重要的会议，出席对象来自不同单位，应设置签名簿，请出席者签署姓名、单位、职务等。

2. 会议内容（Content）：会议纪要最重要的部分。主要包括主持人发言、会议报告或传达、与会者讨论发言、会议决议、下次会议时间、休会时间等。其他会议动态，如发言中插话、笑声、掌声、临时中断以及别的重要的会场情况等，视情况而定可记可不记。

3. 结束语（Ending）：包括会议记录人签名、附件信息和抄送人信息等。

会议纪要的重点包括：

（1）会议中心议题以及围绕中心议题展开的有关活动；
（2）会议讨论、争论的焦点及各方的主要见解；
（3）权威人士或代表人物的言论；
（4）会议开始时的定调性言论和结束前的总结性言论；
（5）会议已议决的或议而未决的事项；
（6）对会议产生较大影响的其他言论或活动。

撰写会议纪要应当注意：1. 概括要全面，要如实反映会议精神。不得随意取舍，不得以偏概全，不能是自己赞同的就多写，不赞同的就略写或不写。2. 要具备一定的分析、综合能力和表达能力。这样，表述上才能做到重点突击、条理清晰、文字简练。3. 会议纪要一般不宜公开发表，如需发表，应征得发言者的审阅同意。

31. 会议议程（简约版）

Group C's Initial Meeting

Date: 1 March, 2012
Time: 10:00 a.m.
Venue: Meeting Room 2

Agenda

1. Apologies
2. Minutes of Last Meeting
3. Matters Arising
4. Concept Study Report
5. Allocation of Tasks
6. Time scales and Deadlines
7. Common Procedures and Approach
8. Any Other Business
9. Date and Time of Next Meeting

C 组第一次会议

日期：2012 年 3 月 1 日
时间：上午 10:00
地点：第 2 会议室
会议议程

1. 道歉声明
2. 上次会议的会议纪要回顾
3. 提出新事项
4. 概念学习报告
5. 任务分配
6. 时间限额和截止日期
7. 一般程序和方法
8. 其他事项
9. 宣布下次会议时间

MEETING AGENDA

Project Name: SYSTEM Z Redesign Phase

Purpose, Objectives and Elements of the Meeting: ***

Risk Identification Workshop

Expected Attendees:	**Date & Time:**	14 December, 1997
A. Smith (Chair) J. Wilder J. Lyon R. Lakey J. Grimes G. Jackson P. Labelle J. Hughson	**Place:**	Tower C, Room 701

Agenda Item		**Person Responsible**	**Time**
1.	Introduction Review purpose of workshop.	A. Smith	2 mins
2.	Risk Management Process Review the basic definition of risk and the approach to risk management established for the SYSTEM Z project.	A. Smith	15 mins
3.	Risk Identification Brainstorming Actively participate in a non-judgemental think-tank session to identify risks in each type and category and produce an initial list of risks. (The list will be assessed, prioritised, and maintained after the workshop.)	All	90 mins

List of Attachments:

Copy of risk management standards and procedures.

会议议程			
项目名称：Z 系统重新设计阶段			
会议意图、目标和构成：***			
风险确认研讨会			
受邀人员：		日期和时间：	1997 年 12 月 14 日
A. 史密斯（主席）J. 怀尔德 J. 林恩 R. 雷吉 J. 格林姆斯 G. 杰克森 P. 拉贝尔 J. 胡森		地点：	C 楼 701 房间
讨论事项		负责人员	时间
1.	开场介绍 回顾开会目的	A. 史密斯	2 分钟
2.	风险管理进程 回顾风险的基本定义以及为 Z 系统项目设定的风险管理办法	A. 史密斯	15 分钟
3.	与会者提出各种项目风险 积极参与智囊团会议，对错罔论，确定各种各类风险，并将其列成一份初始清单。（会后该清单将经过评估，确定重点，并得到维护。）	全体与会人员	90 分钟
附件列表：			
风险管理标准和程序文件。			

32. 董事会会议纪要

Minutes of meeting of Board of Directors, Gamma Systems Inc

Time: 23 February, 2009

Venue: Central Conference Hall

Additional persons attending the meeting: Professor Dan Drew, financial consultant

Preliminary statement by Chairman.

Chair stated that projections for financial year were on target. Professor Dan Drew was introduced to the Board as the new financial consultant for Gamma Systems Inc.

Item 1: Approval of expenditure for new building at Cleveland premises.

…

Prof. Drew was invited by the Chairman to speak to the meeting regarding the financial commitments for the project. Prof. Drew referred to information sheets and confirmed the expenditure and proposed line of credit was viable.

Meeting asked to approve expenditure. Vote was unanimously in favor.

(Signed)
Name of recorder of minutes
(Date)

伽马系统公司董事会会议纪要

时间：2009 年 2 月 23 日
地点：中央会议大厅
新增与会人员：财务顾问　丹·德鲁教授

主席开场发言。
主席表示，财政年的规划是完全正确的。丹·德鲁教授作为伽马系统公司的新任财务顾问被介绍给董事会。
议项 1：　通过克利夫兰地区新楼开支。
……
德鲁教授受主席之邀，在会上就工程的资金事宜发表讲话。德鲁教授查阅了相关资料，并确定开支方案和之前计划的信用额度是可行的。
会议提议通过开支方案。投票表决一致通过。
（签名）
（记录人姓名）
（日期）

33. 公司全体年会会议纪要

MINUTES OF JOINT ANNUAL MEETING OF HOUSE CORPORATION

MEMBERS AND DIRECTORS

The joint annual meeting of members and Board of Directors of the House Corporation was held on *** at ***.

The President certified that proper notice of the meeting had been given as provided by the Bylaws and that the required quorum of members was present.

The President acknowledged the attached agenda of the meeting and gave his report. The following officers made their report to the members: ***

The first order of business was the election of the Board of Directors. The following persons were nominated: ***

The following persons were elected to serve on the Board of Directors: ***

_____ was elected as Chairman of the Board, who then convened the Board of Directors Meeting.

The following persons were nominated and duly seconded by the members of the Board of Directors for the described office:

President: _____

Vice President: _____

Secretary: _____

Treasurer: _____

Assistant Officers: _____

Upon vote, the following persons were elected by the Board of Directors as officers of the House Corporation:

President: _____

Vice President: _____

Secretary: _____

Treasurer: _____

Assistant Officers: _____

The Treasurer made a report as to the income and expenses; he presented a Budget for the year; discussions were made.

Upon motion the meeting of the members and the Board of Directors was duly adjourned at ***.

MINUTES CERTIFIED BY: _____

房屋公司员工和董事会集体年会纪要

房屋公司员工和董事会集体年会于 *** 在 *** 举办。

董事长确定，会议的准确通知已经通过《细则》发布，法定与会人员也已到场。

董事长确认了附加的大会议程并做了报告。以下领导给与会者做了报告：***

大会的首个议程是选举董事会成员。以下人员得到了提名：***

以下人员被选举为董事会成员：***

_____ 被选举为董事长，随后召开了董事会会议。

以下相关职位人员经由董事会成员提名并正式递交大会：

经理：_____

副经理：_____

秘书：_____

财务主管：_____

助理专员：_____

经过选举，以下人员被董事会选为房屋公司高级职员：

经理：_____

副经理：_____

秘书：_____

财务主管：_____

助理专员：_____

财务主管就公司收支情况做了报告；他展示了今年的预算，与会者就此展开了讨论。

房屋公司员工和董事会集体年会按时于 *** 休会。

纪要证明人：_____

34. 部门会议纪要

**** UNIVERSITY

Department of Computer Science and Engineering

Department Meeting

Minutes of the 43rd Department Meeting of the Department of Computer Science and Engineering held on 26 April, 2012 at 10:05 a.m. in Room 7332, Conference Room, 7/F, Phase I, Academic Complex, **** University.

Absent on leave:	Dr. Helen C Shen
Absent with apologies:	Dr. Zhaoping Li
	Mr. Ricci Ieong
	Mr. Terry Lau
	Mr. Frank Luk
	Dr. David Rossiter
	Miss Mandy Chan (student representative)
	Miss Eva Chen (student representative
	Mr. Cyril Kwok (student representative)
	Mr. Eric Hui (student representative
	Mr. Dickson Tong (student representative)
	Mr. Peter Yang (student representative)

With the exception of the above, all faculty members of the Department attended the meeting. In addition, Dr. Matthew Yuen, Associate Dean of Engineering, and Miss Angela Yu (recorder) were also present.

1. APPROVAL OF MINUTES OF THE LAST MEETING

1.1. Minutes of the last meeting were approved as an accurate record.

2. DISCUSSION OF TEACHING

   2.1. Background

   2.1.1. The Chairman highlighted the background leading to this brainstorming session on teaching/learning issues. Subsequent to the formal release of the ABC report in early April, a special session was held by the Senate in which members exchanged their opinions on various issues related to the teaching/learning quality of the University, and special attention was given to address issues brought up in the Report by the ABC panel. It was decided then that a number of follow-up sessions be held by the Senate with a view to formulate positive actions in response to the Report. Before the next special session is held, departments/schools are requested to convene special meetings to canvass opinions of their faculty in general so that constructive ideas can be gathered for further consideration by the Senate.

   2.1.2. It was stressed that the purpose of the discussion is not to address the specific comments in the Report. The Report should be taken as a stimulus that leads to our self reflection on teaching performance–what we have done so far in teaching and what should be done to improve ourselves. The ABC visit were intended to help us setting up the framework for teaching/learning quality control assurance and to improve the quality of teaching and learning.

   2.2. Discussion

   2.2.1. The Chairman kicked off the discussion by sharing his thoughts on teaching with the faculty. He attempted to formulate his self-evaluation as a teacher by asking himself the following questions:

- Have we gone over our student evaluation comments?
- Have we used them constructively?
- How often have we visited our labs?
- Have we helped our TAs if they are inexperienced in teaching?
- How often have our TAs attended our lectures?
- How often have we met with our TAs to plan/discuss?
- How often have we and other section instructors met to plan/discuss?
- Have we reviewed the A-Level syllabi when we teach entry-level course?
- Have we reviewed the syllabi of the prerequisites to our courses?
- Have we reviewed the courses to which our course is a prerequisite?
- Have we worked out the exam paper ourselves beforehand?
- Have we worked out the assignments ourselves beforehand?
- Have we approached students in our class and asked for feedback?
- Have we visited our computer labs in the evening before project due dates?
- Have we mumbled to ourselves walking out from our class, "I should have prepared better?"

      2.2.2. While discussing the validity of the above questions, one member pointed out that although they were good questions for the faculty to ask themselves in evaluating their own teaching performance as individuals, they failed to address the major weakness in our teaching process as identified in the Report. The deficiency in the teaching of out university is seen as an absence of a structured, orderly and systematic approach to monitor the teaching programmes of its departments. Each department carries out its teaching responsibility in a different way, and there is no central co-ordination in the assurance of teaching quality.

4. ADJOURNMENT OF MEETING

    4.1. There being no other business, the meeting was adjourned at

1:15 p.m.

Jack Chen
May 11, 2012

**** 大学
计算机系

系内会议

此为计算机系第 43 次系内会议纪要。会议于 2012 年 4 月 26 日上午 10:05 在 **** 大学教学区一号楼 7 层会议室 7332 房间召开。

休假缺席人员：　　　　　　海伦·C·申博士
因故缺席人员：　　　　　　李照评博士
　　　　　　　　　　　　　里奇·杨先生
　　　　　　　　　　　　　特里·刘先生
　　　　　　　　　　　　　弗兰克·陆先生
　　　　　　　　　　　　　大卫·罗希特博士
　　　　　　　　　　　　　曼迪·陈女士（学生代表）
　　　　　　　　　　　　　艾娃·陈女士（学生代表）
　　　　　　　　　　　　　西里尔·郭先生（学生代表）
　　　　　　　　　　　　　埃里克·许先生（学生代表）
　　　　　　　　　　　　　迪克森·汤先生（学生代表）
　　　　　　　　　　　　　皮特·杨先生（学生代表）

除上述人员以外，我系全体教师都参加了会议。此外，工程系副主任马修·袁和记录员安吉拉·余也在场。

1. 通过上次会议的会议纪要
   1.1. 上次会议的会议纪要作为一份准确的记录而得到通过。
2. 教学讨论
   2.1. 背景
       2.1.1. 主席强调了本次教学事务讨论会的背景。自 ABC 报告于 4 月上旬发布以来，参议院就召开了一次特殊会议，与会者就有关大学教学质量的各种问题交换了意见，ABC 专题小组撰写的报告中提出的问题受到了高度重视。会上决定，为制定积极措施，回应报告中的问题，参议院将有后续会议。在下次特别会议召开之前，各校各系须召开特别会议对教职员工的大致意见进行讨论，以便参议院为进一步的考虑收集建设性观点。

  2.1.2. 会上强调，讨论的目的并非解决报告中的具体问题。报告应当作为一个引子，引导我们反思教学——我们的教学迄今有何成就，还有那些可以提高的地方。ABC 专门小组此行的目的是要帮助我们建立教学质量控制保证框架，提高教学质量。

 2.2. 讨论

  2.2.1. 主席与教师们分享了他关于教书的思考，讨论由此开始。他试图通过自问以下问题，来对教学工作进行自我评价：

- 我们仔细看了学生对我们的评论了吗？
- 我们都有效利用教学评估了吗？
- 我们多久去一次实验室？
- 我们帮助了那些经验不足的助教了吗？
- 我们的助教多久来上一次我们的课？
- 我们是否经常与助教见面制定计划或是展开讨论？
- 我们是否经常和其他课程的教师一起做计划或是讨论？
- 当我们教授初级课程的时候，是否重温了高级课程的教学大纲？
- 我们是否重温了所教课程的一些基础课程？
- 我们教授基础课程的时候，是否重温了相关的高级课程？
- 我们是否自己提前出好了试卷？
- 我们是否自己提前想好了要布置的作业？
- 我们是否与学生交流并向他们索要反馈？
- 在项目截止的前一个晚上，我们是否去过计算机实验室？
- 走出教室的时候，我们是否喃喃自语："我本该做更好的备课"？

  2.2.2. 在讨论上述问题是否有效之时，一位教师指出，虽然这些对于教师个人自评来说是好问题，但是它们无法解决报告中指出的我们教学过程中存在的主要不足。我校教学的缺点，是缺乏一种有结构、有秩序、系统化的监督各系教学项目的方法。各系完成教学任务的方式各不相同，在保证教学质量方面缺乏一个中心协调机制。

4. 休会

 4.1. 由于没有其他问题，会议于下午 1:15 结束。

杰克·陈
2012 年 5 月 11 日

Unit 7　新闻稿　　　　　　　　　　Press Releases

　　新闻稿（Press Release）是一份文稿，由公司／机构／政府／学校等单位发送予新闻传媒的通信文件，用以公布有新闻价值的消息。通常会通过官方网页、电子邮件、传真、书信（电脑打印）等形式分发给报章、杂志、电台、电视台（电视网络）、通讯社的编辑，亦有专业公司提供分发商业新闻稿的服务。

　　新闻稿异于新闻。新闻是由新闻记者撰写的事实陈述，并在媒体上出版；而新闻稿是新闻参考来源之一，发稿人不介意新闻社原稿照登，不过新闻记者会编辑题材，撰写新闻的稿件。

　　新闻稿的内容其实与通知或广告等其他文体无异，只是在形式上稍微有些变化，以符合其新闻的特征。新闻稿的结构包括：

1. 标题：简要、突出、吸引人。
2. 导语：用来提示消息的重要事实，使读者一目了然。
3. 主体：随导语之后，是消息的主干，是集中叙述事件、阐发问题和表明观点的中心部分，是全篇新闻的关键所在。
4. 结语：一般指消息的最后一句或最后一段话，是消息的结尾，它依内容的需要，可有可无。
5. 背景：是事物的历史状况或存在的环境、条件，是消息的从属部分，常插在主体部分，也插在导语或结语之中。

　　在新闻稿的首段，一般需有详细新闻地点、发生时间，并在其后加破折号引出第一段。且首段往往顶格写。

35. 新品发布

It's Bluefin Tuna Month
at Angelo's Flsh House

The Bluefin Are Running Again,
And They're Making Their Way to Diners at Angelo's

SEASIDE VILLAGE, N.Y., July 27, 1996–Angelo's Fish House will celebrate bluefin tuna season by adding 8 special bluefin dishes to its renowned menu.

Bluefin Tuna Month will feature special appetizers, entrees and salads from the kitchen of chef/owner Angelo Marzunni. They will be available to diners only during the month of August, when the bluefin make their annual run along the coast of Long Island.

"The bluefin is one of the greatest eating fish-meaty, delicate, and delicious," said Chef Angelo. "Unfortunately, they're only available for a short time. We want to celebrate the season by giving our customers the chance to enjoy this giant of the deep."

The special Bluefin Tuna Month menu will include:
♣ Blackened Barbecue Tuna–Chef Angelo's signature dish.
♣ Planked Tuna – grilled and smoked over mesquite
♣ …

Copies of Chef Angelo's Blackened Barbecue Tuna recipe are available for publication by contacting Bill Jackson at (516) 555-9000.

Angelo's Fish House, located on the water at 848 Main St. in Seaside Village, has been serving innovative seafood cuisine since 1982, It is open Tuesday-Sunday for lunch and dinner. Reservations suggested.

金枪鱼月
安格鲁鱼味餐馆

金枪鱼又来啦!
它们正游向安格鲁鱼味餐馆的饭桌

滨海村,纽约州,1996年7月27日——安格鲁鱼味餐馆将在其闻名遐迩的菜单上添加八道金枪鱼菜,以庆祝金枪鱼季。

金枪鱼月将主打本餐馆老板兼厨师安格鲁·马尔阻尼烹制的开胃菜、主食和色拉。这些菜品只在八月的餐桌上呈现,因为这时金枪鱼正经历它们一年一度的长岛海岸之旅。

"金枪鱼多肉、细腻、美味,是最好的食用鱼之一,"安格鲁厨师说,"可惜的是,它们出现的时间太短了。我们想给顾客一个品尝这种深海大鱼的机会,以庆祝这一鱼季。"

金枪鱼月的特殊菜单将会包括:
• 黑椒烤金枪鱼——安格鲁厨师的招牌菜

- 板烧金枪鱼——在豆科灌木上熏烤而成
- ……（从略）

若要出版安格鲁厨师的黑椒烤金枪鱼的烹饪方法，请拨打电话（516）555-9000 联系比尔·杰克森。

安格鲁鱼味餐馆坐落于滨海村主街 848 号（水上）。本餐馆从 1982 年起便开始提供新颖的海鲜美食。餐馆营业时间为每周二至周日午饭和晚饭时。建议有需要的食客预订餐位。

36. 人事任命

Contact: XXX
Sally Smith
President of FlagBenders USA
(203) 555-5200

**Flagbenders USA Names Jim Sweeney
Vice President Of Sales**

**Former Polemark Marketing VP Will Oversee
Growing Sales Rep Network**

WEST VALDEVA, Conn; December 10, 1996–FlagBenders USA, manufacturers and designers of custom flags and banners, has named Jim Sweeney as its new Vice President of Sales.

Mr. Sweeney, who had been Vice President of Marketing at rival Polemark, will be in charge of managing and increasing FlagBenders' network of sales representatives and distributors. FlagBenders, which has focused exclusively on the Northeast, will expand its efforts nationally. Mr. Sweeney will spearhead this drive.

"The expansion of our sales rep and distribution team further strengthens our ability to meet the needs of our customers," noted Sally Smith, President of FlagBenders USA. "Jim Sweeney's comprehensive understanding flag and banner sales and marketing will greatly benefit FlagBenders, our sales network, and our clients."

Before joining FlagBenders USA, Mr. Sweeney oversaw marketing for Polemark, where he put together that company's distribution network. While at Polemark, he won the 1991 Innovation Award from the International Banner Marketing Association.

Prior to Polemark, he worked for Mutual Outdoors, which creates outdoor advertising for a wide variety of companies.

Mr. Sweeney has an MBA in Marketing from State University, and a BA in Psychology from Le City College.

He and his wife Francis live in Beauville, Conn.

联系人：XXX
萨利·史密斯
舞旗者（美国）公司总裁
电话：（203）555-5200

舞旗者（美国）公司任命吉姆·司文尼为
销售部副经理

前波尔马克公司营销部副经理将会监管
发展壮大的经销商网络

西瓦尔德瓦，康涅狄格州；1996年12月10日——舞旗者（美国）公司，传统旗帜的生产和设计者们已经任命吉姆·司文尼为公司销售部副经理。

司文尼先生曾在我公司的竞争对手波尔马克公司担任营销部副经理一职，他将负责管理和改善舞旗者公司的销售代表和经销商网络。舞旗者公司一向专营东北部市场，现将市场扩大到全国范围。司文尼先生将引领这一盛举。

"公司销售代表和经销商队伍的扩张增强了我们的实力，使我们能够更好地满足客户的需要，"舞旗者（美国）公司总裁萨利·史密斯指出。"吉姆·司文尼对旗帜和横幅的销售和宣传了解全面，这将对我们公司、销售网络以及我们的顾客大有裨益。"

加入舞旗者（美国）公司之前，司文尼先生负责波尔马克公司的营销部门，他将该公司的经销商网络进行了整合。在波尔马克公司时，他获得了1991年国际旗帜营销协会颁发的创新奖。

在加入波尔马克公司之前，他在户外互动公司工作，为各种公司提供户外广告。

司文尼先生在州立大学获得了市场营销 MBA 学位，在城市学院获得了心理学学士学位。

他和妻子弗朗西斯现居康涅狄格州的波维尔市。

37. 宣布新规定

Contact: XXX
Buck Johnson
The Green Way
(212) 555-5600

New York City Businesses Must Prepare

for Commercial Recycling Regulations

NEW YORK, N.Y.; August 15, 1993–New York City businesses will face a new set of commercial recycling regulations effective September 30, and must be prepared to institute aggressive programs to comply with the new law, urges The Green Way, Inc., a leading recycling consultant based in New York City.

Under Local Law 87, effective September 30, commercial properties in New York City will have to separate out certain items from their garbage for recycling. The law affects all properties, including food and beverage outlets and all other businesses, as well as some residential premises.

"Trash separation and recycling need not be painful tasks for businesses," noted Harris Brockley, President of The Green Way. "In fact, we urge companies to go even further and institute full recycling programs. Properties that have already done so not only comply with the new law, but are able to improve their bottom line costs through lower carting fees."

The Green Way recently published a white paper detailing both the new regulations, and its implications for different businesses, including office buildings, hotels, and department stores.

A building can implement a mixed recycling program (a lesser version of a full program) and still comply with the new regulations. But because commingled recyclables are not very valuable, this option often does not impact carting costs, The Green Way notes.

联系人：XXX
巴克·约翰森
绿道公司
电话：（212）555-5600

纽约市的商人们需要为
商业回收条例做准备

  纽约市，纽约州；1993年8月15日——纽约市的重要回收咨询公司绿道公司敦促，纽约市的工商业从9月30日起将会迎来新的一套商业回收条例，商人们必须建立大的回收项目，适应新的法律。

  根据当地于9月30日起生效的87号法律，纽约市各商铺必须从其垃圾中分类出一些物品以供回收之用。这项法规将影响所有的商铺，其中包括食品和饮料外卖店和其他所有经营，一些小区零售店也不例外。

  "垃圾分类和回收无需成为商业的负担，"绿道公司总裁哈里斯·布洛克利说，"事实上，我们甚至鼓励公司更进一步，制定完全回收的计划。已经这么做的公司不仅适应了新法，还通过降低运送垃圾的费用而减少了开支。"

  绿道公司近日出版了一份白皮书，详细介绍了新法规及其对不同行业的要求，包括办公楼、酒店和百货商店等。

  一栋大楼可以实行一套混合回收项目（及简化版的完全回收项目），同时还符合新法规。但绿道公司也指出，由于这些混合的回收品并不值钱，这一选择往往不会影响到运费。

Unit 8　致词

Speeches

致词（Speech）是一种讲话稿，主要包括欢迎词（Welcoming Speech）、欢送词（Send-off Speech）、告别词（Farewell Speech）、答谢词（Thank-you Speech）等。

在正式场合接待或是招待客人时，主人一般总要说几句热情友好的话，以表示对客人的欢迎，这种话就是欢迎词。主人致了欢迎词后，客人也要说几句话，以表示对主人的感谢，这种就是答谢词。当客人要离别时，主宾又一次欢聚一堂，相互致词，表示祝愿和依依不舍之情，以增进友谊。这时，主人的话就是欢送词。客人在离开之前还要对大家说一些话，这样的致词就是告别词。

致词一般是有先前文稿做准备的，是致词人讲话的依据。由于这种文稿最终要用语言表达出来，因此在写作的时候需要考虑到它的口语成分、表情成分、情感成分等等。此外，撰写致词文稿的时候还应注意：

1. 礼貌：切忌用词粗俗，根据场合采用不同的礼貌用语。在注意热情、礼貌的同时，又要把握尺度，不卑不亢，做到优雅的平等。

2. 清晰：要围绕主题进行清楚的阐述，避免前后矛盾。

3. 长短合适：根据场合的不同，要适当选择不同的致词长度，既要完整、清晰、有力地展示自己心中的情感，又不能忘记外界，滔滔不绝，或是戛然而止，不冷不热。

38. 表示欢迎

Ladies and Gentlemen,

We feel very much honored to have such a distinguished group of guests come all the way from the United Kingdom to visit our company.

We will do all we can to make your visit a rewarding one. Today, we will introduce you to our new research center and our main factory. Please do not hesitate to ask any questions you may have.

At last I want to extend my warmest welcome to all of you, and sincerely hope that your visit here will be really fruitful.

女士们，先生们：
　　我们非常荣幸，能够欢迎从英国远道而来的贵宾。
　　我们将会竭诚为你们服务，使诸位不虚此行。今天，我们将会带诸位参观我们新建的研发中心和大厂房。若有任何问题，尽可提出。
　　最后，我想致以最热烈的欢迎，衷心希望诸位的访问硕果累累。

39. 表示欢送

Ladies and Gentlemen,

　　How time flies! It was three weeks ago that we gave Mr. Cooper a hearty welcome. Now we are here to bid him farewell.

　　It is the second time for Mr. Cooper to visit our company, so he is our old friend. During his visit, he had a deeper understanding of our company and decided to carry out further cooperation with us. And for our part, we are amazed by his insightful views and professional suggestions.

　　Finally, we take the opportunity to request him to convey our profound friendship and best regards to his people.

　　Now let's give the floor to Mr. Cooper!

女士们，先生们：
　　时光飞逝！三周前，我们给库伯先生举行了欢迎仪式。此刻，却到了言别的时候了。
　　这是库伯先生第二次来到我公司参观，因此他也算是我们的老朋友了。在他访问期间，他对我们公司有了更为深入的了解，也决定与我们展开进一步的合作。而我们也为其深刻的观点和专业的建议而惊叹。
　　最后，我们要借此机会请库伯先生将我们的深情厚谊与崇高敬意转达给他的同胞。
　　现在，有请库伯先生给我们讲话！

40. 表示告别

Ladies and Gentlemen,

Our visit to Beijing has come to an end and we will leave for the UK soon.

Before our departure, it gives me a great pleasure to say a few words here to express our appreciation for the hospitality you accorded us during our stay in Beijing. This visit was full of interesting things and memorable events. It is a fruitful trip and it opens a new chapter of our cooperation.

The Chinese people are smart, hardworking, modest, brave and prudent, which gave us very deep impression. My colleagues and I are looking forward to the pleasure of greeting you in the UK in the near future, so that we can push the relationship between us a step further.

Thank you again, we wish you good health and every success in the future.

女士们，先生们：
　　我们的北京之旅就要告一段落了，我们马上就要回到英国。
　　在离开之前，我们很高兴能够表达我们的感激之情，诸位在我们的北京之行期间给予了热情的款待。此次行程充满了趣事和难忘的回忆。这是一次富有成果的旅程，它给我们双方的合作开启了崭新的篇章。
　　中国人民是智慧的、勤劳的、谦逊的、勇敢的、审慎的。这让我印象深刻。我和我的同事都期待着能够在英国欢迎诸位的来访，这样我们双方的关系就能够更上一层楼。
　　再次谢谢诸位。祝你们身体健康，事业有成。

41. 表示勉励

Dear All,

Next year is going to be a very busy year for all of us here at Nita. You are going to find the market very challenging indeed.

As you know, our sales have increased by 50% last financial year and

I must thank you all in the sales department for doing a fine job. However we cannot rest on our laurels. According to what I have heard through the grapevine, our competitors are going to do their best competitive edge. With your enthusiasm and good strategy, I am sure you can do even better next year. Mr. Devadas will soon be informing you of the sales target for the next year.

The year is ending and I am sure all of you are looking forward to your bonuses. I have instructed Miss Hong to get them ready and you should have your bonuses before Christmas. Enjoy the moment and strive for a better year!

亲爱的员工们：

明年对我们倪塔公司的人来说，将会是非常忙碌的一年。你们会发现，市场将变得云谲波诡。

众所周知，上一财政年，我们的销售业绩提高了50%。为此，我必须向销售部的诸位同仁表示感谢，感谢诸位创造的佳绩。然而，我们不能停留在已经取得的荣耀上。据我了解到的消息，我们的对手将要奋力一搏。诸位都有工作热情，也有良好的策略，我相信明年你们一定可以做得更好。德瓦达斯先生很快就会告诉你们我们明年的销售目标。

今年就要接近尾声了，我相信诸位都期待着你们的奖金。我已经交代洪小姐把奖金准备好，圣诞之前你们就可以领到奖金了。让我们享受此刻，并为更好的来年奋斗吧！

42. 表示感谢

Remarks of President Jiang Zemin after the Successful Bid of 2008 Beijing Olympic Games

Dear Comrades,

I, on behalf of the Central Party Committee and the State Council, would like to offer three sentences:

First, warm congratulations on Beijing's successful bid for the 2008 Olympic Games;

Second, heartfelt gratitudes to the contributions made by all the Chinese people and to the support of International Olympic Committee as well as friends from all around the world in Beijing's bidding efforts;

Third, it's my hope that joint efforts of Chinese people and people from the rest of the world will be made to ensure a successful 2008 Olympic Games!

Just one last word. Welcome friends from all over the world to come to Beijing and enjoy the Olympics in 2008. Thank you all!

北京申奥成功后江泽民总书记在中华世纪坛的致词

同志们：

  我代表党中央国务院讲三句话：

  第一句，对北京申办奥运成功表示热烈的祝贺；

  第二句，向全国人民为北京市申办奥运所做出的贡献，同时向国际奥委会及世界的各界朋友对中国申办奥运会的支持表示衷心的感谢。

  第三句，希望全国人民和各界的人们一起奋发努力，一定要把2008年的奥运会办成功！

  最后，欢迎世界各界朋友2008年光临北京参加奥运会，谢谢！

43. 表示祝贺

Ladies and Gentlemen, Dear Mr. Chan,

  It is a special moment tonight. On behalf of all the employees of ABC Company, I am going to extend my warm congratulations on Mr. Chan's appointment to the general manager of the Great China District!

  My colleagues and I are delighted to see that the years of service you have given to our company at last have been rewarded in this way and we join in sending you our very best wishes for the future.

  Congratulations!

女士们，先生们，亲爱的陈先生：

  今晚非同寻常。我代表ABC公司的全体员工，对你晋升大中华区总经理一职表示热烈的祝贺！

我和我的同事非常高兴地看到，你多年来为公司的付出终于以这样的方式得到了回报。我们祝你在今后的事业中一帆风顺。

祝贺你！

Unit 9　其他行政文书

Other Official Writings

　　行政文书是多种多样的，绝不仅仅是本部分之前所介绍的一些，还包括命令、决定、规定、计划等等。由于许多问题极具中国特色，在国外较为罕见或是呈现方式不同，本单元不一一列举，只举3个例子，分别是规定、预算和计划。

　　规定（Regulation）是强调预先（即在行为发生之前）和法律效力，用于法律条文中的决定。作为文件类的规定就是领导机关或职能部门为贯彻某政策或进行某项管理工作、活动，而提出原则要求、执行标准与实施措施的规范性公文。规定具有较强的约束力，而且内容细致，可操作性较强。

　　规定由首部和正文两部分组成。
1. 首部。包括标题、制发时间和依据等项目。
    1) 标题。一般有两种构成形式：一种是由发文单位、事由、文种构成；另一种是由事由和文种构成。
    2) 时间和依据。用括号在标题之下注明规定发布和签发的时间和依据。有的规定是随"命令"、"令"等文种同时发布的。
2. 正文。正文的内容由总则、分则和附则组成。

　　一般来说，比较简单的规定只需要标题、内容和发文单位即可。内容在一段总述（在何背景下做出此规定）之后，往往直接一点一点列出，非常清晰明了。

　　预算（Budget），预算是一种收支计划。
　　预算包含的内容不仅仅是预测，它还涉及到有计划地巧妙处理所有变量，这些变量决定着公司未来努力达到某一有利地位的绩效。既然是计划，那么就可以像列表一样地列出来。大公司的预算往往比较庞大，要写出好多页，而对于一般的小公司或者小店铺，则较为简单。但是，不管字数多少，写作时都要项目明确、考虑充分、具有可操作性。

　　计划（Plan）是一种重要文体，其实用程度更是非常大，有时人们甚至对自己都常常列出各种各样的计划。包括上面的预算，严格来说也可以算是一种计划。

营销计划（Marketing Plan）是指，在对企业市场营销环境进行调研分析的基础上，制定企业及各业务单位的对营销目标以及实现这一目标所应采取的策略、措施和步骤的明确规定和详细说明。

企业营销计划的内容一般包括：
1. 计划概要。
2. 营销状况分析：这部分主要提供与市场、产品、竞争、分销以及宏观环境因素有关的背景资料。
3. 机会与风险分析
4. 拟定营销目标
5. 营销策略
6. 行动方案
7. 营销预算
8. 营销控制

注意：写作时，可根据具体公司单位的不同需求来增加或是删减上述部分。计划一定要实用，具有可操作性，不要为了写作而写作。列出营销计划的目标只有一个，就是促进销售，这是要写作者明确的。

44. 规定

NON-SMOKING POLICY
Board of Governors for Higher Education
State of Rhode Island and Providence Plantations

INTRODUCTION

In light of the new evidence available on the hazards of smoking, both to smokers and to non-smokers, the Board of Governors for Higher Education hereby establishes a non-smoking policy, which applies to all workplace, recreational, and residential areas within the buildings and facilities under the jurisdiction of the Board of Governors. This policy shall direct the actions at the University of Rhode Island, Rhode Island College, the Community College of Rhode Island, and the Rhode Island Office of Higher Education.

POLICY

1. There shall be no smoking in all buildings and facilities under the jurisdiction of the Board of Governors for Higher Education, except in areas specifically designated by the president/commissioner of the institution/agency.

2. If permitted, smoking can be allowed only in specifically designated areas in which the air exchange is directly with the outside atmosphere and not with the atmosphere in any other part of the building or facility.

3. There shall be no smoking in the rooms in which meetings or conferences sponsored by the Board of Governors for Higher Education and/or the University of Rhode Island, Rhode Island College, the Community College of Rhode Island and the Rhode Island Office of Higher Education are held.

4. All buildings and facilities will be clearly posted with "non-smoking area" signs at the entrances.

5. Through the Rhode Island Department of Health, information on smoking cessation programs and policies will be made available to all interested employees.

6. The prohibitions of this policy shall not apply to the use of tobacco products as part of a pre-approved, limited classroom demonstration or a pre-approved research project.

7. The Board of Governors non-smoking policy shall be distributed to all employees and students under its jurisdiction and shall be posted at each institution/agency.

8. This policy supersedes the current smoking/non-smoking policies adopted by the public institutions of higher education; existing policies should be revised to be in keeping with this Board of Governors policy.

9. The Board of Governors non-smoking policy shall become effective as of July 1, 2012.

禁烟规定
高等教育理事会
罗得岛暨普罗维登斯种植园

简介

　　由于最近证实吸烟对吸烟人士和周围人士皆有害，高等教育理事会兹设立禁烟规定，理事会管辖范围内一切工作场所、娱乐区、住宅区均需遵守。该规定对罗德岛大学、罗德岛学院、罗德岛社区大学和罗德岛高等教育办公室等均有指导作用。

规定细则

　　1. 在高等教育理事会管辖范围内的所有建筑和设施内均不得吸烟，由学校/机构的校长/委员专门指定的吸烟区除外。
　　2. 若得允许，只可在与外界有直接空气流通的指定区域吸烟，与建筑或设施其他部位有直接空气流通的区域不得吸烟。
　　3. 在由高等教育理事会和／或罗德岛大学、罗德岛学院、罗德岛社区大学和罗德岛高等教育办公室主办的会议会场内不得吸烟。
　　4. 所有相关建筑和设施入口均需明确张贴"严禁吸烟"字样。
　　5. 关于禁烟项目和政策的信息将通过罗德岛卫生局提供给感兴趣的员工。
　　6. 本规定不针对得到事先批准且有限的课堂展示，或得到事先批准的研究项目。
　　7. 本禁烟规定须对理事会辖区内所有员工和学生发放，还须在每个学校/机构张贴。
　　8. 本规定取代公共高等院校现行的吸烟／禁烟规定；现有规定须经修订，以符合本规定。
　　9. 本规定自2012年7月1日起生效。

45. 预算

Budget of X Store, 2008

　　X Store is basing their projected baking, baked goods and coffee sales on the financial information provided to them by Y Company. Internet sales were estimated by calculating the total number of hours each terminal will be active each day and then generating a conservative estimate as to how many hours will consumers be purchasing.

Cost of Goods Sold: Total cost of goods sold for coffee and baked goods-related products was determined by the "retail profit analysis" we obtained from Y Company. The cost of bakery items is 20% of the selling price. The cost of Internet access is $250 per month, paid to *** for networking fees. The cost of e-mail accounts is 25% of the selling price.

Fixture Costs: Fixture costs associated with starting X Store are the following: 2 computers and wireless hubs $3,000, two printers $1,000, one scanner $400, one espresso machine $10,700, one automatic espresso grinder $895, two coffee/food preparation counters $1,200, one information display counter $1,400, one drinking/eating counter $900, sixteen stools $1,600, six computer desks/chairs $3,400, stationery goods $500, two telephones $200, decoration expense $14,110, for a total fixture cost of $39,305.

Salaries Expense: The founder of X Store, Mr. Jack White, will receive a salary of $24,000 in year one, $36,400 in year two, and $49,040 in year three.

Payroll Expense: X Store intends to hire six part-time employees at $5.75/hour and a full-time technician at $10.00/hour. The total cost of employing seven people at these rates for the first year is $7,240/month.

Rent Expense: X Store is leasing a 1,700 square foot facility at $0.85/sq. foot. The lease agreement X Store signed specifies that we pay $2,000/month for a total of 36 months. At the end of the third year, the lease is open for negotiations and X Store may or may not re-sign the lease depending on the demands of the lessor.

Marketing Expense: X Store will allocate $5,000 for promotional expenses at the time of start-up. These dollars will be used for advertising in local newspapers, magazines and online in order to build consumer awareness.

Insurance Expense: X Store has allocated $1,440 for insurance for the first year. As revenue increases in the second and third year of business, X Store intends to invest more money for additional insurance coverage.

Legal and Consulting Fees: The cost of obtaining legal consultation in order to draw up the paper work necessary for an LLC is $1,000.

Taxes: X Store is an LLC and, as an entity, it is not taxed. However, there is a 15% payroll burden.

Accounts Payable: X Store acquired a $24 000 loan from a bank at a 10% interest rate. The loan will be paid back at $750/month over the next three years. The $9,290 short term loan will be paid back at a rate of 8%.

2008年X店财务预算

X店将其正在烤制和已经烤制完成的食品及咖啡的销售预测建立在Y公司提供的财务信息之上。网络销售的估算是通过计算每位终端用户每日在线的时间，然后对顾客网购的时间做出一个保守的估计。

已售商品的成本：咖啡和烘烤食品的总成本取决于我们从Y公司获得的"零售利润分析"。烘烤食品的成本是其售价的20%。联网花费是每月250美元，上交给***公司。电子邮件账户成本是零售价的25%。

固定开支：X店运作的固定开支如下：2台电脑和无线集线器共3 000美元，2台打印机共1 000美元，1台扫描仪共400美元，1台咖啡机共10 700美元，1台自动咖啡研磨机共895美元，2个咖啡/食物准备柜台共1 200美元，1个信息显示柜台共1 400美元，1个饮食柜台共900美元，16个凳子共1 600美元，6个带椅电脑桌共3 400美元，办公用品共500美元，2台电话共200美元，装修费共14 110美元；所有固定开支共计39 305美元。

经理工资：X店创建者杰克·怀特先生将在第一年收到24 000美元的薪水，第二年收到36 400美元的薪水，第三年收到49 040美元的薪水。

员工工资：X店准备雇佣6名兼职服务员，工资为5.75美元/小时；1名全职技师，工资为10美元/小时。以此工资标准，第一年的员工工资成本将达7 240美元/月。

租金成本：X店以每平尺0.85美元的价格租用了1 700平尺的设施。X店签订的租赁合同上规定我店每月支付2 000美元的租金，共支付36个月。第三年末，租约将可容商讨，租约将根据出租人需要，决定是否让X店续租。

营销开支：X店将用5 000美元作为开店初期的宣传开支。这些资金将被用作在当地报纸、杂志和网站纸张贴广告，告知消费者。

保险开支：X店已拨出1 440美元作为第一年的保险费用。随着第二年和第三年的收入增加，X店将扩大投保范围。

法律和咨询开支：起草有限责任公司所需的文件需要聘请法律顾问，其花费为1 000美元。

税收费用：X店是有限责任公司，作为实业，无需缴税。然而，员工工资需要交纳15%的税。

应付账款：X店从银行以10%的利率得到了24 000美元的贷款。贷款将在未来三年内以每个月750美元的数量偿清。9 290美元的短期贷款将以8%的利率偿清。

46. 营销计划

（由于公司企业制定的各类计划往往较长，故此特选择一篇营销计划的提纲作为范例进行展示。）

Marketing Plan (Outline)

- Executive summary

- Industry analyses

  - SWOT: strengths, weaknesses, opportunities and threats

  - Porter 5 forces analysis: customers; your own company; current and future competitors; suppliers; and the regulatory environment

- The target market

  - Target market demographics: income levels; interests; activities; living environment; other geographic descriptions; psychological mindsets; political affiliations; family situations; age ranges; tastes; etc.

  - Industry or societal trends that affect your customers

  - Your target customers' needs and wants, and corresponding product benefits

- Marketing strategy

  - Overall objectives and mission statement

  - Positioning relative to competitors and in eyes of customers

  - General strategies to reach objectives and fulfill mission

  - Marketing mix, including specific marketing programs

- Products
   - Pricing strategies
   - Distribution channels
   - Promotions, advertising and other marketing programs
- Forecasts
   - Size of target market and growth projections
   - Sales growth projections
- Financial analysis
   - Pro forma profit and loss (P&L) for each product and in total: sales forecasts, cost of goods, marketing budgets, fixed overhead projections, profit margins
   - Breakeven analysis
   - "What-if" scenarios (sensitivity analysis)

营销计划（提纲）

- 经营总结
- 行业分析
   -SWOT：优势（strengths），劣势（weaknesses），机遇（opportunities）和威胁（threats）
   - 波特5项分析：客户；自身；当前和未来的竞争对手；供应商；监管环境
- 目标市场
   - 目标市场人群分析：收入水平；兴趣；活动；生活环境；其他地理特征；心理特征；政治倾向；家庭情况；年龄分布；口味；等等
   - 影响客户的行业趋势和社会趋势
   - 目标客户的需要以及相应产品的利润
- 营销策略
   - 总目标和使命陈述
   - 关于竞争对手和在消费者心目中的定位
   - 达到目标和完成使命的总策略
   - 全套营销策略，包括具体营销项目

- 产品
- 定价策略
- 销售渠道
- 促销、广告和其他营销项目
■ 预测
- 目标市场的规模和成长情况预测
- 销售增长预测
■ 财务分析
- 每件产品以及所有产品的可能盈亏情况：销售预测，产品开销，营销预算，固定间接费用预测，利润率
- 盈亏相抵分析
- 危机应对（灵敏度分析）

特别奉献

一　重要政府部门中英对照

State Development Planning Commission 国家发展计划委员会
Ministry of Railways 铁道部
Ministry of Communications 交通部
Ministry of Information Industry 信息产业部
Ministry of Water Resources 水利部
Ministry of Agriculture 农业部
Ministry of Foreign Trade and Economic Cooperation 对外贸易经济合作部
Ministry of Culture 文化部
Ministry of Health 卫生部
State Family Planning Commission 国家计划生育委员会
The People's Bank of China 中国人民银行
National Auditing Administration 审计署
the National College Entrance Examination 全国高考
Ministry of Science and Technology 科学技术部
State Ethnic Affairs Commission 国家民族事务委员会
Ministry of Public Security 公安部
Ministry of State Security 国家安全部
Ministry of Supervision 监察部
Ministry of Civil Affairs 民政部
State Economy and Trade Commission 国家经济计划委员会
Ministry of Education 教育部
Ministry of Justice 司法部
Ministry of Finance 财政部
Ministry of Personnel 人事部
Ministry of Labour and Social Security 劳动和社会保障部
Ministry of Land and Resources 国土资源部
Ministry of Construction 建设部

二　世界主要国家和地区名称中英对照

Albania 阿尔巴尼亚

Algeria 阿尔及利亚

Afghanistan 阿富汗

Argentina 阿根廷

Egypt 埃及

Ethiopia 埃塞俄比亚

Ireland 爱尔兰

Anguilla 安圭拉

Republic of Albania 阿尔马尼亚共和国

Democratic People's Republic of Algeria 阿尔及利亚民主人民共和国

Islamic State of Afghanistan 阿富汗伊斯兰国

Republic of Argentina 阿根廷共和国

United Arab Emirates 拉伯联合酋长国

Arab Republic of Egypt 阿拉伯埃及共和国

Ethiopia 埃塞俄比亚

Ireland 爱尔兰

Republic of Austria 奥地利共和国

Commonwealth of Australia 澳大利亚联邦

Islamic Republic of Pakistan 巴基斯坦伊斯兰共和国

Republic of Paraguay 巴拉圭共和国

State of Palestine 巴勒斯坦国

Federative Republic of Brazil 巴西联邦共和国

Republic of Belarus 白俄罗斯共和国

Republic ov Bulgaria 保加利亚共和国

Kingdom of belgium 比利时王国

Republic of Iceland 冰岛共和国

Republic of Poland 波兰共和国

Belize 伯利兹

Kingdom of Bhutan 不丹王国
Democratic People's Republic of Korea 朝鲜民主主义人民共和国
Kingdom of Denmark 丹麦王国
Russian Federation 俄罗斯联邦
French Republic 法兰西共和国
Vatican City State 梵蒂冈城国
Republic of the Philippines 菲律宾共和国
Republic of Finland 芬兰共和国
Republic of Congo 刚果共和国
Republic of Colombia 哥伦比亚共和国
Republic of Costa Rica 哥斯达黎加共和国
Grenada 格林纳达
Greenland 格陵兰
Republic of Georgia 格鲁吉亚共和国
Republic of Cuba 古巴共和国
Guam 关岛
Cooperative Republic of Guyana 圭亚那合作共和国
Republic of Kazakhstan 哈萨克斯坦共和国
Republic of Haiti 海地共和国
Republic of Korea 大韩民国
Kingdom of the Netherlands 荷兰王国
Canada 加拿大
Kingdom of Cambodia 柬埔寨王国
Cayman Islands 开曼群岛
State of Kuwait 科威特国
Republic of Croatia 克罗地亚共和国
Republic of Kenya 肯尼亚共和国
Lao People's Democratic Republic 老挝人民民主共和国
Republic of Lebanon 黎巴嫩共和国
Republic of Liberia 利比里亚共和国
Great Socialist People's Libyan Arab Jamahiriya 大阿拉伯利比亚人民社会主义民众国
Republic of Lithuania 立陶宛共和国

Grand Duchy of Luxembourg 卢森堡大公国

Republic of Rwanda 卢旺达共和国

Romania 罗马尼亚

Republic of Madagascar 马达加斯加共和国

Republic of maldives 马尔代夫共和国

Malaysia 马来西亚

Republic of Mali 马里共和国

United States of America 美利坚合众国

Montserrat 蒙特塞拉特

People's Republic of Bangladesh 孟加拉人民共和国

Republic of Peru 秘鲁共和国

Federated States of Micronesia 密克罗尼西亚联邦

Union of Myanmar 缅甸联邦

Kingdom of Morocco 摩洛哥王国

United States of Mexico 墨西哥合众国

Republic of Namibia 纳米比亚共和国

Republic of South Africa 南非共和国

Antarctica 南极洲

Federal Republic of Yugoslavia 南斯拉夫联盟共和国

Republic of Nicaragua 尼加拉瓜共和国

Republic of Niger 尼日尔共和国

Federal Republic of Nigeria 尼日利亚联邦共和国

Kingdom of Norway 挪威王国

Pirtuguese Republic 葡萄牙共和国

Japan 日本国

Kingdom of Sweden 瑞典王国

Swiss Confederation 瑞士联邦

Saint Lucia 圣卢西亚

Republic of the Sudan 苏丹共和国

Republic of Turkey 土耳其共和国

Turkmenistan 土库曼斯坦

Brunei Darussalam 文莱达鲁萨兰国

Republic of Uganda 乌干达共和国

Ukraine 乌克兰

Oriental Republic of Uruguay 乌拉圭东岸共和国

Republic of Uzbekistan 乌兹别克斯坦共和国

Spain 西班牙

Western Sahara 西撒哈拉

Independent State of Western Samoa 西萨摩亚独立国

Hellenic Republic 希腊共和国

Republic of Singapore 新加坡共和国

New Caledonia 新喀里多尼亚

New Zealand 新西兰

Republic of Hungary 匈牙利共和国

Syrian Arab Republic 阿拉伯叙利亚共和国

Jamaica 牙买加

Republic of Armenia 亚美尼亚共和国

Republic of Iraq 伊拉克共和国

Islamic Rupublic of Iran 伊朗伊斯兰共和国

State of Israel 以色列国

Republic of Italy 意大利共和国

Republic of India 印度共和国

Republic of Indonesia 印度尼西亚共和国

United Kingdom of Great Britain and Northern ireland
大不列颠及北爱尔兰联合王国

British Virgin Islands 英属维尔京群岛

British Indian Ocean Territory 英属印度洋领土

Hashemite Kingdom of Jordan 约旦哈希姆王国

Socialist Republic of Viet Nam 越南社会主席共和国

Republic of Zambia 赞比亚共和国

Republic of Zaire 扎伊尔共和国

Republic of Chad 乍得共和国

Gibraltar 直布罗陀

Republic of Chile 智利共和国

Central African Republic 中非共和国

People's Republic of China 中华人民共和国

Chapter 06

日常事务

　　应用文使用范围广泛,不仅仅局限于公文范畴,在我们日常生活中也离不开它。生活中的应用文看似细小、琐碎,却恰恰证明了它们的重要性和实用性。只要有信息需要传递,就需要应用文。日常生活中我们常看到的应用文有:便条、通知、启事、海报、广告、字据、账单、声明、抱怨信、索赔信、检举信、说明书、情书等等。说起来大家都非常熟悉,但如果要用英文将这些应用文写出来,又会是怎样呢?变成英文后,这些文体会发生什么细微的变化呢?我们在写作时又需要注意些什么呢?本章将选取一些非常具有代表性的文体,将答案一一揭示出来。

Unit 1　便条和通知

Notes & Notices

　　便条（Notes & Messages）是一种简便的书信，类似于我们说的留言条。便条形式丰富，可以是意见、托事等。日常生活中的多数便条都格式简单、内容简短、用词通俗，体现出很强的随意性和生活气息。便条的内容一般包括：
1. 时间（一般写在右上方）；
2. 收件人姓名；
3. 正文（交代具体事项，如托事、抱怨、请假等，往往很短，一两行足矣）；
4. 署名。

　　通知（Notices & Announcements）在之前的章节中已经有过介绍。通知的运用范围是非常广泛的，不仅仅适用于企事业单位，在我们的日常生活中也无处不见——学校有通知，居委会有通知，路边小店有通知，电视上也有通知……因此了解通知，学会写通知，是非常重要的。

　　通知的标题可以直接用 NOTICE，也可以以具体事由作标题，但要足够简洁。通知的内容一般有两种：一种为陈述某一事实，希望大家了解；另一种则带有对被通知者的某种要求。通知要求言简意赅、措辞得当、时间及时。通知的具体内容包括：
1. 标题。
2. 称呼：写被通知者的姓名或职称或单位名称。在第二行顶格写。
   （有时，因通知事项简短，内容单一，书写时略去称呼，直起正文。）
3. 正文：另起一行，空两格写正文。正文因内容而异。
4. 落款：分两行写在正文右下方，一行署名，一行写日期。

1. 便条（日常交流）

Feb. 16, 2010

Dear Peter,

  Many thanks for your gift. The dictionary is what I need most at present.

Lily

亲爱的皮特：
  非常感谢你的礼物。这本字典正是我目前最想要的！

丽丽
2010 年 2 月 16 日

2. 便条（意见）

Dec. 8, 2011

Dear Mrs. Green,

  These nights I just can't get asleep because your house is too noisy. It's okay to turn the music on at night, but could you please turn it off after 12 o'clock? I don't think I sleep too early. Sorry for this but thanks a million for your kind cooperation.

Your neighbor

亲爱的格林女士：
  最近几个晚上我无法入眠，因为您家太吵了。您要晚上开着音乐，这没有关系，但您能不能不要在 12 点之后还开着？我不觉得这个时间早了。不好意思打扰了，但您若能配合，我将不胜感激。

您的邻居
2011 年 12 月 8 日

3. 便条（建议）

Oct. 5, 2009

Dear Mike,

　　I notice that your desk has been in a mass for a couple of days. I suggest that you clean it up as soon as possible, because I may affect your efficiency.

Mr. Keats

亲爱的麦克：

　　我注意到你的办公桌已经乱了好几天了，建议你尽快整理一下，因为这可能会影响到你的工作效率。

济慈
2009 年 10 月 5 日

4. 便条（托事）

Sept. 4, 2009

Dear Mrs. Liao,

　　There will be someone sending me a piece of newspaper tomorrow morning, but I will be away then. Could you please take that for me? Thank you a lot!

Li Jianbo

亲爱的廖女士：

　　明早将会有人给我送一份报纸，但我不在家。请问您能否帮我领取？非常感谢！

李建波
2009 年 9 月 4 日

5. 学习通知

NOTICE

There will be a seminar on October 14th, 2011 studying the important thought of "Three Represents" at 3:00 p.m., in Meeting Room No.2. All the teachers of the Department of International Economics are required to be there on time.

Department of International Economics
Oct. 12th, 2011

通知

我系将于 2011 年 10 月 14 日下午 3 点在第二会议室召开学习"三个代表"重要思想研讨会。国际经济系全体教师务必准时参加。

国际经济系
2011 年 10 月 12 日

6. 讲座通知

The Department Office
NOTICE OF LECTURE

Lecture Speaker: Prof. Zhu Zhijun
Subject: The Rhythm and Rhyme of Ancient Chinese Poems
Time: Wednesday, October 12, 2011, at 2:00 p.m.
Place: Room 429

October 10, 2011

系办公室
讲座通知

主讲人：朱之君教授
演讲题目：中国古典诗歌的节奏和韵律
时间：2011 年 10 月 12 日（周三）下午 2:00
地点：429 教室

2011 年 10 月 10 日

7. 参观通知

NOTICE

Attention please. A visit has been arranged for May 5 to the Panyu

Industrial Zone.

Those who wish to go, please gather at the main gate. The coach is to leave at 8:00 a.m. punctually.

Reception Office
April 28, 2009

通知

请注意！我处 5 月 5 日将安排参观盘鱼工业区。

有意参加的同志请于大门处集合。我们的汽车将于早上 8 点准时出发。

接待处
2009 年 4 月 28 日

8. 喜报

Good News!

According to the performance report sent by the National Examination Office for Foreign Languages Colleges, of all the 56 sophomore English majors taking the Test for English Majors Band 4 dated April, 2010, 100% of the students passed the exam with 94.64% of them make their grades above 70. While nationally speaking, the average grades have witnessed a slight drop, the average grades of our English majors have seen a rise of 5.4 points, which amount to 81.20 points, 15.37 points higher than the national average. Moreover, our grades in all specific parts of the test such as listening, writing and reading are higher than those of the English majors of the other universities or foreign language-oriented colleges. This marks the best performance of our English majors in recent years.

In addition, 59 sophomore no-English majors in our university took the test with a passage rate of 100% and average grades of 75.71, and 81.36% of the passed students are with grades higher than 70. Their average grades and the grades of all specific parts of the test are all higher than those of the non-English majors of other foreign language-oriented colleges nationwide.

We hereby extend our congratulations to all those who passed and performed well in the test! And many thanks and congratulations to dear teachers of the English Department!

Academic Affairs Office
English Department
China Foreign Affairs University
Nov. 18th, 2010

英语专业四级成绩喜报

　　根据高等学校外语院校考试办公室下发的成绩通知单,在 2010 年 4 月进行的英语专业四级考试中,英语系 2008 级 56 名同学参加了此次考试,通过率为 100%,优良率为 94.64%,在全国外语院校平均分比去年略微下降的情况下,我院学生平均分提高了 5.4 分,为 81.20 分,高出全国外语院校 15.37 分,各单项成绩均高于全国院校和其他外语院校英语专业学生的成绩,为近几年来最好成绩。

　　我院本科 2008 级非英语专业 59 名同学参加了此次考试,通过率为 100%,优良率为 81.36%,平均分为 75.71。平均分和各单项成绩均高于全国其他外语院校非英语专业学生的成绩。

　　在此,特向我院在本次考试中取得优秀成绩和获得通过的同学表示祝贺!向英语系老师表示祝贺和感谢!

外交学院教务处、英语系
2010 年 11 月 18 日

9. 放假通知

NOTICE

　　Tomorrow will be the New Year's Day. There will be no work for 3 days. All the managers and workers are expected to take part in the celebrations to be held in our factory tomorrow. Work will be resumed on January 4.

Office of General Manager
Dec. 31, 2011

通知

　　明天就是元旦节了。我们将放假 3 天。欢迎所有经理和员工参加我们明天在工厂举办的庆元旦活动。我们将于 1 月 4 日复工。

　　总经理办公室

2011 年 12 月 31 日

10. 停水通知

NOTICE

Notice is hereby given that the water supply is not available from 7:00 a.m. to 11:00 p.m. tomorrow, owing to repair of the water pipes. We greatly apologize for any inconvenience this may cause.

*** Committee
Feb. 9, 2007

停水通知

由于需要修缮水管，明天上午 7:00 至晚上 11:00 将会停水，特此通知。对于此次停水给您带来的不便，我们深表歉意。

*** 居委会
2007 年 2 月 9 日

Unit 2　启事

Notices

　　启事（Notices）是一种公告性的应用文，从某种意义上说，也可以归为通知的一种。公司、部门或个人要说明事情或提出要求，都可以简明扼要地写成启事，张贴于布告栏、公共场所或者刊登在报刊、杂志上。常见的启事有寻物启事（Lost）、出售启事（Sale）、征稿启事（Contribution Wanted）、出租启事（Room to Let）、鸣谢启事（Acknowledgements）、更正启事（Correction）等等。一则启事一般包括以下步骤：

1. 上方正中为启事名称，如 NOTICE，Acknowledgements，Change of Address 等；
2. 在低于启事名称的右上方标注日期，当然，在实践中也有不少启事是将日期放在左下方或是右下方的；简单的启事有时可以省去时间；
3. 正中写启事内容，不用称呼，一般包括：目的、内容、形式、要求、意义等；若内容较多，可分条写；
4. 右下方署名。

11. 寻人启事

Help Wanted

　　My father, Lv Jun (see the picture), has been missing. He has some mental diseases and can hardly take care of himself. He is 168cm with a little white hair. On the day he was missing, he was wearing a brown jacket and a pair of black trousers. The whole family is now very worried about his safety. If anyone happens to see him, please contact us as soon as possible. We are willing to give 2,000RMB if anyone help us out! Thank you!

　　Phone: 1111111.

Mr. Lv
August 15, 2010

寻人启事

  我的父亲吕军（此图为照片）走失了。他有精神疾病，几乎无法照顾自己。他身高 168 厘米，有些许白发。走失当天穿着一件棕色夹克和一条黑色裤子。现在全家都非常担心他的安全。若有人看见他，请马上联系我们。我们愿意出 2 000 元作为酬谢！谢谢！

  联系电话：1111111。

吕先生

2010 年 8 月 15 日

12. 寻物启事

Lost

June 5, 2010

  Red leather purse, 15 by 9 in. Cafeteria No.3. Lost on June 3. Please contact me as soon as possible if anyone finds it. Many thanks!

  Phone: 1111111.

Loser

寻物启事

  本人于 6 月 3 日在三号餐厅遗失一红色皮包（15×9 英尺）。请拾到者速与本人联系。万谢！

  联系电话：1111111。

失主

2010 年 6 月 5 日

13. 招领启事

Found

  I happened to find a black purse in the reading room of the library. The loser is expected to come to my dorm to claim it. My dorm number is 405, Building 2.

Finder

October 25, 2009

招领启事

  本人在图书馆阅览室拾到一个黑色钱包。请失主来我的宿舍领取。我的寝室在 2 号公寓，405 房间。

发现者
2009 年 10 月 25 日

14. 征婚启事

  MALE 34, sincere, honest and reliable, with professional occupation, seeks female 24~30, for friendship and socializing, hopefully leading to romance, single mums welcome. Call me on 1111111.

  男性，34 岁。为人真诚、老实、可靠。有正当职业。寻 24~30 岁女性，可交友、社交，若合适可进一步发展。单身母亲亦受欢迎。有意请联系 1111111。

15. 开业启事

Establishment of A Branch

April 8, 2012

  The Chairman and Directors of Austin Industries, Inc. are pleased to take the opportunity to announce the official opening of their Dellas Branch at *** on Sunday, April 12, 2012.

Board of Directors
Austin Industries, Inc.

开业启事

  奥斯丁工业公司的董事长和董事高兴地宣布，奥斯丁的德拉斯分公司将于 2012 年 4 月 12 日在 *** 街正式开业。

董事会
奥斯丁工业公司
2012 年 4 月 8 日

16. 停业启事

NOTICE

Notice is hereby given that owing to renovation, our shop will not be open to the public until further notice.

ABC Store
July 12, 2011

停业启事

由于我店重新装修，现暂停对外营业。具体开业时间另行通知。

ABC 店
2011 年 7 月 12 日

17. 更名启事

Change of Company Name

Please be informed that from January 1, 2011, Jin Cai Co. , Ltd will be replaced by Jin Cai Investment Co. , Ltd.

The Office
December 20. 2010

更名启事

从 2011 年 1 月 1 日起，晋才有限公司将更名为晋才投资有限公司。

晋才公司办公室
2010 年 12 月 20 日

18. 出租启事

Room to Let

Located near *** Park. Double room suitable 2 students sharing. Cooking facilities, share bathroom. Non-smokers only. RMB 1600 each month, excluding water/electricity.

Phone: 1111111.

Miss Liu
Sept. 12, 2011

房屋出租

    *** 公园附近。双人房，适合 2 个学生居住。有炊具，公共卫生间。吸烟人士请绕道。租金每月 1600 元，不包水电。

    联系电话：1111111。

刘小姐
2011 年 9 月 12 日

19. 求租启示

Room Wanted

    I am a senior student of ABC University. I am now preparing for the exam for postgraduates. In order to study in a quiet environment, I would like to rent a room near my school. If anyone has a single/double room with air-conditioning, a bathroom, cooking facilities and a washing machine, and if the rent is lower than RMB 1500/month, please do not hesitate to contact me.

    By the way, if any student who also wants a quiet room, we can share so that the pay will be lower.

    Phone: 1111111.

Mr Xie
Oct 2, 2011

求租

    本人是 ABC 大学的学生，现阶段正在备战考研。为能有一个安静的学习环境，本人欲在学校附近租一个房间。若您有带空调、浴室、炊具和洗衣机的单人或双人房间，并且租金低于 1500 元 / 月，请马上联系我。

    此外，若还有同学也需要一个安静的房间，我们可以共用，这样费用就降低了。

    联系电话：1111111。

谢同学
2011 年 10 月 2 日

20. 搬迁启事

Change of Address

Oct. 8th, 2010

We are pleased to take the opportunity to announce that we have moved our office to 1 Real Road. The old premises have proved inadequate to cope with the ever-increasing demand made upon by our numerous clients.

ABC Company

迁址启事

借此机会，我们高兴地宣布，ABC 公司的办公室已经迁至瑞尔街 1 号。由于我们客户众多，需求日长，旧址已经无法满足需要。

ABC 公司

2010 年 10 月 8 日

21. 鸣谢启事

ACKNOWLEDGEMENTS

June 23, 2008

During the organization of this Industrial Park, the Organizing Committee accepted considerable help and support from the local government, bank and other nongovernmental units. Now we'd like to offer our sincere thanks to them for their fruitful aid.

*** Industrial Park

Organizing Committee

鸣谢

在本工业园展览组织期间，组委会受到了来自当地政府、银行和其他非政府组织的大力帮助和支持。现组委会对他们富有成效的帮助表示衷心的感谢。

*** 工业园

组委会

2008 年 6 月 23 日

22. 更正启事

CORRECTIONS

In the issue No. 45 of our magazine, the caption for the photo at the right-hand bottom of p. 16 should read: The workers of the *** Chemical Fertilizer Plant are going all out to develop production.

更正启事

本刊第 45 期第 16 页右下方照片的的说明词应改为：*** 化肥厂工人全力发展生产。

Unit 3　海报　　　　　　　　　　Posters

　　海报是一种带有装饰性的宣传广告，有时配以绘画等以引人注目。海报往往是手写的，内容多是人们喜闻乐见的有关娱乐方面的消息，如影讯、球赛、晚会等。英文海报的格式多种多样，语言也比较生动活泼，一般不是很正式，常常使用简短句、省略句、缩写形式等。海报最大的特点是常常有一句口号或是警句，或是有一句号召性的句子。

　　有关影讯、球赛等的海报，可以采用分条书写，一一列出活动的内容、时间、地点等基本信息，清晰明了，让人印象深刻。如：

MOVIE

Name:

Time:

Place:

Fare:

　　晚会海报除写明时间、地点外，还可根据具体情况列出详细的节目单，包括名称及表演者。

　　除此之外，还有讲座海报、社团开会海报、商品拍卖海报等，都需根据具体情况进行写作，以简练、清晰、深刻、有吸引力和号召力为方向。

23. 学术报告类海报

LECTURE

Subject: Asian Women in Hollywood and Beyond

Speaker: Professor Elaine H. Kim

Hostess: Pro. Shi Jian

Time: Thursday, 12 May, 2011, 15:00~17:00 p.m.

Place: Room 360, Main Building

Sponsor: the English Department, American Study Center

讲座

主题：好莱坞内外的亚洲女性

主讲人：埃兰·H·金 教授
主持人：石坚 教授
时　　间：2011 年 5 月 12 日（周四）15:00~17:00
地　　点：主楼 360 教室
主　　办：英语系、美国研究中心

24. 文艺晚会海报

ANNIVERSARY CELEBRATION

　　The ABC Co., Ltd. takes pleasure in announcing that the 10th anniversary celebration of our company is to be held in the assembly hall on Friday, 11 November, 2011, at 7:30 p.m.. The programs include recitations, cross-talks, songs, dancings, plays, etc. Come and join us!

ABC Company
8 November, 2011

公司周年庆祝晚会

　　ABC 公司高兴地宣布，我公司成立 10 周年庆祝晚会将于 2011 年 11 月 11 日（周五）晚 7:30 在礼堂举行。晚会节目包括诗朗诵、相声、演唱、舞蹈、小品等。欢迎参加！

ABC 公司
2011 年 11 月 8 日

25. 体育比赛海报

INTERNATIONAL VOLLEYBALL MATCH

China vs the USA
Time: Oct. 27　3:00 p.m.
Venue: Capital Gymnasium
Please apply at General Affairs Department for tickets
All Are Welcome!

国际排球赛

中国 vs 美国

时间：10月27日下午3:00
地点：首都体育馆
请到总务处购票
欢迎观看！

26. 电影海报

XSense Presents
FILM SHOW
TITANIC (3D)
A Classical Love Story with A New Look
May 2nd, Friday
XSense CINEMA
Doors open 7:15 p.m.
Starts 7:30 p.m.

X感影院呈现
电影
泰坦尼克号（3D版）
爱情经典，全新演绎
5月2日 周五
X感电影院
开门时间：晚7:15
播放时间：晚7:30

27. 社团开会海报

SOCIETY MEETING

　　Attention! The Classical Poetry Society is holding its last meeting for this semester. All our members are expected to be present. The agenda includes annual report and summary, plans for next semester and the election of new leaders. After the meeting, we will go for a big dinner in ABC Restaurant and then go to a nearby KTV. The meeting will be held at 3:20 p.m. this Friday in Classroom 354. We will be waiting for you!

Classical Poetry Society
Dec. 11, 2011

社团例会

请注意！古典诗歌社将召开本学期最后一次例会。所有社员务必参加。会议议程包括年度报告和总结、明年社团工作计划和社团领导换届选举。会后我们将到 ABC 餐馆聚餐，随后到附近的一家 KTV 唱歌。例会将于本周五下午 3:20 召开，开会地点是 354 教室。不见不散！

古典诗歌社
2011 年 12 月 11 日

Unit 4　广告

Advertisements

广告（Advertisements）是商家有计划地通过媒体传递商品或劳务信息，以达到宣传促销、介绍业务等目的的大众传播手段。广告的分类方法很多，根据不同的方法可以分出各种类型。就内容来看，常见的有产品广告、业务广告、招聘广告等等。

产品广告在各类广告中所占比例最大。为了把产品具体生动地介绍给消费者，达到引起注意、唤起兴趣、增强欲望、促使行动的目的，这类广告从内容到形式均十分讲究。选词造句精巧别致，极富感染力。频繁使用省略句、简单句、祈使句等。有些还经常运用双关、拟人、对比、比喻、重复等修辞。由于传播广告的媒介不同，因此广告的长度也会不同。张贴在外的广告一般较短，若是发布在报刊、杂志上的介绍性广告则较长。

业务广告主要是用来介绍公司的业务范围，但同时又能起到宣传公司、树立企业形象的作用。因此业务广告除包括一般性的业务介绍外，还应设法突出公司、企业的特色。

28. 店铺广告

Greatbooks Special Offers

Greatbooks is pleased to announce great savings. We have a huge range of offers on fiction, non fiction, biographies, reference books, and classics.

The Orion Classics series

These Orion series books include all the great classics: Tolstoy, Dickens, Shakespeare, Shaw, Wordsworth, Bacon, Chekov, in fact everything from Aesop to Zola, all $3.95!

Orion Biographies

The Orion biographies are reprints of earlier biographies which are now almost impossible to get. These are the main sources for the modern biographies, and they're quite dazzling reading. Also $3.95, great value!

Film stars: Audrey Hepburn, Sophia Loren, Boris Karloff, and many more.

Politicians: Churchill, De Gaulle, Roosevelt, Stalin, Trotsky, Lenin, Mao Tse Tung, Gandhi, the whole range of 20th century political movers and shakers.

Historical Bios: Napoleon, Robespierre, Wellington, Nelson, Talleyrand, The Hanover Dynasty of Britain, Bismarck, a huge selection of titles.

Non Fiction

There are so many books we'll stick to subjects as a description: History, science, military, environment, sciences, philosophy, culture, travel... you name it, we have it.

Fiction

We have all the current New York Times best sellers, on a regular basis.

Orders with Greatbooks

We've got one more trick up our sleeve. You can order any book you like, even if it's out of print, and we'll find it for you if it can be found. We'll give you some quotes for prices, and you make the decision to buy.

You can call us anytime to check what we've got, or check out our website, www.greatbooks.com.

Happy reading,
Greatbooks

大阅书店特供

大阅书店惊喜特供！小说、非小说文学、传记、参考书、传世经典……凡所应有，无所不有！

猎户经典系列图书

猎户经典系列图书包括所有的经典名著：托尔斯泰、狄更斯、莎士比亚、萧伯纳、威廉·华兹华斯、培根、契诃夫……事实上，从伊索时代到左拉时代，所有图书，一律3.95美元！

猎户名人传记系列图书

猎户名人传记系列图书都是早期传记的重印版,当时的原件已难以复得。这些都是现代传记的主要来源,将给你带来一场阅读盛宴。所有图书,一律3.95美元,物超所值!

电影明星:奥德雷·赫本、索菲亚·罗兰、波利斯·卡洛夫……星光璀璨。

政治人物:丘吉尔、戴高乐、罗斯福、斯大林、托洛茨基、列宁、毛泽东、甘地……尽览20世纪政坛风云人物。

历史名人:拿破仑、罗伯斯庇尔、威灵顿公爵、纳尔逊、塔列朗、英国汉诺威王朝、俾斯麦……收录齐全。

非小说

我们的图书品目繁多,仅以类别概括为:历史、科学、军事、环境、哲学、文化、旅游……只有你想不到的,没有你找不到的!

小说

我们常年供应《纽约时报》时下最畅销书目。

好书不愁订

大阅书店还有惊喜!您可以订购您喜欢的书,即便此书已经停印,只要我们找得到,我们就一定帮您挖出来!我们将会给您订购的图书统一要价,看着合适了您就购买。

我们随时提供图书咨询热线服务,您也可以登录我们的网站 www.greatbooks.com 查询图书。

祝您阅读愉快!

大阅书店

29. 促销广告

BELLS ELECTRICAL

Shop 14, Anywhere Shopping Mall
Phone: 2234 4554
E-mail: fred@bellselectrical.com
HUGE CUTS IN PRICES ON THESE ITEMS!

Hicrust Toaster ovens	$49.95
Simsung Microwaves	$39.95
Simsung Heaters	$8.95
Tuffany Kettles	$9.95
Dawson mini vacuums	$29.95

COMING SOON TO BELLS ELECTRICAL:
　　The top of the range Pinosonic Steam Cleaner will be arriving in store in February. This is the "Cleaners Dream" as seen on the Shopping Channel, the all in one cleaning unit for your home.

铃儿电气

地址：天涯海角商城，14号店铺
电话：2234 4554
E-mail: fred@bellselectrical.com
以下产品大减价！

Hicrust 牌烤箱	$49.95
Simsung 牌微波炉	$39.95
Simsung 牌电暖气	$8.95
Tuffany 牌电水壶	$9.95
Dawson 牌迷你吸尘器	$29.95

快来铃儿电气店：
　　Pinosonic 牌蒸汽清洁器高端产品将于二月到达本店。该产品是购物频道上的"家庭主妇梦中宝贝儿"，一件在手，家务不愁！

30. 服务广告

Beat The Heat
Leave The Mowing To Us!
ABC Lawn Mowing Service
Affordable, Dependable, Insured
Residential, Commercial
FREE ESTIMATE
(XXX) XXX-XXXX

一边儿歇着去
把修草的事情交给我们！
ABC 割草服务
经济、靠谱、有保障
住宅、商务，来者不拒！
免费评估

电话：(XXX) XXX-XXXX

31. 出租广告

House for Rent

Beautiful Home for Rent in Lakewood, Next to Fort Lewis and American Lake.

Beautifully remodeled split-entry on sleepy culdesac, just up the hill from American Lake, and just a couple minutes from Fort Lewis. New kitchen with new gas range, dishwasher and refrigerator, new baths, carpeting, roof, windows, paint, and even a new fireplace insert in this large four bedroom, three bath home. Huge family room and very private back yard. About a five minute drive to Lakewood Center for shopping, and also just over the hill from the historic town of Steilacoom.

Type	Rent
Price/Rent	$1650.00 /month
Rooms	4bd/3ba
Sq Feet	2000
Street	123 Test Lane
City	Lakewood
Contact	555-555-5555 samplead@posthousing.com
Posted On	March 10, 2008 (Monday)

房屋出租

湖林市漂亮房屋出租！毗邻福特路易斯区和美洲湖。

　　曲径通幽处，岔道入口唯美翻修；依山傍水，数分钟可到福特路易斯区。崭新厨房配备全新煤气炉、洗碗机、电冰箱，浴室、地毯、屋顶、窗户、墙画一律全新，更有全新内嵌式壁炉设于四间卧室和三间浴室。宽敞的客厅，私密的后院，到湖林购物中心仅五分钟车程，翻山即到历史古镇斯德雷昆。

种 类	出 租
价格/租金	$1650.00/月
房间	4卧室/3浴室
面积	2000平尺
地点	123特斯特路
城市	湖林市
联系方式	555-555-5555 samplead@posthousing.com
发布日期	2008年3月10日（周一）

Unit 5　字据、账单与租赁　I.O.U., Receipt & Bill & Renting Issues

　　字据主要有借据（I.O.U.）和收据（Receipt）。

　　借据是借钱或是借物时所留的凭证。借钱借据一般要注明I.O.U.字样，是"I owe you"的缩略语，即"我欠你"的意思，翻译过来可以是"今借到"。右上方标注借款日期。在低于日期的左上方或正文后以To...注出被借人姓名，右下方则为借款人姓名。

　　收据是收到所交或归还的欠款或物品的一种凭证。格式与借据相同，正文多采用"Received from..."句型，可以翻译成"今收到"。

　　账单（Bill）是记载货币、货物出入事项的单子，一般是预先印制好的，多为表格形式。填好时间后，一般只要逐项填写相应情况即可。

　　房屋租借是我们日常生活中的热点问题。租赁房屋一般都有一个租赁合同，而合同一般较长，因此本文暂不赘述。这里为读者朋友们提供房主和房客的信件各一封。信中不仅涉及了房屋租赁的一些基本法律信息，还可以从字里行间看出双方当时的心情。

32. 借据

模板

August 3, 2011

To Mr. Song Junai,

　　I.O.U. Eight Thousand yuan (¥ 8,000), to be paid within four months form this date.

　　　　　　　　　　　　　　　　　　　　Gao Qiang

宋军爱先生：

　　本人欠您人民币八千元（¥ 8 000），自今日起四个月内还讫。

　　　　　　　　　　　　　　　　　　高强
　　　　　　　　　　　　　　　　　2011年8月3日

33. 收据

January 4th, 2009

 Received from Mr. Li Jianxi the sum of twenty thousand yuan (¥ 20,000)only.

            Chen Zhiyi

今收到李建喜先生人民币两万元（￥20 000）整。

            陈之怡
           2009 年 1 月 4 日

34. 账单

Haoxianglai Restaurant	
Number of People:	Number of Table:
Menu: 1. ABC 2. DEF 3.GHI	Unit Price (￥): 34, 25, 46
Total Amount(￥): 105	

好想来餐馆	
人数：	桌号：
菜单： 1. ABC 2. EDF 3. GHI	单价（￥）： 34, 25, 46
共计（￥）： 105	

35. 房主告知房客租约即将到期

Dear Mr. Herbert,

 I mean to terminate the Lease Deed of my House No. 1-5-9 which will take effect on 12th February, 2011 because my son is coming back and he may need it.

 I write this letter to inform you beforehand, be able to prepare your things and arrange those needed things before leaving my house. Also for you to be able to look for a new house where you and your family will stay in.

So, I am requesting that you leave my house on or before February 1, 2011 and provide me with empty possession of your things.

Hope that you will respond to my request. If you have any queries feel free to contact me, my number is 925-273-5624.

Sincerely thank you,
Michael C. Lance

尊敬的赫伯特先生：

由于我的儿子即将回来，他也许需要住的地方。我希望终止我的第 1-5-9 号租约，这份租约将于 2011 年 2 月 12 日到期。

这封信是想预先提醒您，以便您能够在离开房子之前准备好东西，安排好需要做的事情。同时，也让您有时间再找一间房子，给您和您家人居住。

我希望您在 2011 年 2 月 1 日前离开我的房子，不要留下您的东西。

希望您能对我的要求予以回应。如果您还有什么问题，请随时联系我，我的电话是 925-273-5624。

真诚地感谢您
迈克尔·C·兰斯

36. 房客要求续约

Dear Mr. Lance,

I write this letter to inform you that I will still continue to lease your apartment. The lease contract that I have right now indicates that my contract will end on the 24th of this month.

Though my college years have ended already, I still want to lease your apartment for the reason that I want to work in your locality and I am very contented with my stay in your apartment.

With regards to this matter, please do advise me the soonest if I can still lease your apartment so that I can relax my mind of looking for another apartment if I can't get a new lease contract from you.

Thank you very much for your time.

Yours Truly,

Lula D. Nguyen

亲爱的兰斯先生：

　　我写这封信是想告诉您，我将续租您的房子。现有的房契上显示我们的租约在本月 24 号就要到期了。

　　虽然我的大学已经读完了，但我仍然想租用您的房子，因为我想在附近工作，而且这儿的居住条件也让我十分满意。

　　关于这一请求，如果我能继续租用您的房子，请尽快告诉我，这样我就可以不用因为担心无法续约而苦于寻找另外一个住处了。

　　感谢您抽出时间阅信。

卢拉·D·古延 谨上

Unit 6　约会

Appointments

约会（Appointment）即预约会面，指预先约定时间地点会面的活动。约会往往是出于某种目的，如吃饭、聊天、娱乐等。如果约会对方是熟人，则语言方面可以非常轻松随意；如果是商务伙伴等，则需要用较为正式的语气。约会写作需注意：
1. 格式和一般信件一样；
2. 要写明约会原因、时间、地点；
3. 语气可以是强烈要求的，可以是商量的，也可以是建议的，主要看与对方的熟悉程度；
4. 如果约会时间较为仓促，则一般通过电子邮件或是手机短信发送。

37. 朋友约会

Dear Carla,

My birthday falls on 22 April and I am counting the days of happiness. I am waiting for my friends and family to gather at my home on 22 April and shower wishes on me. On this special occasion, I Cordially you to be present with me. Looking forward to see you on that day. I will send you the details later.

Yours lovingly,
Benne Dickson

亲爱的卡拉：

4月22日就是我的生日了，我现在正一天天算着幸福日子的到来。我等待着朋友和家人在4月22日在我家欢聚一堂，用生日的祝福将我席卷。值此特殊的时刻，我真诚地邀请你来参加我的生日聚会。期待在生日那天见到你。过后我会给你送来详细信息。

你的 本·迪克森

38. 恋人约会

Sweetheart,

  Would you like to take a walk tomorrow night in Peace Park? I heard there would be a movie show then. What about making it at 6:00 p.m. at the gate? If you want to come, tell me as soon as possible!

Affectionately Yours,
Mike

亲爱的：

  明晚你想到和平公园走走吗？我听说到时那儿有播放电影。我们 6 点在公园门口见如何？如果你想去，快点儿告诉我！

爱你的 麦克

39. 闺蜜约会

Hi Jane,

  There will be a fashion show in the cinema the day after tomorrow. Would you like to come with me? If you would, I'll go and ask for some details. Do not hesitate to tell me if you want to go!

Yours,
Lily

简：

  嗨！电影院后天会举办一场时装秀。你想和我一起去吗？如果你要去，我就去问问具体情况。决定了就马上告诉我！

你的 丽丽

40. 和长辈约会

Dear Mr. Brown,

  How are you these days? I have been struggling with the thesis and I find some problems with the literature review part. If you don't mind, can I come to your office to seek some advice from you? And what about 8:00

tomorrow morning?

I look forward to your early reply. Thank you so much!

             Sincerely yours,
             Jordan

尊敬的布朗先生：

  您最近过得好吗？这些天我一直在忙论文的事情，在文献综述部分卡住了。如果您不介意的话，我可以到您办公室向您寻求些建议吗？明早 8:00 如何？

  静候佳音。非常感谢！

             乔丹 谨上

41. 和晚辈约会

Dear Kate,

  Tomorrow I will invite some of my old friends to a casual dinner. They are all professors in the field of Chinese literature. I have told them that there is an American girl in my class who loves Chinese culture very much, and they are quite interested to see you. Are you interested to come? Don't forget to tell me if you do. It will be in the ABC restaurant at 6:30 p.m.. Looking forward to seeing you!

             Sincerely yours,
             Cai Yude

亲爱的凯特：

  明天我会邀请我的几个老朋友一起吃顿便饭。他们都是汉语文学领域的教授。我给他们说我班上有个非常喜欢中国文化的美国姑娘，他们都很想见见你。你有兴趣来吗？如果你有兴趣，请记得告诉我。我们吃饭的地点是 ABC 餐厅，时间定在下午 6:30。希望你能来！

             蔡禹德

42. 商务约会

Dear Mr Thomas,

  This letter is in response to the telephonic conversation we had last

Saturday regarding our business meeting. I am writing to confirm our appointment that we made over the telephone on 15th February, 2012 at 6:00 p.m. in your office.

I am preparing for the meeting and I will be there for the meeting in your office on 15th February, 2012 at 6:00 pm. Please go through the meeting agenda once and suggest for any changes if required.

Please read all the enclosed documents and get all the information required so that we can make our meeting much more productive.

If you have any doubt or question related to our appointment, feel free to contact me at 4556346260 or through e-mail at faltu@zalaltu.com.

I am looking forward for our meeting.

Yours truly,
Allen B Bennett

尊敬的托马斯先生：

此信是对上周六我们关于商务会见的电话谈话的回复，目的是想和您确认，我们电话里约定的时间是 2012 年 2 月 15 日下午 6:00，地点就在您的办公室。

我正在为这次见面做准备，我将在 2012 年 2 月 15 日下午 6:00 到您的办公室。请您看一看日程安排，若有任何变动，请告知。

请阅读所有附件并了解所有需要的信息，以便我们的会见能够更加富有成果。

若您对我们的会见还有什么疑问，请随时联系我。我的电话是 4556346260，邮箱是 faltu@zalaltu.com。

期待与您见面。

艾伦·B·本纳特 谨上

Unit 7　授权书

Authorization Letters

　　授权书（Authorization Letters）是由当事人准备的，赋予了一位他信任的人一项权力——当他没有时间、条件或在精神或健康上出现问题，以致不能做某事时，替他作出某项决定，如买卖物业、银行存支、交税及交其他单据。授权书的种类多种多样，有些是为生活中的琐事授权，有些则是涉及法律责任的大事。本书列举了三个为生活中的一些较小的事情而进行授权的授权书，还列举了一篇医疗授权书和一篇法律授权书。

　　授权书的写作根据不同的类型而异。但总体的要求是：
1. 语言要正式；
2. 授权何事交代清楚；
3. 授权的范围；
4. 说明被授权人会出具的相关证明材料，如身份证等；
5. 语言要简洁有力。

43. 授权他人领取物品

Dear Mr Jesse,

　　I, Sandy Rawal, hereby authorize my Driver, Champalal, to pick up goods from your showroom and sign related documents on my behalf. I am also sending my two IDs for identification purposes. He will check the number of packages and also verify the relevant documents. Please allow him complete access to all the documents and packages. He will arrive on next Monday, 17th September, 2011 at 9:00 a.m. at your showroom.

　　Please feel free to ask me for any clarifications needed.

　　Thank you very much.

Respectfully yours,
Sandy Rawal

尊敬的杰西先生：

　　我，珊迪·洛尔，兹授权我的司机山帕拉从您的寄存室里代领物品，并代表我在相关文件上签字。我还将送去我的两个身份证件作为认证身份之用。他还将检查包裹号并核实相关文件。请允许他接触所有文件和包裹。他将于 2011 年 9 月 17 日（周一）上午 9 点到达您的寄存室。

　　如有需要，请随时联系我澄清相关事宜。

　　非常感谢。

珊迪·洛尔 谨上

44. 授权代领薪水

Dear Sir/Madam:

　　I, the undersigned, authorized my brother, Rodel Rosario, to claim my payments from your company on my behalf. He hereby presents at least two cards for identification purposes.

　　This authorization applies to all payments dated from July 2008 up to August 2008. It does not include past August 31, 2008 without my written authorization.

　　If you have any questions, you may contact me at (047) 791-2911.

Sincerely,

Ericson Rosario

敬启者：

　　我，艾瑞克森·罗莎里奥，授权我兄弟罗德·罗莎里奥代表我本人到您公司领取我的薪水。他将至少出示两张身份证以证明身份。

　　这份授权书适用于任何 2008 年 7 月至 2008 年 8 月的薪水。若没有本人的书面授权，这份授权书并不涵括已经过去的 2008 年 8 月 31 日的薪水。

　　若还有任何问题，请通过电话（047）791-2911 联系我。

艾瑞克森·罗莎里奥 谨上

45. 授权某人进入自己家

Dear Mr. Brooke,

Good day! I am writing to you regarding the internet connection plan that I have subscribed to just the other day. I am giving you the authority to work on my home to install the plan.

I understand that it will take you at least seven days to fully install my internet connection. I am hoping that I could start using the plan by then.

I have enclosed here my first down payment amounting to $100.00, which will serve as the fee for installation. You are welcome to start setting up the connection anytime. I will just be waiting for your arrival. I hope you can get started right away so that my children won't have to pay for internet rental services anymore.

Please call if there are any changes or questions you may have at my contact number 987-6543.

Sincerely Yours,
Jenna Smith

尊敬的布鲁克先生：

您好！此信是关于不久前我申请的联网计划。兹授权您进入我家进行网络安装。

我知道您完全装好需要至少七天。我希望在那之前我能用上互联网。

随信附上 100 美元的第一笔定金作为安装费用。随时欢迎您前来安装，我会恭候您的光临。我希望您能马上安装，这样我的孩子们就不必再交钱租网了。

如果您有任何变动或者疑问，请通过电话 987-6543 联系我。

杰娜·史密斯 谨上

46. 医疗授权书

Medical Treatment Authorization Letter

TO WHOM IT MAY CONCERN:

As the guardians of Mr. John Smith, we authorize the bearer of this letter to approve medical treatment for our father. We entrust our father's condition to the physician assigned to our father's medical treatment.

Guardian 1
Jenny Smith
Work Phone: 592-0323
Mobile Phone: 0903420-4234

Guardian 2
Bryan Smithg
Work Phone: 893-9323
Mobile Phone: 0903-410-4234

PATIENT'S PERSONAL INFORMATION
Date of Birth: October 16, 1943
Blood Type: Type AB
Known Allergies: Oily and fatty foods
Being Treated For

These Chronic Conditions: High blood pressure, consecutive heart attack events, other complications such as inflammation in the eyes.

Doctor: Dr. Jenna Smith
Doctor's Contact number: 542-3242

Thank you,

_____

Guardian 1's signature

Guardian 1's Full Name

_____

Guardian 2's signature

Guardian 2's Full Name

Subscribed and sworn to before me this 29th Day of May 2010.

_____ Notary Public

_____ County, New York

(Doctor's Hospital Incorporation)

2482-942-424

医疗授权书

敬启者：

  作为约翰·史密斯先生的监护人，我们授权院方批准对我们的父亲进行医治。我们将我们父亲的身体状况委托给院方分配给他的医生。

监护人 1
杰尼·史密斯
工作电话：592-0323
手机：0903420-4234

监护人 2
布莱恩·史密斯
工作电话：893-9323
手机：0903-410-4234

病人的个人信息
生日：1943 年 10 月 16 日
血型：AB
已知过敏食物：油腻食物
病情：
患有以下慢性病：高血压、连续心脏病发作、其他并发症，如眼部发炎。

医生：杰娜·杰克森

医生联系电话：542-3242

谢谢

_____
监护人 1 签名
监护人 1 全名

_____
监护人 2 签名
监护人 2 全名

于 2010 年 5 月 29 日在本人见证下签署并确认

_____ 公证人
_____ 县，纽约州

（医生所属医院）
2482-942-424

47. 法律授权书

Dear Ms. Smith,

　　Good day! I am writing to inform you that I am giving you the authority to act as my attorney on the case that I filed against the Brown Suits Company. I understand that your rate is at $300 per hour. I have enclosed a $3,000 check that serves as my first payment.

　　Please send me the billings if ever it exceeded 100 hours. I will have to approve them first. You recall that you assured me that this case should not cost me more than $30,000.

　　Please sign in the space provided at the bottom if you agree with the terms stated in this letter. However, if you have other preferences, please contact me as soon as possible so we can settle our arrangements. You can reach me at 232-9493.

　　Thank you very much.

Sincerely
Susan Bourne

亲爱的史密斯女士：

　　您好！我特来通知您，我授权您在我起诉布朗服装公司的案件中担任我的律师。我知道您的薪资标准是每小时 300 美元。我已随信附上一张 3 000 美元的支票，作为我的第一笔预付款。

　　如果您在此案上的用时超过 100 小时，请将账单交给我，需先经过我的批准。记得您向我保证这一案件的花费不会超过 30 000 美元。

　　如果您同意此信中陈述的款项，那么请在信下的空白处签名。然而，如果您还有其他方案，请马上与我联系，以便我们安排妥当。我的电话是 232-9493。

　　非常感谢。

苏珊·布恩 谨上

Unit 8　其他　　Other Writings

日常生活中的写作种类千千万万，限于篇幅，无法一一介绍。为满足大家的需求，在此特集中一些其他常见文体模式，以飨读者。

48. 建议书（给个人）

Dear Ralf,

I have received your letter from school and am glad to know that you are becoming responsible enough to decide on your career.

You are now in the school final year and are about to launch into more independent education in college. You know that a generation divides us as the norms and conditions of social life were different in my days. But all I can say as advice is that you must select a career wisely. The first consideration is your interests. You can only succeed and feel happy when you do something you enjoy. Employment must be both gainful and satisfying. Then you must read up on the latest development in the field you are aiming at and acquaint yourself with men and women in the profession of that specialization. When mind and heart function in unison, success is inevitable.

No career is more or less important. It takes different people to set in motion the machinery of life. I thought your interests lay in the field of making T.V. films. Your very good communication skills, your active participation in school plays and the prizes you have won in oratorical competition make point in that direction. So a career in Mass Communication and T.V. film production prove lucky for you. If you succeed and make it that field, fame and fortune will both follow.

Think thousand times before taking any final decision in the case of your career. Anyhow we want you to be a man of success.

We all know that you are matured enough to think for yourself.

With all the best wishes
Your loving father

亲爱的拉夫：

　　我已经收到了你从学校寄来的信，很高兴看到你已经有足够的责任感，对你自己的职业做出选择。

　　你现在已经处于高中的最后一年，即将进入更加独立的大学教育阶段。你知道，我们之间隔了一代，我上学时的社会生活的规范和条件与现在迥异。但是，我能给你的建议就是，你必须明智地选择一条职业道路。首先你要考虑你的兴趣点。只有你的职业是你的兴趣所在，你才能成功并感到快乐。工作必须既能让你学到东西，又能让你得到满足。其次，你必须紧跟你目标职业领域的最新进展，熟悉在这一行业工作的人士。当你的思想和心灵协调一致，成功将向你走来。

　　职业不分贵贱。生活的机器需要不同的人维持其运转。我想你的兴趣应该是影视制作。你有良好的沟通技巧，积极参加学校的戏剧演出，还在演讲比赛中得奖，这些都说明了你有从事影视制作的潜质。所以从事大众传媒和影视制作是个不错的选择。如果你在这个领域取得了成功，那就名利双收了。

　　在择业问题上一定要三思而后行。无论怎样，我们都希望你取得成功。

　　我们知道，你已经长大了，可以为自己的未来考虑了。

祝万事顺意
爱你的爸爸

49. 建议书（给单位）

模板

Dear Mr. Goldberg,

　　Further to our earlier discussion on Meteor Organization's current project, we now submit a proposal from Forever Young Ltd for your consideration. We believe Forever Young Ltd is your right candidate to collaborate with Meteor Organization in marketing your products globally, with its high quality services, commitment, and expertise.

　　From our enclosure, you will approve of Forever Young Ltd's impressive business strategies, which have heaped outstanding feedback from our clients in past projects for the outstanding services rendered to Forever Young's esteemed clients. Enclosed is a listing of our esteemed clientele for your perusal.

Forever Young is capable in adjusting and focusing on current and effective strategies while tracking the current market sentiments to benefit Meteor Organization in your sales strategies for your new product launch.

We look forward to hearing positively from you for further collaboration.

Yours Sincerely,
Cindy Larlaton

尊敬的哥德伯格先生：

先前我们谈论了流星公司目前的项目，现在，我们将常青公司的建议提交给您，供您考虑。我们相信，有着高质量服务、责任感和专业技术的长青公司是流星公司将产品打入国际市场的不二合作之选。

从我们的附件中，您会看到长青公司令人印象深刻的商业战略，这使其从以往项目的客户那儿得到了众多良好反馈，长青公司的尊贵客户们对享受到的服务称赞有加。附件中有我们尊贵客户的名单，供您过目。

长青公司能够在适应和专注于当前战略和有效战略的同时，跟踪当前市场意见，让流星公司在新品发布后的销售战略上获益。

我们期待关于进一步合作的积极消息。

辛迪·拉拉顿 谨上

50. 抱怨信（质量低劣）

Dear Sirs,

On 1 September I bought one of your "Big Benny" alarm clock from Tiffanie Jewelry in London. Unfortunately I have been unable to get the alarm system to work and am very disappointed with my purchase.

The manager of Tiffanie has advised me to return the clock to you for correction of the fault. This is enclosed.

Please arrange for the clock to be put in full working order and return it to me as soon as possible.

Yours faithfully,
Charles White

敬启者：

　　9月1日，我在伦敦蒂凡尼珠宝店购买了贵公司的"大本尼"闹钟。不幸的是，这个闹钟的闹铃没办法正常使用，我对这次购物非常失望。

　　蒂凡尼的经理建议我将闹钟寄给您维修。现已随信寄去。

　　请将闹钟修好后尽快寄给我。

查尔斯·怀特 谨上

51. 抱怨信（多收运费）

Dear Sir,

　　Thank you for your letter of 5 July. As you wish to know why we have placed no orders with you recently, I will point out a matter which caused us some annoyance.

　　On 21 April last year we sent you two orders, one for USD 290 and one for USD 150. Your terms at the time provided for free delivery of all orders for USD 400 or more, but although you delivered these two orders together we are charged with the cost of carriage.

　　As the orders were submitted on different forms, we grant that you had perfect right to treat them as separate orders. However for all practical purposes they could very well have been treated as one, as they were placed on the same day and the delivery at the same time. The fact that you did not do this seemed to us to be a particularly ungenerous way of treating a regular long-standing customer.

　　Having given you our explanation, we should welcome your comments.

Yours sincerely,
Noah Lee

敬启者：

　　感谢您7月5日的来信。由于您想知道最近为何我们没有从贵处订购，我特告知一件让我们颇为不快之事。

　　去年4月21日，我们在贵处下了两份订单，一份是290美元，另一份是150美元。根据当时的条款，只要订单满400美元即可免运费，但虽然您将两份订单的货物一起运送，我们还是被收取了运费。

　　由于两份订单是分别下的，我们承认您完全有权利对它们进行分开处理。

然而，从实用角度出发，它们本完全可以被当做一件物品来对待，因为两份订单是同一天下的，运送也是同时的。而贵处的处理方式在我们看来，是对一位老顾客极不厚道的做法。

解释完毕，欢迎赐教。

诺亚·李 谨上

52. 索赔信（人寿保险）

Dear Mr. Patrick,

I enclose the completed and signed claims form and a copy of my late stepmother's death certificate, as you requested.

I would appreciate it if you could pay the settlement in one lump sum and as soon as possible. I still have a lot of unpaid medical and other assorted bills to be settled. Thank you.

Sincerely,

Arthur Blander

尊敬的帕特里克先生：

根据您的要求，我寄去了一份填好并签名的索赔表以及一份我已故继母的死亡证明。

若您能尽快一次付清赔款，我将十分感激。我还有许多尚未付清的医疗和各种其他账单需要结算。谢谢。

亚瑟·布兰德 敬启

53. 索赔信（车险）

Dear Mr. Verden,

I am writing this letter in regards with the insurance claim for my car. My insurance policy number is 2563965. The details of the car accident are mentioned below:

On 20 June morning I parked my car in front of my office, in the parking area. There was a car that tried to park between two cars, but it was no enough space and it hit my car from behind. The result is that the body from behind got smashed. I checked my insurance papers and I could see from there that I am eligible for claim. I have already met a representative from your company and filed the report. As I was informed you will contact me regarding the insurance matter.

I would like to inform you that I haven't received any correspondence, any calls from your company regarding this matter in spite of my reminders during the last 4 days.

Kindly ask you to pay close attention to the matter.

Sincerely,

Arthur Blander

尊敬的威登先生：

此信特来为我已上保险的汽车进行索赔。我的保险单号是2563965。车祸细节如下：

6月20日上午，我将车停在我办公室前的停车位里。有辆车试图停在两车之间，然而空间却不够了。那辆车便撞到了我的车的后面。结果我的汽车后面被撞碎。我检查了我的车险文件，发现我还能够进行索赔。我已经与贵公司的一位代表见了面，并将报告存档。我被告知您将就这份保险赔偿与我取得联系。

特此通知您，尽管过去的4天里我数次提醒贵处，但尚未从贵公司收到任何回函，接到任何电话。

烦请关注此事。

亚瑟·布兰德 谨上

54. 索赔信（意外险）

Dear Mr. Orlando,

One of my sales executive, Mr. James, had his arm broken when a motorcycle knocked into him while he was walking along the road in Shanghai on 8 November. He also suffered concussion and bruises. The culprit vanished from the scene before anyone could get his motorcycle number.

Mr. James is now warded in the Shanghai *** Hospital. I enclose a copy each of the police report and the medical report.

Mr. James is insured under your scheme P211. Could you please send us a claims form so that we can make claims for his hospital bills and other losses?

Thank you.

Sincerely,
Arthur Blander

尊敬的奥兰多先生：

11月8日，我公司的一位销售主管詹姆斯先生在上海的街上走路时，被一辆摩托车撞伤了胳膊。他还被撞出了脑震荡和瘀伤。人们未及记下车牌号，肇事者就已经从现场逃逸。

詹姆斯先生目前正在上海***医院住院。随信附上警方报告和医院报告各一份。

詹姆斯先生购买了贵公司P211方案的保险。烦请给我们邮寄一份索赔表，以便我们对他的医院账单以及其他损失进行索赔。

谢谢。

亚瑟·布兰德 谨上

55. 售后服务承诺书

After-sales Service Letter of Commitment

All products purchased in our company are guaranteed to keep in good repair for one year. If quality problems happen in guarantee period, our company will maintain for free. Additionally, our company provides technical support and fittings for life. After-sales service isn't restricted by time and we will assign technical personnel to solve your problems immediately after receiving telephone and hear feedback idea of users and deal with them in time. If you are caught in some problems when using our products, welcome to contact us at any time.

售后服务承诺书

凡购买我公司产品保修一年，在质保期内出现质量问题，本公司免费维修，终身提供技术支持及配件。售后服务不受时间限制，在接到电话后立即派人解决，听取用户反馈意见并及时处理。如果您在使用我们的产品时遇到问题，欢迎随时与我们联系。

56. 免责声明

DISCLAIMER

This report is solely prepared for XXX Systems Corporation and for the purpose of assisting in an internal enquiry. All duties and liabilities (including without limitation, those arising from negligence or otherwise) to any other parties are specifically disclaimed. This report and any information or any part thereof may not be released to any other parties without our prior written consent which consent may be given on such terms as we deem appropriate including a term of confidentiality and non-reliance.

免责声明

此报告专为ＸＸＸ系统公司编制，仅用于ＸＸＸ系统（中国）公司内部查询协助之目的。特此做出免责声明，不对任何其他方负有任何责任（包括但不限于因疏忽或其他原因所产生的责任）。未事先征得我方的同意，不得将此报告和信息以及其中的任何部分披露给任何其他方。此处的同意指的是基于我方认为适宜条款基础上的同意，包括适宜的保密条款和互不依赖条款。

57. 道歉声明

The Apology Statement of Tiger Woods

Good morning and thank you for joining me. Many of you in this room are my friends. Many of you in this room know me. Many of you have cheered for me or you've worked with me or you've supported me.

Now every one of you has good reason to be critical of me. I want to say to each of you, simply and directly, I am deeply sorry for my irresponsible and selfish behavior I engaged in.

I know people want to find out how I could be so selfish and so foolish. People want to know how I could have done these things to my wife Elin and to my children. And while I have always tried to be a private person, there are some things I want to say.

Elin and I have started the process of discussing the damage caused by my behavior. As Elin pointed out to me, my real apology to her will not come in the form of words; it will come from my behavior over time. We have a lot to discuss; however, what we say to each other will remain between the two of us.

I am also aware of the pain my behavior has caused to those of you in this room. I have let you down, and I have let down my fans. For many of you, especially my friends, my behavior has been a personal disappointment. To those of you who work for me, I have let you down personally and professionally. My behavior has caused considerable worry to my business partners.

To everyone involved in my foundation, including my staff, board of directors, sponsors, and most importantly, the young students we reach, our work is more important than ever. Thirteen years ago, my dad and I envisioned helping young people achieve their dreams through education. This work remains unchanged and will continue to grow. From the Learning Center students in Southern California to the Earl Woods scholars in Washington, D.C., millions of kids have changed their lives, and I am dedicated to making sure that continues.

But still, I know I have bitterly disappointed all of you. I have made you question who I am and how I could have done the things I did. I am embarrassed that I have put you in this position.

For all that I have done, I am so sorry.

……

I recognize I have brought this on myself, and I know above all I am the one who needs to change. I owe it to my family to become a better person. I owe it to those closest to me to become a better man. That's where my focus will be.

I have a lot of work to do, and I intend to dedicate myself to doing it. Part of following this path for me is Buddhism, which my mother taught me at a young age. People probably don't realize it, but I was raised a Buddhist, and I actively practiced my faith from childhood until I drifted away from it in recent years. Buddhism teaches that a craving for things outside ourselves causes an unhappy and pointless search for security. It teaches me to stop following every impulse and to learn restraint. Obviously I lost track of what I was taught.

As I move forward, I will continue to receive help because I've learned that's how people really do change. Starting tomorrow, I will leave for more treatment and more therapy. I would like to thank my friends at Accenture and the players in the field this week for understanding why I'm making these remarks today.

In therapy I've learned the importance of looking at my spiritual life and keeping in balance with my professional life. I need to regain my balance and be centered so I can save the things that are most important to me, my marriage and my children.

That also means relying on others for help. I've learned to seek support from my peers in therapy, and I hope someday to return that support to others who are seeking help. I do plan to return to golf one day, I just don't know when that day will be.

I don't rule out that it will be this year. When I do return, I need to make my behavior more respectful of the game. In recent weeks I have received many thousands of e-mails, letters and phone calls from people expressing good wishes. To everyone who has reached out to me and my family, thank you. Your encouragement means the world to Elin and me.

I want to thank the PGA TOUR, Commissioner Finchem, and the players for their patience and understanding while I work on my private life. I look forward to seeing my fellow players on the course.

Finally, there are many people in this room, and there are many people at home who believed in me. Today I want to ask for your help. I ask you to find room in your heart to one day believe in me again.

Thank you.

老虎·伍兹的道歉声明

早上好,感谢各位的出席。在这间房间里的都是我的朋友,都很了解我,都是曾经为我欢呼或者与我一同工作或是曾经支持我的人。

如今你们每个人都有充分的理由批评我。我想要对你们每个人说,我对于我不负责任和自私的行为感到非常抱歉。

我知道人们都想知道为什么我可以这么自私和愚蠢,人们想知道我怎么能对我的妻子埃琳和孩子们做出这样的事。尽管我一向试着做一个有隐私的人,但是有些事情我还是想说出来。

埃琳和我已经开始讨论关于我的行为所造成的不良影响。埃琳已经指出了很多,我对她的歉意已经难以用言语来表达,而需要用我今后的行动来证明。我们有很多事情需要商量,尽管如此,我们之间的言语只有我们两个人知道。

我也意识到我的所作所为会给今天到场的各位带来多大的伤害。我让你们失望了,让我的粉丝们失望了。对于你们,特别是我的朋友们,我的行为真的令我在你们心中的为人大打折扣。对于曾经跟我一起工作的人们,在个人行为和职业上我都令你们失望了。我的所作所为也给我的商业伙伴们造成了相当大的担忧。

对于每一个为我奠定基础的人,包括我的团队、董事会、赞助商和最重要的是我们帮助的孩子们。13年前,我的父亲和我就希望能够通过教育帮助孩子们实现他们的梦想。这个宗旨从来没有改变过,也会继续发展下去。从南加州的学生学习中心到华盛顿的厄尔·伍兹奖学金,上百万的孩子们通过教育改写了他们的人生,我会继续致力于这项事业得以延续。

与此同时,我知道我曾经的行为让他们感到深深的失望。我让你们开始质疑我是一个怎样的人和怎么能做出那样的事。我感到很惭愧将你们陷入了这样的境地。

对于我曾经做错的一切,我感到很抱歉。

……

我知道这一切是因为我造成的,我也知道最需要改变的那个人是我。这是我亏欠家人和那些最亲近我的人的,我应该做个更好的人,这是我将来的重心。

我有很多事情要做,我会全身心地投入其中。其中之一是佛教,这是我小时候母亲就教导我的。人们也许还不知道我出生在佛教家庭,从小就有的信仰竟然在最近的几年被我抛到一旁。佛祖教导我对于身外之物的渴望是痛苦和失去安全感的根源所在。这让我明白应该克制冲动,学会自制。显然过去的我忘记了这些曾经学过的东西。

如今我要向前看,我会继续寻求帮助因为我已经学会了要怎样才能彻底改变。从明天开始,我要继续接受更多的恢复和治疗。感谢埃森哲的朋友们和理解我为什么要在今天说这些的正在比赛的球员们。

在治疗中我学到了正视自己心灵和在职业运动员生活中找到平衡的重要性。我需要重新找回自己的平衡点，挽救那些对我来说最重要的东西——我的婚姻和孩子们。

这也意味着需要其他人的帮助。我学会了从治疗伙伴中寻求支持，我希望有一天能够帮助那些需要帮助的人。我确实打算某一天重返高尔夫，我只是不知道那一天什么时候到来。

我不排除可能会是今年。当我真的回来，我会让我的行为更加体现出对这项运动的尊重。在最近几周我收到了成千上万的祝福邮件、信件和电话。对于每一位关心我和我家人的人们我感到深深的谢意。你们的鼓励对于埃琳和我就是全世界。

我也要感谢美巡赛长官芬臣和球员们，为他们对我处理私生活问题给予的耐心和理解。我很期待将来能与他们在球场上重逢。

最后，今天到场的很多人和没有到场但一直相信我的人们，我希望你们能够在心里留出一个空间给我，相信某一天我能够再次赢得你们的信任。

谢谢你们。

58. 求助信

Dear Uncle,

How are you?

Next week an English speaking contest will be held in the city. A classmate of mine and I will take part in it on behalf of my school. I am excited but also nervous, because it is a good chance to improve my English. But I have no experience. Although I have been preparing for the contest, I am still not confident. As an expert in English, what would you advise me to prepare for the contest?

I plan to pay a visit to you this Saturday morning. I wonder whether you will be free then. If not, could you tell me the suitable time? I am eager to get your instruction. I will appreciate any of your help.

Your niece,
Yang Mei

亲爱的叔叔：

您好！

下周市里举办英语演讲比赛，我和一位同学将代表学校参加比赛。我感到既兴奋又紧张，因为这是一个提高英语的好机会，但我没有经验。我一直在为比赛做准备，可仍然没有把握。作为一个英语专家，您建议我为比赛准备些什么呢？

我打算这周六上午去您家，我想知道到时您是否有空。如果没空，能告诉我您什么时候方便吗？我渴望得到您的指导。非常感激您的帮助。

您的侄女 杨梅

59. 举报信

Dear Editor,

   I recently came back from a tour to Kunming and I would like other readers to be aware of the pitfalls.

   First, the tour was advertised to be a luxury tour and therefore much more expensive than tours of similar itinerary. We stayed in a shabby hostel that should have been a three star hotel. The sheets were not changed daily and the blankets had holes. Cockroaches ran on the floor and the bathroom door couldn't shut.

   As for the meals, we had to eat in the same restaurants with tourists who only paid half the fee that members in my group paid, and the dishes were identical.

   The contract said we would be going to different scenic spots in air-conditioned luxury coaches. In fact, we were packed into noisy, bumping buses that vegetable venders wouldn't take to town. These buses broke down at least twice a day during our 3-day stay in Kunming.

   We protested, but it was of no use. If you want to know the name of the agency, it is Sounds Great.

Yours truly,
Mr. Wang

尊敬的编辑同志：

我最近刚结束昆明旅游，希望提醒其他读者注意一些小陷阱。

首先，广告中说这次旅行是一次豪华之旅，因此它要比其他类似行程昂贵。我们居住在一件破旧的招待所里，可能是一家三星级旅店吧。这家旅店的床单不是每日更换的，毯子上还有破洞。蟑螂满地乱爬，浴室的门还没法关。

至于饭菜，我们不得不与出资仅达我们一半的其他游客在同一家餐馆吃饭，而且还是一样的饭菜。

合同上说，我们将乘坐豪华型空调长途车去不同的景点。事实上，我们被塞进了吵闹不堪、颠颠簸簸的巴士，这样的巴士就算是菜贩子都不愿意坐到城里。这些巴士在我们为期三天的昆明之行中至少每天得坏掉两次。

我们表示反抗，但无济于事。如果您想知道这家旅行社的名字，那么它叫"听起来很美"。

王先生 谨上

60. 倡议书

Green Initiative

To protect the earth, the ecology and the environment is the due responsibility of every citizen.

Actions speak louder. We, builders of the 21st century, should take actions from now on with each trivial matter. In this connection, I propose:

1. Taking active and earnest steps to make work places, residential districts and public areas green, beautiful and clean. Reduce or abandon the use of one-time plastic utensils to effectively control pollution generated in our daily lives.

2. Ensuring personal hygiene. No spitting and littering.

3. Calling for joining hands to reduce pollution. Carrying out trash separation and recycling to prevent the repollution of trash.

4. Everyone is a green advocator. Effective actions should be taken to influence people around us and to change the surrounding environment.

5. In Trees-Planting Days, members of the Sunshine Club should launch collective trees-planting activities. A "Sunshine Forest" should be created to

show our care for the earth.

  Citizens of the 21st century, we need actions! Let's join our hands and hearts and create for our world a green future!

绿色环保倡议书

  爱护地球、维护生态、保护环境是每一个公民义不容辞的责任。

  "心动不如行动"，我们二十一世纪的建设者就从现在做起，从身边的每一件小事做起。为此，我向大家倡议：

  1. 积极、认真搞好工作生活区域、公共场所的绿化、美化、净化，少用或不用一次性塑料用具，有效控制日常生活中产生的污染。

  2. 养成讲卫生的好习惯，不随地吐痰，不乱扔垃圾。

  3. 倡导"人人动手，减少污染"，开展垃圾分类回收，防止垃圾的二次污染。

  4. 人人都是绿色宣传员，用我们的实际行动影响周围的人，改变周围的环境状况。

  5. 植树节阳光俱乐部成员集体植树活动，建一个"阳光林"，向地球表一份爱心。

  二十一世纪的世纪公民，行动起来！让我们心手相携，共同为我们的地球缔造一个绿色的明天！

特别奉献

一 常见食物名称中英对照（二）

Potato 马铃薯	Okra 秋葵
Carrot 红萝卜	Chillies 辣椒
Onion 洋葱	Sweet potato 蕃薯
Aubergine 茄子	Spinach 菠菜
Celery 芹菜	Beansprots 绿豆芽
White Cabbage 包心菜	Peas 碗豆
Red cabbage 紫色包心菜	Corn 玉米粒
Cucumber 黄瓜	Lemon 柠檬
Tomato 蕃茄	Pear 梨子
Radish 小红萝卜	Banana 香蕉
Mooli 白萝卜	Grape 葡萄
Watercress 西洋菜	Peach 桃子
Baby corn 玉米尖	Orange 橙
Sweet corn 玉米	Strawberry 草莓
Spring onions 葱	Mango 芒果
Garlic 大蒜	Pine apple 菠萝
Ginger 姜	Kiwi 奇异果
Chinese leaves 大白菜	Starfruit 杨桃
Leeks 大葱	Honeydew-melon 蜜瓜
Mustard & cress 芥菜苗	Cherry 樱桃
Green Pepper 青椒	Date 枣子
Red pepper 红椒	lychee 荔枝
Yellow pepper 黄椒	Grape fruit 葡萄柚
Coriander 香菜	Coconut 椰子
Dwarf Bean 四季豆	Fig 无花果
Flat Beans 长形平豆	Glutinous rice 糯米
Iceberg 透明包心菜	Plain flour 中筋面粉
Lettuce 萵苣菜	Self-raising flour 低筋面粉

Whole meal flour 小麦面粉	Monosidum glutanate 味精
dark Brown Sugar 红糖	Chinese red pepper 花椒
Custer sugar 白砂糖	Salt black bean 豆鼓
Icing Sugar 糖粉	Sea vegetable or Sea weed 海带
Rock Sugar 冰糖	Green bean 绿豆
Noodles 面条	Red Bean 红豆
Instant noodles 方便面	Black bean 黑豆
Soy sauce 酱油	Red kidney bean 大红豆
Maltose 麦芽糖	Dried black mushroom 冬菇
Sesame Seeds 芝麻	Pickled mustard-green 酸菜
Sesame oil 麻油	Silk noodles 粉丝
Oyster sauce 蚝油	Rice-noodle 米粉
Pepper 胡椒	Star anise 八角
Red chilli powder 辣椒粉	Wantun skin 馄饨皮
Sesame paste 芝麻酱	Red date 红枣
Tofu 豆腐	Mu-er 木耳
Creamed Coconut 椰油	Dried shrimps 虾米

特别奉献

二　重要标识英文表述法

1. Business Hours 营业时间
2. Office Hours 办公时间
3. Entrance 入口
4. Exit 出口
5. Push 推
6. Pull 拉
7. Shut 此路不通
8. On 打开 (放)
9. Off 关
10. Open 营业
11. Pause 暂停
12. Stop 关闭
13. Closed 下班
14. Menu 菜单
15. Fragile 易碎
16. This Side Up 此面向上

17. Introductions 说明
18. One Street 单行道
19. Keep Right/Left 靠左／右
20. Buses Only 只准公共汽车通过
21. Wet Paint 油漆未干
22. Danger 危险
23. Lost and Found 失物招领处
24. Give Way 快车先行
25. Safety First 安全第一
26. Filling Station 加油站
27. No Smoking 禁止吸烟
28. No Photos 请勿拍照
29. No Visitors 游人止步
30. No Entry 禁止入内
31. No Admittance 闲人免进
32. No Honking 禁止鸣喇叭
33. Parking 停车处
34. Toll Free 免费通行
35. F.F. 快进
36. Rew. 倒带
37. EMS（邮政）特快专递
39. Open Here 此处开启
40. Split Here 此处撕开
41. Mechanical Help 车辆修理
42. "AA" Film 十四岁以下禁看电影
43. Do Not Pass 禁止超车
44. No U Turn 禁止掉头
45. U Turn Ok 可以 U 形转弯
46. No Cycling in the School 校内禁止骑车
47. SOS 紧急求救信号
48. Hands Wanted 招聘
49. Staff Only 本处职工专用
50. No Litter 勿乱扔杂物
51. Hands Off 请勿用手摸
52. Keep Silence 保持安静
53. On Sale 削价出售
54. No Bills 不准张贴
55. Not for Sale 恕不出售
56. Pub 酒店
57. Cafe 咖啡馆，小餐馆
58. Bar 酒吧
59. Laundry 洗衣店
60. Travel Agency 旅行社
61. In Shade 置于阴凉处
62. Keep in Dark Place 避光保存
63. Poison 有毒／毒品
64. Guard against Damp 防潮
65. Beware of Pickpocket 谨防扒手
66. Complaint Box 意见箱
67. For Use Only in Case of Fire 灭火专用
68. Bakery 面包店
69. Keep Dry 保持干燥
70. Information 问讯处
71. No Passing 禁止通行
72. No Angling 不准垂钓
73. Shooting Prohibited 禁止打猎
74. Seat by Number 对号入座
75. Protect Public Propety 爱护公共财物
76. Ticket Office 售票处
77. Visitors Please Register 来宾登记
78. Wipe Your Shoes And Boots 请擦去鞋上的泥土
79. Men's/Gentlemen/Gents Room

男厕所

80. Women's/Ladies/Ladies' Room 女厕所

81. Occupied （厕所）有人

82. Vacant （厕所）无人

83. Commit No Nuisance 禁止小便

84. Net (Weight) 净重

85. MAN：25032002 生产日期：2002 年 3 月 25 日

86. EXP：25032002 失效期：2002 年 3 月 25 日

87. Admission Free 免费入场

88. Bike Park(ing) 自行车存车处

89. Children and Women First 妇女、儿童优先

90. Save Food 节约粮食

91. Save Energy 节约能源

92. Handle with Care 小心轻放

93. Dogs Not Allowed 禁止携犬入内

94. Keep Away From Fire 切勿近火

95. Reduced Speed Now 减速行驶

96. Road Up. Detour 马路施工，请绕行

97. Keep Top Side Up 请勿倒立

98. Take Care Not to Leave Things Behind 当心不要丢失东西

99. Please Return the Back After Use 用毕放回架上

100. Luggage Depository / Left Luggage 行李存放处

Chapter 07

电邮与短信 E-mails & Messages

在日常生活中，除了纸质的信函，人们往往大量地使用电子方式传递信息，如通过电子邮件、短信、飞信、微信、米聊等等。尤其是现在，随着科技的高速发展，各种电子、网络交流方式层出不穷，日新月异，大有让人应接不暇之势。即便是在一个社交网站，人们往往都需要与网友进行大量的信息交流活动。在这样一个信息爆炸的时代，事实上除了国家机关、企事业单位等为表示正式、严肃和对对方的尊重而需要保持纸质信件的传统外，基本已经很少有人还一直依赖纸质书信了。

如果说时代发展太快，很多新玩意儿实在没法跟上，那么一些基本的电子类文书还是要掌握的。本章就将向读者朋友们介绍如何写英文的电子邮件以及短信。其实电子邮件的写作方法和之前介绍的信件是极为相似的，因此前面介绍的众多信件很多都可以以电子邮件的形式发送出去，可以说是"换汤不换药"。而短信要突出其"短"，用语方面非常随意，实质上是简短的留言。希望大家时刻跟随时代的脉搏，死死"hold 住"，千万别"out"了。

Unit 1　电子邮件

E-mails

电子邮件（electronic mail，E-mail），是一种用电子手段提供信息交换的通信方式，是 Internet 应用最广的服务。通过网络的电子邮件系统，用户可以用非常低廉的价格，以非常快速的方式，与世界上任何一个角落的网络用户联系，这些电子邮件可以是文字、图像、声音等各种方式。同时，用户可以得到大量免费的新闻、专题邮件，并实现轻松的信息搜索。

电子邮件是整个网络间以至所有其他网络系统中直接面向人与人之间信息交流的系统，它的数据发送方和接收方都是人，所以极大地满足了大量存在的人与人之间的通信需求。

电子邮件的特点和优点如下：

1. 价格优势。通过 Internet 发送电子邮件的费用比传统通信方式便宜得多，距离越远越能显示这个特点。一般来说，电子邮件都是免费的。
2. 速度。电子邮件与传统邮件相比较，最大的优势就是速度快。电子邮件是近似以光速来传送的，把电子邮件发送到地球的任何地方对电子邮件来说所花的时间差别是毫秒级的。
3. 方便。电子邮件能减少通讯过程的环节，提高通信的效率。以前，若要发一封信，必须先写好信件，装入信封，把信投到邮箱中。如果使用电子邮件，只要学会与电子邮件有关的操作就行了。
4. 一信多发。在 Internet 中，通过邮件清单发信到若干人手中只需几分钟和几毛钱，而传统的通信方式就无能为力了。
5. 邮寄实物以外的任何东西。电子邮件的内容可以包括文字、图形、声音、电影或软件。

电子邮件 E-mail 通常只包括以下两部分：

1. 信头（Heading）：有些人只把发件人和收件人的地址写在相应的地址栏里，然而有些人会把他们的全名也写下来。在发件人地址栏下面，你可能也会看到抄送（Cc），它代表副本送，你可以把其他你要发送邮件的人的地址写进去。在标题栏，要为收件人提供足够的信息，同时注意做到简明扼要，一目了然，帮助收件人迅速识别邮件内容。常见格式如下：

To：（收件人）_____

From：（发件人）_____

Subject：（主题）_____

Cc：（副本送）_____

2. 正文（Message）：包括称呼、正文、结束语和签名等。正文有缩进式和齐头式两种。但电子邮件往往不用缩进式，用齐头式，即每一行都从左面顶格写起。齐头式信件正文的每段之间，一般要空一行，使每个段落分开，非常清晰明了。在纸质书信中，商务信件大都也采用齐头式的写法，而美国人写信一般用齐头式的为多。

电子邮件中应包括要询问的问题、要发送的文件、要陈述的观点、要征询的意见、要给予的建议、要推销的产品。

一封好的邮件应该简明扼要、层次清晰、逻辑性强。要点出现在最开始，其他信息都和要点相关，这样收件人不需费劲就能知道邮件的主题。但是在组织信息时也会存在困难，不妨考虑下面因素：

- 尽量让收邮件的人能很好地理解邮件信息，一定要明确这封邮件的目的，并且设想收件人看到这封邮件时可能产生的疑问。
- 语言一定要精炼，删除多余的信息。
- 写作思路清晰易懂，过渡自然，不要东聊一个话题，西聊一个话题，这样会使收件人困惑，也会使你困惑。
- 一封电子邮件最好只关于一个话题或主题，每封邮件都针对一个收件人（群）。如果想在一封信内发送所有信息，在开头列出要点，然后用标题帮助收件人（群）迅速地找到具体的细节。如果写的内容太复杂，最好独立成一个文本然后作为附件发送，而邮件仅提供简要的说明。
- 在署名时，如果收件人不是熟人，则最好写上自己的职位和公司名称。

1. 公司对客户

To: _____
From: _____
Subject: _____
Cc: _____

Dear Ms. Bella,

　　Your automobile insurance policy will soon be due for renewal. So perhaps this is a good time to find out how you can get the same coverage for less money and with assurance of the best in service.

　　Just fill in the enclosed form describing your present coverage, and we'll quote our rates and conditions. At the same time, we'll tell you just what our policyholders think of our response, especially during emergencies. Our agency is small and our service is personal and attentive.

Sincerely Yours,
Rosalie Oprah

收件人：_____
发件人：_____
主题：_____
副本送：_____
亲爱的贝拉女士：

　　您的汽车保险单很快就要到期了。因此也许现在是时候看看有没有保险既可以提供相同的承保范围，又可以减少费用，还可以提供最好的保险服务了。

　　请在附件中的表格中填写您现在的保险范围，我们将开出我们的价格和条件。同时，我们会告诉您客户对我们服务的反馈，尤其是在紧急情况发生时的服务。我公司规模不大，因此我们的服务是私人的、周到的。

诚挚的 罗沙尔·奥普拉

2. 公司对公司

To: _____
From: _____
Subject: _____

Cc: _____

Dear Sir/ Madam,

We thank you for so promptly delivering the gas coke ordered on 1 March. Although we ordered 5 tons in 50 kg bags, only 80 bags were delivered. Your carrier was unable to explain the shortage and we have not received any explanation from you.

We still need the full quantity ordered and shall be glad if you will arrange to deliver the remaining 20 bags as soon as possible.

Yours faithfully,
Johnny Dane
President
ABC Company

收件人: _____
发件人: _____
主题: _____
副本送: _____
敬启者:

感谢贵处迅速运送了我们于3月1日订的煤气焦炭。可是,虽然我们订购了5吨的货,用含量为50千克的袋子装,但是我们只收到了80个袋子。贵处的货运人员无法解释货量的不足,而我处也尚未得到贵处的任何解释。

我公司仍然需要订购的全数货物。倘若贵处能尽快安排运送余下的20包货物,我们将十分高兴。
诚挚的 约尼·丹
ABC公司总裁

3. 客户对公司

To: _____
From: _____
Subject: _____
Cc: _____

Dear Mr. Martin,

I am writing this e-mail to aware you about a problem with your product. On 10 July, 2011, I had bought an ABC vacuum cleaner; model number VC012 from your Hill Road Branch.

Unfortunately, this vacuum has not performed well as per my expectations because it is unable to suck whole dust from carpet. I am disappointed because this vacuum is too noisy as well as consumes more electricity. It takes a long time in cleaning with the help of this vacuum.

To resolve the problem, I would appreciate you to replace this product as soon as possible or refund my money back. Later I will send you copies (do not send originals) of my records including receipts, guarantees, warranties, contracts, model and serial numbers, and any other documents.

I look forward to your reply and a resolution to my problem, and will wait until 15th of July before seeking help from a consumer protection agency. Please contact me via e-mail or by phone at 032-4566-669.

Thank You,
Sincerely,
Rebecca Jones

收件人：_____
发件人：_____
主题：_____
副本送：_____

尊敬的马丁先生：

此信特来告知，贵公司的产品有质量问题。2011 年 7 月 10 日，我在贵公司的希尔路分店购买了 ABC 吸尘器，型号是 VC012。

不幸的是，这台吸尘器并未如我所期望的那样，它无法将地毯上的灰尘完全吸入。这个吸尘器不但声音很大，还更加费电，使我大失所望。用它来打扫卫生要花掉很多时间。

为解决这一问题，望贵处能帮我换一台吸尘器或是退款。稍后我会寄去各种材料的复印件（不含原件），包括收据、保证书、担保、合同、模型和序列号，以及其他文件。

期待您的回复，也期待我的问题得到解决。若 7 月 15 日贵处还没有给我回复，那么我将到消费者保护机构寻求帮助。请通过邮件联系我，或是拨打电话 032-4566-669。

  谢谢。

诚挚的 贝贝卡·琼斯

4. 发给关系较好的业务伙伴

To: _____
From: _____
Subject: _____
Cc: _____

Dear Trevor,

You were most thoughtful to send me a battery-operated thesaurus and spelling corrector after you visited our offices last week. It is a most remarkable device and I have placed it in a prominent position on my desk, where I assure you it will get plenty of use. I write at least a dozen letters a day to friends and business associates. Since I am not the world's best speller, I frequently have to look up words in my old, dog-eared dictionary, a time-consuming process. Now, thanks to you, I can eliminate that step with a mere push of the buttons and write more letters in less time.

We enjoyed our discussion, which should prove to be most fruitful for all of us, and we look forward to your next visit.

With best regards,
Leola Meir

收件人：_____
发件人：_____
主题：_____
副本送：_____

亲爱的特雷瓦尔先生：

  上星期您来过我办公室后，回头送给我一部电子同义词词典和拼写矫正机，真是想得太周到了。这可真是个"神器"，我已经把它堂而皇之地放在了办公桌上。我可以向您保证，它将得到充分的利用。我每天写给朋友和商业伙伴的信，少说也有一打。由于我不是拼写专家，因此要经常翻那旧得卷角的字典，煞是耗时。现在，多亏了你，我只要轻轻一按，就可以省去查字典的痛苦，而且用更少的时间写更多的信。

　　我非常满意我们的讨论。事实将证明，这次讨论对我们所有人都是成果丰硕的。我们期待着你们下次的造访。

美好的问候
里欧拉·梅尔

5. 发给下属

To: _____
From: _____
Subject: _____
Cc: _____

Dear Patricia,

　　The company is having a buffet dinner at 6 p.m. next Friday 20 December for the Christian employees and their friends. So I immediately thought of you. Please come and join in the fun.

　　Don't bring anything but yourself and be prepared to sing the whole night long because David is bringing his guitar to back us.

　　Let Julia know by Tuesday if you can make it so that she will have an idea of how much stuff to order.

Sincerely,
Anthony Walker

收件人：_____
发件人：_____
主题：_____
副本送：_____

亲爱的帕特里西亚：

　　公司将在下周五（12月20日）晚6点为信基督教的员工和他们的朋友举办一场自助晚宴。我马上就想到了你。欢迎前来和我们共度美好时光。

　　除了你自己，啥都别带了。大卫要把他的吉他带来给我们助兴，所以你得准备欢唱整晚了。

请在周二前告诉茱莉亚你是否参加，以便她安排。

诚挚的 安东尼·沃克

6. 发给同事

To: _____
From: _____
Subject: _____
Cc: _____

Dear Mrs. Cindy,

Congratulations on the birth of your first child on 1 May. I am sure that you and your husband must be very excited at the arrival of a beautiful baby boy. The other colleagues are pretty excited too and from what I heard, they are planning to pay you a visit soon. So be prepared to receive a lot of congratulations and presents.

The boss himself asked me to convey his congratulations too.

Yours sincerely,
Jonathan Stevie

收件人：_____
发件人：_____
主题：_____
副本送：_____

亲爱的辛迪：

恭喜你 5 月 1 日产下了自己的第一个孩子。我相信你和你的丈夫都对这个漂亮男孩儿的降生感到兴奋不已。其他的同事也都感到非常兴奋，据我所知，他们打算马上到你那儿登门拜访。所以，你就准备着潮水般的祝贺和礼物吧。

老板也让我转达他的祝贺。

诚挚的 岳娜桑·史迪威

7. 发给亲人

To: _____

From: _____
Subject: _____
Cc: _____

Dear Uncle,

  We would like to invite you to my wedding on this coming 10th of August, 2011 at Golden Green Parish Church at exactly 10:00 in the morning. The wedding reception will follow at the famous Athena Palace Hotel.

  You are my uncle so we would like you to be part of this important event of mine. It is the biggest day of my life and I will feel it a pleasure if you come with your blessings. Please bring your family with you. We would be very glad to see you in this event. You can contact me on the same number or give me a message through e-mail to confirm your attendance.

  We are hoping for your presence in this event and we will appreciate it a lot if you can find some time to attend this momentous day of me. Thank you so much.

Truly yours,
Joy L. Bush

收件人：_____
发件人：_____
主题：_____
副本送：_____

亲爱的叔叔：

  我们想邀请您参加即将到来的2011年8月10日上午10点整在金绿教区教堂举办的我的婚礼。随后的婚礼招待会将在著名的智慧女神宫酒店举行。

  您是我的叔叔，所以我们希望您参加我的这一人生大事。这是我人生中最重要的一天，若能有您的祝福，我将倍感欣喜。请把家人都带来，能在婚礼上见到你们，我们将非常高兴。若您要确认您是否到场，请用相同的电话号码联系我，或是通过电子邮件给我发条信息。

  我们期待着您的出席，如果您能在百忙之中参加我的婚礼，我将不胜感激。非常感谢。

你的 乔伊·L·布什

8. 发给心仪恋人

To: _____
From: _____
Subject: _____
Cc: _____

To My Sweetheart,

    I am very happy to tell you that I have fallen in love with you since 1st of July at 7:00 p.m. I saw you at railway station and your first gaze make me crazy. I am deeply in love with you just like a fish in water. I would like to present myself as your future lover. I am crazy to be your boy friend. I want to make history and our love story will be written in Guinness book of world record. Please give me a chance to prove myself as your true lover. If you have any problem then we will make a love contract of two months. During these two months, you will observe my behavior and love for you and after completion of probation if you satisfied we can carry on otherwise I will leave you.

    I will do everything to make you happy. I am ready to take continuous love training and will work hard to improve my performance. I am sure that after analyzing improvement you will surely give me promotion from lover to spouse.

    I want to invite you on coffee to discuss our mutual interest. I request you to respond this letter within 15 days after receiving this letter. Please tell me, if you don't like to take this offer.

Hoping in desperation for your love,
Jonathan Godwin

收件人：_____
发件人：_____
主题：_____
副本送：_____
小甜心：

很高兴地告诉你，从 7 月 1 日晚上 7 点我在车站见到你，我就爱上了你，见到你的第一眼就让我迷炫。我深深地爱上了你，就像鱼儿在深深的水里游。我想成为你未来的男友。我想做你的男友都想疯了。我想创造历史，我们的爱情故事会被写进吉尼斯世界纪录。请给我个机会，让我证明我是真的爱你。如果你有任何问题，我们可以定一份两个月的恋爱契约。在这两个月内，你可以观察我对你的言行举止和爱。试用期一结束，如果你还满意，我们就继续；否则我就滚蛋。

我会绞尽脑汁让你开心的。我已经做好准备，狂补爱情课，我还要努力提高表现。我相信通过分析我取得的进步，你肯定会给你的男友一个晋升的机会，让我做你的老公。

我想请你喝杯咖啡，聊聊彼此的兴趣爱好。我请求你在收到此信后的 15 天之内给我回复，如果你不想赴这个咖啡之约的话，请告诉我。

渴望你的爱，

乔纳森·高德文

9. 发给朋友

To: _____
From: _____
Subject: _____
Cc: _____

Dear Kate,

We are happy that you could make it to our wedding anniversary. James's and yours presence made a lot of difference to our special day. Thanks for making the day all the more memorable with your company. You are very near to our heart and your presence means a lot to us.

In addition, thank you for the beautiful antique wall painting gifted by both you and your husband on our anniversary. I am waiting to flaunt it on our bedroom wall of our new home.

Please accept appreciation from both of us.

Thank you once more for making us feel so unique and making us so important.

Hoping to meet you soon.

Mr & Mrs Conklin

收件人：_____
发件人：_____
主题：_____
副本送：_____

亲爱的凯特：

　　你能参加我们的结婚周年纪念日，这使我们非常高兴。詹姆士一家和你家的礼物给我们的纪念日增添了不少光彩。感谢你们的陪伴，使这一天更加值得纪念。我们的心离得很近，你们的礼物对我们来说意义重大。

　　此外，感谢你们夫妇送来的漂亮的古壁画。我正等着把它挂在我们新家卧室的墙上，好好炫耀一番呢。

　　我们俩对你们表示感谢。

　　你们让我们感到自己如此与众不同，感到自己如此重要，再次感谢你们。

　　希望早日再见。

孔克林夫妇

Unit 2　短消息　　　　　　　　　　　　　Short Messages

　　短消息（short message）是通信公司提供的一种独特的沟通方式。与语音服务不同，它通过短消息服务中心在网络和手机间传递的是文字、图形等可视信息，使沟通更温馨、更完美。短消息是伴随数字移动通信系统而产生的一种电信业务，通过移动通信系统的信令信道和信令网，传送手机短消息文字或数字短消息，属于一种非实时的、非语音的数据通信业务。它是由用户通过手机或其他电信终端直接发送或接收的文字或数字信息，一般来说，短消息的字数会有一定的限制，那就是为什么它叫"短消息"了。现在，我们还会看到诸如"飞信"这样的服务，使得信息的发送可以通过计算机进行，不仅更为方便快捷，还可以省去短信的费用。

　　短消息特点：
- 信息传达完整全面；
- 短消息具有独特的信息到达方式及信息存贮特点；
- 有效节省话费；
- 具有独特的沟通方式，有利于情感交流。

　　这些与生俱来的特点，使短消息具备了传递准确可靠、迅速及时的优点，具备了影响人们习惯的基本条件！

　　书写短消息时应注意：
1. 主题突出：问候祝福、交待事情等目的明确。
2. 简明：双方都明白的事情注意用词简洁。同时，可以大量使用缩写、网络语言、表情符号等比较快速、俏皮的文字形式。如 u 代表 you，ur 代表 your，pls 代表 please，4 代表 for 等等。
3. 得体：短消息的语言、内容必须注意场合及双方的身份，一般要注意礼貌、语言文明。
4. 有文采：好的短消息应讲究文采，要特别注意修辞手法的运用。
5. 有创意：精彩的短消息应有精巧的构思，才会让人过目不忘。

10. 发给亲人

Pa, I've got 95 in the exam. Remember ur iPad :-D

老爸,我考试拿了95。别忘了你答应给我买的 iPad :-D

11. 发给爱人

Darling, I'm already in Beijing. This time I'll remember to bring u & Jack some gifts. Love u. ♥ 3 ﻭ

亲爱的,我到北京了。这次会记得给你和杰克带点礼物的。爱你。♥ 3 ﻭ

12. 发给朋友

Wanna play basketball? 3 o'clock, playground. Give me a reply.

打球吗?下午三点,操场。收到回复。

13. 发给同学

I've got a cold & can't go to class today. Can u bring the handouts 4 me? thx!!!

我今天生病了,不能去上课了。你能帮我带材料吗?多谢!!!

14. 发给老师

Miss Liu, I'm Zhu Linhui. I failed to book the train ticket for Sept. 3rd so that I may be late for school. I don't wish this to happen but there are too many passengers and it's out of my control. I'll try to book the earliest ticket possible to get back. Terribly sorry!

刘老师,我是朱临辉。由于我没能订到9月3日的火车票,因此我可能无法按时到校。我不希望这样,但乘客实在太多了,我也无可奈何。我会及早订到票回校的。非常抱歉!

15. 发给同事

I forgot to take the name list. Would u pls take it to the manager's office 4 me? Thx~

我忘了带名单了。你能帮我带到经理办公室吗？多谢啦~

16. 发给上级

Mr. Brown, I've e-mailed you the revised agenda. Please call me if you have any problem.

布朗先生，我已经把修订好的日程表发送到您的邮箱了。如果有任何问题，请给我电话。

17. 发给下级

Thx for the wishes. I'll be giving a party this Friday, would u like to come?

感谢你的祝福。这周五我要开个聚会，你想来参加吗？

18. 短信祝语

Best wishes for the year to come!
恭贺新禧！

Good luck in the year ahead!
祝吉星高照！

Live long and proper!
多福多寿！

Rich blessings for health and longevity is my special wish for you in the coming year.
祝你在新的一年里身体健康，多福多寿。

May many fortunes find their way to you!
祝财运亨通!

May you come into a good fortune!
恭喜发财!

I want to wish you longevity and health!
愿你健康长寿!

Take good care of yourself in the year ahead.
请多保重!

On this special day I send you New Years greetings and hope that some day soon we shall be together.
在这特殊的日子,向你致以新年的祝福,希望不久我们能相聚在一起。

On the occasion of the New Year, may my wife and I extend to you and yours our warmest greetings, wishing you a happy New Year, your career greater success and your family happiness.
在此新年之际,我同夫人向你及你的家人致以节日的问候,并祝你们新年快乐、事业有成、家庭幸福。

I would like to wish you a joyous new year and express my hope for your happiness and good future.
祝新年快乐,并愿你幸福吉祥,前程似锦。

May the New Year bring many good things and rich blessings to you and all those you love!
愿新年带给你和你所爱的人许多美好的事物和无尽的祝福!

Good luck, good health, hood cheer. I wish you a happy New Year.
祝好运、健康、佳肴伴你度过一个快乐新年。

With best wishes for a happy New Year!
祝新年快乐,并致以良好的祝福。

I hope you have a most happy and prosperous New Year.
谨祝新年快乐幸福，大吉大利。

May the seasons joy fill you all the year round.
愿节日的愉快伴你一生。

Allow me to congratulate you on the arrival of the New Year and to extend to you all my best wishes for your perfect health and lasting prosperity.
恭贺新禧，祝身体健康、事业发达。

特别奉献

一　网络常用符号及其释义

@>>—>>— 请收下这束漂亮的玫瑰
B-) 笑的人带着眼镜哩
8-) 眼镜族的笑
:-) 最基本的笑脸，微笑，高兴
:-D 开口大笑
^_^ 灿烂的笑容
:] 傻笑
^o^ 大笑
*^÷^* 得意的笑（有上下唇的哟）
*^◎^* 呵呵大笑（嘴唇好厚）
3:] 动物的微笑
3:[动物的冷笑
:-) 喜极而泣
*<|:-) 圣诞老人
&:-) 头发是卷曲的
{:-) 中分的发型
=| 一只猩猩
:-P 吐舌头
3:=9 哞……这是一头牛
?_? 什么？
:-O 惊叹
<:-P 吐舌头
°o° 晕倒，不省人事
_ 看花了眼
*_^ 挤挤眼
;-) 抛媚眼啦！
:-... 心碎泪流
*^?^* 羞羞
*^o^* 哦～，呵呵傻笑
*^◎^* 呵呵大笑（嘴唇好厚）

*^÷^* 得意的笑（有上下唇的哟）
* ∩_∩ * 献上最可爱的笑
+:-) 神甫的微笑
:-D 对你笑
:-1 平淡无味的笑
:j 暧昧的笑
:l 冷淡的微笑
:-9 舔着嘴唇笑
|-) 眯眼笑／还是快睡着
:—— 邪恶戏谑的嘴脸
|-D Ho Ho 笑
8-) 眼镜族的笑
|-P 捧腹大笑
:< 难过的苦笑
@?@ 悲，晕
+?+ 流泪，感动
:~) 喜极而泣
;_; 哭泣
:-{ 抿着嘴，如泣如诉
:-... 心碎泪流
-(哭泣
u_u 假仙，羞羞
:-! 不屑一顾
*^@^* 乖～（还含个奶嘴哦）
:-(*) 恶心，要吐
⊙0⊙ 目瞪口呆
+?+ 超级感动，眼泪不停
@o@ 哇～
?< 好刺激
ˇ?ˇ 不以为然

:-C 非常沮丧
<:-P 吐舌头
>-r 做鬼脸
¨?¨ 嗯~，思考中
>:-< 要气炸了
-:7 有所不悦
!-) 睁一只眼，闭一只眼
|-O 打哈欠
-,) 独眼龙眨眼睛
+<:-| 修女乎/神甫乎
*<|:-) 圣诞老人
...—... SOS！HEP！救命啊！
+-(:-) 主教大人
:- 不修边幅，头发胡子乱七八糟
×?× 糟糕
*:O) 小丑呀
-#,:-X 我就是不说，看我嘴都封住了
O-) 焊工或戴水镜的潜水员
:%)% 满脸青春痘
:-& 我舌头打结了
:*) 酒糟鼻子
＞？＜＝ 不
-(=) 我有大门牙
-:)8 打着领结，帅！
-:6 吃了酸东西
+?+ 受不了
:-/ 犹豫不决
-:{#} 戴着牙齿矫正器
-:8(大猩猩
-:[- 反胃了
:|] 留着一字胡
-:<] 留着八字胡
-:-= 留着日本胡
-:@ 留着络腮胡
:-} 涂了口红了

:=| 一只狒狒？
:>) 好大鼻子
<:-)<<| 宇航员呀
:-? 抽着烟斗呢
=:-) 庞克族
:i 吸烟族
@:-) 一头卷发
8:-) 眼镜推到头顶才够帅！或者是头戴蝴蝶结的女生。
-(哼，不看我
:-{} 擦口红
X-< 惨不忍睹
}:-(风大时戴着假发
[:-] 戴着耳机呢
#-) 参加了一个大PARTY，一夜没睡，睁不开眼了
[:|] 机器人
#:-) 太随便了，头发都不梳
|-| 打坐练功
(-: 左撇子
%-) 呵呵，跌破眼镜
:-[吸血鬼
%-} 我没醉……呵呵
%-) 瞪着萤幕很久
:-E 暴牙的吸血鬼
-:) 不小心剃掉一边的眉毛
(-) 头发都盖眼睛了，该理发了
&:-) 我是自然卷的头发
{:-) 中分的发型
:-& 暗示此人正生气呢
:~) 流鼻涕
8:-) 小女孩
(:-) 大光头
O :-) 一个天使
:-|K- 打着领结呢

(:I 理论家
:^(鼻子都打歪了
@:-) 戴头巾
@-) 独眼龙？
:-0 不要吵
:-X 保密
|-| 睡着了
X-(翘辫子了
:_Q 抽烟者
@= 核生化武器
E-:-) 火腿族
]:-)8 魔术师
:-? 抽雪茄
C=:-) 大厨
]:O_ 母牛
(8-o 秃子见鬼
(^o^)/ 再见
-6% 脑死
?_? 什么？
(^_^)v 和平
:-@ 尖叫
:=) 两个鼻子
:-# 戴牙套
+-:-) 教皇
:V) 另一边鼻梁断了
:^) 鼻梁断了
:-[抿着嘴，一副如泣如诉的神情
(-_-) 神秘笑容
(:)-) 哈哈！这是一个小蛙人，戴着潜水镜在偷笑
(:-(紧皱眉头，又愁眉苦脸
(:-D 真是大嘴巴，多嘴
(:<) 吹牛大王
(:>>-< "打劫！把手举起来！"

(0-< 面无表情，目光呆滞
*-(闭着眼睛的独眼巨人（希腊神话）
o-) 睁着眼睛的独眼巨人（希腊神话）
*:** 不修边幅的人，头发、胡子都乱七八糟的
-) 嘘！这是我们之间的秘密，千万不要跟别人说
-} 嘴歪眼斜的
8:-I 魔术师，不寒而栗也像卡通画的食人族
8:] 大猩猩
:-I 带着一脸不屑的笑容
:-" 嘟哝着嘴
:-# 抱歉，这是秘密，我答应人家不说的
:-% 银行家、股票玩家用的笑
:-I 我感冒了，妈妈不许我出去玩
...~*.*~... 女生高兴得笑翻时甩着辫子
=^.^= 脸红
~~~~>_<~~~~ 大声哭用力哭
:-* 生气 / 嘟着嘴巴
:-7 火冒三丈，已经快吃人了，还不快闪开
:-}} 很迷人的翘胡子
:$ 我生病了
:-e 失望的笑容
<:I 小傻瓜
<<:>>== 乌贼
<<<<(:-) 是帽子推销员，想不想来顶高帽儿？
>:< 已经快发狂、要气炸了
>>:(很愤怒
~~:-(极度愤怒，都快要爆炸了

特别奉献

二 最新汉语潮词英译

婚奴 wedding slave
房奴 mortgage slave
宅男 Otaku
宅女 Otaku girl
卧槽族 job-hugging clan
赖校族 campus dwellers

甲型 H1N1 流感 influenza A virus subtype H1N1
躲猫猫 hide-and-seek
闪孕 quick pregnancy
山寨版 heap copy
装嫩 act young